MAGICAL RELIGION
AND
MODERN WITCHCRAFT

MAGICAL RELIGION
AND
MODERN
WITCHCRAFT

James R. Lewis, Editor

STATE UNIVERSITY OF NEW YORK PRESS

Published by
State University of New York Press, Albany

For information, address State University of New York Press,
State University Plaza, Albany, N.Y., 12246

Production by Marilyn P. Semerad
Marketing by Nancy Farrell

Library of Congress Cataloging-in-Publication Data

Magical religion and modern witchcraft / James R. Lewis, editor.
    p. cm.
    Includes bibliographical references and index.
    ISBN 0-7914-2889-3 (hardcover). — ISBN 0-7914-2890-7 (pbk.)
    1. Magic—History—20th century. 2. Witchcraft—History—20th
century. 3. Paganism—History—20th century. 4. Goddess religion-
-History—20th century. I. Lewis, James R.
BF1571.M34 1996
299—dc20   95-42351
                                              CIP

10 9 8 7 6 5 4 3 2 1

CONTENTS

INTRODUCTION

It is the night of the Winter solstice. In San Francisco, there are bonfires everywhere: strung along the beaches, blazing on Twin Peaks, on all the high places. In the parks and on rooftops, small groups gather around cauldrons. There are no mass meetings, only circles. . . . They have all they need to make magic: their voices, their breath, each other.

Through the long night, they chant each other's names. They sing hymns to the newborn sun, to the eternally revolving Goddess. They pour libations and give thanks—especially the very old ones, who remember when it was different:

"I am thankful that in this city, no one goes hungry."

"I am thankful that in this city, no one is left to die alone."

"I give thanks that I can walk the dark streets without fearing violence."

"I give thanks that the air is clean, that life has returned to the waters of the bay, that we are at peace."

—Starhawk, *The Spiral Dance*

IN THESE WORDS STARHAWK, a popular spokesperson for the Neo-Pagan movement, offers us a profoundly moving vision of the future: It is a future without violence or deprivation, in which the blight of industrial pollution has been removed and mutual care has come to play a central role in human relationships. It is also a future in which humankind has returned to the Old Religion, conceived of as heartfelt worship of the Goddess and respect for the Earth as her principal embodiment.

In contemporary Neo-Pagan gatherings, the sympathetic observer can sense that modern witches magically create tiny islands in which this optimistic vision may live, even if for but the brief span of the ritual. Believing themselves in league with greater spiritual forces striving to restore natural balance to the Earth, most feel little need to promote their views in public arenas. And, rarely building up such visible institutions as organized churches, they go unnoticed by the outside world. Instead, Neo-Pagans meet together in a variety of informal settings—forests, fields, and suburban living rooms—to quietly craft their world.

Neo-Paganism is a growing phenomenon, but how large of a movement are we really talking about? Using several different indicators, Aidan Kelly, a scholarly insider, estimates three hundred thousand serious participants. This estimate does not include the many sympathizers and fellow travelers who are involved around the fringes of the movement, nor does it include the many feminist spirituality groups and men's movement groups who draw inspiration from contemporary New-Paganism.

How has a movement of this size thus far eluded sustained scholarly scrutiny? Over the past several decades, mainstream academics have periodically generated articles on various aspects of Neo-Paganism, but this sporadic research has not been significant enough to constitute the basis of a recognized subfield of study. The lack of meaningful research can be understood as a function of academic prejudice. Scholars who study the occult have continually had to deal with the disdain of their colleagues. Irving Zaretsky, in a major work on non-mainstream religious movements published over two decades ago, noted that, "Not a few social scientists consider the untraditional and unconventional aspects of human social life . . . to be ill suited for serious scholarly endeavor."[1] Such attitudes have pushed research on the occult to the margin, and have left us without an adequate framework to grasp the meaning of modern Witchcraft.

Where did Neo-Paganism originate? Modern Witchcraft has several different starting places. None, however, have been as influential as Gerald Gardner's blending of liturgical elements from ceremonial magic with the speculative scholarship of Margaret Murray—a creation that came into being as an active new religion in England around the time of the second world war. Claiming roots in ancient British Paganism, Gardner's brand of Witchcraft gained a broad following, both in Europe and America. And, while few contemporary Wiccan groups are orthodox Gardnerians, the influence of Gardner is omnipresent in the Neo-Pagan subculture.

Like its more visible sister the New Age, the Neo-Pagan movement is populated by significant numbers of baby-boomers—people who two decades earlier were participating in the phenomenon known as the counterculture. As the counterculture faded away in the early seventies, many former "hippies" found themselves embarking on a spiritual quest—one that, in many cases, departed from the Judeo-Christian mainstream. Thus one of the possible ways of dating the beginnings of contemporary Neo-Paganism as a significant movement is from the period of the rather sudden appearance of large numbers of unconventional spiritual seekers in the decade following the sixties.

Contemporary Neo-Paganism is diverse and decentralized. Beliefs differ widely, yet it is nevertheless possible to delineate certain common themes. Modern witches believe in the efficacy of magic as a non-ordinary means of impacting events in the everyday world. Also, as mentioned above, the Divine is viewed as being primarily female (the Goddess), and is simultaneously monistic and polytheistic. The Earth is respected as the Goddess's principal embodiment, a belief entailing ecological consciousness and responsibility. Unlike most other traditions, Neo-Pagans do *not* view release from the physical world as the goal of the religious life. Rather than a burden, life in the body is viewed as good, and physical pleasure is a blessing that should be sought rather than avoided. However, even these ideas and values, while generally accepted, would not meet with universal agreement (a wide variety of views are tolerated, reflecting the movement's extreme anti-authoritarianism, which sometimes borders on anarchism).

What draws people to become involved in modern Witchcraft? While answers to this question are diverse, it should be clear from the above discussion that many aspects of contemporary Neo-Paganism are intrinsically attractive. Most serious participants would say that they were *born* pagans rather than converted—that the movement made immediate sense to them, and that they felt at home from the very beginning of their involvement. From an outside observer's perspective, it is clear that—however sincere their current practice—many participants initially become involved out of a revolt against some other aspect of their environment. In some cases they revolted against traditional Christianity; in others they revolted against the impersonal worldview of modern secularism. The very term "Witchcraft" has something scandalous about it, as if to become a witch is to embrace the *shadow* self (though it would be more accurate to say that they embrace the *amina*) of contemporary society.

As a religious vision, contemporary Neo-Paganism draws heavily upon what historian of religion Mircea Eliade referred to as the

Myth of the Eternal Return. According to Eliade, the passion of the religious mind is to seek rapport with sacred power. This can be accomplished spatially by drawing close to spots where the Divine has manifested, or temporally by recreating—in ritual—the world as it was "in the beginning," when gods and goddesses walked upon the earth. In most strands of Neo-Paganism, the world of the Beginning was the pre-Christian world, which contemporary Neo-Pagans tend to romanticize as a kind of paradise, uncomplicated by pollution, instruments of mass destruction, political oppression, etc. This attractive vision of earlier time periods is evoked in ritual, as well as in other day-to-day activities of practicing Neo-Pagans. Starhawk's vision of the future cited above draws on the power of this romanticized view of the past.

With respect to interpretations of the movement, many participants feel that they have been misportrayed by the handful of academic researchers who have studied them, but in the past few Neo-Pagans were prepared to meet mainstream scholars on their own turf. This situation has, however, radically changed. At the time of this writing, there are many Neo-Pagans who have completed (or who are completing) graduate degrees in religious studies or in other, relevant disciplines. The extent to which insiders have undertaken mainstream academic training was unknown to this editor at the inception of the present project. After becoming aware of the changed situation, it was decided that a significant portion of the current volume should contain the reflections of thoughtful participants. The result is a highly diverse collection of documents, ranging from poetic theology to the observations of detached outsiders. Most readers will, I believe, find this diversity of perspectives stimulating in formulating their own views of the Neo-Pagan movement.

☆   ☆   ☆

Part one of the present volume consists of three chapters which explore the contemporary Neo-Pagan worldview, particularly as that worldview relates to the Goddess, the central locus of Wiccan sacrality. Part two tackles the dimension of Neo-Pagan praxis as it manifests in magic and ritual. Unlike other religious movements which emphasize doctrine and belief, witches tend to stress liturgy and specific kinds of magical practices.

Part three contains two chapters that examine certain phases of the movement historically, both in terms of its empirical history and its mythological history, as well as a chapter that looks at magical religion as a response to modernity. In striking contrast to the many misportrayals of Neo-Paganism as being without moral-ity, part four examines this movement's complex ethical dimension.

Part five examines the unusual topic of Neo-Paganism's inter-sections with Christianity, both as these two traditions conflict with each other, as well as how they overlap. Finally, part six concludes with a pair of bibliographical chapters that survey and critique earlier studies on the movement.

NOTE

1. Zaretsky, Irving I. and Mark P. Leone, eds., *Religious Movements in Contemporary America*. Princeton, NJ: Princeton Univ. Pr., 1974.

Part I

The Goddess and the Witches' Worldview

1

THE CONTEMPORARY NEO-PAGAN REVIVAL

Judy Harrow

THE RE-EMERGENCE OF THE GODDESS in our times is the fruit of a more general Neo-Pagan renaissance that began in England early in this century and was brought to the United States by English immigrants in the early 1960s.[1] In the 1970s, the great metaphor of the Goddess was adopted by some segments of the feminist community.

Up to this point, the scholarly community seems only to have been aware of women whose Goddess affiliation is secondary to their feminist ideology, a large and creative subset of the Goddess movement. Those of us who came to the Goddess through ecological or other concerns—and especially Goddess-oriented men—have remained far more invisible. But the Goddess is, as all true religious symbols, multi-vocal. Certainly she is about the empowerment of women and the gentling of men, but she is about a great deal else as well.

The latest estimate is that there are over 250,000 Goddess-worshipers of all kinds in the United States, but religious scholars have paid startlingly little attention to our thinking or our doings. One of the reasons for this is that so few of us have the skills to participate in scholarly discussions. Unfortunately, for two reasons, this is not likely to change.

One is that most institutions of theological education are firmly Christian or Jewish based, and primarily intended to be training schools for future clergy. Even for Jewish and Christian feminists, this is a big problem. Until recently, and still in some of the more retrogressive branches, women have been excluded from the clergy, and therefore from theological training. So traditionally women have been denied access to the tools needed to bring women's perspectives and concerns into the discussion.

The problem is somewhat different for Neo-Pagans of either gender. By now there are theological schools that admit women and even admit religious "outsiders." But most of the courses offered are still in Christian or Jewish studies. No criticism is intended. These traditions have need and right to train their future clergy, and so the schools have every reason to emphasize their own roots. But few Neo-Pagans can afford to invest the time in material that is, to us, irrelevant, in order to learn the methodology or acquire the credential.

Also, many of the Neo-Pagan traditions, my own definitely included, adamantly oppose the creation of a paid, professional clergy. It's difficult and risky for anyone to establish an academic career in any field these days, and the field of religious studies is particularly inhospitable to mavericks. Most of us must earn a livelihood, and so few of us can afford to pay the tuition fees or put in the years to get a degree that may well never lead to a job. Carol Christ, probably the leading spokesperson for the Goddess movement among academic theologians, found the Goddess *after* she was well into her scholarly training (Christ 1987, 93–101).

Christ won't be the only one like that, of course, but there will never be very many. More to the point, these are the ones whose Goddess orientation is most likely to be propelled by an angry rejection of patriarchal institutions. Those of us who never got that close to the patriarchy in the first place, whose religious choices were made earlier and less reactively, are more likely to stay invisible. So Neo-Pagans remain underrepresented, and what representation we have is by a skewed sample—not by anybody's ill intent, but by the way the system works.

Mary Jo Weaver has described the history of scholarly understanding of Neo-Paganism in terms of a debate between the reformist and revolutionary wings of the feminist theology, with Rosemary Ruether representing the reformists and Carol Christ the revolutionaries (Weaver 1989). That dichotomy, between those feminists who choose to work within existing religious institutions and those who instead seek to build an entirely new religious practice was popularized by Carol Christ and ("reformer") Judith Plaskow in their very important 1979 anthology *Womanspirit Rising* (1979, 9–11). It seemed useful at first, but soon proved oversimplified and divisive, and has been specifically repudiated by Plaskow and Christ in their newer anthology, *Weaving the Visions* (1979, 6–8).

Neo-Pagan priestess Margot Adler points out that *all* of us, Christians, Jews, Pagans or whatever, are using our source materials selectively and interpreting them in accord with our own experiences and values (Adler 1989, 97–100). So all of us are creating new religions or creating our religions anew. The Neo-Pagan effort is simply less contiguous in time with its antecedents than some of the others. All of us have something to teach and something to learn. All of us can offer each other support and even appropriate and respectful challenge.

Such challenge has been offered to the Goddess movement over the years by Christian feminist Rosemary Ruether, one of the very few to take us seriously enough to engage us. (For just one example, *The Spiral Dance* by Starhawk [1979] is certainly one of the most important books about contemporary Goddess worship. Yet in the decade following its publication, only *one* review of that book appears in the *Religion Abstracts*. That review is by Ruether [1980c].) Whatever miscommunications we may have had with Ruether pales before such a total lack of communication by her colleagues.

And, indeed, while many Goddess-worshipers have seen Ruether's comments as "hostile," over the years I have perceived them as a sort of "tough love." Ruether consistently supports our right to seek alternatives and affirms the validity of our quest (1987, 460–461). She challenges us to examine what she perceives as our weak spots. Sometimes she really is pointing out weaknesses in our thinking, other times the problem is simply with how we present ourselves. Of course, there are times when I seriously disagree with her analysis. But even then, I feel, the exercise of responding to her challenges helps me understand, define, and express what I believe. When Neo-Pagan religious thinking comes into its maturity, we will owe Rosemary Ruether a debt of thanks that we will then be happy to pay. I would like now to examine some of her main criticisms more closely.

1. Ruether accuses Neo-Pagans of rejecting the Bible without ever really having studied it. She says that our unthinking rejection indicates a kind of lingering "unresolved dependency," in that we are not able to regard the Bible as one among many possible sources and open-mindedly search it for what is usable (1980b, 22–25).

Carol Christ responds that she believes Ruether's "real problem" is that we do not make biblical ideas the basis for our work. Christ points out that for Jews and Christians "the Biblical vision has never been understood to be one vision among others from which one can—on the basis of human judgement—select that which is useful and reject that which is not. The Bible has always been understood as *the* vision which is the source and norm for all authentic vision" (1980a, 29).

I'm inclined to agree with Christ. Ruether seems to hold a hidden assumption that we ought to consider the biblical traditions *first*, and then, after culling them, perhaps draw on other traditions as a supplement. That is the method of her excellent books *Sexism and God-Talk* (1983) and *Gaia and God* (1992). It is an entirely appropriate method for Christian and Jewish feminists, but not for Neo-Pagans.

Most Neo-Pagans are first generation, so we look like a religion of converts—and Ruether seems to be asking us to prove that we have thoroughly studied our various birth traditions, most of which are Christian or Jewish, to justify our conversion. But in reality few of us feel like converts. We say "you don't *become* Pagan, you discover that you always were." Our experience is that of finding a name for the spirituality that had moved us all our lives, and a community of friends with whom we can learn, grow, and celebrate (Darcie 1993). This "Pagan homecoming" experience, to which Margot Adler devotes an entire chapter of her book *Drawing Down the Moon* (1986, 14–23), is almost a cliché among us. We never set deep roots in our families' religions. Most of us don't know the Bible well enough to be hostile to it. We're just indifferent.

But if the Bible really is just one source among many, why should it be the first one we try? Since I am not trying to salvage for myself a Jewish or Christian identity, I need not begin with those sources. I accept no obligation to justify my choice of another Path by proving that I first searched the Bible. I am free to select from all these many sources according to my own affinities. Pagan materials—the religious symbols, stories, and practices of Nature-oriented, Goddess-worshiping, polytheistic and shamanic peoples from pre-Christian Europe and the contemporary Third World—have the same rightful claim on my first attention that the Bible does on Ruether's. Her criticism boils down to nothing more than this: we act by our own priorities instead of by hers.

For those of us who have some knowledge of the Bible, there are other, more serious barriers to using it as a source. In her effort to find a usable past within the Bible, Ruether culls those parts of the prophetic-messianic tradition that are critical of privileged establishments and liberating to those who have been marginalized and oppressed by class. I would not criticize her for using the Bible selectively, particularly since she has consistently stated that selective use is her method. But are the rest of us bound to view the Bible only through Ruether's screens?

The Hebrew Bible relates with approval many incidents of genocide during the original occupation of the land, followed by generations of repression of lingering Pagan tendencies among the people. The initial genocide, at least, Ruether acknowledges in her most recent book, *Gaia and God* (1992, 118–119). But, after the success of the invasion came the long mopping up operation, which Ruether ignores.

As Christ points out, the inspiring prophetic statements about social justice appear in close proximity to nasty, vindictive attacks on polytheists, Nature-worshipers, and the people of the Goddess. "For every prophetic injunction against those who 'sell the needy for a pair of shoes' (Amos 2:6), there is a threat against those who 'worship on every high hill and under every green tree' (Hosea 4:13)" (Christ 1980a, 29). The prophets were primarily leaders and spokesmen for the "Yahweh only" party of religious intolerance.

This sad history, and its subsequent religious enshrinement, is one of the major roots of bigotry in the West. I hope Ruether will someday come to understand why those of us who worship on the high hills under the green trees are so offended by this context that even the admittedly "good parts" are not usable for us.

I've been particularly disturbed by Ruether's statement, as recent as 1987, that our Gods are slavemasters whereas hers worked to create the world and then established the Sabbath to model a rhythm of work and rest for ordinary folk (p. 463). In 1980, Carol Christ told her that ours is a "modern, syncretistic religion" in which traditional elements and contemporary experience are "all filtered through the lens of feminism" (1980b, 12). In 1983, I devoted a great part of my review of Ruether's *Sexism and God-Talk* to a description of all the many sources I draw on in addition to the theology of the ancient Near Eastern monarchies (Harrow 1980, 10–13). We told her: we pick and choose just like she does. Doesn't she listen?

Or perhaps she doesn't want to listen. Selecting what's usable from tradition may be perfectly legitimate when constructing a nurturant spiritual practice for today's needs and today's consciousness. It's a very different matter to select the nicest part of my own tradition and the meanest part of yours, then juxtapose them to your disadvantage. The word for that is cardstacking. For example, Judith Plaskow describes how Jesus can be made to look like a feminist ahead of his time by those who want to blame patriarchal society exclusively on the Jews (1980, 11–12). A Neo-Pagan who wanted to do something similar might contrast Brigit, the healer and blacksmith, with the kind of petty, jealous tyrant who could turn a woman into a rock formation because, in the middle of fleeing from a catastrophe, she stopped to show concern for her dying neighbors.

Let the nasty zero-sum game stop here. As polytheists, we Neo-Pagans are not looking for the "One Truth"; we need not discredit each others' ways. Instead of throwing the more unpalatable parts of our respective traditions up to each other, let's recognize that all of us are reconstructing. Let's begin to compare notes about how to choose and how to reinterpret.

2. Ruether consistently accuses us of historical inaccuracy and claims that we have no authentic continuous tradition (1980a, 843–844).

For any Christian to fault us for the discontinuity of our tradition, even if this were true, would be a particularly blatant case of blaming one's victim. But, in fact, although generations of missionaries and worse took their best shot at cultural genocide, continuous living traditions that are Pagan, polytheistic, Nature- and Goddess-worshiping are all around us. Yes, indigenous European religion was largely truncated. But in New York, where I live, over a million people practice Santeria, a syncretistic faith whose major root is the old faith of tribal Africa. A significant and growing minority of Native Americans are still traditional faithkeepers, as are some of the Asian tribal peoples recently transplanted here because of disasters at home.

The steadfastness of these and other Third World "paleo-Pagans" is for European and Euro-American Neo-Pagans a source of great inspiration. A new generation of anthropologists, some of them native themselves, is making more accurate information about tribal religions available to us. Sometimes we can use this information to supplement the shredded remains of our own Pagan heritage. Meanwhile, even from the Near East, better archaeological methods, and new ways of construing evidence long available, are giving us some hints about the religious practices of the pre-literate past, which was also pre-imperial.

In the final analysis, none of this matters, because history is, for us, only a source of inspiration, to be selectively drawn on like all other sources. What religion is really about is not history, but myth—teaching stories that may or may not be factual, but that carry our deepest values. Mary Jo Weaver points out that our origin myths actually serve us as utopian myths, expressing our hopes for a very different and far better future (Weaver 1989, 42–43). Margot Adler says if we have no history "so be it. It's not such a bad fate to be a provider of positive visions in a time of difficulty and darkness" (1989, 98). I can only echo her "so be it!"

I also have to say that Ruether is applying the standard of history selectively. She often talks about her own God that brought the slaves out of Egypt. While this may be an inspiring model for liberating action, the Exodus event has—to put it kindly—no better archaeological evidence behind it than Marija Gimbutas's theories of a peaceful and egalitarian Old Europe (1982, 1987, 1991). If Christians and Jews can use dubious history as empowering myth, so can the rest of us.

3. Ruether says that our movement grows out of nineteenth-century romanticism, which has, in the past, led to nationalism, and, in its worst excesses, to Nazism (1980c, 1987).

Although at face value, this charge may seem like the crudest form of mudslinging, it points to a complicated story that is painful to remember, but dangerous to forget. The fact is that the romantic movement of the nineteenth century did inspire a revival of interest in the ancient religion of Germany. Then Allied peace overtures that led to the end of World War One were cynically abandoned in favor of the vindictive Treaty of Versailles. In Germany, the sense of betrayal was kept raw by real deprivation, caused when the treaty exacerbated the effects of a worldwide Great Depression. Resentment opened the way for the Nazis, and their cancerously inflated form of nationalism.

Himmler and other Nazi leaders saw that the old religious symbols, which were already becoming familiar because of the prior religious revival, could be used as emotionally loaded rallying points for their evil schemes. The swastika itself was once an entirely clean symbol for the sun. Fifty years after the demise of Nazism, the swastika is still completely unusable as a religious symbol because of its Nazi associations. Something ancient and sacred was polluted. The Nazis coined the term "Neo-Pagan." We can't deny it; we can only mourn and rage.

Teutonic tribal religion is far from inherently Nazi. The same pantheon, the same core values, form the ancient Pagan heritage of

England and Scandinavia, which resisted Nazism, and that of Germany, which succumbed. Today, some American Neo-Pagans feel drawn to the Norse mythos, because of family roots or simply because, through the Anglo-Saxon tribes, that religious sensibility lies at the heart of our language and our culture. Most are appalled and embarrassed by the Nazi connection. Yet even from other Neo-Pagans they face some prejudice, and even more from outsiders (Adler 1986, 273–282).

Few people have known about the Nazi's Neo-Pagan involvement. (American Neo-Pagans, already suffering from unfair and incorrect association with Satanism, have generally been grateful for this.) Unfortunately, even fewer know the whole story. The more authentic groups within the German Neo-Pagan revival refused to collude with what was for them, as for us, blasphemy. As soon as the Nazis took power, in 1933, non-cooperating native Germanic religious groups were banned. Several of their leaders went to the camps, as did German leaders of anti-Nazi political factions (Thorsson 1989, 21–26).

Contemporary American Norse Pagans do not support Nazism any more than Ruether, who is a Catholic, supports the Inquisition. Just as the Nazis once sent authentic Norse Pagans to the camps, so the Inquisition, with only a name change, harasses and silences Catholics involved with Liberation Theology and Creation Spirituality. When we all learn to judge people by their behavior instead of their associations, we will find enriching friendships and empowering alliances in surprising places.

Just as people should not be easily labelled "fascist," neither should ideas. Fascism is very different from a wholesome sense of attachment to local landscapes and communities, which Ruether considers to be nationalism. Actually, even nationalism is only a problem when we assume that "different" necessarily means either "better" or "worse." In a polytheistic, partnership-oriented worldview, I can love my own land, language, and folkways without disrespecting yours. Fascism and imperialism are what happens when the culture of domination—of ranking—is taken to sick extremes. They are real dangers.[2]

But there are complementary, and equally real, dangers to eroding the sense of people and place. I experience the Earth as one living organism, and I call her my Holy Mother. But I also know that very local and grassroots activities are the best ways to take care of ourselves and to protect her. Some historians believe that one of the motivations for the European witch hunts was to break the cohesion of peasant communities, so that people could be more easily driven from the land. Those first clearances and enclosures made it possible to begin the industrialization of agriculture, while the people thus displaced were driven into the first grim factories (Starhawk 1982, 182–219).[3]

Thus began the road that led to present-day eco-rape. The consolidation process has continued and accelerated. Today, the actual damage is usually done by multi-national corporations, now even further unleashed by NAFTA. Decisions that drastically affect local ecologies and communities are too often made by men who have never seen those places. "Think globally, act locally" has become one of the slogans of the green movement, bio-regionalism one of its key theories.

Our challenge, then, is to hold the abstract sense of the Whole and the concrete sense of place in dynamic balance. In our time, the loss of either one is a threat to the Earth's survival. We must maintain an appropriate, and balanced, sense of rootedness in place and people.

4. Ruether says our beliefs and practices can lead us back to old-fashioned gender-role stereotyping, or even to female supremacy and the marginalization of our men (1980b, 25; 1980a, 844–845).

Unfortunately, I have to agree with Ruether on this point. It's not just a possibility that some types of Goddess rhetoric may lead either to the scapegoating or exclusion of men or to the imposition of limiting gender stereotypes on all of us. Both of these problems have actually happened among Neo-Pagans at times. Until we learn to find both Goddess and God in all people, regardless of their gender, all we can do is reverse patriarchal oppression—and that's no real improvement. It's tempting to settle for vengeance instead of transformation, yes, but this temptation is no greater among Goddess-worshipers than anybody else.

Ruether herself gives us a remarkably clear and compassionate description of separatist rage in her *Sexism and God-Talk.*

> ... The acceptance of liberating anger and the reclaiming of basic self-esteem allow a woman to look honestly at the situation that has shaped her own life. She is able to acknowledge her own compliance with the systems that have diminished her humanity. The shackles of this system on her mind and energy begin to shatter, and she gains the courage to stand up against them.
>
> This breakthrough experience is the basis for the development of consciousness. Women read their own history within the history of patriarchy. They become aware of the depths of the system that

has entrapped them and discover a hidden history of women of the past. They reclaim their own history as witnesses to an alternative possibility and also become increasingly conscious of the complexity of the global socio-economic system that subjugates women. The difficulty of the task of emancipation becomes clearer. It is no longer just a matter of settling accounts within interpersonal relationships.

This expanded consciousness deepens one's sense of alienation and anger so that one senses oneself ready to 'go mad' with alienation and anger. Males take on a demonic face. One begins to doubt their basic humanity. One desires only to be with women, to distance oneself from the whole male world with its myriad games. Most women are afraid of this deeper anger and alienation and stop well short of experiencing it. Their immediate ties of survival and service to men and children are too deep. Moreover, they believe that 'loving everyone' and affirming everyone's humanity disallows the experiencing of this anger.

This creates a parting of the ways between feminists—those who are willing to experience this deeper alienation and anger and those who draw back from it. Those who enter into deeper alienation become the 'bad feminists,' the separatists, lesbians, radicals. Those who take a more moderate stance are tempted to get 'brownie points' for not being like those 'bad feminists.' Yet the depths of anger and alienation to which women point are not inappropriate. It really has been 'that bad.' Unless one is willing to take the journey into that deeper anger, even to risk going a little mad, one really will never understand the evils of sexism. The great importance of a feminist thinker like Mary Daly is precisely that she insists on taking herself further and further into that journey and insisting that others who wish to be honest follow her. She lays before our eyes the 'passion drama' of female crucifixion on the cross of male sexism.

The journey into that deeper anger does not mean that one needs to remain there permanently. . . . Only by experiencing one's anger can one move on, with real integrity, to another level of truth. One is able, with freedom, to refuse a reversed female chauvinism that would cause one to loose touch with the human face of males and to begin to imagine that women alone are human and males are evil and defective. . . . (1983, 186–188)

The rage process happens in the Goddess-worshiping community, as it does in every feminist grouping, just as Ruether describes it. And, wherever it happens, some women work through it, while others get stuck. Those who get stuck can, in theory, hurt men. In reality, all they can do is create some very small, restricted enclaves that exclude men. Since men have equality and more in most places, few men will even notice.

As Ruether says, rage is a stage we must work through. Victims of any kind of oppression need to experience rage, but those who get stuck in it are in trouble, both psychologically and spiritually. Some women have been more hurt by patriarchal oppression than others. For them, a period of relative isolation from men can provide safe space in which to heal. However, it's something like putting a cast on one's leg: perhaps necessary for healing, but harmful if maintained too long or used when not needed.

But I believe Ruether is making a completely unjustified assumption when she groups separatists, lesbians, and radicals together as the "bad feminists." I am no more willing to concede the term "radical" to the separatists than I am willing to concede the term "feminist" itself. Radical means "from the roots." I insist, as radically as I know how, on the complete equality and full participation of both genders.

More important, lesbianism is not just a result of deep anger and alienation against the patriarchy. It isn't about the patriarchy at all. Lesbianism is the affirmative sexual and affectional preference of the women concerned. Neither is lesbianism the same thing as separatism. A woman who prefers women as sexual partners still may live in a world containing both genders, and can work, play, or worship with men. After all, why should all the other parts of our lives be spent only with people we might consider as sexual partners?

In any case, most Neo-Pagans are not separatists. Some of us resent it when either separatists or people who are not Goddess-worshipers assume that we must be, or when some declare that Goddess worship is "women's religion," as though Mother Earth had no sons. We believe in the full participatory equality, the partnership, of the genders. Our rituals model partnership, and our gatherings are open to all. Another Christian feminist writer, Virginia Ramey Mollenkott, has described how she once expected the Goddess movement to discriminate against men, but eventually learned that we do not (1982, 1043–1046). After all these years of contact, I would hope for a similar statement from Ruether.

5. Ruether says we have no adequate explanation for the existence of evil in the world (1980d, 209).

She said that back in 1980. For the most part, she is correct. The goal of Neo-Pagan spirituality has been to increase our attunement with Nature. Our primary sacred model is the Triple Goddess—Maiden, Mother, and Crone—symbolizing the continuous cycle of life. Much of human suffering comes from the impersonal processes of change, which are inherent in Nature. We experience some changes as pain and loss. Humans call such changes evil, but they are not. Resentment and resistance to the inevitable only increases our suffering. Instead, Pagans try to make peace with the Crone's part of the cycle: with darkness, night, winter, aging, and death. These make a space for birth and growth. The destruction of individuals allows the survival of the Whole.

In our time, human greed has thrown Earth's body out of balance. Her survival is threatened. We need to understand that to destroy Her is inevitably to destroy ourselves. All humankind needs to face the reality that the part is not the ruler of the Whole, and to learn to live in balance. This is the most important concept Neo-Pagans can offer to the general culture. We dare not turn aside from the Crone's stern and loving face. Still, Ruether is correct. While the Crone's action, and our unthinking resistance, explain much of human suffering, they do not explain all of it.

What describes one area of experience very well may not have much to do with another. It is foolish to generalize inappropriately, foolish to insist that *all* of what we call evil is simply natural. In the last century, this kind of thinking manifested itself as Social Darwinism, an excuse for the greedy to fatten off the suffering of others. "Whatever is, is right," is a slogan created by bullies who want to keep the rest of us quiet. In those times and places where people believe that *all* suffering comes from attachment and desire, or that the way to peace is submissive acceptance, the result has been gross social disparities and massive deprivation for most people.

Some human suffering, and just about all eco-rape, is not natural but caused by greed and malice. People dominate and exploit other people individually. Domination and exploitation are also built in to many of our social structures. When we confuse human greed and malice with impersonal natural processes, we deprive ourselves of a standard of justice and foreclose even the possibility of righting the wrongs.

While few Neo-Pagans would actually deny the existence of active human evil, we have emphasized developing acceptance of natural losses to the point of ignoring other kinds of suffering. That's reason enough for Ruether to worry. When she, and other friendly adversaries, confronted me with this concern, I realized I had no answer for them or for myself. So some of my students and I decided to look for one. We began by convening what became known as "the evil workshop." This was a free-form discussion on the origins and nature of evil that we hosted at several Neo-Pagan gatherings. We intended to discover the range of ideas about evil that people in our community had, then to evaluate them and try to create some sort of reasonable integration.

We pursued our "evil project" for a couple of years with no result. Then a particularly perceptive young man had that flash of perception for which we all had been preparing. Our elaborate efforts ended at once, as his insight was so obvious that it seemed self-evident once it arrived. The basis for all human-created evil, he realized, is a rip in the fabric of empathy. As long as we hold the consciousness that all life is not only Sacred, but fully inter-connected, we know that to deprive others by taking more than our share is to hurt ourselves. The illusion of separateness is what makes greed possible. Malice, intentionally causing harm to oth-ers, follows frustrated greed.

So the two different understandings of suffering finally come together. We suffer when we want more than our share from Nature. We cause suffering to others when we want more than our share from the human community. To want more than one's share, from humankind or from Nature, is the way of the dominator culture. Learning to live in balance, in partnership, as part of a greater Whole, is the way to reduce the needless suffering we cause to ourselves and to others.

This is consistent with Neo-Pagan ethics, the core statement of which is "an it harm none, do what you will." The second clause is usually interpreted to forbid making needless rules against harmless behaviors, especially since pointless restriction is itself a form of harm. The first clause directs us to consider the effects of our actions on those around us and on the Whole. Empathy is the touchstone by which we discern whether our behavior may be harming others, and by which we keep our actions and our lives in balance.

Living in balance is not the same thing as passive acceptance of whatever happens on the theory that the boss has his reasons that pass our understanding, or that it's all illusion anyhow. When somebody wants to dominate, wants to take more than his or her share from me or from Nature, keeping the balance means setting the limits.

If empathy is the touchstone for living in balance, then we must ask how damaged empathy can be restored. All around us are calloused people. Privileged white men are scarred by the patriarchy's training in toughness and competition. The children of the ghetto are scarred by daily exposure to violence. Everywhere, sensitivity is further dulled by drugs: crack cocaine or fine cognac.

To be empathic in an insensitive culture is to risk a terrible vulnerability. But restraining the greedy is just a stopgap. Real transformation can only come as more people allow empathy to direct more of their behaviors. How will this tide be turned? We don't yet know. We await—and expect—an answer.

CONCLUSION

In sum, it seems that few religious scholars up to now have heard of the contemporary Neo-Pagan movement at all. A limited and skewed picture of us has been presented to the academic community. Even fewer are thinking about what our reappearance means, about what insights our very different worldview might offer to a culture and a planet in crisis.

Some of this invisibility is our own doing. We are unskilled in formal theological discourse, and those skills are not easily come by. Not only are we more comfortable among our own, but there are real risks to visibility. The fires of Inquisition no longer burn, but some of our people have lost their jobs, their apartments, or even the custody of their children. Here in supposedly liberal New York, I had to fight for five years for my right as a member of the clergy of a minority religion to perform legal marriages (James 1985, 2–3). The cult scare of a few years ago, and the ritual abuse panic of today, both tactics to discredit the different, have left their bitter traces.

Yet four Goddess-worshiping groups participated as co-sponsors in the 1993 Parliament of the World's Religions.[4] We shared our rituals and told our story to perhaps more religious leaders in one week than in the prior fifteen hundred years.[5] A man who had just attended our full moon ritual at the parliament told me how happy he was to have been at our "coming out party." Yes, it was that, and it was time.

NOTES

1. For more information on the history of contemporary Neo-Paganism, see: Ashcroft-Nowicki, Dolores, ed. *The Forgotten Mage: The Magical Lectures of Colonel C. R. F. Seymour* (Wellingborough, Northhamptonshire: Aquarian, 1986); Kelly, Aidan A. *Crafting the Art of Magic: A History of Modern Witchcraft, 1939–1964* (St. Paul: Llewellyn, 1991); Russell, Jeffrey B. *A History of Witchcraft: Sorcerers, Heretics and Pagans* (London: Thames and Hudson, 1980); and Valiente, Doreen. *The Rebirth of Witchcraft* (London: Hale, 1989).

2. For a full explanation of the concepts of "partnership culture," "linking," "dominator culture," and "ranking," all of which are very important in contemporary Neo-Pagan thinking, see Riane Eisler, *The Chalice and the Blade: Our History, Our Future* (San Francisco: Harper and Row, 1987).

3. This is an appendix called "The Burning Times: Notes on a Critical Period in History."

4. They were Circle Sanctuary, Covenant of the Goddess, the Earthspirit Community, and the Fellowship of Isis.

5. See Covenant of the Goddess *Newsletter* 18 no. 7 (Autumn Equinox 1993), a special issue on the Parliament of the World's Religions.

REFERENCES

Adler, Margot. 1986. *Drawing Down the Moon: Witches, Druids, Goddess-Worshippers and Other Pagans in America Today.* 2d ed. Boston: Beacon Press.

———. 1989. "A Response to Weaver and Hackett." *Journal of Feminist Studies in Religion* 5, no. 1 (Spring 1989): 97–100.

Christ, Carol P. 1980a. "A Religion for Women: A Response to Rosemary Ruether—Part One." *WomanSpirit* 6, no. 24 (Summer 1980): 29.

———. 1980b. "A Religion for Women: A Response to Ruether—Part Two." *WomanSpirit* 7, no. 25 (Fall 1980): 12.

———. 1987. *Laughter of Aphrodite.* San Francisco: Harper and Row.

Christ, Carol P., and Judith Plaskow, eds. 1979. *WomanSpirit Rising.* San Francisco: Harper and Row.

Darcie. 1993. "Coming Home: Reflections on Conversion to Wicca," in Chas S. Clifton, ed., *Modern Rites of Passage*, pages 105–125. St. Paul: Llewellyn.

Gimbutas, Marija. 1982. *The Goddesses and Gods of Old Europe.* Berkeley: University of California Press.

———. 1987. *The Language of the Goddess: Images and Symbols of Old Europe.* New York: Van der Marck.

———. 1991. *The Civilization of the Goddess: The World of Old Europe.* San Francisco: Harper Collins.

Harrow, Judy. 1983. "Review of Ruether, *Sexism and God-Talk.*" *Harvest* 4, no. 1 (October 1983): 10–13.

Mollenkott, Virginia Ramey. 1982. "An Evangelical Feminist Confronts the Goddess." *Christian Century* 99, no. 32 (10 October 1982): 1043–1046.

Plaskow, Judith. 1980. "Blaming Jews for Inventing Patriarchy." *Lilith* 7 (Fall 1980): 11–12.

Plaskow, Judith, and Carol P. Christ, eds. 1979. *Weaving the Visions.* San Francisco: Harper and Row.

Ruether, Rosemary Radford. 1980a. "Goddesses and Witches: Liberation and Countercultural Feminism." *Christian Century* (10–17 September 1980): 843–844.

———. 1980b. "A Religion for Women: Sources and Strategies." *WomanSpirit* 6, no. 24 (Summer 1980): 22–25. (Reprinted with permission from *Christianity and Crisis*, 10 December 1979.)

———. 1980c. "Review of Starhawk, *The Spiral Dance.*" *Christian Century* 97 (20 February 1980): 208–209.

———. 1980d. "The Way of Wicca." *Christian Century* 97 (20 February 1980): 209.

———. 1983. *Sexism and God-Talk: Toward a Feminist Theology.* Boston: Beacon Press.

———. 1987. "Female Symbols, Values and Context." *Christianity and Crisis* (12 January 1987): 460–463.

———. 1992. *Gaia and God: An Ecofeminist Theology of Earth Healing.* San Francisco: Harper Collins.

Scott, James. 1985. "By the Power Invested in Me." *Liberty* (July–August 1985): 2–3.

Starhawk. 1979. *The Spiral Dance.* San Francisco: Harper and Row.

Thorsson, Edred. 1989. *Rune Might.* St. Paul: Llewellyn.

Weaver, Mary Jo. 1989. "Who Is the Goddess and Where Does She Get Us?" *Journal of Feminist Studies in Religion* 5, no. 1 (Spring 1989): 49–64.

2

WHO ON EARTH IS THE GODDESS?

Morning Glory and Otter G'Zell

"Well, for instance, who is this All-Mother you're always talking about?

"Why, you are, Edward . . . The All-Mother. You're the All-Mother, I'm the All-Mother, that little bird singing out there, it's the All-Mother. The All-Mother is everything. The All-Mother is life . . ."

—Mark Reynolds, *Of Godlike Power*

THE PRIMAL AND SUPREME DIETY of the ancient world, the oldest and most universally worshiped, was the Great Mother, Mother Earth. Images of her date back to Aurignacian Cro-Magnon peoples from twenty-seven thousand years ago, and are found all over the Eurasian continent from Spain to Siberia. For thousands of years before there were any male gods, there was the Goddess, and her worship continued unabated clear up until its violent suppression by Iron Age patrism. When and where the worship of the Mother prevailed, women and Nature were held in esteem. The Chinese called her Kwan Yin; the Egyptians knew her as Isis; the Navajo call her Changing Woman. To the Greeks she was Gaea, and to many black peoples she is Yemanja. She is Aphrodite, the Goddess of Love, and she says: "All acts of love and pleasure are my rituals." She is also the ancient Crone who gives us both wisdom and death.

The Goddess is diversity. She represents both darkness and light and her worship is the reconciliation of opposites. We recognize no such thing as a "Good Goddess" or an "Evil Goddess." Death is part of the natural cycle as night follows day and we accept it with grace as her final gift. The search of Balance is the goal of her people, and it is achieved by the acceptance of multiple paths and truths. Dion Fortune once commented that all goddesses are manifestations of the One Great Goddess whose identity is as the universal feminine spirit of Nature.

Because of the diversity of the Goddess, she is seen as manifesting in many different aspects. She is often called the Triple Goddess, which refers to her link in the fertility cycle where she appears as Maiden, Mother, and Crone. Some ancient cultures personified this triplicity as the waxing, full, and waning moon, and other three-faced Goddess aspects are familiar to us as the Fates, the Graces, the Furies, the Muses, or even as Faith, Hope, and Charity. Another familiar division of her aspects is into Mother and Daughter (Demeter and Persephone), or as Sisters/Lovers (Fauna and Flora). Such polarities are also important in her worship— sometimes the polarity can exist with two different aspects of the Goddess representing both poles, but more commonly it is the great gender polarity, for the Goddess is a deity of sexual loving.

She is Ishtar, the eternal lover who awaits with eager arms the mortal man brave enough to risk her immortal favor. Many men have worshiped her as a lover, but she can never be possessed, for she belongs only to herself. She is Partnenos, the eternal virgin (in the patriarchal meaning "of her own household"). She represents the strong woman—not dominant, but independent. Her lovers are not truly human but divine. She has been the beloved of many gods, and though jealous male gods eventually suppressed her worship, she shared the co-rulership of Heaven and Earth for thousands of years of marital bliss. She is the inescapable yin necessary for the cosmic balance of yang yin. Symbols associated with her (the Tree of Life, the Sacred Serpent, the Labyrinth) are found in all parts of the globe, at the heart of all the Mysteries, and underlying all the later accretions of successive religions. The search for her is the search for our deepest ancestral roots.

> I am the star that rises from the twilight sea.
> I bring men dreams to rule their destiny.
> I am the eternal Woman; I am She!

The tides of all souls belong to me—
Touch of my hand confers polarity—
These are the moontides, these belong to me.
(Fortune, "Charge of the Moon Goddess")

HONOR THY MOTHER

In all the cultures where she is still worshiped, there is no confusion over her identity—she is Nature, and she is the Earth. She is not an atavistic abstraction, not a mystical metaphor, not a construct of consciousness. Her body is of substance as material as our own, and we tread upon her breast and are formed of her flesh. "Walk lightly on the bosom of the Earth Mother," says Sun Bear, and traditional Native Americans agree. Cherokee shaman Rolling Thunder emphasizes that "It's very important for people to realize this: the Earth is a living organism, the body of a higher individual who has a will and wants to be well, who is at times less healthy or more healthy, physically and mentally" (Boyd 1974). Frank Waters, author of *Masked Gods* and *Book of the Hopi*, makes the same point:

> . . . To Indians the Earth is not inanimate. It is a living entity, the mother of all life, our Mother Earth. All Her children, everything in nature, is alive: the living stone, the great breathing mountains, trees and plants, as well as birds and animals and man. All are united in one harmonious whole.

Renowned historian Arnold Toynbee, writing on "The Religious Background of the Present Environmental Crisis," has also observed that:

> For pre-monotheistic man, nature was not just a treasure-trove of 'natural resources.' Nature was, for him, a goddess, 'Mother Earth,' and the vegetation that sprang from the Earth, the animals that roamed, like man himself, over the Earth's surface, and the minerals hiding in the Earth's bowels, all partook of Nature's divinity. (1972, 58)

Before ever land was,
Before ever the sea,
Or soft hair of the grass,
Or faith limbs of the tree,
Or flesh-colored fruit of my branches,
I was—
And thy soul was in me.
(Swinburne, "Hertha")

THE GAEA THESIS

In order to understand the nature of the All-Mother, we must first understand our own origins. Each of us began our individual life as a single fertilized cell, or zygote. In the process of its innumerable divisions and multiplications, that cell kept dividing up and redistributing the very same protoplasm. That protoplasm which now courses through all of the several trillion cells of your adult body is the very same substance that once coursed through the body of that original zygote. For when a cell reproduces, the mother cell does not remain intact, but actually *becomes* the two new daughter cells. And this is why, no matter how many times a cell fissions in the process of embryological development, all the daughter cells collectively continue to comprise but one single organism.

We may imagine that, should our cells have consciousness akin to our own, they may very well fancy themselves to be independent entities living and dying in a world that to them would seem to be merely an inanimate environment. However, we know them to be in fact minute components of the far vaster living beings that we ourselves are.

Over four billion years ago, life on Earth began, as do we all, with a single living cell containing a replicating molecule of DNA. From that point on, that original cell, the first to develop the awesome capacity for reproduction, divided and redivided and subdivided its protoplasm into the myriads of plants and animals, including ourselves, that now inhabit this third planet from the Sun.

But no matter how many times a cell fissions in the process of embryological development, all the daugher cells collectively continue to comprise but one single organism. All life on Earth comprises the body of a single vast living being—Mother Earth herself. The Moon is her radiant heart, and in the tides beats the pulse of her blood. That protoplasm which coursed through the body of that first primeval ancestral cell is the very protoplasm that now courses through every cell of every living organism, plant or animal, of our planet. And the soul of our planetary biosphere is she whom we call Goddess (Zell, 1973).

> First life on my sources
> First drifted and swam.
> Out of me are the forces
> Which save it or damn.
> Out of me man and woman,
> and wild-beast and bird.

Before God was, I am.
(Swinburne, "Hertha")

> . . . Be the terror and the dread of all the wild beasts and all the
> birds of heaven, of everything that crawls on the ground and all the
> fish of the sea: they are handed over to you (Gen. 9:2–3).

Since the time of the Exodus, thirty-five hundred years ago,
Western civilization has been pursuing a course that has taken it
further and further from the Mother. The three great monotheistic religions of the West, Judaism, Christianity and Islam, have
from their beginning activity suppressed the worship of the Goddess, and have tortured and brutally murdered millions of her people.
Today, she is all but forgotten in the hearts of her children, and
her body lies raped and ravished in the wake of human progress.
The Goddess is the concept of feminine divinity incarnate. The
denial of feminine divinity results in the oppression of all women,
including Mother Nature. The thesis of Toynbee's essay "The
Religious Background of the Present Environmental Crisis" is, in
Toynbee's words,

> that some of the major maladies of the present-day world—for in-
> stance the recklessly extravagant consumption of nature's irreplace-
> able treasures, and the pollution of those of them that man has not
> already devoured—can be traced back in the last analysis to a reli-
> gious cause, and that this cause is the rise of monotheism. (1972, 63)

Where are You, then, Mother,
Whose strength was before
All other powers? Your name
Is the only freedom.
(Sen, *Grace and Mercy in Her Wild Hair*)

Pantheism is the view that everything in Nature is alive, and
that all living is Divine. The simplest explanation of Divinity, then,
is as "an energy field created by all living things. It surrounds us,
it penetrates us, it binds the galaxy together" (*Star Wars:* "The
Force"). Thus a pantheistic theology of Immanent Divinity ("Thou
Art God/dess") contrasts sharply with the theology of Transcendent Divinity ("God is Out There") presented by most of the "World's
Great Religions." Unlike the God worshiped by Christians, Mos-
lems, and Jews, the Goddess is not an all-powerful, indestructible,
non-physical being who created the world and exists apart from it.
"The All-Mother is Life. . . ." She is the very soul of the Earth,
and she lives or dies as all life on this planet lives or dies.

Mother, not maker;
Born, and not made.
Though her children forsake her,
Allured or afraid,
Praying prayers to the God of their fashion
She stirs not for all who have prayed.
Oh my children, too dutiful
Towards Gods not of me,
Was I not enough beautiful?
Was it hard to be free?
For, behold, I am with you,
am in you, and of you—
Look forth now and see!
(Swinburne, "Hertha")

"EARTH MOTHER, YOUR CHILDREN ARE HERE!"

Current environmental crises are legion. Chlorofluorocarbon chemicals are destroying the ozone layer in the atmosphere; industrial pollution is creating the greenhouse effect which will melt the polar ice caps, drowning the coastal regions; and the destruction of the rainforests and the pollution of phytoplankton in the seas is causing worldwide droughts. The problems are so vast and the politics of greed and corruption are so complex that it will truly take a miracle to reverse such global destruction. The only thing that can save us is a total and electrifying change of consciousness. Nothing short of a worldwide realization of our planetary situation will bring home the desperation of our plight. We must activate our Gaean identification so that we regain our shattered empathy with the Spirit of Nature. We must become one with the Earth Mother in order to feel her pain/our pain and make it stop before the cancer we have become reaches the terminal phase.

The word *religion* derives from the Latin *re-ligio*, "relinking." The very purpose of true religion, then, is to heal the rifts and alienations that have caused us to become separated from the divine Source of Being: the rifts between humanity and Nature; between matter and spirit; between mind and body; between man and woman; between our own egos and the Soul of Nature. Recent books analyzing the trends of our wayward world have, with increasing frequency, been calling for a return to worship of the Mother. Many wistful comments made by writers such as Merlin Stone, Mary Daly, James Lovelock, Judy Chicago, Dolores LaChapelle, Rene

Dubos, Daniela Gioseffi, Paolo Soleri, Elizabeth Gould Davis, Arnold Toynbee, Joseph Campbell, Marija Gimbutas, and Riane Eisler reflect a craving for such a religious revival. The truth is that such a revival has been going on for some time now—since the early 1960s—in the form of what we call the Neo-Pagan movement (from Latin *paganus*—"peasant" or country dweller—Paganism now refers to all nature religions). To the two hundred thousand or so Neo-Pagans who have been actively practicing and publishing for more than a quarter of a century, the greatest mystery of this religion is its continuing obscurity and invisibility to those such as the above-mentioned writers, who continue to publish books advocating such a movement as this, while remaining ignorant that it is already in effect. The new Paganism encompasses many Nature-oriented groups such as Feraferia, Church of All Worlds, Madrakara, Bear Tribe, Venusian Church, Pagan Way, Church of the Eternal Source, Odinic Fellowship, Reformed Druids, Earth Church of Amargi, and Children of the Earth Mother.

The largest contingent of modern Goddess-worshipers, however, is found in Witchcraft, or Wicca. Wicca is a pre-Christian European Pagan magical tradition: European shamanism. The violent suppression to the point of eradication of the followers of Wicca by the Inquisition can only be compared to the Jewish Holocaust of Nazi Germany (estimates of the number of martyrs run as high as nine million!), but today the Craft is making a powerful comeback on the wings of the re-emergent Goddess.

The Neo-Pagan movement, and especially feminist Witchcraft, has recently been joined by increasing numbers from the women's spirituality movement, by many thinkers from the Deep Ecology movement, and even by such radical environmental activists as Earth First! members. These are some of the forces that form the core of the movement to restore the Earth Goddess to her rightful place; a movement that has its roots in the combined studies of feminism and ecology and is the logical spiritual application of such studies. If witches can be priestesses of feminism, then Neo-Pagans are the chaplains of the ecology movement. The overall movement, though variously called Ecofeminism and Ecosophy, is truly an attempt at expressing Gaean Spirituality.

These three streams of spirituality—Deep Ecology, Goddess Spirituality, and Neo-Paganism—have met and mingled with Native American, Hawaiian, and other ancient spiritual teachings and fused somewhat with the more nebulous New Age movement. What is struggling to be born from this blending of pathways is a truly planetary religious metaphor that will transcend all the tradition-specific patterns in the same way the idea of Neo-Paganism absorbed and united a multiplicity of wildly differing but basically polytheistic religious groups in the 1960s and 70s. Perhaps what we are looking for could be called Gaean religion, because at the heart of our Unity is our identity as children of the same Mother—Gaea herself, Mother Earth. It is said that it's a wise child who knows its own Mother!

A brief digression on etymology here: Who is Gaea, that we would name a movement after her? The name *Gaea* is the Greek name for the Earth Mother Goddess, she who was created by light and by love from the primal cosmic chaos. Pierced by the arrows of Eros, Gaea gave birth to all the plants, animals, gods and goddesses, and of course the human race. So Gaea is the Mother of us all according to ancient Greek mythology.

From the moment that the people of Earth achieved the ability to observe the image of our planet spinning in all her radiant blue-and-white splendor through the black velvet night, we have been impelled towards planetary identification. We must inevitably begin to think of ourselves as one planet, one people, one organism. The power of that image alone unites us, not to mention the concept that the past three-and-a-half billion years of terrestrial evolution resembles one vast embryogenesis. Something is developing, hatching, unfolding as a self-reflexive mind capable of contemplating its own existence. Gaea developed increasingly complex eyes and extensions of her eyes/our eyes in order to contemplate her own image. And now, having seen herself through our satellite eyes, she is awakening to consciousness. She has a face, an identity, and now even a name, and so we inevitably come to identify ourselves through her as Gaean.

A Gaean movement would be deeply committed to communication and education. Many tribal people and many of the old nature-based folk religions such as native Australians, Hawaiians, Siberians, Tibetans, and Americans have come to the brink of extinction rather than allow the mysteries of their sacred rites to pass outside their tribes. Others have realized the need to become more eclectic if they are to survive.

The Gaean movement is presently small and largely unrecognized, since it is anarchic and not evangelical, but it has tremendous potential in having no single head and presenting a genuine answer to so many of the world's problems. Its vision is, in fact, an idea whose time has come. Yet there are still many obstacles, and revolutions in consciousness rarely happen overnight. The greatest forces operating against a new Gaean renaissance are inertia and apathy—the watchwords of the 1970s and 80s. But winds of change are blowing and by the time the century turns we will see that once again the Goddess is alive and Magick is afoot!

> And you who think to seek for me—
> Know that your seeking and yearning will avail you naught
> Unless you know the Mystery:
> That if that which you seek you find not within you,
> You shall never find it without.
> For behold: I have been with you from the beginning,
> And I am that which is attained at the end of desire.
> ("Charge of the Star Goddess")

REFERENCES

Boyd, Doug. 1974. *Rolling Thunder.* New York: Delta.

Reynolds, Mack. 1966. *Of Godlike Power.*

Toynbee, Arnold. 1972. "The Religious Background of the Present Environmental Crisis." *International Journal of Environmental Studies,* vol. 3.

Waters, Frank. "Lessons from the Indian Soul." *Psychology* 9.

Zell, Tim. 1973. "The Gods of Nature; The Nature of Gods." *Gnostica* 15.

3

EMERGENT NATURE SPIRITUALITY: AN EXAMINATION OF THE MAJOR SPIRITUAL CONTOURS OF THE CONTEMPORARY PAGAN WORLDVIEW

Dennis D. Carpenter

IN THIS CHAPTER, I examine the spiritual contours of the worldview inherent in contemporary Paganism. "Paganism," as I use the term, refers broadly to an emerging spiritual movement comprised of overlapping forms of spirituality referred to by many names (e.g. "Neo-Paganism," "Paganism," "Neo-Pagan Witchcraft," "Witchcraft," "the Craft," "Wiccan Spirituality," "Wicca," "Wicce," "Wiccan Religion," "the Old Religion," "Goddess Spirituality," "Nature Spirituality," "Nature Religion," "Earth-Based Spirituality," "Earth Religion," "Ecofeminist Spirituality," and "Euro-American Shamanism"). As reflected in the above listing of these terms, atypical capitalization will be utilized throughout this chapter with words having spiritual significance. Original usages, spelling, and capitalization will be used in citing quotations of others' writing even if different from the style I have chosen.

The literature that has dealt with contemporary Paganism is relatively limited. Two of the most influential writers on this subject are Margot Adler (1986, 1989) and Starhawk (1982, 1987a, 1987b, 1989a, 1989b, 1990). Unique in being practitioners as well as scholars of contemporary Paganism, their work will provide the foundation for examining and clarifying the fundamental spiritual contours of the Pagan worldview. I have chosen these texts because of the influential role they play in the current interest in Paganism as well as the substantive manner in which they articulate the various themes inherent in the Pagan worldview.

This chapter begins with a discussion of relevant background contexts. First, I will define spirituality and describe it within the context of postmodernism. I will summarize the main themes of postmodern spirituality as described by David Ray Griffin (1988a, 1988b, 1990) and Charlene Spretnak (1987a, 1987b, 1989, 1991) in order to determine the ways in which these themes are descriptive of contemporary Paganism. Since little has been written regarding the spiritual contours of the Pagan worldview, the presentation of postmodern spiritual themes provides a framework for the discussion of contemporary Paganism. Second, I will provide a brief overview of Paganism, including an examination of the bases for textual reconstruction. As I will demonstrate, Paganism relies more on insight derived from personal spiritual experience than from standard religious texts or a central religious authority. Third, I will provide a brief historical summary of Paganism, culminating in the description of Paganism as an example of a new religious movement.

Once these background contexts have been developed, I will identify and describe the major spiritual contours of the Pagan worldview. I have selected, as important for examination, the themes of interconnectedness, immanence and transcendence, animism and spiritism, monotheism and polytheism, magic, the sacred circle, and cyclicity. Following this, I devote a section to the implications of these spiritual themes, including the re-enchantment of Nature and the emphasis on personal spiritual experience. As I will demonstrate, various aspects of the natural world (e.g., the seasonal cycles) represent central elements in the spiritual contours of the Pagan worldview, which is why Paganism is frequently referred to as Nature Religion or Nature Spirituality.

In summary, the main purposes of this chapter are to describe the major spiritual contours of the contemporary Pagan worldview, to illustrate how these spiritual themes are symbolically related to Nature, and to consider the similarities between contemporary Paganism and postmodern spirituality. Clarity regarding the spiritual components of the Pagan worldview is important in conducting further investigation of the spiritual practices and experiences of Pagans. Also, clarification of the spiritual worldview should lend insight into the significance of Paganism in present-day society and its relationship to other contemporary social and spiritual movements.

In writing this chapter, I have drawn from published works as well as from my personal experiences as participant-observer. I have been involved in Paganism for ten years, working for the past eight years at Circle Sanctuary, a Wiccan church, a global Pagan educational/networking organization, a sacred Nature preserve, and a healing center. One of my primary job responsibilities has been editing *Circle Network News*, a newspaper/journal in which Pagans share their ideas stemming from scholarship and experience. My personal experiences as well as a review of the literature have led me to identify the major spiritual contours of the Pagan worldview selected for examination in this chapter. In addition, the discussion of Paganism within the context of postmodern spirituality was pursued because many of the themes within postmodern spirituality appeared similar to those within contemporary Paganism. While I speak of the Pagan worldview throughout this chapter, I must emphasize that Paganism refers to a diverse collection of individuals and spiritual forms. In some respects, my perceptions of the Pagan worldview represent an idealized formulation which may differ from the views of others who call themselves "Pagans."

BACKGROUND CONTEXTS

SPIRITUALITY WITHIN THE POSTMODERN CONTEXT

In the broadest sense, this chapter focuses upon spirituality, defined succinctly by Griffin as "a person's ultimate values and commitments, regardless of their content" (1988a, 2). In this definition, spirituality does not necessarily concern the Sacred or the Divine. In contrast, Spretnak provided definitions of spirituality that do include the Sacred or the Divine. She defined spirituality as "the focusing of human awareness on the subtle aspects of existence, a practice that reveals to us profound interconnectedness" (1987a, 24). Spretnak further described spirituality as the "sense of the sacred—our human perception of the larger reality, ultimate mystery, or creativity in the universe" (1991, 2). Drawing from these definitions, the term "spirituality" is used in this chapter to refer to the ultimate values, beliefs, and experiences that reflect human perceptions of the Sacred and give life meaning.

According to Griffin (1988b), postmodernism refers to a diffuse sentiment that humanity can and must go beyond modernity, i.e., the worldview that developed out of the seventeenth-century Galilean-Cartesian-Baconian-Newtonian science. On the positive side, the modern worldview has done quite well in providing explanations for observable phenomenon based on the epistemology of empiricism (i.e., the modern scientific method) and has produced unparalleled achievements in the areas of scientific discovery, industry, and technology (Krippner 1988). Griffin developed the argument that this modern worldview has also influenced spirituality. He identified individualism and dualism as characteristics central to the understanding of spirituality within a modern context, although such features are not necessarily connected to the Sacred according to his definition of spirituality. From a philosophical perspective, Griffin defined "individualism" as:

> the denial that the human self is internally related to other things, that is, that the individual person is significantly constituted by his or her relations to other people, to institutions, to nature, to the past, even perhaps to the divine creator. (1988a, 3)

Griffin contrasted premodernity with modernity by pointing out that the emergence of modernity involved a major shift from the communal orientation of premodernity to an individualistic self-understanding. Griffin used the term "dualism" to refer to the essential separation of the human soul, mind, or self from the rest of creation, as well as the separation of non-human Nature from any sort of sentience or spirituality. Griffin identified this notion of non-sentient Nature as providing the ideological justification for the domination and exploitation of nature during the era of modernity. Griffin further claimed that the mechanistic picture of Nature, basic to the mind-and-nature dualism, represented a denial of Divine immanence in Nature.

One of the basic arguments for needing to go beyond modernity that underlies the urgency of the situation rests in "the awareness that the continuation of modernity threatens the very survival of our planet" (Griffin, 1988b, xi). While modernity has brought about advances in scientific discovery, industry, and technology that has improved the lives of many, these advances have had their costs. Spretnak (1991) described such costs by enumerating the threats to human survival and global well-being that modernity has brought about, which include ecocide, nuclear arms, globalization of unqualified growth economies, the plunder of indigenous peoples' cultures and homelands, the loss of meaning beyond consumerism, the loss of community and connectedness with other people, and the loss of a secure sense of embeddedness in the rest of the natural world. These costs may be attributed to the uncontrolled growth of industry and technology, as well as to characteristics of the modern worldview. As mentioned previously, Griffin (1988a) believes that the view of Nature as mechanical and non-sentient has contributed to the ecological crisis (an idea that will be further developed in this chapter in the discussion of the re-enchantment of Nature).

Griffin (1988b) advocated "constructive" or "revisionary" postmodernism in which a postmodern worldview is constructed through a revision of modern premises and traditional concepts, involving a unity of scientific, ethical, aesthetic, and religious intuitions. Griffin went on to say that this constructive, revisionary postmodernism involved a creative synthesis of modern and premodern truths and values, including premodern notions of a divine reality, cosmic meaning, and an enchanted Nature. Spretnak advocated a similar form of postmodernism, called "ecological" postmodernism, which she described as:

> passage beyond the failed assumptions of modernity and a radical reorientation that preserves the positive advances of the liberal tradition and technological capabilities but is rooted in ecological sanity and meaningful human participation in the unfolding story of the Earth community and the universe. (1991, 4)

Griffin (1988a, 1990) identified a number of specific themes characterizing postmodern spirituality and social thinking and the attempt to overcome the shortcomings of modernity, including: (*a*) the reality of internal relations or interconnections, i.e., individual identity is constituted by one's relationships to body, family, culture, and the larger environment; (*b*) a nondualistic relation of humans to Nature and of the Divine reality to the world, by which humans experience an organic sense of oneness with Nature and with other life forms; (*c*) the immanence of both the past and the future in the present, acknowledging the value of past knowledge and traditions as well as concern for the future; (*d*) the universality and centrality of creativity, meaning that the shape of the world is determined by the cocreativity of the Divine and all of Earth's creatures, including humans; (*e*) postpatriarchy, recognizing the equality of the sexes on all levels including metaphorical perceptions of the Divine based on gender; (*f*) communitarianism (versus individualism and nationalism), advocating that social policy be directed toward the preservation and re-creation of various forms of local community including family, religious organizations, bioregions, and cultural regions; (*g*) the "deprivatization" of religion, involving the rejection of the autonomy of morality, politics, and economics from religious values, as well as the acceptance of religious plurality based upon equality; and (*h*) the rejection of materialism, in the sense of economism, meaning the subordination of social, religious, moral, aesthetic, and ecological interests to short-term economic interests.

This postmodern context described by Griffin (1988a, 1990) and Spretnak (1991) is relevant to the discussion of contemporary Paganism because, as will be shown, Paganism represents an attempt to incorporate premodern notions of divine reality, cosmic meaning, and an enchanted Nature into present-day life. Also, the Pagan worldview will also be shown to have direct implications regarding the relationship of humans to the rest of Nature in the global Earth community.

INTRODUCTION TO CONTEMPORARY PAGANISM

Contemporary Paganism does not represent a solidly unified religious tradition with a universally accepted set of standard texts, beliefs, and practices. As was pointed out in the introduction to this chapter, a variety of descriptive labels have been used to describe overlapping forms of spirituality included within the broad category of Paganism. Those who use the word "Pagan" to describe themselves can be generally described as drawing upon religions, philosophies, and mythologies with pre-Christian roots. Differences exist regarding which pre-Christian spiritual traditions and mythologies are used for inspiration and what form current spiritual expression takes. Among the premodern cultures represented in the contemporary Pagan renaissance are Egyptian, Roman, Greek, Celtic, Scandinavian, and Native American.

Wiccan Spirituality, or Witchcraft, has been the dominant influence in the growth of contemporary Paganism. Wiccan Spirituality is believed to be the re-emergence, in the twentieth century, of the pre-Christian religion of Western Europe. (This historical context will be further developed in an upcoming section.) Some practitioners use the terms "Paganism" and "Wiccan Spirituality" interchangeably, while others use "Paganism," as I have chosen to do in this chapter, as a term referring broadly to an emerging spiritual movement comprised of overlapping forms of spirituality, of which Wiccan Spirituality is an example. The use of "Paganism" as the more general label is advocated by Starhawk: "The Old Religion—call it Witchcraft, Wicca, the Craft, or with a slightly broader definition, Paganism or New Paganism—is both old and newly invented" (1982, xii). Similar usage is reflected in Adler (1986) and Fox (1979). Due to its dominant influence, I will make special reference to aspects of Wiccan Spirituality in order to help identify general themes characterizing the worldview inherent in contemporary Paganism. I will focus on these general themes rather than addressing the ways in which the individuals who call themselves Pagans and/or Wiccans may differ.

BASES FOR TEXTUAL RECONSTRUCTION OF PAGANISM

Various writers have stressed that contemporary Paganism does not have a clear textual heritage, and this lack is identified as a valued feature by many of those involved. According to Starhawk,

> Witchcraft or the Old Religion is not based on dogma or a set of beliefs, nor on scriptures or a sacred book revealed by a great man. Witchcraft takes its teachings from nature, and reads inspiration in the movements of the sun, moon, and stars, the flight of birds, the slow growth of trees, and the cycles of the seasons. (1989b, 16–17)

Adler also described most contemporary Pagan religions as having few creeds and no prophets. She further pointed out that such religions are "based on seasonal celebration, the cycles of planting and harvesting, on custom and experience rather than the written word" (1989, 153). Since such religions are based on myth and metaphor rather than literal understanding. Adler suggested that contemporary Paganism is similar to a poem or work of art.

According to Drengson, the ancient Pagan ways were Nature religions that represented evolving and creative cultural processes rather than binding obligation to texts or central authority. While an ongoing obligation to texts can involve a creative process, this was apparently not the sort of creativity valued in earlier Nature religions. "Stories, rituals, dancing and songs kept [ancient Pagans] . . . attuned to the ongoing, creative processes of Nature, for all that they needed to know to survive and thrive was continuously being revealed by the ongoing processes of Nature within and around them" (Drengson 1988, 21). Obviously, life in contemporary society is very different from that in ancient times and it could be argued that attunement with Nature is not enough for survival in today's complex social systems and urban environments.

Nevertheless, those interested in contemporary Paganism recognize that human survival is jeopardized if the relationship with and teachings from Nature are overlooked.

Weaver elaborated on the relationship between the lack of a clear textual history and present-day practice from the perspective of Goddess Spirituality:

> If we take the formula, "first the appearance, then the dance, then the story," to specify the proper relationship among theophany, ritual and theology, then we can say that the theophany is prehistoric and not textually recoverable; that rituals are now being created and "rediscovered" by believers in a celebration of diversity; and that the theology has just begun to be written. (1989, 63–64)

Weaver's views also emphasize the creative aspects of contemporary Paganism.

As demonstrated in this section, emphasis and value is placed upon attunement to and inspiration from Nature rather than upon dogma, central authority, sets of beliefs, and sacred texts. Furthermore, creativity and experiential celebration are viewed as central to the spiritual life of Pagans. While some Wiccan and other Pagan churches have identified beliefs and structure as part of their organizational development and legal interface with secular society, emphasis continues to be on personal spiritual experience rather than imposed dogma. In some respects, this emphasis on personal spiritual experience could be regarded as an aspect of the modern emphasis on individuality as described by Griffin (1988a), because the focus is more on the spiritual experience of the individual rather than the spiritual life of a community. The question then arises regarding whether this emphasis on personal spiritual experience may be regarded as postmodern in any way. If such experiences contribute to acknowledgement of the postmodern themes to be discussed further in this chapter as well as stimulate social action to help solve the problems of the modern world and the global community, then they may be considered postmodern. If such experiences only serve the individual through gratifying a sense of self or providing pleasure, then they may be considered modern.

THE HISTORICAL CONTEXT OF CONTEMPORARY PAGANISM

The Premodern Heritage
Despite the implied value placed on the lack of a religious textual heritage providing the inspiration for the spiritual life of contemporary Pagans, many Pagans are also struggling to understand their

spirituality within particular historical perspectives in order that it might have historical and cultural legitimacy. Adler described this struggle to recover a spiritual heritage:

> Neopagans are searching among the archaic images of nature, among the ruins of traditions lost, in order to find, revive, and re-create the old polytheistic nature religions. The fascination with long dead pagan traditions is part of a search for cultural roots. Since most Neopagans are white, they often look toward Europe, just as Alex Haley looked to Africa. Neopagans are searching among these traditions and creating new religions. (1989, 151)

Adler also noted that "modern Wicca descends in spirit from precisely those fragments of pre-Christian beliefs and practices that nobody denies: myths, poetry, the classics, and folk customs" (1986, 87). The search for such spiritual heritage is complicated by the fact that Christian religious and political dominance resulted in the destruction of much of the pre-Christian Pagan heritage.

As mentioned previously, Griffin (1988b) maintained that a constructive, revisionary postmodernism involves a creative synthesis and revision of modern and premodern truths and values, including premodern notions of a divine reality, cosmic meaning, and an enchanted Nature. Spretnak implied such a revision of the premodern when she said that "the contemporary renaissance of Goddess spirituality draws on a growing body of knowledge about historical Goddess religion but is shaped and energized by the living practice, which is both personal and communal, ancient and spontaneous" (1991, 133). Starhawk also alluded to such a revision when she summarized the historical evolution of Witchcraft and Paganism:

> Its roots go back to the pre-Judeo-Christian tribal religions of the West, and it is akin in spirit, form, and practice to Native American and African religions. Its myths and symbols draw from the woman-valuing, matristic, Goddess-centered cultures that underlie the beginnings of civilization. It is not a religion with a dogma, a doctrine, or a sacred book; it is a religion of experience, of ritual, of practices that change consciousness and awaken power-from-within. Beneath all, it is a religion of connection with the Goddess, who is immanent in nature, in human beings, in relationships. Because the Goddess is here, She is eternally inspirational. And so Witchcraft is eternally reinvented, changing, growing, alive. (1982, xii)

While Spretnak and Starhawk both imply the revision of premodern truths and values, the manner in which the premodern is accessed within a modern context remains open for investigation.

Adler described what she called the "Myth of Wicca" which represents a summary of what has been regarded by many Wiccans as the historical evolution of their form of spirituality. Adler presented the following account of the Myth of Wicca:

> Witchcraft is a religion that dates back to paleolithic times to the worship of the god of the hunt and the goddess of fertility. One can see remnants of it in cave paintings and in the figurines of goddesses that are many thousands of years old. This early religion was universal. The names changed from place to place but the basic deities were the same. When Christianity came to Europe, its inroads were slow. Kings and nobles were converted first, but many folk continued to worship in both religions. Dwellers in rural areas, the Pagans and "Heathens," kept to the old ways. Churches were built on the sacred sites of the Old Religion. The names of the festivals were changed but the dates were kept. The old rites continued in folk festivals, and for many centuries Christian policy was one of slow cooption. During the times of persecution the Church took the god of the Old Religion and—as is the habit with conquerors—turned him into the Christian devil. The Old Religion was forced underground, its only records set forth, in distorted form, by its enemies. Small families kept the religion alive and, in 1951, after the Witchcraft Laws in England were repealed, it began to surface again. (1986, 45–46)

As illustrated in this descriptive account, Witchcraft is allegedly a very old religion that was suppressed by the process of Christianity gaining religious and political predominance in Europe. Some individuals have argued that, despite the variety of attempts to eliminate it, Witchcraft has survived intact into the twentieth century, as described in the next section.

Twentieth-Century History

Several individuals were responsible in the first half of the twentieth century for promoting the basic historical outline reflected in Adler's Myth of Wicca (e.g., Gardner [1954] 1970, [1959] 1971; Graves 1948; Leland [1897] 1974; and Murray [1921] 1971, [1931] 1970). The works of Murray and Gardner are particularly important and merit further attention here.

Margaret Murray was a British anthropologist who claimed to have discovered the existence of a pre-Christian religion which she called the ancient religion of Western Europe. Murray ([1921] 1971) studied the evidence from the witch trials of Britain, including the legal records of the trials, pamphlets giving accounts of individual witches, and the works of inquisitors and other writers that she believed showed the beliefs, organization, and ritual of a previously unrecognized cult. Murray called what she discovered "Ritual Witchcraft" or the "Dianic Cult" and maintained that this represented the religious beliefs and ritual of those known in the medieval times as "witches." Murray maintained that the deity of this cult was incarnate in a man, a woman, or an animal. She described a male deity in the shape of a man with two faces which she related to an Italian God called Janus or Dianus, to a God in southern France, and to one in the English Midlands. Murray claimed that the feminine form of the name Dianus, which she identified as "Diana," could be found throughout Western Europe as the name of the female deity or leader of the witches. Because of the prevalence of the deities Dianus and Diana, Murray called the ancient religion she claimed to have discovered the Dianic Cult.

Considerable debate centers around the legitimacy of Murray's claims that a pre-Christian religion called "Witchcraft" had survived intact into modern times. In the foreword of the 1971 reprint of Murray's 1921 book, Sir Steven Runciman described how Murray's work was generally discounted by those who could not accept her claims for various theological reasons and by anthropologists who claimed that she jumped to conclusions which her data did not support. Regardless of the legitimacy of her claims, Murray's work helped inspire the rebirth of Paganism by creating a context of alleged historical authenticity and continuity which individuals such as Kelly (1991) believe provided the inspiration for later work by Gerald Gardner.

The 1951 repeal of the Witchcraft Acts of 1735 (which had forbidden Witchcraft in England) set the stage for Gerald Gardner, in 1954, to publish *Witchcraft Today*. In this book Gardner lent credibility to Margaret Murray's claims that Witchcraft was an ancient religion surviving into modern times by claiming that he was a witch initiated into a Witchcraft coven whose traditions had been passed along from generation to generation, surviving even the Inquisition of the Middle Ages. Debate exists in the literature regarding whether Gardner was actually initiated into a coven of continuous lineage as he described it or whether he created the tradition he wrote about by synthesizing what he read from a number of previously published sources, including the works of Margaret Murray.

Interested in the relationship between the foundational myths and the actual history of Witchcraft, Kelly (1991) utilized interviews with important figures in this history as well as exhaustive textual analysis to investigate the authenticity of Gerald Gardner's claim that he was initiated in 1939 into one of the last surviving covens in England. Even though Kelly concluded that no evidence existed to suggest that Gardner was actually initiated into such a coven and that Gardner actually pieced together material from the variety of texts produced by Leland, Murray, Graves, and others, Kelly credited Gardner as the creative genius behind an important new religious movement in the twentieth century.

Adler noted that a change had occurred by 1975 regarding acceptance of the Myth of Wicca:

> Many Witches no longer accepted the Murrayite thesis totally. While some still talked of "unbroken traditions," few of them thought Gardner—or anyone else—had a direct line to the paleolithic. And people in the Craft [i.e., Witchcraft] were beginning to regard the question of origin as unimportant. Most had become comfortable with the idea of creativity and originality as the springboard to the Craft. As more and more of the Wicca came to see that there was no such thing as a totally unbroken or uncontaminated tradition, they began to reassess the meaning of their movement. (1986, 87)

While Adler noted that many Wiccans and other Pagans have changed their views regarding the historical authenticity of their spiritual traditions, it should be noted that this subject remains a touchy issue for some Wiccan denominations within Paganism. Some practitioners still believe that they are practicing the Old Religion as it existed in premodern times and has been handed down through initiatory lineage. The conclusions of Kelly (1991) have met with considerable negativity among many Gardnerians due to his assertion that direct ancient initiatory lineage does not exist within Gardnerian Witchcraft. Apparently, this is a significant issue due to the legitimacy that such history provides. Such lineage may also provide, for some practitioners, a sense of privileged status upon being initiated into such a very old and esoteric tradition. This debate may never be settled and it may not be important to settle this conflict. While premodern themes provide the foundation for this movement, it is the manner in which such themes are reworked to be appropriate in a contemporary context that is of greatest relevance to the significance of Witchcraft as a postmodern form of spirituality.

While considerable creative inspiration for contemporary Paganism occurred prior to the 1960s in the work of those individuals already mentioned, the seeds of this movement really took root during the 1960s and began to grow most profusely during the 1970s and 1980s. Illustrating the recentness of this history, the two most influential books on the contemporary interest, *Drawing Down the Moon* by Margot Adler and *The Spiral Dance* by Starhawk, were not published until 1979. In the same year, Selena Fox published the first *Circle Guide to Wicca and Pagan Resources*, which also helped herald in a new era of interest and involvement in Paganism and was instrumental in stimulating cooperative networking among practitioners of different forms of Paganism. In the 1986 revision of *Drawing Down the Moon*, Adler referred to a position paper presented by Selena Fox at a 1978 Pagan conference in Georgia. In that paper, Fox said:

> [In 1978] the "Earth Religions Movement" was undergoing its rite of passage, its coming of age, after passing through a rocky adolescence. The future would include: an increase in the number of Pagans willing to appear in the media and willing to take an active, public position; an increase in the number of Pagan newsletters and published books; an increase in communication between different traditions and groups; an increase in festivals and conferences; an increase in contact between Pagan and Craft groups and other "new age" groups; the emergence of self-supporting Craft communities, businesses, and enterprises; and the sharing of music and art. (Adler 1986, 417)

Adler evaluated Fox's predictions by saying "in 1986, this wish list is simply an accurate tally of things that have in fact happened" (p. 417). Since 1986, Paganism has continued to grow at a rapid pace, with the areas of growth that occurred in the first half of the 1980s showing continued growth on through the second half of the 1980s and into the present.

Contemporary Paganism as New Religion
Contemporary Paganism represents a synthesis of historical inspiration and present-day creativity. While the authenticity of historical claims can certainly be questioned, such claims nevertheless provide inspiration for the current evolution of new forms of spirituality. Jones and Matthews identified an important reason underlying the current interest in Paganism:

> Paganism has re-emerged within Western twentieth-century society for a good reason, for though it draws upon the past, it is designed for living in the present. Its reappearance at this time is a spiritual corrective to what many see as the head-long hurtle towards planetary destruction. (1990, 13)

This depiction by Jones and Matthews of Paganism emerging out of threats of planetary destruction is similar to the views of Griffin (1988b) and Spretnak (1991) regarding postmodern spirituality as a response to threats of environmental catastrophe.

Starhawk described Paganism as a new religion, while acknowledging its ancient roots:

> As we have seen, Goddess religion is unimaginably old, but contemporary Witchcraft could just as accurately be called the New Religion. The Craft today, is undergoing more than a revival, it is experiencing a renaissance, a re-creation. Women are spurring this renewal, and actively reawakening the Goddess, the image of "the legitimacy and beneficence of female power." (1989b, 22–23)

Kelly also placed Paganism within the context of new religion in maintaining that "Gardner was engaging in what is actually a well-known sort of religious behavior: the inventing of a new history for one's community is a way of searching for meaning and authenticity" (1991, 179). Kelly further provided perspectives on Paganism as a new religion:

> The current scholarly view is that the creating of new religions is a normal, healthy, and universal activity by which creative people (that is, the educated middle class, not the outcasts) in all societies attempt to meet their own religious needs; and as such, its existence does not need any further explanation. Furthermore, if all religions begin at some time and place as new religions, then the study of new religions is not a luxury; it is not the study of fringe sects, marginal people, epiphenomena, weird hippies, and so on. Rather, it is the study of characteristics central to all religions. (p. 3)

While Kelly's assertion that creative people are from the educated middle class and are not outcasts can certainly be questioned, he does describe the creative aspects of religious development.

As mentioned before, in her discussion of the Myth of Wicca Adler (1986) described the prevalence of creativity and originality as the springboard to Witchcraft. As shown in this section, Starhawk (1989b) and Kelly (1991) also pointed out the creative aspects of Paganism as new religion. Orion (1990) found Pagans to be creative individuals and the movement to be one that fosters the acquisition and use of creativity, and concluded that the core quality characterizing all approaches in Paganism is creativity. Consistent with these viewpoints, my observations have led me to the conclusion that many Pagans are involved in such spiritual paths because of the creative freedom to pick and choose various viewpoints, beliefs, and practices and to integrate them into a spiritual system that meets the needs of those involved. Such creative potential seems to lie at the heart of Paganism as new religion and is similar to the universality and centrality of creativity described by Griffin (1988a, 1990) as characteristic of postmodern spirituality.

So far in this chapter, I have portrayed Paganism as a new religion that involves a revision of premodern truths and values. As demonstrated in this section, creativity seems to play a significant role in this revisionary process. However, the manner in which this occurs deserves further study. The question may also be raised regarding whether contemporary Pagans attempt to synthesize the premodern with the modern or whether they reject the modern in favor of the premodern. Adler (1986) investigated this question and was surprised to discover that the majority of Pagans she encountered were optimistic about the uses of science and modern technology. In addition, these same individuals did not want to return to the past in the process of taking inspiration from it. Adler also discovered that many of those involved in Paganism were employed in technical fields. While such findings suggest that some kind of synthesizing process is occurring, the nature and extent of such tendencies warrant further investigation.

MAJOR SPIRITUAL CONTOURS OF THE PAGAN WORLDVIEW

So far, I have focused on the background contexts for discussing the spiritual contours of the Pagan worldview. I have provided a brief historical summary that culminated in the description of the creative aspects of Paganism as new religion. One of the major points emerging from this discussion is the emphasis on personal spiritual experience rather than standard religious texts or a central religious authority. I have also discussed spirituality within the context of postmodernity in order to provide a frame of reference for examining contemporary Paganism. In the following section, I will describe the major spiritual contours of the contemporary Pagan worldview which I have identified as a result of my personal experiences with Paganism, in addition to a review of the Pagan literature. Throughout, I will identify similarities between the spiritual contours of the Pagan worldview and the themes of postmodernity where appropriate.

INTERCONNECTEDNESS

The theme of interconnectedness represents a fundamental component of the Pagan worldview. Griffin (1990) and Spretnak (1987a) described the theme of interconnectedness within a postmodern context which helps clarify this aspect of the Pagan spiritual worldview. As mentioned before, Spretnak claimed that profound interconnectedness is revealed when human awareness is focused on the subtle aspects of existence. Spretnak described the true nature of being as nondualistic in saying "all is one, all forms of existence are comprised of one continuous dance of matter/energy arising and falling away, arising and falling away" (p. 24). For her, the experience of the true nature of being occurs in "states of grace":

> Experiential, rather than merely intellectual, awareness of the profound connectedness is what I hold to be the true meaning of being in "a state of grace." Awe at the intricate wonders of the creation and celebration of the cosmic unfolding are the roots of worship. (p. 26)

Consistent with the views of Spretnak, Griffin maintained that no feature of postmodern spirituality is emphasized more than the reality of internal relations, the idea that all things are interconnected and that these interconnections are internal to the very essence of the things themselves. Similarly, Starhawk identified one of the core principles of Goddess religion, or Witchcraft, as interconnection which she described as "the understanding that all being is interrelated, that we are linked with all of the cosmos as parts of one living organism. What affects one of us affects us all" (1989b, 10). Fox offered a similar viewpoint when she said, "Mother Earth is the Goddess of Planet Earth. She is the Ecosphere, the totality of all lifeforms and substance here. She is the Web of Life of this world" (1989a, 27). This symbol of the "Web of Life" sometimes depicted as a spider's web or as a web of light around the planet has been used by many Pagans to represent the theme of interconnectedness. The following popular Pagan chant reflects this notion well: "We are the flow, We are the ebb, We are the weaver, We are the web."

IMMANENCE AND TRANSCENDENCE

Related to the theme of interconnectedness, the theme of immanence and transcendence refers to the human understanding about the relation of the Divine to the world. The terms pantheism, panentheism, and deism have been used to refer to this relation.

According to Runes, pantheism means that "the essence of God or the Absolute is completely immanent in the world, i.e. is identical with it" (1983, 157). At the other extreme, "Deism means that God is essentially absent or transcendent from the world" (p. 157). In between these two extremes, panentheism refers to:

> The view that God interpenetrates everything without cancelling the relative independent existence of the world of entities; moreover, while God is immanent, this immanence is not absolute (as in pantheism); God is more than the world, transcendent, in the sense that though the created is dependent upon the Creator the Creator is not dependent upon the created. God thus is held to be the highest type of Unity, viz., a Unity in Multiplicity. (p. 239)

Griffin described panentheism, within the context of the the theme of interconnectedness, as a characteristic form of postmodern spirituality:

> The reality of spiritual energy is affirmed but it is felt to exist within and between all nodes in the cosmic web of interconnections. It is thus dispersed throughout the universe, not concentrated in a source wholly transcendent to it. Postmodernists who speak of God generally affirm a naturalistic panentheism, according to which God is in all things and all things are in God. . . . The relations between things are regarded as internal to them, and as their participation in the universal web of interconnections, which is itself holy or sacred, being the source of all value and power. (1990, 2)

Such panentheism may be regarded as postmodern in the sense of moving beyond the individuation and duality of modernity already described. Sheldrake also revealed a panentheistic perspective when he said, "God is not remote and separate from nature, but immanent within it. Yet at the same time God is the unity which transcends it" (1990, 167).

The concept of the divine feminine, or Goddess, is valued by many Pagans as a metaphor/symbol of the immanent Divine. Starhawk defined "immanence" as "the awareness of the world and everything in it as alive, dynamic, interdependent, interacting, and infused with moving energies: a living being, a weaving dance" (1982, 9). Starhawk further described Divine immanence from a Goddess perspective:

> The Goddess can be seen as the symbol, the normative image of immanence. She represents the divine embodied in nature, in human beings, in the flesh. The Goddess is not one image but many— a constellation of forms and associations—earth, air, fire, water, moon

and star, sun, flower and seed, willow and apple, black, red, white, Maiden, Mother, and Crone. She includes the male in her aspects: He becomes the child and Consort, stag and bull, grain and reaper, light and dark. Yet the femaleness of the Goddess is primary not to denigrate the male, but because it represents bringing life into the world, valuing the world. The Goddess, The Mother as symbol of that value, tells us that the world itself is the content of the world, its true value, its heart, and its soul. (pp. 9–10)

Spretnak stressed the fundamental importance of immanence from a Goddess perspective, while adding a transcendent component. She described immanence as meaning that "the divine—creativity in the universe, or ultimate mystery—is laced throughout the cosmic manifestations in and around us" (1991, 136). Spretnak described transcendence as representing the Sacred Whole, or infinite complexity of the universe, and contrasted this meaning with the transcendent sky god of patriarchal religion. Viewing the Goddess as a metaphor for Divine immanence and the transcendent Sacred Whole, Spretnak maintained that the Goddess "expresses ongoing regeneration with the cycles of her Earthbody and contains the mystery of diversity within unity: the extraordinary range of differentiation in forms of life on Earth issued from her dynamic form and are kin" (p. 137).

Adler (1986) noted that many Pagans maintain a pantheistic perspective, meaning that Divinity is diffused throughout the world and is inherent in all Nature. Starhawk's conceptualization (1982) of the Goddess as a symbol of Divine immanence also demonstrates such a pantheistic perspective. However, upon closer examination of Starhawk's viewpoints, a transcendent aspect emerges within the theme of "unity in diversity." As suggested by Griffin (1990), Spretnak (1991), and Runes (1983), "unity in diversity" is a central theme of the panentheistic worldview, meaning that the Divine is immanent (i.e., interspersed throughout Nature in the web of interconnections), as well as transcendent (i.e., perceived as a unifying whole). According to Fox, "The Goddess is around us and within us. She is immanent and transcendent" (1989a, 3). Fox further described such immanent and transcendent aspects when she said, "I know that Divinity has many facets and I experience this through a variety of Gods and Goddesses. I also honor Divine Oneness, the Unity of All" (1990, 45). Starhawk described the paradoxical aspects of this theme of "unity in diversity":

> A mirror image is a reversed image, the same, but opposite, the reverse polarity. The image expresses the paradox: All things are

one, yet each thing is separate, individual, unique . . . Witchcraft holds to the truth of paradox and sees each view as equally valid. They reflect and complement each other; they do not contradict each other. The world of separate things is the reflection of the One; the One is the reflection of the myriad separate things of the world. We are all 'swirls' of the same energy; yet each swirl is unique in its own form and pattern. (1989b, 39)

In summary, Pagans maintain immanent and pantheistic perspectives in that the Divine is seen as dispersed through Nature and is Nature. To the extent that Pagans also acknowledge the mutual existence of a unifying aspect or transcendent Whole, as have Fox (1989a, 1990) and Starhawk (1989b), they may be regarded as panentheists.

ANIMISM AND SPIRITISM

According to Runes, animism is defined as "the view that souls are attached to all things either as their inner principle of spontaneity or activity, or as their dwellers; the doctrine that Nature is inhabited by various grades of spirits" (1983, 28). In other words, animism refers to "the attribution of a living soul to inanimate objects and natural phenomena" (Simpson and Weiner 1989, 478). Spiritism reflects the characteristics of animism, but adds an element of communicability. According to Runes, spiritism is defined as:

the doctrine that ancestral or other spirits can communicate with man; belief in the existence of conscious, voluntary beings other than of the organic, corporeal type represented by animals and man, such as souls connected with inorganic Nature, disembodied nature spirits, manes or ancestral spirits, demons, celestial beings, angelic beings, deities. (p. 316)

Another term related to animism is "hylozoism" which refers to "the conception of nature as alive or animated, of reality as alive" (p. 149).

Consistent with these definitions and closely related to the theme of immanence, Pagans view all of Nature as alive and imbued with spiritual energy. Adler highlighted the animistic aspects of the premodern world which she believes provides the inspiration for the reanimation of Nature by contemporary Pagans. She described the premodern worldview as one which "did not conceive of a separation between 'animate' and 'inanimate.' All things—from rocks and trees to dreams—were considered to partake of the life force" (1986, 25). In addition to this notion of all natural phenomena as living, many Pagans believe that communication is possible between humans and various aspects, or spirits, of the animated natural world.

Over the years, I have heard these concepts of an animated world and communication with it revealed in a number of ways by Pagans. Many report having experienced interspecies communication with other life forms such as plants, trees, and animals. Many also report connecting with power animals, or animal spirits, which serve as spiritual helpers or guides. Another commonly reported set of experiences involves connecting with special places of spiritual power in Nature. Reflected in these experiences are the beliefs that Nature is alive, that various aspects of Nature maintain an autonomous sense of spirit or consciousness, and that communication can occur between humans and these aspects of Nature. Fox illustrated such themes when she said, "The Wiccan Religion is animistic in that every human, tree, animal, stream, rock, and other forms of Nature are seen to have a Divine Spirit within" (1989b, 1). Fox went on to say that "many Wiccans have personal communication and friendships with various animals, plants and other lifeforms" (p. 1). DiZerega (1988) offered an experiential account that clearly reflects such viewpoints. DiZerega described his experiences during a ritual invocation to the Goddess: "Suddenly, very suddenly, the atmosphere surrounding us changed. A presence permeated the area, and was experienced by most there as very powerful, very feminine, very nurturing, and very loving" (1988, 24). DiZerega went on to indicate that subsequent stronger experiences convinced him that the powers of Nature will often respond when approached: "Experiential evidence suggests to me that these beings are separate from us. Their communication frequently works with symbols carrying levels of meaning not easily described through discursive reason."

Fox described her relationship with the natural world which links the themes of interconnectedness and animism:

> I am a Pagan. I am a part of the whole of Nature. The Rocks, the Animals, the Plants, the Elements, and the Stars are my relatives. Other humans are my sisters and brothers, whatever their races, colors, genders, ages, nationalities, religions, lifestyles. The Earth is my Mother and the Sun is my Father. I am a part of this large family of Nature, not the master of it. (1990, 44)

The implications of such viewpoints regarding the human relationship to the rest of Nature will be discussed further in the section about the ecological aspects of the contemporary Pagan worldview.

Consistent with the view of all Nature as alive, Pagans revere the Earth as a living being, often referring to the Earth as Mother Earth (Fox 1989, 1990) or Gaia (also spelled Gaea), after the primordial Greek Earth Goddess (Farrar and Farrar 1987). Lovelock (1979) also referred to this Greek Goddess in coining the term "Gaia Hypothesis" to refer to the interconnectedness of all life on Earth and to the Earth's ecosphere exhibiting the behavior of a single living organism through self-regulation. In describing Paganism, G'Zell said that "it is a living religion that deals not only with environmental issues but re-incorporates the Female Divine Principle in the form of Gaea, seen not only as a living planet but as a living Goddess" (1990, 11). Sheldrake further expanded on the animistic nature of this "living earth concept" to include the whole universe:

> The organismic or holistic philosophy of nature which has grown up over the last sixty years is a new form of animism. It implicitly or explicitly regards all nature as alive. The universe as a whole is a developing organism, and so are the galaxies, solar systems and biospheres within it, including the Earth. (1990, 125)

Sheldrake cited the vision of the Earth from space provided by astronauts and cosmonauts as well as the realization that human economic activities are altering the global climate as underlying reasons for the re-emergence of the premodern view of the Earth as a living being in contemporary times. While the capability of viewing Earth from space is made possible by modern technology, the impact such images have had may be regarded as postmodern in the manner in which they have helped shift human perception away from the notion of individual separateness and toward the notion of the planet as an interconnected living whole within the vastness of space. These images of a finite blue-green sphere hanging in the darkness of space have also contributed to humans once again understanding the biosphere as a living system and to a rethinking of the relationship between humans, technology, and the environment. Such perceptions of the Earth and all of Nature as alive and interconnected constitutes a fundamental tenet of Paganism that fosters a sense of compassion and an obligation to save the environment (which will be discussed further in a later section).

MONOTHEISM AND POLYTHEISM

According to Runes, polytheism is the "theory that Divine reality is numerically multiple, that there are many gods; opposed to monotheism" (1983, 258). Monotheism, in this case, refers to the theory that Divine reality is characterized by one God, usually believed to be transcendent. Adler offered the following definition of polytheism from the Nature-based perspectives of Pagans:

> The idea of polytheism is grounded in the view that reality (divine or otherwise) is multiple and diverse. And if one is a pantheist-polytheist, as are many Neo-Pagans, one might say that all nature is divinity and manifests itself in myriad forms and delightful complexities. (1986, 25)

Considerable variation exists regarding whether individual Pagan practitioners and Pagan groups can be described as monotheistic and/or polytheistic. As already described in the discussion of "unity in diversity" as it relates to the theme of interconnectedness, one of the most prevalent points of view is the result of synthesizing the polytheistic and monotheistic perspectives, in recognizing the diverse, multiplistic aspects of the Divine, but also acknowledging a unifying aspect. Fox described such a synthesizing perspective:

> The Wiccan religion is monotheistic in that there is an honoring of Divine Unity. It also is polytheistic in that Wiccans honor the Divine through a variety of female and male deity forms—Goddesses and Gods which are aspects of the Divine Female and Divine Male and their Unity. (1989b, 1)

Adler claimed that feminist Witches often hold a monotheistic viewpoint, worshiping the Goddess as the One. She further pointed out that many Wiccans "might well be considered 'duotheists,' conceiving of deity as the Goddess of the Moon, Earth, and sea, and the God of the woods, the hunt, the animal realm" (1986, 35). For the most part, at least some component of the Pagan worldview may be described as polytheistic and involves working with gods and goddesses from a variety of cultures, past and present, throughout the world. A good example of the range of deities and cultures is reflected in two books by Janet and Stewart Farrar. In their first book, published in 1987 and entitled *The Witches' Goddess*, the Farrars included descriptions of more than a thousand goddesses from past and present cultures on all continents. Similarly, in their second book, published in 1989 and entitled *The Witches' God*, the Farrars listed more than a thousand gods from similar times and geographical distributions.

Many Pagans metaphorically relate the concept of human sexuality and gender to the Divine as suggested already by the use of the terms "god" and "goddess" in this chapter. The polarity of the masculine and the feminine is viewed as important by many Pagans, including Jones and Matthews who believe that such polarity "allows for the creative resolution of any dilemma through the interplay of equal and opposite principles, in contrast to the requirement of merely accurate submission to the One True Way which is all too easily characterizes monotheistic, hierarchical religion" (1990, 33–34). Consistent with the previously mentioned views of Fox (1989b) regarding monotheism and polytheism, Crowley discussed the concept of polarity within the context of the "unity in diversity" theme when describing the personification of the male and female in the form of the God and Goddess. According to Crowley, "All Gods are different aspects of the one God and all Goddesses are different aspects of the one Goddess, and . . . ultimately these two are reconciled in the one divine essence" (1989, 12). Such recognition of the Divine as female as well as male is very common in Paganism and is similar to the postmodern theme of postpatriarchy noted by Griffin (1988a, 1990).

Some Pagans view the polytheistic aspects of the Divine as similar to Jungian archetypes within the collective unconscious. Crowley took this view: "We contact the divine archetypes through the ritual and through the enactment of the ancient Pagan myths which express eternal truths about humanity and the universe it inhabits" (1989, 12). However, Farrar and Farrar (1989) cautioned against viewing the gods and goddesses as only representing archetypes of the human collective unconscious. Instead, they maintained that the gods and goddesses exist as living, active faces of the ultimate Unknowable and ensoul the archetypes.

As suggested in this section, considerable variation exists regarding the extent to which Pagans may be considered monotheists and/or polytheists. In addition, variation exists regarding how these monotheistic and polytheistic components are manifested in spiritual practice. Some Pagans direct their worship toward a single aspect of deity; many focus their worship upon a Goddess-God pair; and others direct their worship to an entire pantheon. Some work with a pantheon rooted in a particular culture, while others work with a pantheon which includes goddesses and gods from many cultures.

MAGIC

Perhaps one of the most significant factors distinguishing Wiccans or Pagans from other contemporary individuals who share similar spiritual viewpoints on the themes mentioned above is the value placed upon magic. Based upon the theme of interconnectedness, but going beyond it, magic involves the recognition that each part of the interconnected whole affects every other part (Starhawk 1989b). Given this model, many Pagans believe that magic can be used to gain insight from, as well as to influence, other aspects of the interconnected whole. Some variance could be expected regarding the extent to which those involved in the overlapping forms of spirituality comprising Paganism move beyond the basic recognition of interconnectedness to try actively to influence other parts of the interconnected whole. While some who agree with this basic recognition may question the ethics of using a spiritual perspective for more ego-centered benefits, most Pagans operate under the ethical principle of "An it harm none, do what you will." While such an ethical foundation certainly permits the use of magic for ego-based purposes, my observations over the years suggest that many Pagans utilize magic in more altruistic ways, focusing on the healing and well-being of others as well as the planet as a whole.

With the notion of influencing other parts of the interconnected whole in mind, Starhawk described magic as "the art of sensing and shaping the subtle, unseen forces that flow throughout the world, of awakening deeper levels of consciousness beyond the rational" (1989b, 27). She went on to say that ritual serves a magical function in stimulating an awareness of the hidden side of reality and awakening long-forgotten powers of the human mind. Starhawk further maintained that magical rituals are used to create states of ecstasy, of union with the Divine, as well as to achieve material results such as healings.

Adler offered a description of magic that involves a collection of techniques utilizing the capabilities of the human mind to achieve desired effects:

> We might conceive of these techniques as including the mobilization of confidence, will, and emotion brought about by the recognition of necessity; the use of imaginative faculties, particularly the ability to visualize, in order to begin to understgand how other beings function in nature so we can use this knowledge to achieve necessary ends. (1986, 8)

Implied in this description is the ability of the mind to influence the material world.

In fact, Winkelman (1982) compared magic to experimental parapsychology findings regarding psi and cited evidence to suggest that some aspects of magical practice involve psi. Referring to various definitions presented in the *Journal of Parapsychology*, Winkelman defined psi as a general term used to identify personal factors or processes in Nature that transcend accepted laws and that are non-physical in nature. Krippner further defined psi phenomena within the context of modern science:

> Psi phenomena are usually defined as organism-environment interactions in which it appears that information or influence has occurred that can not be explained through science's understanding of sensory-motor channels. In other words, these reports are *anomalous* because they appear to stand outside of modern science's concepts of time, space, and energy. (1988, 132)

This definition of psi phenomena can also be regarded as an appropriate description of magic as I understand it. Krippner identified a group of parapsychologists who believe that psi phenomena are related to the spiritual nature of humans and indicated that he believed these individuals "to be more in accord with the holistic vision of the postmodern worldview than with the fragmented mythology of the modern worldview" (p. 133). Magic's relationship to the holistic theme of interconnectedness within Paganism is also similar to the postmodern worldview.

Winkelman (1982) noted that some magical practices and beliefs reported by anthropologists share certain of the characteristics found through research to be conducive to psi manifestations, such as altered states of consciousness, visualization, positive expectation, and belief. Orion (1990) asked her respondents to indicate the human faculties through which they believed magic to operate. The responses included one's own power or will, imagination, psychic powers or skills, creativity, and change of consciousness. These are consistent with the factors noted by Adler and Winkelman as central to the efficacy of magic.

As demonstrated in this section, magic can be viewed as stemming from the theme of interconnectedness which is a feature of postmodern spirituality. Based upon my experiences, I would describe magic as the active cultivation of psi abilities. Similar to the beliefs of the parapsychologists identified by Krippner (1988), Pagans tend to view magic as related to spirituality. In fact, many Pagans regard magic as a key component of their spiritual life. Communion with the Divine is desired not only for the sake of the experience, but also for bringing about desired changes in day-to-day life. Such magic can be individualistic in nature by focusing on improving personal life circumstances or it can be very communal and altruistic by focusing on such goals as helping others or bringing about more ecological well-being. Whatever the focus magic might take, most Pagans regard magical practice as an aspect of their spirituality.

THE SACRED CIRCLE

For contemporary Pagans, the image of the sacred circle is fundamental in describing sacred space, serving as a division line between the sacred and the mundane. Adler (1986) called this sacred circle a microcosm of the universe and described it as a protected place apart from the world. Starhawk described in more detail the demarcating function of the sacred circle:

> The circle exists on the boundaries of ordinary space and time; it is 'between the worlds' of the seen and unseen, of flashlight and starlight consciousness, a space in which alternate realities meet, in which the past and future are open to us. (1989b, 72)

Incorporating the theme of interconnectedness, Starhawk also said that living in harmony with Nature is implied in recognizing that "the circle is the ecological circle, the circle of the interdependence of all living organisms" (p. 208). From these statements regarding the image of the sacred circle, two major functions emerge, a separating function as well as an integrating function. First, the circle is used to mark a protective space within which sacred work can be done. In this role, the circle serves to separate the sacred from the mundane, as already mentioned. Second, the circle is used as a symbol of the fundamental interconnectedness of all life forms and the ultimate interconnectedness of the sacred and the mundane.

The concept of the quartered circle is basic to contemporary Paganism. The quartered circle is also common to Native American, African, East Indian, Tibetan, and some other spiritual systems (Starhawk 1989b). As already mentioned, Pagans carry out their individual and group spiritual work within a sacred circle. This circle is commonly marked by the four compass directions, north, east, south, and west. These directions are associated with the four elements of Nature—earth, air, fire, and water—with considerable variation between spiritual systems regarding which direction is associated with each of these elements. A commonly used system incorporates the following associations: north is linked with earth which symbolizes the realm of the physical body and home; east is linked with air which symbolizes the realm of thoughts and communication; south is linked with fire which symbolizes the realm of energy and will; and west is linked with water which symbolizes the realm of emotion and feelings. The center of the circle is linked with the fifth element, spirit, which represents the unity, harmony, and balance of the four directions, of the male and female aspects of the Divine, and of the immanent/transcendent sacred whole. For this particular system, the psychological dimensions associated with each of the elements was developed by Selena Fox and the underlying associations of the compass directions and the elements of Nature came about as a result of Fox's contact with a variety of Wiccan traditions in the early 1970s (S. Fox, personal communication, 24 April 1992). Fox also noted that some Wiccan groups do not incorporate the fifth element, Spirit, as representing a unifying principle—which is consistent with the variation previously discussed regarding the extent to which Pagans acknowledge the theme of "unity in diversity."

CYCLICITY

Starhawk maintained that "the world view of Witchcraft is cyclical, spiral. It dissolves dualities and sees opposites as complements. Diversity is valued" (1989b, 209–210). Such a cyclical worldview is inspired, in large part, by the cycles of Nature. Attunement to Nature is accomplished, in part, by paying special attention to the patterns in Nature determined by the cycles of the sun and moon. According to Sheldrake, "The linking of calendars to the cycles of the moon and sun reminds us of the celestial context of our earthly life, and seasonal festivals celebrate the quality of the time of the year, and give it a sacred dimension" (1990, 186). Consistent with the polarity of the God and Goddess mentioned previously, it is often claimed that the sun symbolizes the male aspect of the Divine and the moon symbolizes the female aspect of the Divine. Particular points during the lunar and solar cycles determine the schedule of spiritual ritual and celebration.

The solar cycle is marked by eight sabbats, or sacred times (often referred to collectively as the Wheel of the Year)—the solstices, equinoxes, and the four points between, or cross quarters. According to Adler, "These festivals renew a sense of living communion with natural cycles, with the changes of the

season and the land" (1986, 111). The God is often conceptualized in a dual manner relating to the waxing and waning of the
sun. One of the more common images, present in premodern
Pagan cultures and surviving in contemporary folklore, is that
of the Oak King and Holly King (Farrar and Farrar 1989). During
the waxing half of the calendar year, as the days grow longer,
the Oak King rules and represents expansion and growth. During the waning half of the year, as the days grow shorter, the
Holly King rules and represents withdrawal and rest. This cycle
of the waxing and waning sun is also related to the cyclical
theme of birth-growth-death-rebirth, especially in northern
European Pagan mythologies which are based on dramatic seasonal changes involving the growth and death of plant and animal life. Such seasonal festivities and symbolism "seek to harmonize
human activities with the natural rhythms of the cosmos" (Jones
and Matthews 1990).

The lunar cycle is generally marked by three phases—the
waxing moon during which it grows fuller, the full moon, and the
waning moon during which it grows smaller. The Goddess is often
conceptualized by Wiccans in a triplicate fashion paralleling these
phases of the moon: the waxing phase represents the maiden; the
full aspect represents the mother; and the waning aspect represents
the crone, or old wise woman. The similarity between the length
of the lunar cycle and the length of the human female menstrual
cycle is usually viewed as part of the rationale behind the association of the moon with the feminine.

As shown here, the cycles of both the sun and moon contribute to cyclical views of life marked by the theme of birth-growth-
death-rebirth. By attuning themselves through ritual and meditation
with the cycles of Nature, Pagans gain greater understanding of
the cyclical processes operating in their own lives. The Pagan
conception of human death parallels these metaphors of Nature
and is viewed as a time of rebirth to new life.

IMPLICATIONS OF THE PAGAN WORLDVIEW

I have described the major spiritual contours of the Pagan worldview
by examining the themes of interconnectedness, immanence and
transcendence, animism and spiritism, monotheism and polytheism, magic, the sacred circle, and cyclicity. In this section, I will
address further implications of these spiritual themes as well as
further relationships with postmodern spirituality.

THE RE-ENCHANTMENT OF NATURE

As demonstrated in this chapter, Paganism emphasizes and values attunement to and inspiration from Nature rather than dogma, a central religious authority, standardized sets of beliefs, and sacred texts. Pagans view themselves as part of the web of interconnections in Nature. In addition, the Divine is viewed, at least in part, as immanent in Nature and all of Nature is considered to be alive. Sheldrake summarized well the implications of such an interconnected and animistic perspective:

> As soon as we allow ourselves to think of the world as alive, we recognize that a part of us knew this all along. It is like emerging from winter into a new spring. We can begin to reconnect our mental life with our own direct, intuitive experiences of nature. We can participate in the spirits of sacred places and times. We can see that we have much to learn from traditional societies who have never lost their sense of connection with the living world around them. We can acknowledge the animistic traditions of our ancestors. And we can begin to develop a richer understanding of human nature, shaped by tradition and collective memory; linked to the Earth and the heavens, related to all forms of life; and consciously open to the creative power expressed in all evolution. We are reborn into a living world. (1990, 198–199)

Sheldrake's descriptions of intuitive experiences of Nature, deep interconnectedness, and the creative power expressed in the living world illustrate the Pagan concept of the Divine in Nature. Such recognition of Divinity has implications regarding the human relationship to the environment. According to Jones and Matthews, "Seeing Nature as an expression of divinity means that Pagans naturally have an ecological awareness of the globe" (1990, 35). The ecologically conscious attitudes and practices emerging from such awareness often stand in contrast to those evolving out of other spiritual traditions. Toynbee cites Genesis I:28 of the Bible as the Christian doctrine regarding the relations between God, humankind, and Nature:

> And God blessed them, and God said unto them, Be fruitful, and multiply, and replenish the earth, and subdue it: and have dominion over the fish of the sea, and over the fowl of the air, and over every living thing that moveth upon the earth. (1973, 6)

Toynbee contrasted this biblical sanction with the deification of Nature reflected in the pre-Christian world, which he described as follows:

Nature was not just a treasure-trove of "natural resources." Nature was, for him, a goddess, "Mother Earth," and the vegetation that sprang from the earth, the animals that roamed, like man himself, over the earth's surface, and the minerals hiding in the earth's bowels all partook of nature's divinity. (p. 7)

Starhawk (1989b) echoed themes similar to those of Toynbee in describing the deification of Nature reflected in contemporary Paganism. She also pointed out that religious models have conditioned humans' understanding of their relationship to the Earth and to other species. In particular, Starhawk maintained that the image of God as separate from Nature has provided the rationale for human destruction of the natural world and exploitation of Earth's resources. She cited the severity of pollution and ecological destruction and the threats to human survival as contributing to the growing awareness of the importance of ecological balance and the interdependence of all life. Starhawk described the Goddess and Witchcraft from an ecological perspective:

The model of the Goddess, who is immanent in nature, fosters respect for the sacredness of all living things. Witchcraft can be seen as a religion of ecology. Its goal is harmony with nature, so that life may not just survive, but thrive. (p. 25)

Central to Witchcraft as a religion of ecology is the concept of immanent value, which refers to the inherent value of all things due to their living, animistic nature and their interconnectedness which is too complex to ever be more than partially described (Starhawk 1987b). Starhawk further described the mandate for action stemming from such a religion of ecology:

When we start to understand that the Earth is alive, she calls us to act to preserve her life. When we understand that everything is interconnected, we are called to a politics and set of actions that come from compassion, from the ability to literally feel with all living beings on the Earth. That feeling is the ground upon which we can build community and come together and take action and find direction. (1990, 74)

Central to this mandate for ecological action is the sense of compassion for all life forms that stems from the understanding of all life as interconnected. Starhawk added that the view that all life is sacred implies that all living things have value beyond their usefulness for human ends.

Starhawk's (1987b, 1990) ideas regarding immanent value are consistent with those of deep ecologists such as Devall and Sessions, who maintained that humans are a part of the organic whole of nature and that "all organisms and entities in the ecosphere, as parts of the interconnected whole, are equal in intrinsic worth" (1985, 67). Devall and Sessions pointed out that ecological consciousness and deep ecology stand in marked contrast to the "dominant worldview of technocratic-industrial societies which regards humans as isolated and fundamentally separate from the rest of Nature, as superior to, and in charge of, the rest of creation" (p. 65). While more in-depth examination of the deep ecology literature may be relevant to this discussion, such exploration is beyond the scope of this chapter.

It seems that the disenchantment of Nature that rose to predominance during the period of modernity resulted from a long and complicated process involving religious beliefs as well as the values of modern science and technology. The important contribution that Paganism, as an example of postmodern spirituality, can make is toward the re-enchantment of Nature. The Pagan and deep ecological vision of the planet and all of Nature as a living interconnected whole seems to offer a clearer ecological mandate than does the modern mechanistic and dualistic worldview which has resulted in human domination and exploitation of Nature. While the modern worldview has provided dramatic successes, the current ecological crises beg for corrective action.

EMPHASIS ON PERSONAL SPIRITUAL EXPERIENCE

Gablik made the following observations regarding spiritual experiences within the context of modernity:

> One of the peculiar developments in our Western world is that we are losing our sense of the divine side of life, of the power of imagination, myth, dream and vision. The particular structure of modern consciousness, centered in a rationalizing, abstracting and controlling ego, determines the world we live in and how we perceive and understand it. Without the magical sense of perception, we do not live in a magical world. We no longer have the ability to shift mindsets and thus to perceive other realities, to move between the worlds, as ancient shamans did. One way to access these worlds is through ritual where something more goes on than meets the eye—something sacred. (1992, 21–22)

Gablik's comments really get to the heart of the Pagan quest for personal experience of the Divine. Jones and Matthews describe such a quest:

Contemporary Pagan individuals and groups . . . are typified by
their easy access to the gods. They are directly in touch with their
deities in a way which has been forgotten since the medieval rulings
which placed Christian salvation in the hands of the clergy, and the
materialistic science which arose as their heir. Paganism has taken
the reins of spiritual power into its own hands. It recognizes that for
each person contact with divinity is possible. (1990, 33)

While some Pagans serve in ministerial roles as priest or priestess
performing a variety of leadership functions, all individuals are
generally regarded as priests or priestesses, acknowledging the notion
that everyone has a personal relationship to the Divine and that a
spiritual intermediary is not necessary for experiencing connections with the Divine.

Consistent with the primacy of spiritual experience and the
material presented previously regarding magic is the idea that the
practices of Pagans are geared toward facilitating altered states of
awareness or shifting mind-sets. According to Adler, "Neopagans
have brought back the rituals and ecstatic techniques—the dancing
and the chanting—but within a nonauthoritarian framework" (1989,
154). I have participated in numerous rituals, all of which contain
such consciousness-changing elements as chanting, singing, dancing, drumming, visualization, and meditation. Starhawk (1989b)
discussed the importance of working with alterations of consciousness and outlined techniques including visualization, ritual, working with self-suggestion, working with dreams, relaxation strategies,
sensory restriction (e.g., scrying in a candle flame, a crystal ball, a
black mirror, a dark mirror, or a bright sword), rhythm (experienced in motion, song, drumming, chanting, or poetic meter), and
spoken trance inductions.

Luhrmann (1989) concluded that four distinctive components
contributed to magical experience, i.e., altered conditions of consciousness—meditation and visualization, linguistic strategies, ritual
strategies, and symbolism. According to Luhrmann, those who engage
in activities such as meditation, visualization, and ritual within the
context of magical practice have experiences of the type that people
feel comfortable calling spiritual or religious. According to Starhawk
(1989b), the effects of working with consciousness-altering spiritual approaches include: opening up paranormal senses, psychic
awareness, and precognition; empathizing and connecting with other
beings and life forms; perception of astral reality; astral projection;
augmenting sensitivity, growth, and creativity; facilitating physical
and emotional healing; and the experience of divine revelation.

Starhawk further described such revelation with the following:

> We invoke and become the Goddess and God linked to all that is.
> We experience union, ecstasy, openness. The limits of our percep-
> tion, the fixation on a single note of the song, dissolve: We not only
> hear the music, but we dance the whirling, exhilarating, spiral dance
> of existence. (p. 157)

Gablik described a kind of visionary mode which occurs under the
conditions of non-ordinary consciousness:

> Myths from all times and cultures are available to us; we touch into
> a seemingly magical dimension from which emanates a sense of the
> mysterious and the sacred; we have experiential access to the past or
> the future, and the limitations of our cultural conditioning are tran-
> scended. (1992, 25)

According to Spretnak (1991), religious scholars generally divide
the experience of divine revelation into the two broad categories of
numinous experiences and mystical experiences. Spretnak defined
numinous experience as involving "awareness of a holy presence
apart from the self, whether it is an encounter with an awesome
numen (the holy) or a loving relationship with a personal 'other' "
(p. 209). Spretnak defined mystical experience as involving "a sense
of unity in multiplicity ('extroverted' mysticism) or unity devoid of
all multiplicity ('introverted' mysticism)." Spretnak reacted to these
categories by saying:

> The scholarly categories do not seem adequate for describing con-
> temporary Goddess spirituality, in which people experience a 'loving
> relationship' with the presence of the Goddess, but that presence is
> perceived as unitive, as the immanent and transcendent cosmic cre-
> ativity within the self and the great whole. (p. 210)

Research into the nature of the spiritual experiences of Pagans
seems warranted by Spretnak's remarks in order to evaluate the
extent to which such experiences conform to current scholarly
perspectives.

Attunement with Nature and other forms of spiritual experience are valued more by Pagans than dogma, central authority,
standardized beliefs, and sacred texts. This section has identified
the Pagan quest for personal experience of the Divine which involves a variety of techniques for facilitating alterations in consciousness. The resulting experiences, considered spiritual or religious,
provide the basis for the spiritual life of those involved. Spretnak
(1991) briefly alluded to the inadequacy of commonly accepted

scholarly categories in describing the experiences of those involved in Goddess Spirituality, and in a more general sense, of those involved in Paganism. In light of the limited amount of information regarding the numinous, mystical, and other kinds of spiritual experiences valued by Pagans and the role such experiences play in spiritual development, further research regarding Pagan spiritual experiences could be illuminating.

CONCLUSIONS

In this chapter, I have examined the spiritual contours of the worldview of a diverse group of people involved in contemporary Paganism. First, I defined spirituality as the ultimate values, beliefs, and experiences which reflect human perceptions of the Divine and give life meaning. I then discussed spirituality within a postmodern context as described by Griffin (1988a, 1988b, 1990) and Spretnak (1991). Throughout this chapter, I examined the similarities between Paganism and postmodern spirituality, which both involve an incorporation of premodern notions of divine reality, cosmic meaning, and an enchanted nature into contemporary life. In addition, interconnectedness, nondualism, panentheism, the centrality of creativity, and postpatriarchy represent postmodern themes particularly descriptive of Paganism. While Pagans seek spiritual inspiration from premodern sources, some evidence suggests that they do not generally reject the positive achievements of science and technology. In addition, many Pagans are deeply concerned about and actively involved in issues such as feminism, racial equality, nuclear disarmament, and ecological preservation. To the extent that Pagans integrate premodern inspiration with efforts to solve the problems of modernity, they be regarded as postmodern. However, further study is needed to determine the extent to which contemporary Pagans synthesize premodern truths and values with modern ideas such that they might be considered postmodern.

I also provided a brief overview of Paganism, including an examination of the bases for textual reconstruction which suggested that Paganism relies more on creativity and insight derived from spiritual experience than on dogma, central authority, standardized beliefs, and sacred texts. Then, I provided a brief historical summary of Paganism which culminated in the description of Paganism as an example of a new religious movement. Once these background contexts were developed, I identified and described the major spiritual contours of the contemporary Pagan worldview.

Selected for examination were the themes of interconnectedness, immanence and transcendence, animism and spiritism, monotheism and polytheism, magic, the sacred circle, and cyclicity. The theme of interconnectedness represents a basic component of the Pagan worldview and involves the recognition of the fundamental interrelatedness of all beings. The theme of immanence and transcendence refers to the human understanding regarding the relation of the Divine to the world. Pagans vary somewhat in their perceptions of this theme, with many best described as panentheists in recognition of both the immanent Divine in Nature and the transcendent unifying Whole. Pagans may be described as animistic in their recognition of all Nature as alive and imbued with spiritual energy. Pagans are also spiritistic in their belief in the ability to communicate with various aspects, or spirits, of the natural world. Pagans tend to vary considerably in their views regarding the singularity or multiplicity of the Divine, as demonstrated in my discussion of the theme of monotheism and polytheism. The theme of magic involves the Pagan recognition of the interconnectedness of all things, as well as the ability to influence other parts of the interconnected whole. Relying on alterations of consciousness, many Pagans believe that they can tap into natural human abilities to spiritually influence events in the natural world. The image of the sacred circle involves the marking of sacred space and represents unity, balance, and harmony. Cyclicity refers to attunement with the cycles and seasons of Nature, in which all of life is viewed in terms of the cyclical theme of birth-growth-death-rebirth.

Following the examination of these spiritual contours of the Pagan worldview, I explored further some of the implications of such spiritual themes, including the re-enchantment of Nature and the emphasis on personal spiritual experience. The Pagan worldview results in a very different picture regarding the human relationship to the rest of the natural world, when contrasted with the disenchantment of Nature which has emerged so dramatically through the modern era. Recognizing their interconnectedness with all aspects of animated Nature, Pagans respect and value the intrinsic worth of all life. Pagans also value a personal experiential relationship to the Divine. Utilizing a variety of approaches to facilitate alterations in consciousness, Pagans seek modes of consciousness conducive to connecting with the enchanted aspects of the immanent divine in Nature as well as the transcendent unity of all life. Attunement to and inspiration from Nature provides the heart of the Pagan spiritual life. It is in recognition of this centrality of Nature to the Pagan worldview and experiences that Paganism is frequently referred to as an example of Nature Spirituality or Nature Religion.

REFERENCES

Adler, M. 1986. *Drawing Down the Moon: Witches, Druids, Goddess-Worshippers, and Other Pagans in America Today.* Rev. ed. Boston: Beacon Press.

———. 1989. "The Juice and the Mystery." In *Healing the Wounds: The Promise of Ecofeminism,* edited by J. Plant, 151–154. Philadelphia: New Society Publishers.

Crowley, V. 1989. *Wicca: The Old Religion in the New Age.* Wellingborough, England: The Aquarian Press.

Devall, B., and G. Sessions. 1985. *Deep Ecology: Living as if Nature Mattered.* Salt Lake City, Utah. Peregrine Smith Books.

diZerega, G. 1988. "Neopaganism and Ecology." *Trumpeter* 5, no. 1: 23–25.

Drengson, A. R. 1988. "Paganism, Nature, and Deep Ecology." *Trumpeter* 5, no. 1: 20–22.

Farrar, J., and S. Farrar. 1987. *The Witches' Goddess.* Custer, Wash.: Phoenix Publishing.

———. 1989. *The Witches' God.* Custer, Wash.: Phoenix Publishing.

Fox, S. 1979. *Circle Guide to Wicca and Pagan Resources.* Madison, Wisc.: Circle Publications.

———. 1989a. *Goddess Communion Rituals and Meditations.* Mt. Horeb, Wisc.: Circle Publications.

———. 1989b. *Introduction to the Wiccan Religion.* Mt. Horeb, Wisc.: Circle Publications.

———. 1990. "I Am a Pagan." In *Circle Guide to Pagan Groups,* edited by Circle Staff. Mt. Horeb, Wisc.: Circle.

Gablik, S. 1992. "The Artist as Enchanter." *Common Boundary* 10, no. 2: 20–27.

Gardner, G. B. [1954] 1970. *Witchcraft Today.* Reprint, New York: The Citadel Press.

———. [1959] 1971. *The Meaning of Witchcraft.* Reprint, London: The Aquarian Press.

Graves, R. 1948. *The White Goddess: A Historical Grammar of Poetic Myth.* New York: Farrar, Straus and Giroux.

Griffin, D. R. 1988a. Introduction: Postmodern Spirituality and Society. In *Spirituality and Society*, edited by D. R. Griffin. Albany, N.Y.: State University of New York Press.

———. 1988b. Introduction to SUNY Series in Constructive Postmodern Thought. In *Spirituality and Society*, edited by D. R. Griffin. Albany, N.Y.: State University of New York Press.

———. 1990. Introduction: Sacred Interconnections. In *Sacred Interconnections*, edited by D. R. Griffin. Albany, N.Y.: State University of New York Press.

G'Zell, O. 1990. "Intimations of Gaea." *Circle Network News* 12, no. 2: 11.

Jones, P., and C. Matthews. 1990. Introduction: The Pagan World. In *Voices from the Circle: The Heritage of Western Paganism*, edited by P. Jones and C. Matthews. Wellingborough, England: The Aquarian Press.

Kelly, A. A. 1991. *Crafting the Art of Magic: A History of Modern Witchcraft, 1939–1964.* St. Paul, Minn.: Llewellyn.

Krippner, S. 1988. "Parapsychology and Postmodern Science." In *The Reenchantment of Science: Postmodern Proposals*, edited by D. R. Griffin. Albany, N.Y.: SUNY Press.

Leland, C. G. [1897] 1974. *Aradia: Gospel of the Witches.* Reprint, New York: Samuel Weiser.

Lovelock, J. E. 1979. *Gaia: A New Look at Life on Earth.* New York: Oxford University Press.

Luhrmann, T. M. 1989. *Persuasians of the Witch's Craft.* Cambridge, Mass.: Harvard University Press.

Murray, M. A. [1931] 1970. *The God of the Witches.* Reprint, London: Oxford University Press.

———. [1921] 1971. *The Witch-Cult in Western Europe.* Reprint, Oxford: Oxford University Press.

Orion, L. L. 1990. Revival of Western Paganism and Witchcraft in the Contemporary United States. *Dissertation Abstracts International* 52: 1799A. (University Microfilms No. DA9128573)

Runes, D. D., ed. 1983. *Dictionary of Philosophy.* Rev. ed. Savage, Md.: Littlefield, Adams Quality Paperbacks.

Sheldrake, R. 1990. *The Rebirth of Nature: The Greening of Science and God.* London: Century.

Simpson, J. A., and E. S. C. Weiner. 1989. *The Oxford English Dictionary*. 2d ed. Oxford: Clarendon Press.

Spretnak, C. 1987a. Green Spirituality. *Resurgence* 124: 24–27.

————. 1987b. Knowing Gaia. *ReVision* 9, no. 2: 69–73.

————. 1989. Toward an Ecofeminist Spirituality. In *Healing the Wounds: The Promise of Ecofeminism*, edited by J. Plant, 127–132. Philadelphia: New Society Publishers.

————. 1991. *States of Grace: The Recovery of Meaning in the Postmodern Age*. San Francisco: HarperCollins.

Starhawk [Miriam Simos]. 1982. *Dreaming the Dark: Magic, Sex and Politics*. Boston: Beacon Press.

————. 1987a. "The Religion of the Great Goddess." *Trumpeter* 4, no. 3: 18–21.

————. 1987b. *Truth or Dare: Encounters with Power, Authority, and Mystery*. San Francisco: Harper and Row.

————. 1989a. "Feminist Earth-Based Spirituality and Ecofeminism." In *Healing the Wounds: The Promise of Ecofeminism*, edited by J. Plant, 174–185. Philadelphia: New Society Publishers.

————. 1989b. *The Spiral Dance: A Rebirth of the Ancient Religion of the Great Goddess*. Rev. ed. San Francisco: Harper and Row.

————. 1990. "Power, Authority, and Mystery: Ecofeminism and Earth-based Spirituality." In *Reweaving the World: The Emergence of Ecofeminism*, edited by I. Diamond and G. F. Orenstein. San Francisco: Sierra Club Books.

Toynbee, A. J. 1973. "The Genesis of Pollution." *Horizon* 15, no. 3: 4–9.

Weaver, M. J. 1989. "Who Is the Goddess and Where Does She Get Us?" *Journal of Feminist Studies in Religion* 5, no. 1: 49–64.

Winkelman, M. 1982. "Magic: A Theoretical Reassessment." *Current Anthropology* 23, no. 1: 37–66.

Part II

Magic and Rituals

4

SPELLS OF TRANSFORMATION: CATEGORIZING MODERN NEO-PAGAN WITCHES

Shelley TSivia Rabinovitch

SCHOLARS LOOKING INTO THE WORLD of Neo-Paganism and/or modern Witchcraft in North America are often faced with a dizzying myriad of titles, covens, temples, and even "churches," all claiming to be populated by "witches."[1] Even the witches themselves do not necessarily agree on what defines a witch.

New religions scholar J. Gordon Melton has typified Wicca as the fastest growing religion in the United States, and my M.A. research on Canadian Wiccans shows that the Neo-Pagan family of religions is the fastest growing group by self-identification (rather than by immigration patterns[2]) in that country. With no central-ized authority or collection of doctrines, it becomes very difficult to make any generalizations about North American Neo-Pagans. However, after substantial research through Canada and the United States, some analysis does seem possible.

Neo-Pagans are usually one or more of the following: ani-mist, pantheist, polytheist, or monist (Adler 1986). The word Pa-gan is derived from the Latin word *paganus*, described as "rustic, peasant," and has historically meant one who was not a follower of one of the three religions often referred to as "People of the Book": Judaism, Christianity, and Islam.[3] Under the latter definition, a

Hindu is a Pagan, as is a Buddhist. For simplicity's sake some Neo-Pagans drop the "neo" when explaining their worldview and refer to themselves as Pagans. Neo-Pagans sometimes view themselves as returning to old religious roots, seeing their form(s) of belief as holistic and balanced (diZerega 1988). These Neo-Pagans are striving to live in some sort of relationship with nature, often personified as Gaia.

Witches (also called Wiccans) are a subset of Neo-Paganism, followers of a Goddess and a God in what they view as a pre- or non-Christian religion from the British Isles. For the purposes of this chapter, a Neo-Pagan witch is a self-identified believer in a Goddess/God-based religion.[4]

NEO-PAGAN WICCA: TRANSFORMATION BY USE OF POWER

The Neo-Pagan movement in North America is extremely diverse, encompassing everything from atheist witches (those who, when interviewed, denied there was any transcendent deity but who worship the immanent "god/dess within every person" to Unitarian Pagans. In order to discuss Neo-Pagan "witches" and see relationships between their myriad self-defined traditions, some form of classification system is required.

Many witches appear to have heard of the religion through other witches they met through hobbies. A large number of witches participate in what might be called "golden-age" type pastimes: the Society for Creative Anachronism (SCA), science fiction fandom (and conventions), *Star Trek* fandom, *Dr. Who* fandom, and comic book fandom.

These hobbies can be typified as manifesting a "future golden age" type of thinking, where Camelot, colonies on other planets, or friendly aliens can exist. Ben-Yehuda (1986) investigates the relationship between occult thinking and the rise in popularity of science fiction, and Whitehead (in Zaretsky and Leone 1974) investigates how occult thinking, science fiction, and Scientology are linked. So one way witches find Wicca and Neo-Paganism is through friends or acquaintances they find in other spheres of interest.

In addition to those who find Witchcraft through hobbies, others find the religion through vegetarian groups, health food stores, and ecological activist groups and periodicals. These individuals find their first links to Witchcraft through their global activism. Feminist contacts also work as the first introduction for many women to Witchcraft. Courses on feminist thought at many

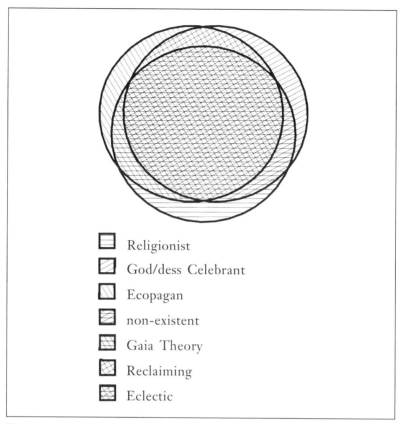

☐ Religionist
▨ God/dess Celebrant
◪ Ecopagan
▧ non-existent
▤ Gaia Theory
◩ Reclaiming
▨ Eclectic

Figure 1

universities often discuss Goddess worship and women, with some teachers inviting a witch to address the class. Although some use these avenues of introduction to Witchcraft, the number one introduction to the religion still appears to be through books.[6]

Concurrent with these three different ways of finding Neo-Paganism appear to be three foci for the witch's transformation of the world around him/her. Neo-Pagan witches can be grouped into three categories, using these foci as pivots for the definitions. Most Neo-Pagans seem to use one of three types of transformation as the main thrust of their cosmology and axiology: Personal ("Religionist"), Global ("Ecopagan"), and Societal ("God/dess Celebrants").

These categories are not fully inclusive, and for this reason the writer has also highlighted the tradition of "Eclectic." Eclectic is not so much a tradition of Neo-Pagan Witchcraft as a melding of many traditions, and it is for this reason that Eclectics are shown as the large central overlap point in the classification system of Neo-Pagans illustrated in this chapter (see figure 1). Eclectics may practice their religion alone, or with others. As the most numerous single appellation for Neo-Pagans and Wiccans across Canada and the United States, all an Eclectic need do is label him/herself as a Pagan and he/she becomes one.

These categories are grouped according to their use of power. An excellent discussion of the various anthropological theories of power can be found in Schultz and Lavenda (1990). They refer to two differing understandings of power based on cultural practices: coercive versus free will.

In the Neo-Pagan worldview there are three and not two manifestations of power: power-over, power-with, and power-from-within (Starhawk 1987). The Neo-Pagan worldview is different from that of Christianity in its expression of where power is vested. The placement of power in the Neo-Pagan worldview helps explain the differences between these different descriptive categories.

When power is viewed as coercive and internally vested in the individual,[7] powerful individuals can use force, violence, and what Starhawk (1987) calls power-over to gain control. When power is viewed as external to the individual, however, a different understanding of human nature is evidenced. Because every person (and in some worldviews every *thing*) is so imbued, there can be no threats of violence to gain power-over. Instead, coercion appears unwise as every person has the same amount of power, no more, no less (Schultz 1990). Neo-Pagans subscribe to the latter theory of power, for whether immanent or transcendent, the gods made all things equal (and by extrapolation, imbued with equal amounts of sacredness and power). This worldview allows for the concepts of power-with and power-from-within to exist (Starhawk 1987).

PERSONAL TRANSFORMATION:
RELIGIONIST WICCAN TRADITIONS

The more "traditional" and "ceremonial" systems of Neo-Pagan worship fall under the category of Religionist. These include, in general, Gardnerian and Alexandrian Wicca; in Canada, the Wiccan Church of Canada; and a large cross section of the Eclectics. The main concerns of these practitioners appear to be a form of worship that acknowledges Divinity as male and female, immanent and transcendent.

These are the groups usually self-labelled as Wiccan (as the term witch straddles the borders of these categories). For the practitioners, their concerns are focused on the Self and the Self's relationship to the Divine (however the practitioner defines Divinity). In the secular sphere, Religionist Neo-Pagans are most concerned with legitimization of their belief systems as a bona fide religion (e.g., earning the legal right to ritually name, marry, and bury its adherents), "proper" forms of worship of the Divine, and embracing Wicca as an alternative to the institutionalized forms of religion current in North America.

Religionist Neo-Pagans are, as a rule, the most hierarchical and codified of the three categories. Gardnerian and Alexandrian Wicca feature three degrees of Initiation, plus positions such as High Priestess,[8] High Priest, Guardian of the Portal (sometimes called summoner), and maiden (sometimes called Handmaiden). Canada's Wiccan Church of Canada actually offers six degrees (of which one is non-ritualized, two feature non-initiatory rituals, and three include initiatory rituals).

Religionist Neo-Pagans are also those who are most dependent on "props" and/or trappings for worship. Alexandrian and Gardnerian Wiccans train for some period of time on subjects which cover the symbolic and "magical" uses of various tools and symbols.

Alexandrians and Gardnerians conduct their rites nude, or skyclad, when possible (northern weather and urban living conditions are often less than optimal for these practices). Certain forms of jewellery and/or colors of clothing (robes and ritual belts called cingula), along with certain stones (amber and jet in most of these traditions) are also regulated.

With the flood of books on Wicca coming out of the United States and Britain in the last ten years, it is quite simple for interested Neo-Pagan to "cookbook" themselves a coven with strong Religionist leanings. As more and more authors espouse the acceptability of self-initiation (including Crowley 1989; Cunningham 1988; Farrar and Farrar 1984; Valiente 1989), eclectic covens and groves of this type are springing up with strong Religionist Neo-Pagan orientation. "Power-over enables one individual or group to make the decisions that affect others, and to enforce control" (Starhawk 1985, 9).

Traditional organized religions are, as a rule, hierarchical in nature (Bibby 1987; Stark and Bainbridge 1985). By comparison,

Stark and Bainbridge (1985) indicate that in some types of cults, no hierarchy or leadership exists at all. To the casual observer, the Neo-Pagan movement is the archetypal non-hierarchical religion, but in some traditions this is not the case.

Those Neo-Pagans active in heavily Religionist Wiccan traditions appear to be, in part, seeking to carve a niche for themselves in an existing power-base. Although the participants themselves would not view their studies towards achieving degrees of initiation as seeking power-over, close study of the mechanisms of initiation granting and the respect resulting seem to indicate otherwise.

Most Religionists are from the more ceremonial branches of Christianity (e.g., High Anglicans/Episcopalians and Roman Catholics). An observer at a Gardnerian circle would find some aspects of the ritual immediately familiar, such as the burning of incense, the colored tower candles, the ringing of a bell at certain points in the ritual, and even the text of the consecration of the elements of Water and Salt (Earth).[9]

The exercising of power-over can be both positive and negative in this situation. In situations where abuse of power is evident, a Wiccan student working towards elevation could be put off or discouraged by the continual denial of the initiation ceremony when the priest/ess in the position of power decides the student is not ready yet. Some candidates can be victims of power-over thinking when those above him/her in the hierarchy refuse to allow access to "oath-bound" information.[10]

Power-over types of Neo-Pagan expression hold the highest potential for abuse. Complaints about individuals being initiated "too early," efforts to invalidate the "lineage" of a given initiate by another more powerful initiate, or other exercises of power over one participant by another are common in Religionist Wiccan groups.

Some of the abuses of power-over within the Religionist systems can become extremely manipulative if taken to extremes. Frequently difficult or impossible to prove (due to the reticence of adherents to speak ill of a person who has power over their religious achievements), allegations of sexual misconduct and/or emotional manipulation are not uncommon by former members of some Religionist groups.

It has been suggested by other scholars that an in-depth personality study of the men in the Religionist groups of Neo-Paganism would probably turn up many traits of physical, sexual, and emotional manipulation. Certainly it is odd that the main speakers for many Religionist traditions are most frequently men (despite the myth of Neo-Paganism and Wicca as a woman's religion), and that in the 1981 Canadian census there were nearly half again as many men as women claiming Pagan status.

One might hazard guesses as to why so many individuals are still practicing in some variant of the hierarchical, power-over styles of Religionist Wicca and Neo-Paganism.[11] Perhaps it is the familiarity that draws the practitioners: the hierarchy and trappings are familiar from church symbolism, and the abusive use of power-over as postulated above would be familiar to one coming from an abusive family background.

GLOBAL TRANSFORMATION: ECOPAGANS

The Trumpeter, a magazine originating out of Victoria, B.C., bills itself as "Voices from the Canadian Ecophilosophy Network." Across the bottom of one issue the following is exclaimed: "Paradox, Completeness, Utopianism, Paganism, Bioexuberance" (vol. 5, no. 1, Winter 1988). Neo-Pagan presence in the environmental movements in Canada and the United States is becoming increasingly evident, as this magazine indicates.

Ecopagans are not as easily identified by their religious beliefs. The researcher is far more likely to find this group of Neo-Pagans through magazines such as *The Trumpeter,* or by making contacts through recycled-goods stores and alternative press publications. Some Ecopagans are active with organizations such as Greenpeace and local humane societies and SPCAs. Others do volunteer work at peace centers in their communities.

Some aspects of the Reclaiming tradition (United States) straddle the categories of Ecopagan and God/dess Celebrant, creating groups with a blended worldview and worship style. Groups such as these focus on both societal and global transformation, with their religious activities inextricably intertwined with their actions within society. With a religious framework that is recognizable as Neo-Pagan, these groups use their reverence for the Goddess and her creations as a springboard for activities such as protests against environmental issues. Where to an Ecopagan the Divine may merely be a euphemism for the life force in all things, to the Ecopagan–God/dess Celebrant subcategory of Wiccan, the Divine exists in all things.

Ecopagans do not seem to focus on legitimizing their religion to governmental authority. Their membership appears to be the lowest of the three categories, although a high proportion of Ecopagans are found from British Columbia down the West Coast of the United States.

Ecopagan worship can be both personal and global in its forms. Ecopagans have been known to participate in protests (such as against clear-cutting efforts in West Coast forests) and hold impromptu rituals when necessary to make a point or reinforce their secular motives with religious/spiritual forces. Most Ecopagans are solitary in their worship rather than communal (in comparison with Religionists), and sometimes a pentacle or a crystal around the neck are the only external signs of internal religious belief.

British scientist James Lovelock popularized the concept of the Earth as a living, sentient single organism with his "Gaia Theory" in the mid-1970s. Through anthropomorphizing the Earth many individuals discover a more basic need to actively intercede on her behalf, as one might help an ailing friend or care-giver. Much of this concept rings true for the Neo-Pagans who have focused their spirituality as Ecopagans, creating a different classification subcategory which straddles the division between Ecopagan and Religionist. This Ecopagan-Religionist blend is often typified by Wiccan and Neo-Pagan groups that focus on environmental or social issues while also featuring degree-based initiatory systems of worship (such as Canada's Pagans for Peace tradition).

> [Power-with is] . . . the power of a strong individual in a group of equals, the power not to command, but to suggest and be listened to, to begin something and see it happen. (Starhawk 1987, 10)

Of the organized religions in North America, the one closest to a functional use of power-with appears to be the Society of Friends (Quakers). Perhaps this is one reason why many Neo-Pagans and Wiccans are active in both religious communities. At least three Ottawa, Ontario, couples were wed in Quaker services, and a small but noticeable minority of the witches also attend Quaker meetings periodically. However, many of these dual-religion worshipers do not indicate their witch identity to their Quaker friends. The level of social activism in some Christian churches appears to be a convenient outlet for some Neo-Pagans to affect change in their world.

Ecopagans appear to be the most power-with oriented of the three Neo-Pagan groupings. Often solitary and/or eclectic in religious practices, they often see themselves as worshiping as they do proactive ecological activities. Power-with is similar in its expression to, for example, a women's co-operative publishing collective.[12]

Most Ecopagans do not see a need for as formalized or hierarchical a structure as some Religionists use for worship. They view themselves as interconnected and interrelated with the world around them and part of one organic wholeness. Ecopagans are the most solitary of the three categories of Neo-Pagans, expressing their religion through their activism in environmental groups and often peace centers.

Interviews with Wiccans throughout North America did not turn up any Ecopagan groups with "degree" structures. Rather, all participants seemed to view themselves as equals and expressed their sense of Divinity as very immanent.

Some feminist and Dianic witches also fall into the power-with categories. Many active and successful women's worship circles also shun titles and hierarchical notions (Budapest 1980), with the nominal title of High Priestess being rotated around the participants (sometimes whoever hosts the circle in her house is the High Priestess for the day).

Power-with Neo-Pagans strive to work and live co-operatively with each other, their surroundings, and the world around them. Gaia, as an expression of the Earth and all things on it, is popular with many Ecopagans. It is again no surprise that feminist and ecology Pagans are merging in some areas, creating an ecofeminist movement. Ecopagans seem to come from varied religious upbringings with very little pattern evident.[13]

SOCIETAL TRANSFORMATION: GOD/DESS CELEBRANTS

God/dess Celebrants are often set apart from the rest of the Neo-Pagan movement by their extremely eclectic form(s). Radical Faeries (male), feminist (female), and Dianic (primarily female) forms of Wicca fall into this category, as do thousands of solitary worshipers and independent spirituality groups.

Influenced by the women's liberation and consciousness-raising movements of the 1960s and 1970s, the God/dess Celebrants are focused on change both within themselves and within the society around them. Many of these Neo-Pagan groups act much like a Quaker meeting for worship, speaking or acting when "the spirit moves them."

Rituals arising out of God/dess Celebrant groups are often very poetic and creative. They focus on the reclaiming and re-empowerment of certain sectors of society such as the gay and lesbian communities, women of color, and so forth. These are perhaps the most creative groups in the modern Neo-Pagan movement.

Most of the God/dess Celebrant groups do not follow set ritual formats, nor do they have specific props and/or clothing. Some groups will use drums and/or rattles for inducing altered states of consciousness, while others will utilize books such as Starhawk's *Spiral Dance* (Starhawk 1979) or the writings of Z. Budapest (1986, 1980) as ritual guidelines.

When the National Film Board of Canada launched the Studio D release by Donna Reed, *Goddess Remembered*, at the Royal Ontario Museum in Toronto, a ritual was featured after the early showing. Run by a small core of God/dess Celebrants, the ritual had to be rerun after the later screening due to the overwhelming demands of the participants. Over 150 men and women attended each of the two circles, held behind the Royal Ontario Museum. The unity of such an eclectic religious movement became obvious as participants within the circle, many from hundreds of miles away, would start up a chant or song which would then be recognized and picked up by others around the circle, including the organizers.

God/dess Celebrants use what they "feel fits" in their rituals, and toss out what seems awkward or stilted. The efforts are to free the participants, and through them society at large, from patriarchal restraints and assumptions endemic to North American culture in the late twentieth century. Many of the groups are comprised of gay and lesbian participants, but mixed-orientation and heterosexual groups of this type are not unknown. While in Winnipeg, Manitoba, this writer interviewed a coven of nine women, all Dianic witches, all heterosexual, and all married.

There is a tangible amount of strain between Religionist Neo-Pagans and God/dess Celebrants due to differing views of what a "witch" should be. Religionists view a witch as one who has spent years studying the mysteries inherent in the religion, practicing rituals, and adhering to the forms and trappings of the religion. They also strongly believe that a Neo-Pagan who does not recognize the Goddess and the God as equals cannot be a Wiccan. No Neo-Pagan traditions are indicated in the subcategory created by the God/dess Celebrant and Religionist classifications, as their cosmologies and axiologies appear to be all but mutually exclusive.

In opposition to this stand, God/dess Celebrants view the Goddess as existing in all things and in all places. They feel that the validity of one's beliefs is expressed in actions and in the heart rather than in external manifestations such as color of candle, of cingulum, or in any form of orthopraxy. For many God/dess Celebrants the Goddess incorporates the elements of male divinity as well as female, so they express the male presence through the Goddess rather than having to anthropomorphize a second form of deity. Understandably, this is a very basic disagreement between the traditions grouped in these classification categories.

Despite strong opposition from the Religionist traditions in the Neo-Pagan movement, God/dess Celebrants are firmly located within the Neo-Pagan movement. These Neo-Pagans are frequently not concerned with hierarchical trappings such as initiations and ranks. The statement, "Thou Art Goddess" (or "Thou Art God") is one of the few common denominators among most of these worshipers, and indicates the highly immanent view of divinity they express. Some God/dess Celebrants (male and female) call themselves witch, but few use the term Wiccan.

> Power-from-within . . . sees the world itself as a living being, made up of dynamic aspects, a world where one thing shape-shifts into another, where there are no solid separations and no simple causes and effects. In such a world, all things have inherent value. (Starhawk 1987, 15)

The groups closely affiliated with God/dess celebration are also the least hierarchical of the various traditions of Neo-Paganism. In some groups, the concept of Deity as immanent is so strong that one finds political witches: one who, atheist or agnostic, uses witch as a political term and internalizes the concept of Divine as Self.

The God/dess Celebrant is often solitary, and also often eclectic in format of ritual. The God/dess Celebrant movement appears to celebrate power-from-within and the groups work in very fluid forms. Many women and men who express their religious philosophy through the power-from-within technique turn to the title of witch as a statement of power, while others will shun any title or label at all.

Where Ecopagans are expressing co-operative power, and Religionist Neo-Pagans are expressing power and belief through hierarchy, God/dess Celebrants are expressing the power of the human being when working in tune with itself. Power-from-within is perhaps the most alien concept to those raised in Christian belief structures, although it is certainly not alien to Christian history.[14] Gnostic thought and mystical experience are typical of power-from-within in a Christian framework (Weber, in Halpern 1983).[15]

The structure of power-from-within allows the acceptance of a Divine presence in all things, and is conducive to respect for all creatures whether science would judge them "living" or not. With beliefs similar in many ways to those of Reconstructionist Judaism, some God/dess Celebrants view the Divine as in-dwelling, while others view Divine as a power or energy alive in all things (whether sentient or not).

Philosophically the practice of power-from-within is akin to some forms of Buddhist thought. However, unlike many Buddhists, God/dess celebration needs no temple or place of worship, shares no doctrinal writings on the religion, and appears to have no theological requirement for communal worship.[16] Many God/dess Celebrants *do* worship in groups, but the groups are unstable in their membership and lack any formalized leadership. God/dess Celebrants celebrate the Divine in Self, the Divine *as* Self, and the Divine as in-dwelling in all things.

The link between feminist thought and God/dess Celebrant worship forms is a logical one. Much of the religious work going on in God/dess celebration is recognizable as stemming out of the consciousness-raising groups formed in the late 1960s and early 1970s in the United States and Canada. The participant's relationship to internal and external stresses, and the choices for handling these stresses, comprise much of the God/dess Celebrant focus. Unlike the participants in the consciousness-raising groups, however, these worshipers use magical thinking and sympathetic magic as an aid in much of their Self-improvement.

HOLISTIC WICCA: ECLECTICS

Eclectics are often trained in a more formalized system of practice, frequently Alexandrian/Gardnerian in style. They then move away from the doctrinal style of belief and adapt and edit what they have learned. These creative Neo-Pagans tailor their rituals and beliefs to suit individual needs. Eclectics are often solitary in nature as they have trouble finding others who are interested in the same type of patchwork religious expression.

Eclectics often practice alone, but at times a small group of Eclectics will band together with similar axiology and cosmology, creating a new "mini-tradition."[17] Others practice a mixture of what they may have been taught from other Neo-Pagans with what they have read and how "the spirit moves them."

By far the bulk of Neo-Pagans and Wiccans in North America are Eclectics. For every practitioner in a recognized system, there appear to be hundreds of Eclectics.

Variation is the lifeblood of Neo-Paganism. For every category there is an Eclectic using elements from various traditions. Neo-Pagans defy classification, and most shun institutionalization. Some Neo-Pagans are blending Amerindian beliefs into their worship; others are borrowing from gypsy lore or African belief systems. It is the vibrancy and the variety within the Neo-Pagan community that makes it a fascinating family of religions to observe and study.

A WITCH ALONE: SOLITARY WORSHIP

This is not so much a tradition of Neo-Paganism as a style of worship. Solitaries pop up in every system listed heretofore: there are solitary Gardnerians, feminist witches, and Eclectics. Some solitaries practice alone because of geographical or tradition isolation (e.g., there are no Gardnerians in a given city), while others choose a solitary path due to dislike of group worship or individuals in a community.

Solitaries often appear in large Neo-Pagan centers in reaction against "monolithic" traditions or due to personality clashes. In small communities solitaries are usually simply too isolated to find others with similar beliefs (e.g., Truro, Nova Scotia, noted for its Bible Hill, is not a place where one might expect to find many Wiccans practicing).

Solitaries, like Eclectics, are a major force in the Wiccan landscape and are often loathe to self-identify to someone as "official" as a census-taker. Solitaries cannot be numbered specifically here as they are usually subsumed in the approximate figures for other traditions.

TRANSFORMING WITH WORDS: THE "WITCH"

When Glinda the Good asks Dorothy, in the movie *The Wizard of Oz*, "Are you a Good Witch? Or a Bad Witch?," the whole world of witches is laid bare before the viewer. Good witches are traditionally referred to as "fairy Godmothers" in collections such as the Grimms' fairy tales, and bad witches are "witches" (without modification).

The use of the word "witch" within Neo-Pagan classifications varies from area to area, depending on various factors. Most Religionists view the term "witch" to denote one who has undergone a formalized initiation within a pre-Christian mystery religion. This attitude is most common in areas where the bulk of the worshipers

have not undergone such a formalized rite of passage but are training towards such.

For Ecopagans, the term "witch" rarely arises. For them the
label Neo-Pagan, or merely Pagan, is sufficient identification with
the pantheistic, nature-oriented beliefs they express. Some Ecopagans
will use the term "Heathen" (e.g., coming from the heath) and do
away with "Pagan" all together.

In God/dess Celebrant groups, "witch" becomes a label for
all participants regardless of initiatory status. Both the gay and
lesbian Neo-Pagan subcultures are adamant in their reclaiming of
the term as a word of power. For the feminist and Dianic witch, it
is often sufficient to say three times into a mirror, "I am a Witch,"
to become one (McFarland 1975; Budapest 1986).

The language of self-identification to outsiders differs from
that used when discussing religion with insiders. Although there is
little East-West contact between covens or groups of practitioners
of Neo-Pagan traditions, information is exchanged through personal movement of adherents and by attendance at festivals throughout
North America. Informants falling into all classifications indicated
they would tell another Neo-Pagan they were a witch (whether
initiated or not), but they would use one of the more neutral terms
in discussion with the general public.

CONCLUSION: TRANSFORMATION OF SELF

Neo-Pagans appear to be striving towards a unity in their worlds:
unity with nature, environment, self and others. To a Neo-Pagan,
power exists in rocks, trees, other Neo-Pagans and indeed, non–
Neo-Pagans (who are usually viewed as equally powerful but
untrained). Balancing one's relationship with all around and the
use of language in healing and empowerment appears to be a major
concern in most Neo-Pagan classifications.

The chore for the researcher into the myriad sects of the
Neo-Pagan world (both Wiccan and non-Wiccan: this chapter deals
primarily with Wicca and ignores other Neo-Pagan occultic groups
such as the Church of All Worlds, neo-Druidic groups, neo-shamanic
circles, Ásatrú/Odinist groups, and so on) is familiarizing oneself
sufficiently with the concepts of power and transformation displayed by a particular group. Once the relationships to power,
transformation, and divinity are analyzed, it should be fairly simple
to place the individual tradition somewhere within the spectrum of
the above-mentioned categories. Once Neo-Pagan sectarianism can

be understood by scholars, the cosmologies and axiologies implied therein will become self-evident for further study and discussion.

NOTES

1. Indeed, even the Church of Satan has referred to its adherents as "witches."

2. Buddhism, Hinduism, and Islam would show a faster ten-year growth rate due to increased immigration patterns from non-Christian countries.

3. This is out of the 1972 *Webster's English Dictionary*. Most dictionaries give similar definitions of the term.

4. Although the more radical Dianic and feminist branches will rarely use God imagery in worship, they nearly always acknowledge the male deity form, or the presence of male power within the Goddess (in the yin/yang form).

5. The SCA works on a romanticized version of the historical past.

6. Many letters from isolated witches indicated that they found it extremely frustrating not to find others "of a like mind" in their communities. As a result, they rely heavily on books for their ritual forms and spiritual ideas.

7. E.g., power which is given to chosen individuals by the Deity when the human follows the Deity's coercive orders (a framework familiar to Jews and Christians) (Schultz 1990).

8. "First among equals" as she is termed in most of the popular literature (Farrar and Farrar 1981, 1984; Adler 1986).

9. "I exorcise thee, O creature of water, that thou cast out from thee all the impurities and uncleanliness of the spirits of the world of phantasm; in the name of Cernunnos and Aradia. . . . Blessings be upon this creature of salt; let all malignity and hindrance be cast forth hencefrom, and let all good enter herein; wherefore do I bless thee, that thou mayest aid me, in the names of Cernunnos and Aradia." (Farrar and Farrar 1981, 37)
This is virtually identical to the blessings of salt and water which appears in some missals for baptismal water.

10. "Oath-bound" is a Wiccan term for secret information. This relates to the oaths sworn during initiation ceremonies that the initiate will not reveal any secrets except to other initiates.
Schultz (1990) would term this sort of power coercive power.

11. Some Religionists are accused of worshiping "God in Skirts" by more Eclectic Neo-Pagans.

12. Schultz (1990) would indicate this is a persuasive form of power.

13. Strict Baptist and atheist are two of the religions of origin indicated by the Ecopagans.

14. Christian mystics such as Hildegarde of Bingen do appear in Christian texts, but rarely.

15. The problem is that most institutionalized forms of Christianity are not prepared to deal with personal experience as religious form. It has been argued that the reason monks and nuns were isolated in their own communities was due to the inability of the institution to deal with experiential religious expression.

16. Neo-Pagans are like all other human beings, however, and often feel a social need to worship with others.

17. A group of Halifax (Nova Scotia) Alexandrians, after relocating in Ontario and adapting their book-oriented religious practices, began to refer to themselves as "Halexandrians."

REFERENCES

Adler, Margot. 1986. *Drawing Down the Moon*. Rev. ed. New York: Viking Press.

Albas, Daniel, and Cheryl Albas. 1989. "Modern Magic: The Case of Examinations." *The Sociological Quarterly* 30, no. 4: 603–613.

Bainbridge, William Sims, and Rodney Stark. 1985. *The Future of Religion*. Berkeley: University of California Press.

Ben-Yehuda, Nachman. "The Revival of the Occult and of Science Fiction." *Journal of Popular Culture* 2. 1986.

Bernard, L. L. 1927. "A Psycho-Sociological Interpretation of Magic." In *Papers and Proceedings: 22nd Annual Meeting, American Sociological Society (Dec. 27–30, 1927)*, vol. 22, pp. 60–73. New York: Johnson Reprint Corporation, 1927.

Bibby, Reginald. 1987. *Fragmented Gods: The Poverty and Potential of Religion in Canada*. Toronto: Irwin Publishing.

Budapest, Zsusanna. 1980. *The Holy Bible of Women's Mysteries*, vol. 2. Oakland, Calif.

———. 1986. *The Holy Book of Women's Mysteries*, vol. 1. Rev. ed. Oakland Calif.

Crowley, Vivianne. 1989. *Wicca: The Old Religion in the New Age*. Wellingborough, England: Aquarian Press.

Cunningham, Scott. 1988. *Wicca: A Guide for the Solitary Practitioner*. St. Paul, Minn.: Llewellyn Publications.

Eliade, Mircea. 1976. *Occultism, Witchcraft and Cultural Fashions.* Chicago: University of Chicago Press.

Farrar, Janet, and Stewart Farrar. 1984. *The Life and Times of a Modern Witch.* Custer, Wash.: Phoenix Publishing.

———. 1981. *Eight Sabbats for Witches.* London: Robert Hale.

Halpern, David A., ed. 1983. *Psychodynamic Perspectives on Religion, Sect and Cult.* Bristol: John Wright.

Johnson, Karen. 1991. *Trusting Ourselves: The Complete Guide to Emotional Well-Being for Women.* New York: Atlantic Monthly Press.

Lehmann, Arthur C., and James E. Myers. 1989. *Magic, Witchcraft and Religion: An Anthropological Study of the Supernatural.* 2d ed. Mountain View, Calif.: Mayfield Publishing Company.

Lewis, Lionel S. 1963–1964. "Knowledge, Danger, Certainty, and the Theory of Magic." *The American Journal of Sociology* 69 (July 1963–May 1964): 7–12.

Luhrmann, Tanya. 1989. *Persuasions of the Witch's Craft.* Boston: Harvard University Press.

McFarland, Morgan. 1975. "Witchcraft: The Art of Remembering." *Quest: A Feminist Quarterly* 1, no. 4 (Spring 1975).

Schultz, Emily A., and Robert H. Lavenda. 1990. *Cultural Anthropology: A Perspective on the Human Condition.* 2d ed. St. Paul Minn.: West Publishing Company.

Shotwell, James Thomson. 1909–1910. "The Role of Magic." *The American Journal of Sociology* 15 (July 1909–May 1910): 781–793.

Starhawk [Miriam Simos]. 1979. *The Spiral Dance: A Rebirth of the Ancient Religion of the Great Goddess.* San Francisco: Harper and Row. (Rev. ed. 1989.)

———. 1987. *Truth or Dare: Encounters with Power, Authority, and Mystery.* San Francisco: Harper and Row.

Valiente, Doreen. 1989. *The Rebirth of Witchcraft.* London: Robert Hale.

Wax, Rosalie, and Murray Wax. 1962. "The Magical World View." *Journal for the Scientific Study of Religion* 1, No. 2 (April 1962): 179–188.

Whitehead, Harriet. 1974. "Reasonably Fantastic: Some Perspectives on Scientology, Science Fiction, and Occultism." In *Religious Movements in Contemporary America*, edited by Irving I. Zaretsky and Mark P. Leone. Princeton: Princeton University Press.

5

RITUAL IS MY CHOSEN ART FORM: THE CREATION OF RITUAL AS FOLK ART AMONG CONTEMPORARY PAGANS

Sabina Magliocco

AMONG CONTEMPORARY NEO-PAGAN and Wiccan groups, ritual is central to both religious worship and creative expression.[1] Numerous scholars have noted this fact (Adler 1986; Luhrmann 1990; Orion 1990; Scott 1980; Truzzi 1972); yet few have examined in detail the process by which ritual traditions are created among Wiccans and Neo-Pagans. Most studies of such groups, working under the Durkheimian assumption that social progress would somehow obviate people's need for ritual, have focused on the *whys* of the ritual process rather than the *hows*, often stressing the function of ritual, either psychological or social, for its adherents. But thus far little has been written on the creative and aesthetic qualities of Neo-Pagan ritual. Folklorists studying folk religions and religious folklore have often focused on festivals, narratives, and sermons within the Christian tradition (Abrahams 1972; Davis 1985; Dégh 1991; Lawless 1988; Magliocco 1993; Rosenberg 1975; Smith 1975). Yet they have thus far largely ignored contemporary Neo-Pagans. A closer examination of the artistic process of ritual creation can shed light on the ways new religions invent themselves, and uncover additional reasons why individuals become attracted to Neo-Paganism.

While many contemporary Neo-Pagans trace the descent of their religion from ancient forms of nature worship that once existed throughout Europe and in Asia, Africa, and North America, scholars generally agree that, though fragments of these religions continued to exist in folk custom, Neo-Paganism essentially constitutes a new religion. Many contemporary Neo-Pagans eclectically combine elements from various folk traditions "to rebuild a whole new culture from a pile of old and new fragments" (Adler 1986, 253). This makes Neo-Paganism an "invented tradition," a term first coined by Eric Hobsbawm to describe the creation of numerous traditions in nineteenth-century Europe following the upheavals of the romantic movement (Hobsbawm 1983). These new traditions sought to define identities or create them where they had not previously existed, and were particularly important to emerging nation-states and to ethnic and regional groups struggling to maintain their identities in contrast to nationalist movements. Hobsbawm stresses that traditions are most likely to be invented during periods of rapid social change. This is in fact the case of Neo-Paganism, which emerged in the United States during the late 1960s, a historical juncture during which social and political movements such as ecology and feminism radically altered the American landscape. Interest in nature spirituality, Goddess-worship, and other tenets of contemporary Neo-Paganism grew out of this social transformation. While as a group they are not class-oppressed (Orion 1990, 168), Neo-Pagans continue to see themselves in contrast to the dominant hegemonic American culture: they are attempting to construct a more meaningful and satisfying moral order that includes respect for the Earth, feminism, racial equality, cultural diversity, and an alternative to conspicuous consumption (Adler 1986; Fox 1980; Orion 1990, 49; Starhawk 1979, 1982.)

The creation of tradition among contemporary Pagans is not unlike the process of identity creation among many ethnic and regional groups attempting to revive or revitalize the culture of their ancestors. Adler (1986, 253) describes it as a predominantly Euro-American movement in which people attempt to rediscover their lost roots through folktales, songs, and dances; Ludeke (1989) and Orion (1990, 49) compare it to Wallace's description (1956) of revitalization movements. Like many such movements, its basic premise is romantic: authenticity is located in an ancient past whose ethos is thought to be close to the Earth and the cycles of nature, which Neo-Pagans see as the central metaphor of their cosmology.

Like the romantic movements of nineteenth-century Europe, Neo-Paganism makes extensive use of folkloric materials to recreate the lost ethos of the past. Many Neo-Pagans have a deep and abiding interest in folklore and are extraordinarily well read in it.[2] While folklore theory is not their primary concern, they are unusually knowledgeable about historical and contemporary folk traditions, especially folk narrative and customs, and consciously make use of this knowledge when shaping new rituals. Among them, I have found individuals who can debate with me the relative merits of the ballad collections of Child, Bronson, and Sharp; who can practically quote from Frazer and Mannhardt; and who recognized in my description of an obscure Sardinian children's Easter custom the Gardens of Adonis described by classical authors. Knowledge of and interest in folk traditions are fundamental to the creative process of ritual construction, as folk materials are among the primary building blocks of ritual.

In addition to making extensive use of folklore, Neo-Pagan ritual is itself folkloric. It has become a truism in the discipline that there are almost as many definitions of folklore as there are folklorists. In this chapter, I am basing my analysis on a composite definition that I find useful in teaching folklore courses: folklore is expressive culture which is creative, occurs in multiple variant forms, exhibits continuity through time and space, usually cannot be traced to a single author, and reflects a community's ethos. Because of folklore's expressive qualities, the boundary between folk*lore* and folk *art* is necessarily arbitrary. I am using folk *art* here because of ritual's broad nature, encompassing verbal folklore, folk music, folk drama, and folk craft in any single performance.

According to these criteria, it is clear that Neo-Pagan ritual can be approached as a form of folk art. It has all the characteristics of folklore as defined by Dan Ben Amos: "artistic communication in small groups" (1972, 13). It is not strongly fixed, but fluid; while it is built around a basic framework (which I will describe later), it is subject to constant innovation and variation according to the personalities of the individuals involved, their moods and desires, the time of year, and multiple other factors. While rituals may be copied from publications or disseminated through organized seminars whose purpose is to teach individuals to become priestesses or priests, the vast majority of Neo-Pagans learns to assemble rituals informally, through observation, contact with other Neo-Pagans, and experimentation. Most Neo-Pagan groups are characterized by a low degree of separation between the ritual leader(s) and the congregation; often a ritual performance is the product of group planning and collaborative decision making.

The focus of this chapter, then, is twofold: to explore and document the creation of ritual traditions and their cultural construction among contemporary Neo-Pagan communities, and to analyze the implications of the uses of academic folklore texts and media interpretations of folklore in the creation of new traditions. As a folklorist, I am particularly interested in individuals' deliberate and conscious use of folkloric materials to create new religious and spiritual traditions, especially rituals. What are the cultural sources for ritual material? What is the underlying structure of Neo-Pagan rituals? How are these elements combined in the communal creative process and in the performance of ritual itself? These are some fundamental questions which this chapter will explore.

RITUAL IN THE NEO-PAGAN COMMUNITY

Among contemporary Neo-Pagans, ritual plays an important role in religious expression. Many rituals are connected with the eight major year-cycle rites generally observed by this group; others take place at the covens' monthly sabbat meetings; still others include life-cycle rites such as handfastings (marriages) and Wiccanings (child blessings). Rituals may also be performed privately, for instance to mark the beginning of an important personal project, or to overcome a bad habit. Large rituals are performed at yearly Neo-Pagan festivals and gatherings. Neo-Pagans ritualize many aspects of life, and are self-reflexively aware of this and sometimes use it as a source of in-group humor: for instance, during a Neo-Pagan festival in the summer of 1993, a member of the clean-up crew announced at a community gathering, "We have a new ritual: please crush your aluminum cans before recycling them!" He proceeded to demonstrate the technique by stomping on a can as though he were performing a dance.

Neo-Pagans' definition of ritual is usually extremely broad. Adler cites one witch's personal definition: "It's a sacred drama in which you are the audience as well as the participant, and the purpose of it is to activate parts of the mind that are not activated by everyday activity" (1986, 141). This is essentially similar to the definition given by ritual scholars such as Turner (1968). "It's art, it's theater, it's sacrament—it's so many things," explains Lhianna Sidhe, a priestess in her forties and a prominent organizer of large rituals at Neo-Pagan gatherings. "Anything can be a ritual," said Lyra, a Rhode Island witch. She proceeded to give an example of an animal sound that she and her partner would make to soothe one another when one or the other was feeling stressed; "That's a ritual," she explained.[3]

While the emic definition of ritual is all-encompassing, I will limit myself in this chapter to the discussion of rituals that are larger in scope—that is, that involve more than the individual or the dyad. Many Neo-Pagans distinguish between rituals for various functions (e.g., worship, blessing, banishing, etc.); however, my purpose here is not to develop a taxonomy of ritual. Since most of these have similar underlying structures and are created and performed according to similar underlying principles, I have chosen not to treat them separately in this chapter, but rather to focus on the creative process of ritual invention itself.

There are various complex reasons why Neo-Pagans choose to foreground ritual in the context of a dominant culture in which such formalizations are becoming less frequent. Ritual is seen as a vehicle for personal and planetary healing and transformation (Orion 1990), important concepts in Neo-Pagan philosophy. Neo-Pagans base their worship on that of ancient pre-Christian religions. Often all that remains of these, both in written sources and in folk custom, consists mainly of rituals or descriptions thereof; we know less about the actual theology, beliefs, or doctrine of ancient Pagan peoples than we do about their rituals. Ritual thus becomes a primary way of enacting and maintaining the presumed historical link between contemporary and ancient Paganism which is at the root of Neo-Pagan teleology. This connection is central even to those who realize the constructed nature of that link. Steven, a priest from Minnesota, explains:

> I don't really believe that modern Paganism in the form that it's in now, or Wicca to be specific, has come down to us from most ancient times in a hands-on succession from the woman who sculpted the Willendorf Mother; I really don't think so. [But] people have been celebrating these folk festivals all along. . . . The rituals stay the same, the interpretation of rituals varies from generation to generation as each is reinterpreted. These are the things people have been doing for thousands of years, and we are the current incarnations of those people doing just what they did in a new way. . .

The link with the past is one ritual vehicle for inducing feelings of timelessness and liminality that can make the ritual experience transcendent. Steven continues:

[T]here's a grove by the Mississippi River where Witches have been doing rituals for 35, 40 years. . . . There was a big ritual going on there one night, the bonfire was going, and people were dancing and singing and the sun was setting and the dogs were barking and the children were running around. That was one of those things where I just stepped back from myself and I had a very strong feeling of . . . timelessness. . . . Suddenly we had stepped out of time, because what we were doing then is what [people had been doing] forever. And what we always will do.

Ritual also provides a way for many Neo-Pagans to feel connected to the natural world. A witch from Ohio explains: "As a Pagan, I'm part of nature; I'm connected to everything, everything's connected to me. [Ritual] keeps me in touch with the cycles of nature. I think all human beings have that instinctive drive to connect with something mysterious. . . . " For this woman, as for many other Neo-Pagans, the divine is immanent in nature; connection with nature is the key to the divine, and thus to transcendence. "What is ritual after all?" she added. "It's a way for us [to try] . . . to connect with the divine and bring it into our understanding. That's what ritual is." The importance of ritual, then, is its power to link individuals to the natural world and to the divine as manifest through nature. Through these links, many Neo-Pagans find meaning which allows them to spiritually transcend the routine of their daily lives. Like many art forms, the ultimate purpose of ritual is transcendence.

RITUAL AS ART

For Neo-Pagans, art and ritual are closely intertwined and virtually inseparable. "Ritual is an art form, just as much as painting or dance or acting," asserts Blacksun in a manual on ritual construction (Blacksun 1982, 3). "Human beings have a need for art, and art is ritual," explained Sharon Devlin, a California witch interviewed by Adler (1986, 141); and Steven, a veteran ritual artist and gifted narrator, told me: "Ritual is my chosen art form." Selena Fox, a Wisconsin priestess, likened ritual to performance art. This is in part because, like many theatrical productions, rituals often require staging, set construction, and elaborate prop and costume design, and Neo-Pagans are intimately involved in their physical creation. But more importantly, it points to a deeper issue in Neo-Pagan philosophy: the issue of creativity. Neo-Pagans value individual creativity to a very high degree; they believe that "an effective artist or craftsperson is, or has the potential to be, a magician" (Orion 1990, 131). Both artists and magicians/witches use imagination and the resources of the unconscious mind to manipulate objects and symbols and make manifest a vision (Orion); Orion describes how she gained the acceptance of the Neo-Pagan community simply through her artwork. It is no accident that some Wiccan Pagans refer to their religion as "the Craft": it is a metaphor for both ritual and artistic work.

For many Neo-Pagans, the aesthetic, emotionally affecting qualities of ritual are very important. Rituals move participants towards transcendence and greater understanding chiefly through their aesthetic charge; this is what allows good rituals to become, according to Selena, "vehicles for changing our consciousness." As Turner and Turner (1982, 205) suggest, the recombination of divergent symbolic elements in an aesthetically significant way through ritual startles people "into thinking anew about persons, objects, relationships, social roles, and features . . . hitherto taken for granted. Previous patterns of thought, feeling and action are disrupted" (1982, 205). Rituals tend to do this not through words, or cognitive meaning, but through dramatic action—affective meaning (Smith 1975, 7).

Neo-Pagan rituals are laden with meaning, but that meaning is couched within an aesthetic, dramatic presentation. Lhianna described how this was achieved in a summer solstice ritual in 1991:

> A few years ago we did a ritual called The Rose and the Thorn, and its theme was the Summer Solstice; it was the wedding feast of the God and Goddess. She was a pregnant goddess; she was veiled because you never ever see the true face of the Goddess. . . . but she had a pink diaphanous gown with roses pinned all over it and she had a crown of roses. . . . And then we invoked the God, and we body painted [John] green . . . ; I had sewn him a loincloth of green leaves. We put put green glitter in his hair, and we glued some of the green leaves coming out of his mouth, so he looked like the Green Man of the Forest. He had bells on his ankles, and when the God was invoked, he came dancing into the circle, and we heard jingle, jingle, jingle! So . . . Here comes the Goddess, she's walking around the circle, and here comes the dancing God, and he's dancing in jingling, and people are sticking their hands out to touch 'em, there's audience participation, unrehearsed! . . . He's this work of art, she's this work of art, it's reality. They're seeing the embodiment of all the worship that they do, they're seeing it right in the circle! . . . A woman told me later, "My child was in that circle and I've talked about the Goddess to her and I've talked about the God to her; this was one time that she could see it and understand it, and she'll never forget it. I don't have to talk any more, 'cause she's seen them."

In this case, the myth of the Goddess and the God and their fruit-ful union, represented by the bounty of nature in summer, was more easily understood and experienced when presented in this artistic, dramatic, and emotionally affecting framework.

THE AESTHETICS OF RITUAL

Like all folk art forms, Neo-Pagan ritual has a well-defined set of aesthetics that operates within the community. Different ritual artists also have their own recognizable styles. Because Neo-Pagans are such a diverse group, not all agree on every aspect of ritual aes-thetics. Some feel that rituals should be varied and spontaneous: "I like to keep things different," said Toraine, a witch in his twenties; "I don't like to do the same ritual week after week. If I wanted that, I'd be Christian." Others prefer a more ceremonial style: "I think it's wonderful that people can just rattle off the Lord's Prayer without even bothering to think about it," said Steven. "I aspire to a time when Pagans can do things without having to be so con-scious about them." While some prefer a more traditional, regi-mented ritual style, such as that of Gardnerian Wicca, others revel in a lighthearted, humorous, playful style manifest in freeform, tongue-in-cheek rituals in honor of chocolate or the comic strip character Bill the Cat.

Yet responses to my questions probing aesthetics were re-markably similar. "Ritual should be a transformative experience," said Lhianna. Like many others, she emphasized the educational value of rituals: "If we don't know more on an internal level after we've left the circle, as well as on the cerebral level, then some-thing has not happened." Yet rituals are more than just educational tools; ideally, they need to affect participants on an emotional level as well. Almost all my respondents felt that ritual should express sincere emotions, that it should come from the heart and not be a meaningless rote performance. "I want to learn something, I want to be moved, I want to feel renewed, I want to feel like I've had some sort of participation in something bigger than myself," one man explained. As Steven was speaking to me about the sense of timelessness and transcendence that the ritual along the banks of the Mississippi had induced in him, I became so moved the hair on my forearms stood on end, and I called his attention to it. "That's it!" he exclaimed. "That's how you know a ritual's good."

Not all Neo-Pagan rituals are equally successful for all their participants in this respect. Some rituals are highly successful for certain individuals, but leave others cold; others just don't "work." Negative examples cited included rituals that go on too long and lose the participants' attention; scripted presentations with little spontaneity and few participatory elements; rituals with invocations that take place entirely in a foreign language such as Old Welsh or Gaelic, and thus are incomprehensible to the majority of the participants; and rituals where little planning has taken place and nobody is sure what is going on. These examples emphasize important Neo-Pagan values: a strong participatory ethic, resistance to certain forms of hierarchical esoterism, and an emphasis on spontaneity, variation, and creativity. "In Wiccan ritual, free will is a really important thing," explained Toraine. "I think that's the art form: being able to include that spontaneity and sincerity in worship in a piece . . . that isn't totally chaotic."

Good ritual does not just happen. It takes organization and artistry, as Toraine suggests, to achieve just the right mix of spontaneity and planning that allows for good ritual to happen. In many ways, ritual is a collaborative performance between the director or facilitator and all of the participants. Lhianna, who often facilitates large rituals, explained: "I like to make sure that not a lot is left to chance, although I don't want to inhibit creativity on the part of the participants, either. . . . Flexibility is essential. . . . I want the people in the group to find the deep places within themselves and feel the freedom of expression."

THE STRUCTURAL FRAMEWORK

The highly participatory nature of rituals is possible largely because most Neo-Pagans have internalized a similar ritual grammar or structure, and this structure underlies nearly all rituals. Like Albert Lord's *guslars* (1960), participants feel free to improvise on this common framework and insert new elements at appropriate times.

This structural framework was probably first outlined by Gerald Gardner in *Witchcraft Today* (1954), and numerous Wiccan publications have printed variations of it (Blacksun 1982; Starhawk 1982; Valiente 1973). But contemporary Neo-Pagan ritual structure probably owes as much to the social movements of the 1960s as it does to Gardner. Books such as Alicia Bay Laurel's *Living on the Earth* (1971) and (with Ramon Sender) *Being of the Sun* (1973) combined ritual techniques with concepts from popular psychology to design "happenings" emphasizing ecological goals; feminist groups, dismayed with what they perceived as the patriarchal nature of Western religions, began to experiment with goddess-oriented worship through ritual (Starhawk 1982). The basic structural framework has by now passed into the folklore matrix of the Neo-Pagan subculture, so that few contemporary Pagans have learned it directly from any publication, but have picked it up informally through contact with other Neo-Pagans and by participating in community rituals.

The core structure is none other than Van Gennep's classic tripartite model of ritual (1909; elaborated by Turner 1968) as separation from daily life (liminality) followed by testing and reintegration into society. While the separation and reintegration phases are self-evident, in the Neo-Pagan case the testing takes the form of the main ritual work itself. Ritual is hard work that requires each participant's undivided attention and tests the strength of the circle; many told me that rituals sometimes do not work if one or more members is unwell, out of sorts, or otherwise unable to dedicate full energy to the task.

Skilled ritualists recognize this tripartite structure and often articulate it as "beginning, middle, and end." Selena, for example, divides the ritual into three parts: preparation and orientation, the work or focus of the ritual, and closure and assimilation. Understanding the core tripartite structure of ritual allows for the development of greater variations, sometimes bypassing certain formal elements of the model altogether.

The following basic outline is accepted by many Neo-Pagans. Ritual begins with the drawing of the circle, sometimes physically, as with chalk or a stick, other times by the presence of the participants standing in a circle. The circle becomes sacred, liminal space (Turner 1968), marked off from the everyday world. The drawing of the circle serves to separate actions that follow from ordinary time and space.

An invocation of the four elements through the four cardinal directions—earth (north), air (east), fire (south), and water (west)—usually follows the opening. Each element/direction corresponds, in Neo-Pagan teleology, to a set of properties or qualities associated with it through the principles of sympathetic magic. Thus earth suggests growing things, material concerns, worldly matters; air, the intellect and thought; fire, passion, the life force, commitment and engagement; and water, emotions, intuition, and the unconscious. These are only basic associations; specifics vary from one individual to another within the ritual context. An invocation of the God and Goddess may follow the salute to the four directions; some ritual artists use additional elements, such as the universe, the planet, spirit or shadow. Through the invocation of elements and sometimes a circular dance or the joining of hands, Neo-Pagans say they "raise the cone of power"—consolidate the combined energies of the participants to focus on the purpose of the ritual. They conceptualize the cone as rising upwards from the participants' bodies.

What follows in the main body of the ritual is the part most likely to vary widely, according to the ritual's purpose, the holy day being observed, the mood of the participants, and countless other variables. Being the least formulaic, this is the part of ritual that necessitates the most planning and is the focus of everyone's attention during ritual planning sessions. Gardnerian-derived practices feature "drawing down the moon," the embodiment of the Goddess in the high priestess, as well as a symbolic Great Rite, the union of the male and female principles in nature symbolized by the priestess plunging the athame, or ritual dagger, into the ritual chalice. Other traditions may include practices such as meditation, focusing and sending group energy towards a particular purpose, or the giving of thanks.

After the main actions of the ritual are accomplished and the energy raised at the beginning has been used or focused on a task, Neo-Pagans say the energy must be "grounded" so the participants can return to the real world. Rituals that end abruptly without closure are thought to be potentially dangerous, since participants have not had a chance to assimilate the ritual experience. Closure is sometimes accomplished through a ceremony known as "Cakes and Ale" in which the group shares food and drink. The ritual may end with one or more formulas which figuratively open the circle and return the group to non-ritual time. One example is:

> The circle is open, but never broken;
> Merry meet, merry part, and merry meet again.

While this tripartite model serves as the basis for most rituals, individuals and covens feel free to modify it according to their needs and wishes. Some cleave tightly to the formal aspects, while others relish in developing new variants.

PRACTICAL CONSIDERATIONS

According to Selena, most rituals need a facilitator, an individual who directs the action from beginning to end and guides the participants through the three stages. While small groups can sometimes dispense with this, a facilitator is particularly important in large group functions where people may not all be familiar with the ritual process and may come from different Neo-Pagan traditions. The facilitator may or may not be a priestess or priest, but he or she usually plans an outline of the ritual ahead of time, and explains the sequence of events to the participants at the beginning of the ritual. Sometimes two or more people may work together to facilitate a ritual, particularly a large group ritual.

Practical considerations are of prime concern when planning the insertion of elements into the underlying structure. One of the main determining factors is the size of the group: certain activities that can be done with small groups become impracticable with larger ones. For large group rituals, which can sometimes have as many as four hundred participants, considerations such as visibility, audibility, and mobility of the participants are important (Fox 1986). These in turn determine the kinds of ritual activities that can be undertaken. While small rituals have an intimate feeling and can be intricate and subtle, playing on the feelings and reactions of the participants, large rituals become more theatrical, with simple action and dramatic gestures taking the place of complex personal interactions.

Selena, who teaches ritualcraft in a yearly school for priestesses, outlined several other important factors to take into account when planning a ritual, including the ages of participants (very old and very young members have special needs), the weather, time, and location, and even the relative amount of time participants must stand. These are important because in order to be successful, a ritual must hold all the participants' attention for the duration. If people focus on other matters because they are bored or uncomfortable, Neo-Pagans say the energy becomes disrupted; the ritual loses momentum and cannot be a vehicle for transcendence or aesthetic expression.

SOURCES FOR RITUAL MATERIAL

To my question about the sources for ritual materials, Raven, a Neo-Pagan from Illinois, replied, "Anything that doesn't run away fast enough" is a potential source. This is not far off the mark. Neo-Pagan ritual artists are adept at combining and adapting materials from widely divergent sources, cultures, historical periods, and media into a harmonious whole; they are by nature *bricoleurs.* I have already established that Neo-Pagans turn to folklore for ritual material and inspiration; here, I intend to demonstrate how this is done.

LIVING FOLK TRADITIONS

A fair amount of source material comes not from books or other media, but from living folk traditions. In this case, the traditions are not invented, but adapted and reinterpreted as folklore has always been. Neo-Pagans may turn to their own family traditions as a source of inspiration, or may continue family practices under the auspices of the new religion. For instance, one witch learned that her grandmother had dyed Easter eggs using onion skins and other scraps from the kitchen; the practice appealed to her because it used natural substances and did not rely on packaged egg colors marketed at Easter. She adapted it for use in her spring equinox ritual. Many Neo-Pagans carve jack-o'-lanterns at Samhain (Halloween), continuing unbroken an American folk tradition. Local or regional folk customs may be adapted in a similar way: for instance, at a Neo-Pagan festival in the summer of 1993, Susan, a witch from New Orleans, gave a workshop entitled "Bayou folklore and Grisgris."[4]

If a family or local tradition is not available, Neo-Pagans may turn to the folk practices of their friends and associates for inspiration. Explained Steven: "I cultivate friendships whenever possible with people from ethnic backgrounds other than my own; as often as I can I attend synagogues and mosques and churches of different persuasions, Hindu temples. . . . " Selena, whose group includes members from a wide variety of ethnic and cultural backgrounds, said, "If I want to do a ritual with a particular ethnic flavor, I'll go to people in that group and ask them about their traditions." She then involves these individuals in planning and facilitating the rite. Here Selena is acting much as a folklorist would, collecting information on a particular folk custom from living individuals (though a folkorist would not make the same use of it as a Neo-Pagan).

ACADEMIC CULTURE

Academicians, particularly folklorists and anthropologists, have provided a treasure trove of information about ritual practices and folk customs that Neo-Pagans feel free to borrow and adapt. Some prominent Neo-Pagans in fact were moved to try their first ritual as a result of classes and academic activities: Starhawk recounts how she performed her first ritual in the context of an anthropology class at the University of California–Los Angeles (1982, 2), and Selena performed her first ritual, a Dionysian rite, as president of the Classics Club at The College of William and Mary (personal communication with S. Fox, 25 July 1993). Selena continues to maintain close ties with the academic community and to consult folklorists and anthropologists on ritual; this is possible because she lives in the range of a large research university, and is not necessarily typical of other Neo-Pagans.

Adler (1986), Orion (1990), and Carpenter and Fox (1993) have shown that Neo-Pagans read more widely than the general population, and my research bears this out. Most have extensive collections of books, both Neo-Pagan and academic, on various aspects of history, religion, folklore, and anthropology; often the first step in ritual construction is reading. As Lhianna said, "If we're pursuing a particular theme, I'll probably pull down every book I have and read that version. . . . " Necessarily, then, ritual material is eclectic, even when individuals are seeking to work within a single ethnic tradition.

Generally, individuals do not limit themselves to a single source; most rely on many. A few notable works my informants mentioned include the Child ballads, the Opies' *The Lore and Language of Schoolchildren*, Robert Graves's *The White Goddess*, Frazer's *The Golden Bough*, Maria Leach's *Standard Dictionary of Folklore and Mythology*, the works of Joseph Campbell and Tacitus's *De Rerum Brittanniae* (for its description of Druids).

Of course, material which inspires Neo-Pagans is often not that which inspires academics, and some of the sources informants cited are now looked upon askance in academia. However, most Neo-Pagans are not interested in the academic validity of their sources, but in their emotional, intuitive validity; thus academic judgments do not affect their choices.

POPULAR PSYCHOLOGY

Throughout Neo-Pagan literature, there are many references to concepts drawn from popular psychology. Of particular interest is the concept of the "inner child," first popularized in the book *I'm OK, You're OK* (Harris 1969) and later picked up by the recovery movement. As early as 1979, Starhawk wrote of the unconscious mind as the "Younger Self" that "directly experiences the world" (1979, 35). She related this part of the psyche to the right side of the brain, the imagination, dreams, and visions—its ways of communicating with the conscious mind, or "Talking Self." Rituals and related exercises are presented as a way of communicating with Younger Self to integrate the unconscious with the conscious. Today, many Neo-Pagans speak of the importance of letting the Inner Child emerge in ritual: "Play [in ritual] is very important. It's the Inner Child stuff; we're all working on our Inner Children, all of us," said Lhianna.

Popular writers such as Joseph Campbell and Robert Bly have diffused the Jungian idea of archetypes into the popular culture; this is another important concept in Neo-Pagan ritual. Various aspects of the Goddess and the God are referred to in conversation as "archetypes" or "archetypal"; one car at a Neo-Pagan festival bore the bumper sticker "Follow Your Bliss!"

Many techniques used in rituals are also borrowed from popular psychology. Creative visualization is regularly used by Selena, for example, to focus participants' attentions on such goals as world peace and healing the planet. Some rituals use dramatic reenactments to help participants deal with past traumas. For example, in one case a seventeen-year-old woman had experienced unwanted sexual overtures during a festival. Her mother, a priestess, designed a ritual to raise the coven's awareness of sexual harassment and to help the young woman overcome the unpleasant experience. Humor played a role in this ritual during which group members at one point recited clichéd pick-up lines, such as, "My wife doesn't understand me," "A man has needs he can't help!" "Wanna come up and see my etchings?" and "Hey baby, what's your sign?" By likening sexual harassers to trolls and ritually banishing them in all four cardinal directions, the group enacted its disapproval of sexual harassment and expressed its support for the young woman.

MASS MEDIA AND POPULAR CULTURE

A surprising number of inspirations come to Neo-Pagans from the mass media and popular culture. I spoke with numerous Neo-Pagans who favor certain programs, especially *Star Trek* and its spin-offs *Star Trek: The Next Generation* and *Deep Space Nine*. The customs and practices of aliens in this series seemed to particularly inspire some. Reportedly, one coven has developed an elaborate set of rituals based on Vulcan mythology. To what extent Neo-Pagans overlap with the extensive realm of *Star Trek* fandom has not yet been determined, however.[5]

For some with cable television, the Discovery channel has proved a source of materials. Lyra, a priestess who trains other priestesses, reported that she draws ritual elements from the ethnographic films shown regularly on the network.

Cartoon character Bill the Cat, from Berke Breathed's comic strip "Outland" (previously "Bloom County"), has furnished inspiration for a humorous ritual performed yearly in his honor at a large midwestern Neo-Pagan festival. At the same festival, another lighthearted ritual honors rock artist Jimi Hendrix. Sometimes consumer products can furnish material upon which to build a ritual: plastic troll dolls partially inspired (and were used as props in) the ritual designed to raise awareness about sexual harassment in which sexually predatory offenders were likened to trolls.

FESTIVALS, NETWORKING, AND PAGAN PUBLICATIONS

Neo-Pagan festivals are probably the single most important vehicle for the transmission of ritual forms, and have been key in the development of a Neo-Pagan folk culture. Numerous gatherings occur yearly, some specific to one region, others drawing national or international participation. Most of these include a number of large rituals designed to bring the community together during the event. Many also include sessions specifically designed to teach ritual techniques to aspiring priestesses and priests. These encounters can result in fast and efficient dissemination of specific rituals, ritual elements, and techniques. Some Neo-Pagan organizations run ritual training workshops separately from festivals; these are obvious sources for inspiration and materials. In addition, many Neo-Pagans network with like-minded others in their geographic area; these encounters can result in borrowings of ideas.

Currently, there are over one hundred Wiccan and Neo-Pagan newsletters in the United States alone. Many of these encourage reader contributions in the form of essays, poetry, visual artwork, and ritual, and serve as sources for ritual ideas for many readers. They also serve as vehicles for disseminating rituals within the larger Neo-Pagan community. Readers can also turn to any number of books on ritual and magic, offering everything from precise rituals with chants and songs to suggestions for making up your own. Now Neo-Pagan tapes and videos demonstrating rituals are available through some of the publications, and can serve as a further source for inspiration. Finally, computer bulletin boards and networks with an occult focus (such as ARCANA) can sometimes serve as vehicles for spreading ritual ideas and forms.

INTERNAL SOURCES: INTUITION AND IMAGINATION

Ultimately, perhaps, the individual's own intuition and imagination are the most valuable tools for ritual construction. They are especially necessary in the process of *bricolage*—combining disparate elements gleaned from divergent sources into an artistic and coherent whole. Numerous respondents reported finding inspiration for ritual in dreams, meditation, or trancework. Sometimes these insights reveal themselves to be remarkably similar to an existing folk tradition the artist had not known about before. Selena explained, "Folkways that I've sometimes used have first appeared in a dream or a vision or a flash of intuition [and] I've later found, when I've talked to other people who are practitioners or gone to the books, that this is something that's connected with a particular culture or a particular heritage."

Other times, moving and aesthetic expressions happen in rituals without planning. It is difficult to isolate their source or to plan for them; they happen because of a mixture of spontaneity and serendipity, much as exciting and wonderful moments may happen during a class. One can say that they seldom happen in a poorly planned classroom, or in one with an incompetent teacher or unprepared students; yet it is difficult to describe the exact mix of ingredients that causes them to occur. They are often not the doing of the facilitator or organizer at all, but come from the participants themselves. The collaborative nature of the ritual performances makes such moments possible.

THE COMMUNAL CREATIVE PROCESS: A CASE STUDY

I have already established that most rituals are co-performances in which both the facilitator and the participants have active roles; this spontaneity is one of the most appealing facets of Neo-Paganism for its adherents. In some cases, however, rituals are planned and created by an entire community, with each member making active contributions, in what can only be called a process of communal creation. This process is most apparent in small, intimate covens or groups that have been working together for some time. In such cases, members plan rituals together in the same way that a group would plan a party, with each member contributing ideas, props, and labor, and the group reaching a consensus as to how the ritual will take shape. At a time in which traditional religions are moving away from formalism in religious expression and excluding some of the more participatory aspects of ritual, the participatory nature of Neo-Pagan rituals is an important factor in attracting many creative individuals.

The process of communal creation can also take place at the larger Neo-Pagan festivals, and it is a case of this type that I will describe here. The ritual took place in the context of one of the large Neo-Pagan festivals which is held yearly at midsummer in the upper Midwest. In the summer of 1993, the festival had over six hundred participants from various Neo-Pagan traditions. Participants were camped in a large valley in a private natural park and campground; a ritual fire burned continuously in a firepit, and the valley was lined with multicolored tents. A festive atmosphere prevailed throughout the week-long event; large rituals were held almost every night around the ritual fire, and in addition groups of campers held private rituals following their chosen traditions. During the day, participants could attend numerous workshops on ritual planning and creation where the fundamentals of ritualcraft were taught.

The gay/lesbian/bisexual mythologies group met in the afternoon of the fifth day of the festival. It was facilitated by Toraine, a young gay man from Indiana. For some Neo-Pagans, particularly those who trace their descent from Gardnerian practice, the union of the Goddess and God, the female and male principles in nature, is a central metaphor which is enacted repeatedly in ritual. Many lesbian and gay Neo-Pagans feel this metaphor is heterosexist and denies the legitimacy and even the existence of homosexual love and union. The purpose of the meeting was to design a ritual that would express gay/lesbian/bisexual Neo-Paganism in a non-heterosexist way.

The meeting began with Toraine soliciting myths and narratives that participants felt had a gay, lesbian, or bisexual ethos. Interestingly, nearly all of the contributions came from classical mythology and literature. None of the narratives are, according to traditional interpretations, about homosexuality; yet the narrators forged those links themselves, interpreting the stories according to their imagination and political agenda. One woman recounted the story of Artemis and her devotee Amethyst, who was returning from Artemis's shrine; to protect her from Dionysius's drunken fury, Artemis transformed her into a stone. Dionysius spilled wine from his goblet over it, turning it the color of Amethyst. The woman explained that she believed Artemis had protected her devotee because they were lovers. She went on to explain that this is the origin of lavender or purple as a color symbolizing homosexuality. A man alluded to the epic of Gilgamesh, in which the deity sends the wild man Enkidu as a companion for Gilgamesh the king; he felt that the two men were clearly lovers. The story of Zeus and his cup-bearer Ganymede was told implying that Zeus loved Ganymede in a homosexual way. Also mentioned as gay/lesbian mythic prototypes were Damon and Pythias, Queen Boadicea, the three Fates, and the Hindu goddesses Durga and Lakshmi.

The most fully developed narrative was told by Toraine, a master storyteller whose style blends dramatic enactments with witty asides. It is the Sumerian myth of the descent of the goddess Inanna, who follows her dead lover into the underworld and becomes trapped there herself. Her worried supernatural relatives create two genderless, faceless beings to go to her rescue; being faceless and genderless, only they can descend without themselves succumbing to death. They are of course successful in retrieving Inanna, and Toraine explained that they are the prototypes for gays and lesbians, who served as acolytes in the temple of the goddess Inanna in ancient Sumer.

The storytelling was used to generate ideas for ritual activities. For example, Toraine explained that during the medieval Witchcraft persecutions, homosexuals were also victimized, and were used to light the pyres on which the witches were burned to death; this was, according to his explanation, the origin of the slang term "faggot" to mean homosexual.[6] The group decided to make a small bundle of sticks, or fagot, which would be burned in the ritual fire in remembrance of those who had suffered persecution because of their sexual orientation.

Participants also contributed poems, chants, and prayers to the planning process. Great attention was given to devising a rite to replace the Great Rite which typically occurs during Gardnerian-derived rituals: instead of having the athame, a symbol of male energy, plunged into the chalice, a symbol of female energy, to express the union of these forces in nature, two athames and two cups would be crossed, and water would be poured over them to signify lesbian, gay, and bisexual energies. Two men and two women were asked to volunteer to pass the cups and athames around to each member of the circle during the ritual; four individuals were chosen to represent the four cardinal directions and invoke their qualities.

The ritual itself took place a short while later in a sunny clearing near the center of the camp. The circle was cast, and each of the four volunteers spoke briefly about the qualities they wished to invoke from that direction. The God and Goddess were invoked; the two cups and two athames, filled with the spirit of the deities, were borne around the circle by the volunteers. The women offered each participant a drink from the cup, while the men touched each participant lightly on the forehead with an athame. Then two participants read original poetry they had written which they thought applied to the occasion. We were each asked to pick up a stick to make the fagot, and as we did so, the facilitators began to chant:

> We're changing everything we're touching, and
> Everything we're touching changes.[7]

As we chanted, we began to march solemnly towards the ritual fire; the facilitators were carrying the fagot composed of everyone's sticks and tied with a red cord. We assembled in a circle around the fire and joined hands. At this point, a spontaneous element occurred: two participants solemnly lit a pair of large sparklers and placed them in the ground on each side of the firepit. A facilitator offered a brief prayer in which we were asked to meditate on the persecution of gays and lesbians through hate crimes, to visualize a more tolerant future, and to focus our thoughts on people afflicted with the H.I.V. virus and those who had gone before them into the Summerland.[8] It was a simultaneously grim and affecting moment, as we all found ourselves remembering friends and relatives, some now gone, and calling out their names.

FOLKLORE, POPULAR CULTURE, AND
THE INVENTION OF TRADITION

All traditions are ultimately created, and all religions invented out of what came before. Neo-Paganism offers us a glimpse into this process as it takes shape. Yet their particular use of sources raises a number of interesting questions about contemporary folklore and its relationship to both academic and popular culture.

Folklorists have distinguished folklore from both academic and popular culture chiefly through its mode of transmission: the intimate, face-to-face situation (Ben Amos 1972, 12; Narváez and Laba 1986, 1). While the folklore of Neo-Pagans—the rituals, narratives, songs, chants, etc. themselves—is frequently transmitted in this way, it is also clear that in the process of creating this folklore, Neo-Pagans draw materials from folk, academic, and popular sources. Academic and popular culture have often been treated by scholars as things quite apart from folklore in an attempt to discriminate between "genuine" folklore and spurious imitations (Dorson 1976). What does Neo-Pagans' invention of tradition reveal about the usefulness or even the applicability of such categories, and how might we better understand it?

First of all, the application of adjectives such as genuine, authentic, and spurious to Neo-Pagan folklore does little to help us understand the folkloric process (Handler and Linnekin 1984, 288). The invention of tradition by Neo-Pagans should by no means be regarded as a distortion of academic knowledge, but rather as an integral part of the process by which folklore is shaped and changed by its practitioners. Recent studies have shown that the concept of tradition is itself culturally constructed (Handler and Linnekin 1984; Wagner 1981); presumed links with the past are never merely a matter of fact, but depend on what is considered evidence from the vantage point of the present (Herzfeld 1982, 3). This applies to the academic tradition of folkloristics, as well: as Herzfeld has shown, attempts by Greeks to construct a national study of Greek folklore drew liberally from both folk traditions and classical sources (Herzfeld 1982). In this respect, folkloristics and Neo-Paganism have many common roots.

Like nineteenth-century national and regional groups, Neo-Pagans are using folklore to establish a precedent legitimating their existence. This is evident not only in the cultural construction of ritual as deriving from ancient Pagan practices, but in the micro-processes of narrative events and ritual planning. Like their romantic predecessors, Neo-Pagans have a political agenda in mind, but not one that demands cultural unity: rather, most Neo-Pagans espouse a liberal viewpoint valuing diversity, multiculturalism, minority rights, feminism, ecology, and world peace.[10] Many Neo-Pagans act on these convictions: Selena's rituals for saving the Earth are often followed by concrete activities to that end, such as trash collection or tree planting.

Michel De Certeau's *The Practice of Everyday Life* (1984) is particularly useful in illuminating the process of the invention of tradition among Neo-Pagans. De Certeau attempts to trace the effects of postmodernity, by which he means the spread of advanced consumer capitalism and the disjunction that often follows it, on the life of common people in everyday situations. He takes for granted that everyday life is dominated by systems of mass media and consumer culture which determine much of the knowledge at people's disposal. But he privileges the role of the individual imagination. Consumers, according to De Certeau, do not simply consume mass culture and consumer goods. Rather, through a process he calls (after Lévi-Strauss) *bricolage*, they pick and choose from among the goods available to them to construct "narratives" which constitute a form of resistance to those of the dominant culture. He calls this process *tactic*. De Certeau's tactic is reminiscent of Marxist interpretations in which folklore is cast in the role of culture of resistance or protest, either contraposing the dominant culture or appropriating elements of it only to turn it against itself. Yet tactic is not the resistance of the class-oppressed, but the cultural play of disaffected urban intellectuals. It resists through playfulness, irony and self-reflexiveness, and opens new possibilities within the dominant culture itself.

I would like to suggest that the flow of information between academic, popular, and folk cultures in the case of these processes of invention is largely due to the operation of folkloric processes in a postmodern context. Carpenter (1993) maintains that the combination of ancient elements with contemporary ones in Neo-Paganism is characteristically postmodern. The "global flows of world information" (Appadurai 1991) have made knowledge that was previously restricted available to a mass audience: anyone can flick on the Discovery channel and witness Australian aboriginal shamans, Native American ceremonies, or Yoruba healing rituals. Once this knowledge is available, it is not difficult for individuals to manipulate it and use it in the invention of folklore, much as people have long been using available academic knowledge to modify folk traditions (Moser 1964). In this context, the invention of tradition by contemporary Neo-Pagans can be seen as tactic, a *bricolage* of disparate forms from the academic and mass continuum to create a folk culture whose ultimate end is to offer an alternative to a consumer culture that can be sterile and numbing.

NOTES

The field work for this project was conducted principally at a large Neo-Pagan festival in Wisconsin during the summer of 1993, and through prolonged contact with one Wisconsin Neo-Pagan community. I would like to thank Selena Fox and Dennis Carpenter for generously allowing me to conduct research for this chapter at both private and public gatherings that they have organized. Thanks are also due to all those who participated in the interviewing for this chapter and helped my research in other ways, including Caillean, Alice Cascorbi, Lady Cybele, Ember, Jake, Kestrel, Lhianna Sidhe, Lyra, Scott, Steve Piziks, Steven Wise, and Toraine. I also thank Sarah Pike for sharing with me her unpublished bibliography on contemporary Paganism.

1. In this chapter, I will use the term "Neo-Pagan" to designate a range of contemporary nature religions, including those who call themselves witches or practitioners of Wicca. I prefer the term Neo-Pagan as it does not exclude those who draw inspiration for their religious practices from non-Wiccan, non-Western polytheistic traditions. I use Neo-Pagan to distinguish contemporary Paganism from that of classical antiquity in bibliographic indexes.

2. Adler (1986), Carpenter and Fox (1993), and Orion (1990) have all noted that Neo-Pagans have a higher educational level compared to the general population, and that they are avid readers. Orion (1990, 154–158) demonstrated that the majority of Neo-Pagans who held academic degrees had studied the arts, humanities, or social sciences. While she does not include folklore in her list of disciplines, knowledge of folklore can come through exposure to other fields as well. Many well-known Neo-Pagans have been amateur folklorists or anthropologists, including Gerald Gardner himself.

3. Folklorists would argue that this is not properly ritual, but a ludic routine which is part of dyadic folklore. See Bendix (1987) and Oring (1984).

4. See Campbell and McIver (1987) for further discussions of the ways in which folk religion and religious folklore may contribute to an interest in Neo-Paganism and other "occult" religions.

5. For a study of *Star Trek* fandon and its folklore, and especially the role women play in it, see Bacon-Smith (1992).

6. There is little doubt that homosexuals, along with Jews and witches, were persecuted for heresy during the Inquisition. This story of the origin of the term "faggot," however, seems to be a folk etymology. "Fagot" meaning bundle of sticks is, according to *Funk and Wagnalls Standard College Dictionary*, derived from Old French *fagot*, a bundle or parcel. "Faggot" as a derogatory term for homosexual comes from the verb *to fag*, "to exhaust by hard work"; it seems to have originated in British boarding schools, where boys who did menial service for other boys in higher classes were known as "fags," "faggers," or "faggots." Toraine's story appears in numerous Neo-Pagan publications, however, including Weinstein (1979, 92) and Mitchell (1977) and can be considered to have passed into the register of Neo-Pagan folklore.

7. Variant of a chant written by Starhawk (1979, 103).

8. Neo-Pagan term for what follows death, borrowed from Celtic mythology.

9. The use of academic writing in the invention of tradition has a venerable history. Much of the nineteenth-century European folkloristics was in fact motivated by romantic nationalist ideologies which located the soul of a people in its folklore. See G. Cocchiara, *A History of Folklore in Europe* (ISHI, 1980).

10. For an account of the political activities of members of a Dianic coven and their relationship to their spiritual beliefs, see Finley (1991).

REFERENCES

Abrahams, Roger. 1972. "Christmas and Carnival on St. Vicent." *Western Folklore* 31 (4): 275–289.

Adler, Margot. 1986. *Drawing Down the Moon.* Rev. ed. Boston: Beacon Press.

Appadurai, Arjun. 1990. "Disjuncture and Difference in the Global Cultural Economy." *Public Culture* 2, no. 2: 1–24.

Bacon-Smith, Camille. 1992. *Enterprising Women: Television Fandom and the Creation of Popular Myth.* Philadelphia: University of Pennsylvania Press.

Bay Laurel, Alicia. 1971. *Living on the Earth.* New York: Vintage Books.

Bay Laurel, Alicia, and Ramon Sender. 1973. *Being of the Sun.* New York: Harper and Row.

Ben Amos, Dan. 1972. "Toward a Definition of Folklore in Context." In *Towards New Perspectives in Folklore,* edited by A. Paredes and R. Bauman, 3–15. Austin: University of Texas Press.

Bendix, Regina. 1987. "Marmot, Memet, and Marmoset: Further Research on the Folklore of Dyads." *Western Folklore* 46: 171–191.

———. 1988. "Folklorismus: The Challenge of a Concept." *International Folklore Review* 6: 5–50.

Blacksun. 1982. *The Elements of Beginning Ritual Construction.* Mt. Horeb, Wisc.: Circle Publications.

Campbell, Colin, and Shirely McIver. 1987. "Cultural Sources of Support for Contemporary Occultism." *Social Compass* 34: 41–60.

Carpenter, Dennis D. 1993. "Spiritual Contours of the Contemporary Pagan Worldview." *Circle Network News* 46 (1992–93): 14–15.

Carpenter, Dennis D., and S. Fox. 1993. Pagan Spirit Gathering 1992 Tribal Survey Results. In *Pagan Spirit Gathering Village Guide 1993*, edited by D. D. Carpenter, S. Fox, and G. Ordaz. Mt. Horeb, Wisc.: Circle Publications.

Child, F. J. 1864. *The English and Scottish Popular Ballads*. Boston: Little, Brown, and Company. (Re-issued in 1956 in New York by Folklore Press.)

De Certeau, Michel. 1984. *The Practice of Everyday Life*. Berkeley: University of California Press.

Dégh, Linda. 1991. "Are Sectarian Miracle Stories Contemporary American Folk Legends? A Preliminary Consideration." In *Storytelling in Contemporary Societies*, edited by Lutz Röhrich and Sabine Wienker-Piepho, 71–89. Tübingen: Gunter Narr Verlag.

Dorson, Richard M. 1976. *Folklore and Fakelore: Essays Towards a Discipline of Folk Studies*. Cambridge, Mass.: Harvard University Press.

Farrar, Janet, and Stewart Farrar. 1985. *A Witches Bible*. New York: Magickal Childe.

Finley, Nancy J. 1991. "Political Activism and Feminist Spirituality." *Sociological Analysis* 52, no. 4: 349–362.

Fox, Selena. 1980. "Pagan Spirit Alliance Pledge." *Circle Network News*.

———. 1992. "Ritualcraft" and "Power Raising in Large and Small Groups." In photocopied packet for School for Priestesses. Mt. Horeb, Wisc.: Circle Publications.

Frazer, Sir James G. 1959. *The New Golden Bough*. Abridged and edited by Theodore Gaster. New York: Criterion Books.

Funk and Wagnalls Standard Dictionary of Folklore, Mythology and Legend. 1984. Edited by Maria Leach. San Francisco: Harper and Row.

Gans, Herbert. 1979. "Symbolic Ethnicity: The Future of Ethnic Groups and Cultures in America." *Ethnic and Racial Studies* 2, no. 1: 1–19.

Gardner, Gerald B. 1954. *Witchcraft Today*. New York: Citadel.

Gennep, Arnold Van. 1909. *Les Rites de Passage*. Paris: Emile Nourry.

Graves, Robert. 1966. *The White Goddess*. New York: Farrar, Straus and Giroux.

Handler, Richard, and Jocelyn Linnekin. 1984. "Tradition: Genuine or Spurious?" *Journal of American Folklore* 97: 273–290.

Harris, Thomas A. 1969. *I'm OK, You're OK: A Practical Guide to Transactional Analysis*. New York: Harper and Row.

Herzfeld, Michael. 1982. *Ours Once More: Folklore, Ideology and the Making of Modern Greece.* Austin, Tex.: University of Texas Press.

Hobsbawm, Eric. 1983. "Introduction: Inventing Traditions." In *The Invention of Tradition*, edited by Eric Hobsbawm and T. Ranger, 1–14. Cambridge: Cambridge University Press.

Lawless, Elaine. 1988. *Handmaidens of the Lord. Pentecostal Women Preachers and Traditional Religion.* Philadelphia: University of Pennsylvania Press.

Lord, Albert. 1960. *The Singer of Tales.* Cambridge, Mass.: Harvard University Press.

Ludeke, Joan. 1989. "Wicca as a Revitalization Movement Among Post-Industrial, Urban American Women." Ph.D. dissertation, Iliff School of Theology.

Luhrmann, T. M. 1989. *Persuasions of the Witch's Craft: Ritual Magic in Contemporary England.* Cambridge, Mass.: Harvard University Press.

Magliocco, Sabina. 1993. *The Two Madonnas: The Politics of Festival in a Sardinian Community.* New York: Peter Lang.

Mitchell, Larry. 1977. *Faggots and Their Friends Between Revolutions.* New York: Calamus Books.

Moser, Hans. 1964. "Der Folklorismus als Forschungsproblem der Volkskunde." *Hessische Blätter für Volkskunde* 55: 9–57.

Narváez, Peter, and Martin Laba, eds. 1986. *Media Sense: The Folklore-Popular Culture Continuum.* Bowling Green, Ohio: Bowling Green State University Press.

Olrik, Axel. 1975. "The Epic Laws of Folk Narrative." In *The Study of Folklore*, edited by Alan Dundes, 129–140. New York: Prentice Hall.

Opie, Iona, and Peter Opie. 1959. *The Lore and Language of Schoolchildren.* Oxford: Clarendon Press.

Oring, Elliott. 1984. "Dyadic Traditions." *Journal of Folklore Research* 21: 19–28.

Orion, Loretta. 1990. "Revival of Western Paganism and Witchcraft in the Contemporary United States." Ph.D. dissertation, State University of New York at Stonybrook.

Rosenberg, Bruce. 1975. *The Art of the American Folk Preacher.*

Scott, Gini. 1980. *Cult and Countercult: A Study of a Spiritual Growth Group and a Witchcraft Order.* Westport, Conn.: Greenwood Press.

Smith, Robert J. 1975. *The Art of the Festival*. Lawrence, Kans.: University of Kansas Publications in Anthropology 6.

Starhawk [Miriam Simos]. 1979. *The Spiral Dance. A Rebirth of the Ancient Religion of the Great Goddess.* (Rev. ed. 1989.) New York: Harper Collins.

———. 1982. *Dreaming the Dark: Magic, Sex and Politics.* (Reprinted 1988.) Boston: Beacon Press.

Truzzi, Marcello. 1972. "The Occult Revival as Popular Culture: Some Random Observations on the Old and Nouveau Witch." *Sociological Quarterly* 13: 16–36.

Turner, Victor. 1968. *The Ritual Process.* Ithaca, N.Y.: Cornell University Press.

Turner, Victor, and Edith Turner. 1982. "Religious Celebrations." In *Celebration: Studies in Festivity and Ritual*, edited by Victor Turner, 201–219. Washington, D.C.: Smithsonian Press.

Valiente, Doreen. 1973. *An ABC of Witchcraft, Past and Present.* New York: St. Martin's Press.

Wagner, Roy. 1981. *The Invention of Culture.* Chicago: University of Chicago Press.

Wallace, Anthony. 1956. "Revitalization Movements." *American Anthropologist* 58: 264–281.

Weinstein, Marion. 1979 (reprinted 1981). *Positive Magic.* Custer, Wash.: Phoenix Publishing.

6

FORGING MAGICAL SELVES: GENDERED BODIES AND RITUAL FIRES AT NEO-PAGAN FESTIVALS

Sarah M. Pike

HUNDREDS OF FESTIVAL-GOERS dressed in dark ankle-length capes or gauze gowns, adorned with feathers and jewelry, and holding fluorescent wands, candles, and sparklers process through the festival field toward the bonfire site. Dancers perform around the fire as it is carefully lit, the flames spreading slowly at first and then blazing to the accompaniment of drumming and excited applause. A large group of men and women drumming and playing percussion instruments cluster along one side of the bonfire. The full sound and energetic rhythms generated by this crowd of musicians urges on dancers as they pass. A number of women in colorful Middle Eastern costume perform belly dances; other women and men dance in a variety of styles, some taking slow swinging steps, others leaping and bounding closer to the flames.

Such is the scene of a late-night fire at a Neo-Pagan festival in New York State. Many Neo-Pagans read themselves out of family groupings and the religious faiths of their parents, necessitating new definitions of self, kinship, family, and religion. Neo-Pagan festivals make available the materials for creating new identities. At festivals, self-creation takes place within and alongside group activities: workshops on astrology, tarot cards, mythology, magic,

Witchcraft, Native American medicine, African drumming, large planned rituals, and late-night ritual fires. This colorful and diverse festival terrain offers a multitude of activities and resources for making new identities. One festival organizer sees these gatherings as "a wondrous revival of the old regional fair except that this region is one of the mind" (Damarru 1992, 3). Most of the workshops and rituals focus on self-improvement "technologies" like ritual skills and visualization, and present information about many different religious and mythology systems.[1]

As Neo-Pagan festivals have developed over the past fifteen years, the varied interests and commitments with which people arrive come into conflict with each other, and in this way, the festivals have become a space in which highly personalized religious identities take shape within and against a temporary community. In contrast to expectations of unconstrained self-expression these festivals are actually highly structured settings. While gendered aspects of self-expression are somewhat more fluid than in the world outside these festivals, they nevertheless replicate that world in many ways.

Many Neo-Pagan groups describe themselves as aggressively non-hierarchical and decentralized; these characteristics allow them to see themselves as offering an alternative to "mainstream" society. The festivals' cultural patchwork reflects Neo-Paganism's "politically correct" self-presentation: inclusivity is stressed, special accommodations are made for minority and marginalized groups, environmental consciousness is emphasized, and recycling has long been a part of most festivals. Furthermore, festival-goers expect festivals to reflect their vision of a more egalitarian, less sexist society. Construction of men's and women's identities within this ritual space is coded in varieties of bodily expression. The languages of movement and body decoration reveal that while ritual work within Neo-Pagan festivals involves gender play and gender reversal, its transformative effects are more limited than participants anticipate.

Because of its egalitarian focus, Neo-Paganism's "other" is authoritarian, hierarchical, and power hungry. However, structures of authority not apparent at first glance become manifest when invisible boundaries within Neo-Pagan festivals are transgressed. Passing through and shaping these boundaries involves conflict and negotiation. Costumes, body painting, degrees of nudity, and styles of dancing and drumming are all ways of expressing conflict, communicating identity, and locating oneself in the community.

Commenting on carnival, Samuel Kinser argues that while social conflict is embodied and expressed by the festival, nevertheless "society coheres through conflict rather than through obedience" (1986). Neo-Pagan festival communities both cohere *and* fragment through conflicts around the ritual fire. The community becomes aware of its own boundaries and limits as it processes conflicts and problems. Ironically, the very conflicts over boundaries and personal safety are what assure participants that festival space *is* safe for self-experimentation. Conflicts over festival fires also reveal the power dynamics repressed, denied, and hidden in order to present Pagan festivals as an alternative experience of community. Reflecting on his research on Brazilian *carnaval*, Roberto DeMatta writes:

> What explains the style of Brazilian carnaval is the necessity of inventing a celebration where things that must be forgotten can be forgotten if the celebration is to be experienced as a social utopia. Just as the dream makes reality even more vehement, carnaval can only be understood when we discover what it must hide in order to be a celebration of pleasure, sexuality, and laughter. (1984)

Festival emphasis on license, sensual enjoyment, and self-expression necessitates that festival-goers "forget" boundaries and rules. They approach the festival as a kind of "vacation" from the outside world. And yet this place apart is not so far away from their everyday lives. While many participants talk about festival as a place where judgments are suspended, alongside this suspension conversations go on about "right" and "wrong" kinds of energy and behavior.

Groups and individuals calling themselves "Pagan" or "Neo-Pagan" began organizing the first festivals and defining themselves as a movement in the late 1960s. Most Neo-Pagans are engaged in a revival and re-creation of what they understand to be pre-Christian nature religions. The majority of these festivals are outdoor camping affairs which are held at private campgrounds or state parks and involve anywhere from fifty to a thousand people; approximately sixty festivals take place across the United States each year. According to a survey taken at Pagan Spirit Gathering in southwestern Wisconsin in 1991, people travelled from all over the United States, Canada, and several European countries to attend the festival. Some participants only attend one or two festivals each year; others, mostly merchants or ritual specialists, may visit several different festivals each month. Participants include college students, computer programmers, architects, teachers, and secretaries, as well as psychics, massage therapists, and astrologers; some festival-goers combine one or more of these identities. Michael, a long-time festival-goer, observes that "there were a wide variety of people . . . [at one festival]: real hippies, people who had straight jobs and looked normal when they left there, and lots of the steps in between. It was a celebration of diversity" (personal correspondence, 9 June 1992). In the Pagan Spirit Gathering survey, participants identified themselves with thirty-two different religious and cultural traditions—as varied as Egyptian, Mayan, Greco-Roman, New Age, Native American, and Yoruba.[2]

Expectations that new identities can be explored at festivals are based on an understanding that festivals are removed from ordinary time and space. Like anthropologist Victor Turner and other scholars of ritual, Neo-Pagans present a dualistic model of ritual and festival as liminal, anti-structural spaces opposed to highly structured everyday society.[3] Neo-Pagans separate the carnivalesque world of festival from everyday life or "mundania." The journey to a festival is to a strange "place apart," a place of license removed from "civilized" society. Folklorist Beverly Stoeltje explains that "in the festival environment principles of reversal, repetition, juxtaposition, condensation, and excess flourish, leading to communication and behavior that contrasts with everyday life" (Bauman 1992, 268). Festivals are places where play and transformation are encouraged. They are exaggerated like the places in dreams. They are surreal landscapes peopled by colorful and bizarre creatures and extraordinary events, "like a Gypsy circus," according to Julia, a fine arts major at a midwestern university (personal conversation, May 1992). For Neo-Pagans, going to a festival is like travelling to a "more real" world of heightened experience and perception. Says Salome, a college senior who has been involved with Neo-Paganism since she was a teenager, "Everything seemed so vivid there. It was like a psychedelic experience. When we came back it was like back in the real world" (personal interview, July 1993).

Annual journeys to these places are both adventures to the exotic and the faraway and pilgrimages to a familiar, home-like, memory-laden place. It seems ironic that Neo-Pagans identify the world *outside* of festivals as the real one, because they describe festival experiences as being particularly vivid and significant. For many participants, festivals are a hyper-reality, an ideal way of being with others, and more real than the world of everyday existence.

Imagining the journey to festival as a pilgrimage or adventure contributes to the building of a different kind of home or community than is available in the everyday lives of many festival participants. Festival-goers speak of the journey to festival as a journey to a special place, or as one man puts it, a journey to "spiritual homeland." In the special 1992 "Pagan Gatherings—Discovering Spiritual Homeland" issue of *Circle Network News,* John Threlfall describes his first trip to Pagan Spirit Gathering as a pilgrimage across the country: "I have come to see my journey across America that summer of 1989 as my own Hajj . . . I was drawn forth on a pilgrimage of my own making, seeking a holy land that, ultimately, I could find only in myself."

Festivals are also imagined to be "mundane" in the extent to which they represent an invented or discovered "family" or "home" that nurtures new identities. For Pagans, the world they represent as being on the fringes of "mainstream" culture often becomes the center of their most meaningful activities.[4] For the second edition of *Drawing Down the Moon,* her landmark study of Neo-Paganism, journalist Margot Adler added a section on Pagan festivals entitled "Pagan Festivals: The Search for a Culture or a Tribe." Here she gives a brief account of the history of Pagan festivals and responds to the question, "Why did festivals catch on?":

> Probably most critical was the fact that outdoor festivals established a sacred time and space—a place apart from the mundane world, where pagans could be themselves and meet other people who, although from a variety of traditions, shared many of the same values. Many festival organizers have told me that the most frequent feedback they receive is the comment "I never knew there were other people who believe what I believe, let alone several hundred at one place. I never knew that I could come totally out of the closet and be what I am openly." The feeling of being at home among one's true family for the first time is the fundamental reason that festivals have spread throughout the country. As one organizer told me. "It's a trip to the land of faery, where for a couple of days you can exist without worrying about the 'real' world." (1986, 424).

The trip is away from home to a magical fairyland as well as towards the home of one's "true" family. Fliers and pamphlets for festivals like Starwood, Wild Magick, and Pagan Spirit Gathering advertise Neo-Pagan festivals as "a Magickal Village," "a global tribal village," "spiritual community," "family," "home." Home thus becomes a place where invented families reside and where people can be themselves in these families.

Festival-goers inhabit festival space in different ways than they inhabit their own homes. Their experience of time changes; they move differently and relate differently to each other. Michael, an architect from the East Coast explains: "Starwood is long enough so that you live there. Your time frame just shifts down and becomes more attuned to the day. You walk slower, act slower . . . There's a sense of just being outside of time . . . You forget that there's an outside world" (personal correspondence, 9 June 1992). Many festival participants speak of the festival as a place out of time, but a "home-like" place where participants can be the kind of children they want to be, can play in the ways schools, parents, and religions of the outside world deny them. Here, where the rules of everyday interaction are suspended, they imagine finding an ideal community and an ideal self.

Festival, writes a festival organizer, is

> an opportunity to step out of our usual model of social interaction. Some of the same things applied, but when you got out there they made it clear that as long as you didn't hurt yourself or anybody else, basically whatever you wanted went. Now, when it comes down to it, that's not true. There were certain things that still held, but it was a lot more open, a lot more free. And even though it wasn't focused, it was providing an atmosphere, a place, a social mechanism by which people could express more of themselves and discover and explore more than they could back home and in their usual motif. (Peter, personal interview, October 1992)

For many festival participants being "at home" in festival space means moving and feeling differently about their bodies, and ritual fires are places where this difference is both discovered and expressed. Festival fires begin at sundown or after the evening's formal ritual and on weekend nights are likely to last until sunrise. Many participants in the late-night fire seem to share the judgment that drumming is the heartbeat of a festival, while others would add that dancing is equally expressive of the festival experience. The blending of and interaction between these two performed languages generates the ritual ethos of festival fires. Dancing usually starts off slowly and builds in response to the skill and enthusiasm of the drumming. As the evening wears on dancers and observers come and go from the darkness at the edges of the ritual circle. Often a group of slowly swaying "trance dancers" forms the circle closest to the fire, while those moving with more energetic steps circle around them. At times when the beat quickens, a few dancers spontaneously leap and run around the fire, spinning with such speed that they draw out smoke and sparks. Many dancers who want to dance in place or do not want to be illuminated by the fire position themselves in the shadows and among the loosely knit outer circle of people standing and watching or talking together in small groups. Some dancers get lost in the drums and movement and forget about the gazes of audience and drummers; some skip after and chase each other or perform with their bodies for the drummers and audience.

This apparent lack of structure and the deluge of images and sounds challenges participants' personal boundaries on a basic physiological level. With their costumed, tattooed, bejeweled, and glistening nude dancers, chanting, drummers and other musicians, smoke and flame, festival fires are a sensual feast. These scenes are far removed from the daily lives of most participants, encouraging participants to find new and different ways of defining themselves. Confusion and uncertainty about self-identity mix with the discovery of hidden selves at festivals and festival fires. Ritual fires seem free of expectations; however, self-expression and self-creation can themselves become a kind of norm. Many festival-goers are reluctant participants at the late-night fire, preferring to observe from the sidelines while not feeling entirely comfortable doing so. In Pagan magazine *Mezlim*'s "Gatherings Issue," Aravah writes,

> On that first night, while my daughter was dancing joyously around the fire, I sat miserably on a log thinking how much I wanted to dance, too. I was so uptight and afraid. Fear. I've dealt with it a lot since then. Mostly the fear of being myself. The rituals and workshops quite often pulled this out of me in one way or another. I realized I couldn't keep running from myself. I didn't WANT to! Scary as it was, I was ready to start being me, not the person I thought I was expected to be. (1993, 41–45)

Men and women who attend festival fires often feel compelled to be someone different from their everyday self. They use the ritual space to explore issues that they bring with them as well as fears that arise during the ritual experience. In the process of self-exploration layers of selves may be peeled off, revealing a central "me." In the same issue of *Mezlim*, Diane Tabor writes, "ritual dance may also be used to work on personal issues which are too threatening or deeply buried to address in our everyday consciousness. Emotions which have been repressed in the interest of preserving our lives and relationships can be allowed expression and worked through in the safe space created by dance" (1993, 14). Festival fires provide an inviting space for self-performance.

Performance enables individuals to play with and express different aspects of their identity: magical practices, sexuality, body image, their particular sense of humor, and their feelings about how they fit into the larger Neo-Pagan movement.

Festival-goers themselves have different understandings of what this ritual space is for. One ritual participant writes in *The Elven Chronicle*, a Neo-Pagan newsletter, about how he uses a festival fire held in a dome-covered circle:

> To me the Thunderdome is a place to set aside my personality with all of its wants, needs, desires, etc. and enter into direct contact with Spirit through drumming and dancing. It is a special place. A space to do special things. I have many opportunities to relate through my 'personality' and enjoy satisfactions available on that level.
>
> Thunderdome is about a different, less frequent type of experience. (1991)

For this drummer, the late-night festival fire furnishes an opportunity to step outside of his everyday personality and to "enter into direct contact with Spirit." While the entire festival experience provides a space away from the patterns of everyday life, late-night fires are another step removed from this other life and the personality one wears there. Boundaries at ritual fires are permeable; they allow for both freedom of expression and a sense of safety. Not everyone attends the fire to do transformative ritual work. Some come to "trance dance" or engage in what they call shamanic journeying; others approach the fire to express themselves with a physical freedom impossible in other social contexts; while other late-night fire participants may be looking for a party atmosphere, provided by the spectacle of dancing bodies and fire-jumping. People with diverse intentions come and go all night and are disruptive in ways they would never be in a more formal ritual. And yet while the fire is not formally bounded like an organized ritual in which guardians and protective spirits are called on to secure a safe space, it is seen as a safe and sacred space:

> dancing "O"s creates a vortex of energy which acts to keep the space safe. The warding effect is amplified when the dancers are aware and focused on their purpose. I know dedicated magicians who will circle the fire for hours keeping the vortex spinning with their movement and their Wills. It is the raising and maintaining of a temple. It is a sacred act. . . . (Tabor 1993, 13–14)

Ritual fires are thus seen by many festival participants as bounded and protected places, temples constructed by intention, music, and dance. But what makes a space "safe" at festivals? From ritual space to personal space, the process of sacralization includes attention to safety and protection. Salome frequently mentioned her concerns about safety during our conversations. She observed that

> anywhere you go there are always going to be people who are going to try and hurt you. But the idea that you're in a place where there's more safety than elsewhere is a nice thing to know . . . it's been a playground for me to be more assertive on and say, "listen, get out of my personal space and get out of it now. I don't want you in my personal space unless I invite you in." Most people will leave you alone then and if they don't then I'm not going to deal with them. Sometimes it's good to have a safe environment where you can just go out of control. (personal interview, July 1993)[5]

Safety and loss of control seem to be in tension, but the festival fire is a place where contradictory intentions and concerns co-exist. Women do talk about feeling "freer" and less inhibited, about being more comfortable in their bodies, but the guardedness that most women are in the habit of maintaining does not easily fall aside. They are forced to define their own limits. And thus the fire becomes an improvisational space, a theater for self-invention. Participants experiment with both expanding and contracting their personal boundaries. Men and women immerse themselves in the performance of their dance, releasing their bodies in ways unique to the festival setting. Artemis, a librarian, told me that dancing is one of the main reasons she goes to festivals. I asked her if there were other places that she enjoyed dancing:

> Not with the freedom that I feel at Lothlorien or at any other festival, Rainbow or whatever, just because I know that nothing I do down there is going to be looked down upon. It doesn't matter how I dance, nobody's going to go "oh my God," and like look at me like that because when I dance I don't think, I just dance and I move and I know from other people that when I dance it's very obvious and it's very attention-grabbing since it's very outrageous. I have problems dancing in other public arenas like bars. I'm not the kind of person who dances with other people. I dance by myself and that can be a problem when going to bars by yourself as a woman, and I get hassled all the time. (personal interview, July 1992)

Many women describe the fire as a space in which they can express their sexuality and the pleasure they take in their bodies without having their movements interpreted as sexually inviting. Like other areas of the festival, erotic dance is fraught with tension because of its seeming lack of rules and boundaries. This community-in-the-making does not have a history or tradition of rules of behavior. Within the ritual space of the late-night festival fire, men and women must negotiate their own boundaries and find ways to communicate those boundaries to other people.

> In most cases, dancers who are dancing for the purpose of generating energy for the fire are not interested in getting picked up, but rather in amplifying the collective energy flow. This is a valuable gift and deserves to be appreciated as such. By calling up the kundalini energy, the dancer becomes a channel for his or her own sexual energies. The feeling aroused in the observers may also be used to contribute to the personal and general energy flow. (Tabor 1993, 13)

As they become more familiar with this peculiar kind of theater, participants master a language of body and gesture that identifies these boundaries. Although Neo-Paganism is often cast as a feminist goddess-centered religion, men as well as women experience changes in body image at festivals. In a letter to *Circle Network News*, a quarterly newsletter published by Wiccan church and "Nature Spirituality resource center" Circle Sanctuary, a festival participant named Godric discusses his first encounter with festival drumming and dancing. At first he felt intimidated by the dancers' grace and remembered a childhood incident in which someone had made him feel ashamed of dancing at a wedding: "for many years, this vague and chilling memory has recurred whenever I've tried or been asked to dance. It turns my feet to stone and my coordination to chaos." Godric describes joining the dancers at Pagan Spirit Gathering as a step toward healing old fears:

> I had absorbed enough PSG atmosphere to realize that fear of ridicule had been banished from this place, along with indoor plumbing and telephones. This time I left my drum at my camp. I noticed people with bodies no less clumsy or attractive than mine dancing in the fire circle, and they didn't look ridiculous. They looked beautiful, happy, entranced, and ecstatic. I closed my eyes and slipped into the pattern of the music, trying it on. It welcomed me. I retreated briefly and left clothing and inhibitions under a nearby tree, then joined the dance.

Godric's story echoes other men's accounts of working with body image around the festival fire. Michael, an architect from the East Coast, self-consciously makes use of the festival fire to explore body movement and sexuality. "While I was going to these festivals, I was working magically to bring sex into my life, not to specifically get sexual experience, but to find it within myself and to learn to express it." I asked him what changes came about in his life as a result of festival-going: "I dance differently. I look at women differently. I look at their faces; I listen to their voices; I'm not afraid of them anymore. I'm not afraid of myself when I'm around them" (personal correspondence, June 1992).[6] For Michael, festivals in general and the ritual fire in particular made possible expressions of a transformed body and different sexual self.

Expressing one's identity at the fire is not, however, simply a matter of shedding inhibitions in a safe space. Individuals shape the terms of their own performance within a framework of common language, in this case a language of gesture and body-marking. Costumes, nudity, and adornment are part of a complex system of coding. People convey with their appearance who they want to be, or at least who they want to be in the festival space. They perform private identities in a public space which is not however as public as the space outside festival boundaries.

Reflecting on Brazilian *carnaval*, Victor Turner describes costuming as "serious play." "It is a Brazilian point of honor that if one is going to wear a costume or fantasia, it must communicate one's most private or intimate fantasy in the most artistic way possible. Repression must be lifted. One might even talk about the aestheticization of the repressed, making the very private public in the mode of beauty" (Turner 1983, 123).[7] I suspect that many festival participants would agree with this observation, although Neo-Pagans also approach costuming as an opportunity to express aspects they lack, a self that embodies characteristics they "need." Men and women cross-dress. Or a woman may clothe herself as a virgin bride, belly dancer, earth mother, or seductress. I asked Peh, a magician and teacher who has designed and facilitated many festival rituals and workshops, why he did not dress up for festivals:

> I don't costume very well. It's not something that I've been able to develop. It's interesting because they push it so much in ELF, you know, to get your fantasy, to get your persona . . . I was walking around last night looking at all these people in wonderful costumes wondering well, what would I wear, what would I look like? What persona would I take? Would I take a strong leather kind of bondage thing or would I take a more feminine one. Maybe I'm so split between them—I know [laughs], maybe I'm so balanced that I don't need either one. (personal interview, August 1992)

Apparent freedom of individual choice is often coupled with awareness of the most acceptable styles. Normlessness prevails on the surface, while hidden norms become apparent at times of conflict and after prolonged observation. Native American jewelry and buckskins, pentagrams and crystals, anything in black or purple, flowery gauze skirts and "ethnic" clothes, leather bodices, boots or other medieval wear borrowed from the dress codes of the Society for Creative Anachronism: all of these are part of a distinctively Pagan style. Experimenting with degrees of nudity may constitute a kind of conformity; it may also indicate a newly discovered acceptance of one's body. Several festival-goers conveyed to me their own sense of discomfort wearing clothes; they felt that nudity, or at least partial nudity, was the expectation and that they were being looked down upon for not conforming to the "un-dress code."

Costumes, piercings, tatoos, body-painting, degrees of nudity, and styles of dancing and drumming are ways of expressing conflict, communicating identity, and locating oneself in the community. Clothing and movement as well as verbal self-description often express festival selves intended to oppose and critique the outside world. Like hidden selves, tattoos and piercings that remain hidden in everyday life are revealed at festivals. Moreover, professional tattoo artists and piercing specialists are present at most large festivals. In "Why We Mark Our Bodies," Tath Zal asserts that "It is the view of many that an unmarked body is an inarticulate form, separated from its social/cultural identity; and, that, only when the body acquires the 'marks of civilization' does it begin to communicate and become an active part of the greater social experience" (1989, 12).

Neo-Pagan bodies articulate specific cultural and religious identities. Nudity makes visible, or at least more striking, jewelry, body-painting, tattoos, and body-piercings. The popularity of piercings and astrological or mythical tatoos among Pagans tends to exert a levelling effect on gender. Common tattoos include the Chinese yin/yang symbol, Celtic knotwork, animals, dragons, unicorns, and astrological signs. Tattoo and piercing artists are both male and female and their clientele seem to be evenly split by sex. Tath Zal reports in the *Mezlim* body art issue that women "tend to select small, delicate tatoos," and men "choose larger designs," but in the festival community I have observed the opposite to be true as often as not (1989). Festival activities provide an opportunity for the display of and discussion about piercings as well as tattoos. Piercings are growing in popularity, though with the exception of ear piercings, they remain less common than tattoos. Many women and men have one or both nipples pierced; I have also seen lip, nose, navel, and genital piercings at festivals.

Around the fire men's and women's bodies are mixed together in groups of drummers and dancers. While at most fires women still make up the majority of the dancers, men are often present in almost equal numbers. Male dancers may be nude as well, or more often, wear a skirt or cloth wrapped around their waists. At a distance the partially nude bodies with their skirts flowing are almost indistinguishable by sex, men moving as gracefully and sensually as women. Many men wear loose flowing skirts, caftans, or brightly colored cloths wrapped around their waists. Putting on clothing marked as female is an ambiguous statement in the festival setting; like nudity it is a rejection of "mundane" style and an assertion of difference, but it doesn't necessarily signal a change in gender or sexual identity. Salome says she likes to see "all the guys running around in skirts. It's nice because they don't have to worry about being called fag. Heterosexual and homosexual men dress in the same type of outfits and it's really nice for people to be able to get in touch with that feminine side of themselves" (personal interview, July 1993).

British cultural studies scholar Paul Willis describes clothing and decor with which groups of hippies and biker boys protest "normality." An important element of their lifestyle is body and decor: "the most direct expression of their nature was in their appearance and their bodily movement" (Willis 1978, 95).[8] At Pagan festivals costumes, rituals, and identities are pieced together from multiple sources. These products of festival liminality are seen to be critical and oppositional comments on the world outside festival space. Here it may be helpful to distinguish between the "liminal" and the "liminoid" as Victor Turner does in his later writings (1982). Liminality, argues Turner, has subversive potential because of its ludic or playful nature. "In liminality people 'play' with the elements of the familiar and defamiliarize them. Novelty emerges from unprecedented combinations of familiar elements" (p. 27).

However, while the liminal gives rise to new symbols and paradigms, Turner claims these feed back into central social structures. The "liminoid" is more effectively subversive because it allows for sustained transformation of individuals and concrete social change. Turner characterizes the liminoid ritual forms of postindustrial society as individualistic and "voluntary"; he opposes these to collective, tribal, compulsory rituals. Thus Turner creates a binary opposition between two kinds of societies, conveying the impression that tribal rites are static, while rites in postindustrial society are progressive: "The tribal liminal . . . can never be much more than subversive flicker. It is put into the service of normativeness almost as soon as it appears" (1982, 45). I would argue that the opposite is as possible. Neo-Pagans also pose an opposition—between festival and mundane worlds—the one subversive and playful, the other maintaining the status quo. The outcome of liminoid experience is not any more likely to be a "progressive" challenge to the status quo or effective social change.

Both liminal and liminoid forms occur within Neo-Pagan festivals and may be present within the same ritual. For instance, ritual fires, while supposedly the most freeform of all festival activities, actually contain structures that replicate gender roles of the outside society. For instance men tend to be the more aggressive dancers and drummers, dominating the ritual space and taking more risks such as jumping over the fire, while women dance more slowly and sensuously. But both men and women tell stories of self-transformation that involve dancing around the fire. In these stories, issues of conflict and points of contention emerge and make the boundary between festival and mundane worlds difficult to distinguish.

While vehemently defending themselves against misconceptions of their gatherings, Neo-Pagans nevertheless maintain the dualistic worldview of their attackers. Attempts to be non-sexist and egalitarian are evident, but coexist with gender dichotomies. Festival-goers imagine themselves to be constructing boundaries and roles which have little in common with the views of suspicious neighbors and hostile Christians. But, in the process of making a festival community, there is much talk of "us" versus "them."

Marginality and outsiderness seem to hold a romantic attractiveness to Neo-Pagans. Nevertheless, within Neo-Paganism there are a range of positionings vis-à-vis the dominant culture; some feel more a part of it than others. Thus an uneasy dynamic develops: Pagans gather at festivals to share a common experience, yet while there they encounter the differences between them. Writes Frank Manning in the introduction to *The Celebration of Society: Perspectives on Contemporary Cultural Performance*, "just as celebration reverses and violates ordinary reality, it also replicates and upholds it. There is a radical contrast within celebration, not just between celebration and the everyday world" (1983, 21).

Neo-Pagans contrast their festival experiences to life in the outside world, but conflicts over boundaries and safety issues emerge within the festival itself. Creating "safe space," for example, involves boundaries, limits, and rules, all of which are approached ambivalently in the permissive festival atmosphere. Individuals make their own boundaries, but personal safety is also a community issue. Because many festivals have dealt with an occasional incident of sexual harassment, festival organizers have attempted to create guidelines for behavior. *The Elven Chronicle*'s "Miss Manners" covers festival etiquette and identifies issues which have caused tension at past festivals. In the spring 1992 issue Ms. Manners' column entitled "Do Me, Do Me, Do Me, Good Touching" confronts the issue of bodily boundaries:

> Let me begin by saying everyone is capable of both experiencing and pressing sexual harassment and rape. While most people would agree that women don't want to be raped, the question of how a woman could possibly rape or sexually harass a man is still up for grabs, so to speak . . . Sexual come-ons, rude flirting and pressing sex can be suffered by both men and women. Just how do you know when someone doesn't like what you're doing? How do you know when your flirting is "Bad touch?" One easy way to tell is if the person says, "Stop," "No thank you, I'm not interested," or "Get your hands off me." It is less easy to tell if the person tries to be "polite" and just avoids you. You might misunderstand and think they are playing hard to get. When in doubt ask, "Excuse me, but I've been flirting with you. Have you enjoyed it?" They only have to say "Yes" or "No." It might be embarrassing if they say not, but it is better than getting kicked out of the festival for sexual harassment.

Ms. Manners' column was written in response to an incident of sexual harassment at a festival. A female festival participant complained to one of the festival organizers about a male festival-goer who would not leave her alone. This organizer attempted to resolve the problem by bringing the two people together for a discussion. The man claimed that the woman, Angela, had attacked *him* and she refused to further discuss the matter. She complained to other members of the festival community that the organizers did not adequately respond to her charges. Some of Angela's female friends boycotted the next festival, protesting that they felt the atmosphere was not supportive of their safety. One festival participant pointed out that Angela could have approached the incident in a way more conducive to Pagan egalitarianism. She might, he suggested, have gathered together a group of women to confront the man in question, rather than choosing as she did to complain to an authority figure—one of the festival organizers.[9] Though alternative ways of resolving conflict are available in this setting, the habitual turn to authority is not easily broken. This incident reveals assumptions about power and authority that are inconsistent with the egalitarian image the festival community presents.[10]

The late-night festival fire may be a space open to improvisation and largely free of organization and structure, yet its very lack of definition often leads to conflicts which reveal the hidden structures of authority operating in this community. An article in *The Elven Chronicle* suggests that drinking parties and sexual activities should take place elsewhere. People are asked in the festival literature not to bring bottles into the ritual space or throw cigarette butts in the fire. Likewise, at Pagan Spirit Gathering, several announcements about the abuse of the ritual space were made at daily "village meetings." One of the most evident conflicts is between some festival-goers who want to use the space for late-night parties and those who want to keep it a sacred space for ritual work. Ms. Manners questions behavior at the late-night festival fire:

> Third shift, as we understand it, is ritual space where the drum's voices are mingled with the ritualists' heartbeats in a trance inducing mixture of beats, silence, sweat, smiles and rhythmic community chants designed to intertwine with the quiet magic of the angels' drumming. . . . Ms. Manners must ask the question: do these lovely angels really want to come to an atmosphere of: loud, show-off blasts on congas; drying wet sox (etc.); cooking hot dogs over the ritual fire (unless it is Friday) . . . overt sexual grabbing; drinking songs; exaltations of how late it is and isn't it great to be part of third shift; getting falling down drunk; suggesting women have no right to drum and should let the MEN do it; and lover's quarrels. Are these really conducive to keeping the community trance energy?

For many festival participants, music and nude dancing signify a celebratory atmosphere where "anything goes," while for other late-night drummers and dancers, the festival fire is a sacred space in which self-transformation occurs. As festival communities attempt to resolve these differences, they engage in a process of self-definition. They decide which activities are acceptable to the community as a whole and which are not.

Conflict makes possible new definitions of self and community. More than simply allowing their "real selves" to come out, festival-goers work on transforming the selves they bring to the festival with them. The fluidity of individual identity in festival culture makes possible experimentation with multiple selves. Yet this Neo-Pagan understanding of the self is in some sense illusory. Certainly festival-goers experience transformative moments, but they tend to downplay the existence of community tensions and ongoing personal struggles. The selves who emerge here are not uncorrupted by the world outside the festival; they bring it with them. Traumas from the past are shared, childhood fantasies are played out. Neo-Pagan festivals exist in a dynamic network of meaning that is both discursive and experiential. Neo-Pagans are highly self-reflective: they engage in a constant commentary on their own actions. Individuals and communities give meaning to the identities expressed in ritual by gossiping, complaining, protesting, and sharing stories of their sensual, bodily experience. Conversations about behavior, sexuality, identity, and spirituality occur before, during, and after rituals, in small group meetings, in newsletters, and in nationally distributed Neo-Pagan periodicals.

Neo-Pagan festivals produce stories that comment on and construct community and individual identities. Storytelling provides a means for both reflecting on and constructing the sensual and bodily experience of ritual fires. The Neo-Pagan approach to ritual exemplifies Victor Turner's notions of "flow" and "reflexivity": "A performance is a dialectic of 'flow,' that is, spontaneous movement in which action and awareness are one, and 'reflexivity,' in which the central meanings, values and goals of a culture are seen 'in action,' as they shape and explain behavior." This dialectic is visibly played out at the festival fire in the relationship between bodily experience and discourse, and the movement of dancers and onlookers from performance to observation.

At a Neo-Pagan festival in midsummer I was standing in the dark outer circle of the festival fire when I was approached by someone I had interviewed that morning. This black-hooded man from an army base in Maine pointed out to me a friend of his who had worked as an exotic dancer. He remarked that she had been feeling very inhibited about taking off her clothes at the festival, and in particular while dancing around the fire. She had explained to him that she wanted to learn how to dance for herself instead of for an audience. Her desire to replace the sense of herself as a performer for the male gaze with less self-conscious movement was realized by the end of the festival. He came up to me later to ask that I watch her dance, that I notice how she seemed to be lost in her own movement without awareness of herself as a body observed. By then she had removed all her clothes and joined the other nude and half-nude dancers closest to the fire. However, she remained both a female body displayed before an audience and a woman dancing for her own pleasure. She made use of the fire to reshape her past and experiment with a new kind of self. Her black-shrouded friend used this opportunity to create a story about her movement between different identities, a story which highlighted for me both the possibilities and limitations of this festival community.

NOTES

1. Most of the large festivals include a diverse range of workshops. The Starwood 1992 program listed the following: "Ancient Goddesses," "Animal Spirit Circle," "Basic Psychic Skills," "Beginning Ritual Drumming," "Chant Sharing," "Create Your Own Goddess," "Druid Songs and Chants," "Healing Circle," "Hypnosis," "Living Your Myth," "Magic, Music and Sacred Massage," "Nature Spirit Magic," "Tibetan Time Travel," "The Way of the Orisha," "Sweat Lodge," and eighty-five other workshops.

2. The "Pagan Spirit Gathering 1991 Tribal Survey Results" lists the following responses to the question "What is your Pagan Path?": Eclectic Wiccan, Eclectic (blends many paths), Celtic Traditional Wiccan, Wiccan Shamanism, Native American Shamanism, Goddess Spirituality, Nature Mystic/Gaian/Eco-Pagan, Druidic/Keltria, New Age, Family Tradition (old style) Witchcraft, Multi-cultural Shamanism, Unitarian Universalist Pagan, Egyptian/Hermetic, Alexandrian Wiccan, Discordian, Gardnerian Wiccan, Druidic, Pantheism, Buddhist, Animism, Radical Fairy, Mayan, Hindu/Yoga, Taoist, Dianic/Feminist Witchcraft, Norse/Scandinavian, Lithuanian/Baltic, Assyrian/Babaloynian/Summerian [sic], Yoraban [sic], Jewish Pagan, Greco-Roman, and Germanic/Teutonic ("Pagan Spirit Gathering 1992 Village Guide").

3. In *Dramas, Fields, and Metaphors: Symbolic Action in Human Society*, Turner contrasts flexible, egalitarian liminal events to the stratified, normal world (pp. 200–201). Neo-Pagans explore a similar contrast in their own literature about festivals.

4. Classic sociological studies of sectarian movements such as Max Weber's *The Protestant Ethic and the Spirit of Capitalism* (1988) have located them as "opposed" to the "world" in the same ways that many Neo-Pagans imagine festivals apart from "mundania." Scholars of new religious movements likewise neglect to recognize the coexistence of apparently contradictory place-meanings. In *Countercultures: The Promise and Peril of a World Turned Upside-Down*, J. Milton Yinger argues that new religious movements demonstrate two trends: "one branch adapting in some measure to the world around it while another pushes strongly against the dominant norms" (1982, 247).

5. Salome put her drug experience in the context of recent literature by Terence McKenna and others about shamanic techniques using psychedelics.

6. I sent Michael a letter containing some follow-up questions to our initial interview and he responded by mailing me a tape in which he elaborated on his original comments. I initiated our conversation by asking why he came to festivals and what he took away from them when he returned home. He then talked frankly and at length about how his experiences at festivals had enabled him to change the ways in which he related to his body.

7. Turner's essay furthermore suggests that license and the expression of "the repressed" are made possible by the highly structured planning that precedes the actual *carnaval*. While much planning precedes Pagan festivals as well, the relationship between structure and antistructure is more parallel than linear; boundary enforcement and boundarylessness may take place simultaneously.

8. Also see Dick Hebdige, *Subculture: The Meaning of Style* (New York: Methuen, 1979) and *Hiding in the Light: On Images and Things* (London and New York: Routledge, 1988).

9. At a festival in New York State this kind of approach was used when a man was harassing women in the women's shower.

10. My account of the story is based on interviews with this festival organizer, Peh, and friends of the woman, Rachel and Jason (summer 1992). I did not interview the couple involved with the incident.

REFERENCES

Adler, Margot. 1986. *Drawing Down the Moon: Witches, Druids, Goddess-Worshippers, and Other Pagans in America Today.* Rev. ed. Boston: Beacon Press.

Aravah. 1993. "The First Festival." *Mezlim* 4, no. 2: 41–45.

Bauman, Richard. 1992. *Folklore, Cultural Performances, and Popular Entertainments: A Communications-Centered Handbook.* Oxford: Oxford University Press.

Damarru, J. Perry. 1992. "A Gathering Primer." *Mezlim* 3, no. 2: 3.

DeMatta, Roberto. 1984. "Carnaval, Informality, and Magic: A Point of View from Brazil." In *Text, Play and Story: The Construction and Reconstruction of Self and Society,* edited by E. M. Bruner, 230–246. American Ethnological Association.

Elven Chronicle. Summer, 1991. Bloomington, Ind.

Kinser, Samuel. 1986. *Representations* 13 (Winter 1986): 1–41.

Manning, Frank. 1983. Introduction. *The Celebration of Society: Perspectives on Contemporary Cultural Performance*, edited by Frank Manning. Bowling Green: Bowling Green University Press.

"Pagan Spirit Gathering 1992 Village Guide." 1992. Mt. Horeb, Wisc.: Circle.

Tabor, Diane. 1993. *Mezlim* 4, no. 2: 13–14.

Turner, Victor. 1974. *Dramas, Fields, and Metaphors: Symbolic Action in Human Society.* Ithaca: Cornell University Press.

———. 1982. *From Ritual to Theatre: The Human Seriousness of Play.* New York: Performing Arts Journal Publications.

———. 1983. "*Carnaval* in Rio: Dionysian Drama in an Industrializing Society." In *The Celebration of Society: Perspectives on Contemporary Cultural Performances*, edited by Frank Manning. Bowling Green: Bowling Green University Press.

Weber, Max. 1988. *The Protestant Ethic and the Spirit of Capitalism.* Gloucester, Mass.: P. Smith.

Willis, Paul. 1978. *Profane Culture.* London: Routledge.

Yinger, J. Milton. 1982. *Countercultures: The Promise and Peril of a World Turned Upside-Down.* New York: The Free Press.

Zal, Tath. 1989. "Why We Mark Our Bodies." *Mezlim,* "Magickal Body Art Issue."

7

AS I DO WILL, SO MOTE IT BE: MAGIC AS METAPHOR IN NEO-PAGAN WITCHCRAFT

Síân Reid

MAGIC FASCINATES THE WESTERN MIND. Echoes of it resonate through our myths, our fairy tales, and our accounts of religious miracles. Examinations and analyses of magic have been a mainstay of both sociological and anthropological research since the formative days of those disciplines, and yet it remains a marginalized practice, acknowledged but dismissed by those whose conceptualizations define the acceptable boundaries of our social world. Magic is fine for Malinowski's Trobriand Islanders, who perhaps do not know any better and who certainly live in a different social and cultural world, says the often unarticulated status quo, but it does not belong in the modern urban West, alongside dishwashers, subway trains, and nuclear power plants.

Yet magic continues to exist. Modern Western magical belief and practice, often described as "occult belief," are not something that fit neatly into most descriptions of how the modern world operates. "Occult belief" is used as a catchall category for characterizing beliefs and practices that are perceived as ranging from the irrational to the absurd. Marcello Truzzi notes,

Revised version of a paper presented to the American Academy of Religion, November, 1993.

> In many ways, the occult is a residual category, a wastebasket for knowledge claims that are deviant in some way, that do not fit the established claims of science or religion. And once such a knowledge claim gains acceptance within establishment science or religion, it loses its status as an occultism. (1976, 245)

Magic is not perceived as a valid or effective way of dealing with life or the universe, because it is not culturally acknowledged as having any "real" existence. Singer and Benassi characterize occult beliefs as a kind of dysfunctional thinking when they comment,

> The psychological mechanisms involved in occult beliefs may represent more dramatic forms of some mundane pathologies of reasoning . . . occult beliefs, which are at the outer limits of irrationality, may throw some light on more ordinary reasoning pathologies. (1989, 383–384).

These traditional, and deeply ingrained, associations between magic and what is "irrational," "deviant," or "pathological" are grossly oversimplified. They arise out of a one-dimensional view of magic that considers only the relationship of the apparent means to the purported ends of a given working. This approach fails both to contextualize the working, and to account for what might make the beliefs or practices persuasive at the level of the individual. To assert that occult belief and/or magical practice represents a reasoning pathology is to imply that those who subscribe to it are guilty of defective reasoning, without allowing for features of their subjective experience which might explain why magical practices are not only reasonable, but a healthy and progressive way of making sense of the universe. The use of magic in the context of Neo-Pagan Witchcraft, a new religious movement which centrally incorporates it as an element of belief and practice, challenges the traditional analysis of magic. It can be suggested, through comparing Neo-Pagan discussions of magic and the self-help literature that is directed towards survivors of abuse, that magical practice may act to produce outcomes very different than those traditionally presumed to be its goal.

TRADITIONAL SOCIAL SCIENCE: THE INSTRUMENTAL APPROACH

Sociologists and anthropologists, and to a certain extent theologians, have gone to extraordinary lengths to distinguish between the often blurred and overlapping concepts of science, religion, and magic, as though to avoid delegitimating the former two by some accidental association with the latter. Durkheim, Weber, and Malinowski all address this debate in some depth, and their example is followed by subsequent generations of researchers and theorists. To overgeneralize and oversimplify the results of these early discussions, the distinctions emerge approximately as follows: Science provides explanations for natural phenomena that can be rigorously tested and empirically proven to be correct or incorrect, and thus provides a means of making accurate statements about the objectively given world. Religion addresses existential quandaries, issues of morality and meaning, and provides explanations about a subjectively experienced world which cannot be empirically tested and which proceeds from assumptions about some kind of supernatural force or realm. Magic is seen to be uneasily caught in the gulf between the two, purporting to affect and describe the natural world, but through means which, because they do not respond well to empirical testing, can only be characterized as somehow super- or supra-natural. Tanya Luhrmann, in her study of the contemporary British magical scene, characterizes most sociocultural approaches to magic as relying on either an "intellectualist" argument, "which explained magic as based upon mistaken belief" (Tylor, Frazer) or a "symbolist" argument, "which explained away the magic by showing how it had little to do with belief" (Durkheim, Leach, Douglas) (1989, 347). These tendencies are still found in much of the current discussion on the subject of magic.

   To take only one example, Rodney Stark and William Bainbridge, in their exhaustively researched book *The Future of Religion*, distinguish between religion and magic on fairly traditional Durkheimian grounds, asserting that "magic does not concern itself with the meaning of the universe, but only with the manipulation of the universe for specific goals" (1985, 30). They define this distinction by differentiating between the kind of *compensators* offered by religion, and those offered by magic.

> *A compensator is the belief that a reward will be obtained in the distant future or in some other context which cannot be immediately verified.* . . . In our system, compensators fall along a continuum from the general to the specific. Specific compensators promise specific, limited reward. The most general compensators promise a great array of rewards or rewards of vast scope. A shaman's promise that, if certain ritual procedures are followed, a person will be cured of warts is a specific compensator. The promise of a happy life is a general compensator. (pp. 6–7, italics in original)

Using this definition of compensator, they assert that "magic deals in relatively specific compensators, and religion always includes the most general compensators" (p. 30). They define religions as *"human organizations primarily engaged in providing general compensators based on supernatural assumptions"* p. 8, italics in original). In distinguishing between magic and science, Stark and Bainbridge are unabashedly Weberian, relying upon the adequacy of the explanations provided given verifiable and replicable knowledge about an objectively given world.

> . . . because magic deals in specific compensators, it often becomes subject to empirical verification. This means that magic is chronically vulnerable to disproof. Claims that a particular spell will cure warts or repel bullets can be falsified by direct tests. . . . The empirical vulnerability of magic also helps us identify the line between magic and science. Here we fully agree with Max Weber (1963:2), who distinguished magic from science on the basis of the results of empirical testing: "Only we, judging from the standpoint of our modern views of nature, can distinguish objectively in such behavior those attributes of causality which are 'correct' from those which are 'fallacious,' and then designate the fallacious attributions of causation as irrational, and the corresponding acts as 'magic.' " Magic flourishes when humans lack effective and economical means for such testing. Indeed, it can be said that we developed science by learning how to evaluate specific explanations offered by magic. (1985, 31)

In the end, they "reserve the term *magic* for compensators that are offered as correct explanations without regard for empirical evaluations and that, when evaluated, are found wanting" (p. 32). Thus, Stark and Bainbridge would seem to land firmly in Luhrmann's intellectualist category, defining magic in terms of inadequate or mistaken beliefs. Because of this focus on the perceived fundamental error of magical thought, Stark and Bainbridge persistently dismiss magic as having no value, especially within the context of modern religion, which is their primary area of examination.

> That the most central compensators of religion are immune to disconfirmation, while the compensators of magic often are disconfirmed, has a profound sociological implication. It leads to the conclusion that there will be a marked tendency for religion and magic to become differentiated, for religious organizations not to deal in magic, and for specialists dealing only in magic to appear in societies. . . . Although the primitive, part-time priest will deal in both, as societies become more complex, the priesthood will move away from providing magical services, for to provide magic is to risk

not only the failure of these services but the implication that, if their magic is false, perhaps their theology is too. Churches do not really need magic, even though a substantial demand for magic persists. Let others with less to lose run the risks of dealing magic. (p. 110)

In our judgment, faiths suited to the future will contain no magic, only religion. This will not, of course, allow them to escape in the long run the forces of secularization—all successful faiths are fated to be tamed by the world. But faiths containing only religion will be immune to scientific attack and thus will avoid the accelerated secularization in effect during recent centuries. (p. 456)

Modern magic pretends to be science or common sense, and thus is seldom recognized for what is it; mainline religious denominations are well rid of it. (p. 528)

By defining magical belief and practice in the way in which they do, Stark and Bainbridge drastically limit the possible explanations for magic's persuasiveness. They reduce magic to being an instrumental procedure, a means of obtaining a certain specified goal. They focus their attention on the end of a magical working: whether or not the stated aim was achieved and whether there could be a scientific explanation for that achievement. They view magic as an isolated act. This is a very traditional approach, but, in terms of examining modern Western magic, probably a very misleading one. It assumes that magic is performed in order to achieve the ends set out in the working, and that the desirability of those ends accounts for the persuasiveness of magical practice. However, it would appear that, in the case of magic as it is performed within the context of Neo-Pagan Witchcraft, although the ends are desired, it is nonetheless the *process* of becoming magical and performing magic that is of the greatest significance, and not necessarily the achievement of the specified ends of any given working.

NEW DIRECTIONS: TANYA LUHRMANN

Neo-Pagan witches consider themselves to be members of a decentralized, Pagan religious movement which draws upon pre-Christian folkore and mythology for its inspiration, and which centrally features magic in its worldview (Adler 1986; Crowley 1989; Marron 1989; Starhawk 1979; Skelton 1990; for additional sources, see references). Examining magic in the context of Neo-Pagan witchcraft is interesting because Neo-Pagan Witchcraft is a modern Western movement (A. Kelly 1990; Luhrmann 1989). By and large, witches were brought up in the scientific, progressive twentieth century, and not raised in a "primitive" culture which advocated or practiced magic as a routine matter. This apparent dissonance between magical belief and modern culture is what sparked Tanya Luhrmann's doctoral research at Cambridge University in England, which was subsequently incorporated into *Persuasions of the Witch's Craft*. Luhrmann comments,

> Magicians are ordinary, well-educated, usually middle-class people. They are not psychotically deluded, and they are not driven to practice by socio-economic desperation. (1989, 7)

> I became interested in modern magic because these particular people seemed to pose difficulties for the standard interpretations of magic. Modern magicians are sophisticated, educated people. They know of a way of explaining nature—science—which has been remarkably successful in its explanation and remarkably antagonistic towards ritualistic magic. They do not come from a background which accepts magic easily and their rites are novel creations; their magic cannot be explained as some burden of the past. They are clearly equipped with the mental equipment to think non-magically. (p. 10)

Luhrmann takes these observations about modern witches, and turns them into a solid ethnography of modern magic in contemporary England. Her goal is to explain the manner in whch magical ideas go from being alien to being accepted and she does this with great facility, drawing upon detailed participant observation research of the Neo-Pagan magical community in London and its environs. Luhrmann's approach to the issue of magic, treating magical practice as part of an interpretive process which acts to both nurture and explain changes in individual experience, rather than as a series of a isolated goal-driven acts, is superior to the "ends-oriented" interpretation offered by more traditional social scientists inasmuch as it allows her a great deal more flexibility to answer her "classic anthropological question: why do they practice magic when, according to observers, the magic doesn't work" (p. 4). Luhrmann's key insight is that the manner in which an individual becomes magical, the magical "context," is as integral a part of the practice of magic as any ends-oriented spell.

Despite Luhrmann's considerable insight into the way in which an individual becomes magical, her study occasionally rings hollow, because she only rarely and very tentatively addresses what might draw people to magical practice that is not a characteristic of the practice itself. That is, she ignores the uniquely subjective motivations for magical practice, although she acknowledges that these must exist, commenting,

> . . . nor are those who practice it [magic] simply an arbitrary sample of the population. They find magic fascinating, sufficiently so that they are willing to explore it at considerable length and at possible risk to their reputation. In some manner, the themes and concepts of the practice speak to them. Something in their personal makeup draws them to the practice, though different desires motivate different individuals. (1989, 86)

This omission in Luhrmann's research can be partially addressed by discussing an aspect of subjective experience common to many witches that was noted in Shelley Rabinovitch's M.A. research on Neo-Pagan Witchcraft in Canada: experience of an abusive or severely dysfunctional background. Although it would be inaccurate and overgeneralized to imply that this kind of background is the only reason individuals become involved in magical practice and/or that all such individuals have been abused—or even that using magical practice to compensate for the effects of an abusive upbringing is a conscious and deliberate choice on the part of the practitioner—magical practice confers certain psychological benefits to survivors of such backgrounds by promoting attitudes and practices also advocated in much of the self-help literature.

STARTLING DISCOVERIES: RABINOVITCH'S RESEARCH

In the summer of 1991, Shelley Rabinovitch conducted a series of semi-structured interviews with Neo-Pagan witches across Canada. Sixty-seven of these were taped, and form the bulk of her descriptive analysis of Neo-Pagan Witchcraft in Canada. Many other people talked to her less formally, offering off-the-record help and insight. Rabinovitch's informants lived in rural and urban areas in almost every part of the country, and were selected on a non-random basis according to their availability, and their willingness to talk to someone who was, in most cases, a complete stranger, about the intimate details of their lives and their religious practice.

One of the most visible themes in the interviews was the prevalence of an upbringing that was perceived to have been unusually difficult or disturbed. Rabinovitch comments, "Two factors were investigated when determining dysfunctional upbringing: firstly, alcoholic parent(s) or drug dependency; and secondly, physical, sexual or emotional abuse (severe) by a family member or an outsider in a position of control" (1992, 99). She goes on to note,

> Of the 40 women interviewed, only 2.5 percent did not undergo some sort of severe trauma as they grew up (one out of 40). Of the 27 men interviewed, only 22 percent did not undergo similar experiences (seven out of 27). . . . Of those reporting some form of abuse, 29 indicated that one or more of their parents were substance-dependent, 46 reported that they had been victims of abuse (either as a child or an adult), and 22 were victims of incest by a blood relative or step-relative. (p. 99)

Although Rabinovitch allowed her respondents to define "dysfuntional and abusive," they were encouraged to elaborate, if they were comfortable doing so, and the narratives that emerged painfully demonstrate that she had uncovered genuine and justified trauma, and not merely ambivalence towards the kinds of affection and punishment that were considered to be normal in the 1950s and '60s. Here are some examples taken from her thesis:

> Both my parents were severely emotionally abusive. . . . and at age 12 or 13 I had both oral and anal sex with a much older boy, a friend of our family. The whole incident was denied by my family when I told, and so it occurred for months. . . . I attempted suicide three times in four years. (male, Nova Scotia)

> (laughing) Yeah, I got it all and I'm not afraid to talk about it: physical, emotional, sexual abuse. My mother was addicted to prescription drugs. . . . With my father there was touching, and genital sex. He did it frequently between when I was, ah . . . 6 and about 12. . . . I was raped too, as an adult, and I was battered by my spouse. (female, Winnipeg)

> Yes, my childhood was violent. I was a ward of the province, was sent to boarding schools, and at times was raised by other relatives. My father raped me numerous times over a few years. . . . I underwent a lot of emotional abuse from my mother who tried to convince me I was crazy when I said what my father had done. . . . They sent me to a hospital after I told, to see what was wrong with this otherwise lovely child that she would make up such stories. . . . My father was an alcoholic, and my mother was hooked on tranquilizers. . . . My father firmly believed he was doing the Lord's work [when he sexually abused the informant]. He had a strange view of God. As an adult, I was raped at 26. (female, Calgary)

> I underwent severe physical abuse. Because all the work was left to me because my mother was not well, I was beaten if the house was not up to scratch. . . . There was also emotional abuse. . . . For

instance, I was caught reading in bed late . . . and as punishment, my mother took away all the light bulbs from my room for TWO YEARS. . . . I was a victim of child sexual abuse from my step-grandfather [molesting, touching around ages 6 through 9]. (female, Victoria) (pp. 100–101)

In some cases, abuse had occurred in adult life, however, most of Rabinovitch's informants detailed additional problems in childhood and adolescence. Only rarely did problems begin after the age of twenty, and in almost all cases, they were not still occurring at the time of the interview.

MAKING THE CONNECTIONS: MAGIC, POWER, CONTROL, AND WHOLENESS

These findings about the prevalence of the experience of trauma and abuse among Neo-Pagan practitioners are significant given the growing body of knowledge about survivors of this kind of experience. The works cited here are directed towards survivors who are in the process of rebuilding their lives, rather than those people merely concerned to discover the prevalence and forms of abuse. Although most of the discussion cited here comes from the sexual abuse literature, which is limiting primarily inasmuch as it is usually directed only towards women, literature aimed at other "survivor" groups, such as adult children of alcoholics, contains many of the same observations and advocates similar approaches to healing.

MAGIC AS POWER AND CONTROL: NEO-PAGAN DEFINITIONS OF MAGIC

The most common observation about abuse survivors is that they tend to have low self-esteem and a severely curtailed sense of agency (Bass and Davis 1988; Kelly 1988; Johnson 1991). Bass and Davis comment, "When you were abused, your boundaries, your right to say no, your sense of control in the world, were violated. You were powerless. The abuse humiliated you, gave you the message that you were of little value. Nothing you did could stop it" (p. 34). Low self-esteem perpetuates the feelings of powerlessness and lack of control that were learned through the abusive situation, or series of situations, even after the abuse has stopped.

Magic is about power and control; so is recovering from low self-esteem. Johnson comments, "In order to feel good about ourselves, we must . . . develop a sense of effectiveness and power, a sense that we can make things happen" (1991, 255). In Neo-Pagan Witchcraft, most definitions of magic are variations on the formulations of two early-twentieth-century ritual magicians—Aleister Crowley and William Butler. Crowley's definition is "Magic is the Art and Science of causing change to occur in accordance with Will"; Butler's is "Magic is the art of effecting change in consciousness at will" (Bonewits 1979, 28–30). Magic is an unorthodox way in which to cause change. Belief in one's ability to perform magic involves coming to accept a belief that one is capable of causing change (that one is powerful) and that the change will occur according to one's Will (that one is in control). Orthodox ways of causing change and taking control, such as reporting abuse and trying to live up to behavior standards, failed for many abuse survivors, and so perhaps it is unsurprising that there is a high concentration of them in a practice that reassures them that there are other means of control, and that they are not failures.

Modern magic is founded upon a specific set of assumptions that are different from the default assumptions of contemporary Western society. The fundamental assumption from which all Neo-Pagan magic proceeds is that thought can affect matter, without the intervention of the thinker's acts (Luhrmann 1989, 117). Magic, as described in Neo-Pagan literature, is the projection of the Will into the world, in order to cause change. "Will is understood by Neo-Pagans as the focusing of desire and the Immanent Deity to achieve goals" (Rabinovitch 1992, 87).[1] Will is not the same thing as desire; Will is something that must be trained into being. This training will be discussed further below.

The premise of magic, that one's thoughts can change one's environment, is a tremendously positive and powerful one for survivors of abuse. It encourages them to alter their perception of themselves from one in which they are victims, to one in which they are not, by holding forth the promise that, if they can do this, an objective reality will emerge in accordance with their construction.

MAGIC AS DISCIPLINE:
SELF-KNOWLEDGE AND TRAINING TECHNIQUES

In Neo-Paganism, effectiveness at magic is believed to be the result of study and practice. Often magic is presented as an ongoing discipline, the foundation of which is self-knowledge. Starhawk, a well-known and respected American witch, writes,

The magical and psychic aspects of the Craft are concerned with awakening the starlight vision, as I like to call it, and training it to be a useful tool. . . . Starlight vision is a natural potential inherent in each of us, but much work is required to develop and train it. . . . But the final price of freedom is the willingness to face that most frightening of all beings, one's own self. (1979, 18–19)

Marian Green, a British magician whose training manuals are frequently used as guidelines in many Witchcraft groups comments,

The reason for concentrating on understanding yourself first of all is because *you* form the core and base upon which your magical training is founded. The more secure this foundation is, the stronger and higher you can build. If you are aware of your own feelings or reactions to a given situation then you will be able to understand the feelings of others. You will become a crystal-clear mirror in which you may see other people reflected. By seeing yourself in your true colours, you will be able to judge others, and knowing your own faults and failings, give them a fair hearing. (1983, 19)

Neo-Pagan magical training begins with knowing one's self, and training one's Will. If these things have not been addressed, it is not believed that any spell one might attempt will have any hope of success. "Knowing one's self" is a complex, introspective process, and training guides suggest a variety of different exercises (Starhawk 1979; Warren-Clarke 1987; Green 1983, 1985). All of these exercises have similar ends in view: to raise awareness about one's own thoughts, beliefs, and reactions to events, and to make one more aware of one's feelings and intuitions. Neo-Pagan magicians believe that through increasing self-knowledge, one increases the effectiveness of one's magical Will, by removing unintended and counterproductive baggage.

This self-discovery process is the same one advocated in the self-help literature directed at abuse survivors. It too encourages intense self-examination, a re-valuation of feelings and an acknowledgement of needs which, because they were never acknowledged as valid in the context of an abusive situation, were suppressed and half-forgotten. Magical training encourages one to accept intuition as a valid form of knowing, and to acknowledge fears and desires so that they will not interfere with Will. Bass and Davis, speaking to survivors, comment, "The best guide for healing is your own inner voice. Learning to trust your own perceptions, feelings and intuitions forms a new basis for action in the world" (1988, 59). They recognize that survivors are often curiously detached from their own inner workings, because reflection

upon them is painful, and they encourage an examination of the
way in which one's subconscious speaks to them in their daily life.

> Within all of us, there is an inner voice that can tell us how we
> feel . . . Everyone experiences her inner voice differently. You may
> have bad dreams. You may get headaches. You may become exhausted.
> You may have a sudden urge to binge on crackers. Or you may
> notice that you've cleaned the house twice in two days. The impor-
> tant thing is not what you experience, but that you recognize it as
> a message. (p. 117)

Bass and Davis also provide exercises, none of which would look
out of place in a handbook of magical training.

But neither magic nor healing is presented as a purely rational process that can be accomplished through logical analysis. Both
the Neo-Pagan magical literature, and the survivor literature put a
heavy emphasis on the non-rational, usually portrayed as an "inner
child" or a "Younger Self." Starhawk identifies the Younger Self
with the unconscious, writing,

> In the Faery Tradition of Witchcraft, the unconscious mind is called
> the Younger Self; the conscious mind is called Talking Self. Because
> they function through different modes of awareness, communication
> between the two is difficult. It is as if they speak different languages.
> It is Younger Self that directly experiences the world, through the
> holistic awareness of the right hemisphere. Sensations, emotions,
> basic drives, image memory, intuition and diffuse perception are
> functions of Younger Self . . . (1979, 21)

Reaching the Younger Self, Starhawk says, is done through symbol, story, and play. The conceptualization of the inner child in
the self-help literature is less figurative, but strongly related. Because many survivors were abused when they were young, they
were stripped of the innocence commonly associated with childhood, and were forced to develop coping mechanisms that locked
off parts of their personalities. In order to heal, they must rediscover and re-integrate those parts of their personality. "Many
survivors have lost touch with their own vulnerability. Getting in
touch with the child within can help you feel compassion, more
anger at your abuser, and a greater intimacy with others" (Bass
and Davis 1988, 58–59). Among the ways that are suggested to
reach the inner child are play, and "rituals" or role-plays designed to give the inner child a sense of safety and security. These
role-plays look startlingly like the "working section" of a magical
ritual, and serve a similar psycho-dramatic purpose; they encour-

age the participant to alter their consciousness in order to work towards change.

The cornerstones of magical technique, which are believed to strengthen and hone one's Will, are meditation and visualization. Meditation is required to train the mind to still extraneous thoughts, so that one can remain focused on a working without undue distractions. Visualization is required to form a clear "mental picture" of the desired ends of a magical working, and to be able to sustain that picture throughout the course of the spell or ritual, even while one is doing something else, like dancing or chanting. Warren-Clarke describes the use of these techniques as follows: "As the process of meditation is to still the mind whilst relaxing the body, so the process of visualization is to utilize that peaceful and relaxed state for the creation of new states and increased awareness through controlled and conscious creation" (1987, 19). Marian Green makes the distinction between the goals of meditation and visualization by saying,

> Meditation is an altered state of consciousness in which you cease to be concerned with the time and place in which you are sitting and enter a world of information affecting various senses. It is an inward-looking, waiting and perceiving state in which impressions and feelings can make themselves felt. It is an essentially passive activity, for apart from continuing to maintain a relaxed and attentive state, you are not directing the material that comes to you. Creative visualization, on the other hand, is a method of directing what you see and of creating, from fragments already in your memory, a new place or condition. It is the most important key to practical magical work and allows you to direct your will effectively, through the images you create. (1983, 37)

The two techniques are usually practiced in tandem, because without the ability to still extraneous thoughts that comes with meditation, effective visualization is difficult due to the everyday distractions of normal consciousness. All magical training and Neo-Pagan Witchcraft texts emphasize the centrality of these skills, and the necessity for continual practice.

Survivor literature also emphasizes the value of these techniques in contributing to one's ability to heal. Meditation allows the individual to have some control over their thoughts, which can be very beneficial when experiencing such common side effects of abuse as anxiety attacks and flashbacks. Working faithfully at meditation means taking a certain amount of time out for one's self every day, and reinforces the notion that the individual *deserves* that time. It is frequently difficult for survivors to allow themselves to do anything just for *them*, as they have internalized the belief that they are not valuable (Bass and Davis 1988; Finney 1992; Johnson 1991).

Visualization is also advocated, sometimes effusively. Lynne Finney writes,

> For survivors of abuse, visualization is a mini-miracle. You can work with your therapist to change negative behaviour patterns by clearly picturing the behaviour you would like to have. You can obtain things you want through visualization and gain confidence in your ability to control your world. You can learn a new sport and meet new friends. And you can create a world of peace and beauty for yourself when you need a respite from thoughts about your abuse. It is a technique worth trying because it can help you change your world in many ways. (1992, 293)

Karen Johnson discusses a behavioral therapy technique used for treating anxiety, "systematic desensitization," that operates through "imaging" or visualizing anxiety-provoking situations in order to build a kind of tolerance to them. "By enduring, or 'surviving' her anxiety, she will gradually overcome her phobia—at least in her mind. Eventually, her visual mastery can then be translated into real life circumstances" (1991, 282).[2] Although Johnson, a trained psychologist, stops short of the claims made by magicians that visualization, in the context of spell-work, can affect the material world to the extent that it can help to provide tangible goods such as money, she certainly acknowledges that a change in the imagination can translate into a change in the "objective" world, one of the central claims of magic.

It is evident, then, that the techniques considered to be central in magical training are also recognized to be valuable therapeutic tools in the context of healing from abuse. Luhrmann recognizes the therapeutic potential of magical practice, even though she does not emphasize it in her study, commenting,

> The power of this involvement has something to do with the therapeutic efficacy of the practice. For many people this symbolic redescription becomes a therapy, a way of making sense of the facts of their experience and of learning how to alter their attitudes towards those experiences or their manner of handling them. Many magicians—though not all—think of their magic as having therapeutic qualities, and I suspect that most of them would think that their magical practice had led to a positive improvement in their sense of well-being. Therapeutic techniques of course are difficult to evaluate, but I had the impression that magic could be beneficial for its

practitioners, and I saw some people became happier and more confident through their practice. (1989, 247–48)

This is not to imply that magical practice is chosen *as a therapy*.
Most Neo-Pagan witches describe the motivations for their involvement in the religion along the lines of "it was something that
just *felt* right" or "it felt like coming home" (Adler 1986; Marron
1989). What is being suggested here is that *one of* the reasons the
religion, and the magical practice associated with it, "feel right" to
many people who have survived abuse is that they address many of
the subconscious needs that arise as a result of those experiences,
even where those needs are not consciously or logically articulated.

DARKNESS, POWER, STRENGTH, AND MEANING

Luhrmann, in her research, was struck by the concept of "darkness" that is found in all branches of Western magical practice that
she encountered. She notes,

> The practical teaching texts [of magic] describe an underworld of
> darkness that must be confronted, entered and accepted before per-
> sonal power can be gained: the abyss whose negotiation confers
> adepthood. The notion of the Goddess within the practical litera-
> ture is a vision of continuity between chaos and order, destruction
> and creativity, in which the way to personal empowerment and selfhood
> leads through the valley of dissolution. The themes which emerge
> from this creative amalgam of different myths, stories and symbols
> are about the nature of power: of the value of losing it to regain it,
> of the knowledge to control it. Those who become magicians are
> compelled by these portrayals. (1989, 86–87)

Because Luhrmann has not identified the elements of personal
experience that have brought people to magical practice, and because "the darkness" as it is conceived of in magic does not have
the consistently negative overtones of what is probably the closest
cultural approximation of it, evil, she finds it a challenge to understand, and to interpet.

> The most challenging concept in magic is this darkness: the deep,
> the destructive, the angry, primordial, irrational. There is no clear
> parcelling out of the issues here, and all participants intellectualize
> them differently . . . Magic, magicians say, is about plunging into
> the terror of the abyss, and through this, acquiring strength. (p. 92)

If it is true that magic is born out of the inner strength that comes
with traversing the "darkness," then survivors of abuse have a head

start. They have already faced the incredible darkness and pain that came out of their experiences. In order to survive the abuse and to develop mechanisms for coping in their daily lives, they had to draw on their own strength, often at an early age, in a way that people who have never experienced profound trauma and loss have not. Bass and Davis note, "You have survived against formidable odds. The same abuse that undercut you has also provided you with many of the inner resources necessary for healing. One quality every survivor can be confident of having is strength" (1988, 39). Liz Kelly adds, " . . . the common, although often implicit, assumption that all consequences of sexual violence are, or remain, negative can be questioned, and attention can be drawn to the possibility that the process of coping with negative effects may, in the long run, have positive outcomes" (1988, 159).

One of the reasons that abuse survivors might be drawn to magical practice, find its portrayals of the darkness "compelling" to use Luhrmann's phrase, is that magic assigns a positive value to the pain they have experienced. It explicitly legitimates a group of experiences that are minimized in the wider society, and acknowledges that, although they are not justified and cannot be condoned, they nonetheless contribute to an individual's growth, to their personal strength and their magical power. One Craft elder, noted for teaching rudimentary magical technique to beginning students, has been heard to despair over trying to train students who have, in her words, " . . . never known any real *pain* in their lives, who have never had to rely strictly on their own resources, who don't know where the deep well of their own power is, or what it feels like. How can you *teach* that?" A common phrase in Witchcraft is "To learn, you must suffer." To have the darkness that is already a part of their experience given a value and made meaningful helps to place it into a perspective that prevents it from continuing to overwhelm and dominate the individual. This perspective is also sought in the self-help literature, and might account for part of the subliminal appeal of magical practice to survivors of abuse.

SPELL-WORK: MAGIC AS WHOLENESS

Spell-work, the utilization of magical theory and techniques in the hopes of producing change in the objective world, is the purported end-goal of magical training. Almost all Neo-Pagan Witchcraft texts will contain either some suggested spells, or some discussion of how a spell is designed. Interestingly enough, despite the fact that, according to magical theory, one should be able to obtain *anything* one desires sufficiently through appropriate magic, and despite the common Western notion that what are most to be desired are money and power, Rabinovitch's interviews revealed that when Neo-Pagan witches do spell-work, it is more often than not healing work, and is usually done for others. She makes the connection between spell-work and a quest for "wholeness," commenting:

> Nearly all Neo-Pagan practitioners of magic indicate they do magic (spellworking in the interviews) for *others*, and usually in some form of beneficent healing . . . Houseblessings, love spells, job spells, and student spells are all aimed at creating an atmosphere of *wholeness*. The practitioner is healing self and the world around her/him in this manner. (1992, 89; italics in original)

This observation, that spell-work in Neo-Pagan Witchcraft is usually not directed towards immediate personal material gain, is easily confirmed through a casual perusal of the literature. Spells for blessing, protection, healing, love and work predominate. Although this is not to say spells for success and for money do not exist, Rabinovitch's research suggests that they are not utilized to nearly the same extent.

Spell-work can be seen to be appealing to survivors of abuse on a number of levels. First of all, it encourages the clear articulation of an end-goal, which must be acknowledged to be desired. It also encourages the individual to focus upon that goal, and direct energy towards its attainment. "A spell," Starhawk writes, "is a symbolic act done in an altered state of consciousness, in order to cause a desired change. To cast a spell is to project energy through a symbol" (1979, 110). Success in spell-work is predicated upon one's unwavering belief that one will attain the visualized end-goal of the spell. Despite the fact that this work is done in what could be considered a "figurative" manner, it is an assertion of agency, and can nonetheless encourage a more positive and confident attitude towards the world. Starhawk explains,

> Spells also go one step further than most forms of psychotherapy. They allow us not only to listen to and interpret the unconscious but also to speak to it, in the language it understands. Symbols, images, and objects used in spells communicate directly with Younger Self, who is the seat of our emotions and who is barely touched by the intellect. We often understand our feelings and behavior but find ourselves unable to change them. Through spells, we can attain

the most important power—the power to change ourselves. . . . . Spells work in two basic ways. The first, which even the most confirmed skeptics will have no trouble accepting, is through suggestion. Symbols and images implant certain ideas in Younger Self, in the unconscious mind. We are then influenced to actualize those ideas. Obviously psychological spells and many healing spells work on this principle. It functions in other spells too. For example, a woman casts a spell to get a job. Afterwards, she is filled with self-confidence, approaches her interviewer with assurance, and creates such a good impression that she is hired. (p. 111–112)

Most Western magicians, however, Starhawk included, do not stop with the assertion that magic operates psychologically. She goes on to write, " . . . spells can also influence the external world. Perhaps the job hunter 'just happens' to walk into the right office at the right time. The cancer patient, without knowing that a healing spell was cast, has a spontaneous remission. This aspect of magic is more difficult to accept" (p. 112).[3]

The way in which magic is believed to affect the objective world, the "world of tables and chairs" so to speak, is through its operation in a universe characterized by connections. The worldview of Western magic is a holistic one, in which everything is connected to everything else by an assortment of material and non-material "levels." An action taken on one level will have effects on other levels; thus, a spell which appears to be performed on a material level, with candles, oils and the like, produces a change on the "astral" level, which will then produce another change on the material level (for elaboration, see Green 1983; Starhawk 1979; Farrar and Farrar 1990; Skelton 1990).[4] This emphasis on the importance of connectedness in Western magical thought can be reassuring and empowering for survivors of abuse, who may have been forced to live with parts of their lives radically compartmentalized and dissociated from other parts of their lives, as is the case, for example, with a bright schoolchild who is being abused at home.

Magic also allows the creation of boundaries, which is identified as an important element of healing from abuse. Bass and Davis comment, "The capacity to set limits is essential to feeling good about yourself. Many survivors have not known how to define their own time, to protect their bodies, to put themselves first, to say no" (1988, 182). Magical practice addresses these particular issues very directly. For instance, all magical work is done within a circle. A "circle" is an area of physical space that has been temporarily set apart and designated as safe. "Safe" or "special" places are probably a feature of everyone's childhood experience, but they are especially significant for those who underwent abuse at a young age, because they represented what little freedom and self-determination could be mustered. Luhrmann notices the similarity between the magician's idea of a circle and the safe spaces of childhood, without recognizing the significance of her observation. She writes, "The magic circle chalks out a space which magicians idealize as special and different, a mixture of the safe and the sacred. . . . It is curiously like the imaginative sacrality of childhood, the special spot behind the armchair, under the desk, out in the woods, the secret place where fairy tales are almost true *and adults are forbidden to enter*" (1989, 226, italics mine). The setting of magical practice re-creates and reinforces feelings of safety and control.

Magic also provides more explicit protection and boundary-setting tools. Just as a circle can be cast around a limited area for the purposes of spell-work, ritual, or meditation, so an entire living space can be "sealed" against negative influence. "Wards" can be set in a room, or around a bed, to protect the sleeper. A person can work to develop "psychic shielding" to protect themselves from the ill-wishing of others, or the "psychic white noise" of day-to-day life. Whether or not these spells have any independent, objective effect, they are psychologically powerful. They reinforce the notions that one is not helpless, that one has the ability to take steps to protect one's self, and that one's living space can be safe and secure, all very important to survivors of abuse.

CONCLUSION: MAGIC AS METAPHOR

Magic, as it is practiced in the context of Neo-Pagan Witchcraft, has little in common with what most sociologists and anthropologists describe as magic. It is not an exchange commodity. It does not foster client relationships. Magic is not performed on a commission basis, for money or bartered goods. The performance of a spell, especially if done for another person, confers no necessary benefit on the magical practitioner other than satisfaction, and possibly enhanced prestige. Traditional sociology is at a loss in trying to explain this kind of phenomenon within the boundaries of its established definitions.

Success at the spell-work, which is what sociologists and anthropologists define as "magic," is believed by modern witches to rest upon mastery of meditation and visualization techniques, which in its turn comes out of a long process of work and study. In the Neo-Pagan community, a person will be described as "very magical" or "very powerful" based on their degree of skill with these techniques, and their mastery of a body of symbolic and esoteric lore, regardless of whether or not they are known to be engaging in spell-work. This perception of magic as residing in the process clearly undermines the traditional definitions of magic. In conflating magic with spell-work, an end-oriented, instrumental tunnel vision, interpreters are missing the point. Magic is not a way to form a one-to-one relationship between an individual and an otherwise unattainable goal; it is an elaborate, dramatic metaphor for the relationship between an individual and the universe, and, like all metaphors, it hovers on the boundary between the figuratively and the literally true, refusing to commit itself firmly on either side. Luhrmann notes,

> In modern magic the fact that the same assertion is both play-claim (context-defining claim) and reality-claim (claimed true for the larger context of 'ordinary' reality) can allow magicians to waver between the literal and the metaphorical when casting a spell: literal, in that the spell is thought to do what the first-order theory says that it will do, and metaphorical, in that the spell is thought to do something else justified by the second-order theory—spiritual, psychotherapeutic, expressive or creative—by representing an inner state in figurative form. This grants ambiguity, an ambiguity quite important for the magician. The seriousness of the claim of magical efficacy makes their practice seem serious and important, yet the play-claim allows the magician to justify magic on other grounds. Regardless of the veracity of its claims, they argue, magical practice is worthwhile because the experiential involvement is spiritually, morally, aesthetically or psychologically uplifting. (1989, 333)

Despite her insight, Luhrmann does not go far enough. It is not only spells that are metaphorical, but all of the interwoven process that is Neo-Pagan magic.

The prevalence of the experience of past abuse among Neo-Pagan magicians should point the interpreter toward what might be perceived as valuable about the practice. Magical practice, and the training that is an integral part of it, provide a context in which life can be lived and experience can be understood. This context emphasizes wholeness, connections, self-knowledge, and personal agency. In Neo-Pagan Witchcraft, it is in examining the context, and not the content, of the practice that one finds the "compensators" provided by magic, and its greatest appeal, especially for survivors of abuse. The magical context specifically encourages attitudes which foster the kind of personal development believed by many to be necessary in order for these survivors to heal. Magic is the art of changing consciousness at will. Healing is the construction and actualization of a personal reality, a consciousness, in which one is a survivor, and not a victim. The two have much in common. Magical practice demands that the practitioner believe in the force of their own Will. It teaches that thinking about things in certain ways can make a difference. It encourages a person to set goals, and to act in very specific ways upon them. It re-empowers people who may have been taught to believe that they had no effective voice, and were incapable of influencing the universe in which they were compelled to live. That at least one category of people can derive such positive benefits from engaging in magical practice should give us pause, and cause us to reflect on earlier assessments of magic.

To label magic as necessarily regressive is to dismiss its therapeutic value, and the possibility that it could represent a progressive development in an individual's worldview. To label magic as a reasoning pathology implies that the only valid mode of thinking is literally, logically, and linearly. What if magic is not a literal description of the universe, but a metaphorical one? In Neo-Pagan Witchcraft, magic is not a collection of ends, it is an assortment of means; it operates as much on the internal landscape as it does on the external world. In this sense, it has a great deal more in common with therapies described in self-help literature than it does with the sort of quasi-scientific instrumental methods for producing change in the external world, which are what is meant when most academics and social scientists refer to "magic." Neo-Pagan magic is a re-empowering, wholeness-producing context which invites us to reconsider harsh dismissals of magic, and to take a different perspective on what is being provided to the practitioner, and how.

Contemporary Western magic inhabits the shadowy realm of metaphor. When a poet says "Beneath the waves of storm that lash and burn, / The currents of blind passion that appal, / To listen and keep watch till we discern / The tide of sovereign truth that guides it all"[5] he is attempting to give insight into the nature of the intangibles "blind passion" and "sovereign truth" through a comparison with more tangible water and storm imagery. The metaphor itself is a bridge between one and the other. Magic is related to science and religion in a similar fashion. Science describes a testable relationship of cause and effect in the material world. Religion provides an untestable meaning-context based in the supernatural. Both describe aspects of the universe in which the individual lives, but in very different terms. A metaphor describes one thing in terms of another, with the hopes of providing insight into both through a process of inference. In Neo-Pagan magic, the intangible in need of description is the untestable context, the world of invisible forces, multiple planes, primordial darkness, astral forms, and magical Will. It is these elements that provide the meaning structure through which the individual interprets their experience. Luhrmann notes,

> Part of the reason people enjoy practicing magic is that it becomes a vehicle for self-expression. Myths and symbols fill magicians' reading and inflitrate their dreams. . . . It is as if magicians learn a new language in which to talk about their world, and gain a new set of possibilities for organizing it. . . . Magicians use symbolism to capture, express or articulate their experience, and in its mixture of precision and evocation it becomes tremendously important to them. (1989, 244–245)

The scientific cause and effect rhetoric of spell-work is like the water imagery of the metaphor; it is there to give shape to an intangible. In this way, Neo-Pagan magic can be seen as being closer to religion, in its provision of general compensators such as a sense of personal potency, than to science, which seeks only to explain the material world. This is not to say that spells are not expected to work on the material world. They are, just as storms and waves are expected to exist, regardless of their application in a metaphorical context. However, changing the external landscape is not all that magic does, even if it sometimes sounds as though that is all it is meant to do. Magic changes the internal landscape as well. A spell is a way to express and manipulate the meaning context of life. If Neo-Pagan magic were only about ends, then repeated failures should be sufficient to deligitimize it. This is certainly the conclusion one can draw from Bainbridge and Stark. However, as Luhrmann's research makes eminently clear, repeated failure is not enough to deligitimize the practice, and indeed, magicians have developed a host of ways to turn what could be perceived as failures into successes. She comments,

> How is it possible for the magician to retain his faith in the face of constant failure? The succinct answer is that failure is perceived to be far from constant, and it is easily explained within the terms of the theory. Success is easy to establish: the goal of the ritual is often

met by the natural process of healing; the freedom to use symbolically associated events and personal experience as evidence allows
the magician to interpret almost any ritual as at least successfully
raising major power. Failure, when identified, is ascribed to the
particular magician—and her belief, goal or technique—rather than
to the general 'theory' . . . Magicians do not confront the spectre
of constant failure. They banish it. (1989, 141)

Neo-Pagan magic, in practice, is not as clear-cut as the theorists
would like. While appearing to provide specific compensators through
the obvious device of spell-work, it also provides more general
compensators through the network of training practices and beliefs
underlying that spell-work. The content and the context cannot be
easily divorced to fit some arbitrary definitional exigency. Either
we must reconsider traditional assertions about the nature and
function of magic, or we must redraw the boundaries between magic
and religion once again.

NOTES

1. Despite Rabinovitch's reference to "Deity," contemporary magic
is not necessarily performed within a theistic context, although in Neo-
Pagan Witchcraft, this is often the case. Sometimes the well of power
which Rabinovitch labels "Immanent Deity" is conceptualized as the collective unconscious, or as the infinite radiant Is, or the world soul.

2. In order to see the extent of the similarities between the ways in
which visualization can be construed as a therapy, compare Johnson's
behavioral desensitization with Luhrmann's discussion of guided meditation narratives as a potential therapy. Luhrmann writes,
    Therapy seems to work when someone externalizes, or labels, some
internal feeling and then is able to transform it, though how and why that
happens seems quite unclear. Narratives could be therapeutic because of
the way in which someone finds a central character or symbol moving, the
way in which they identify with it. . . . If the character undergoes some
change you again imagine the change based on your own experience, and
perhaps imagine yourself through some experiences you have not had, or
not dealt with properly. The narrative then becomes a practice-ground, a
dry run to handle feelings and responses in new ways. (1989, 249)

3. Bainbridge and Stark discuss the relationship of magic to improved conditions with reference to chance, not psychology.
    " . . . All therapies seem to work because of regression towards the
mean and the random ebbs and flows of life. People who seek a therapy
at a 'bad' time in their lives (which is when they have a motivation to seek
it) are likely to find that their lives soon improve—just as most people will

recover from many kinds of illness whether they receive medical treatment or not. Thus it is that magic has always gained and regained its plausibility. Magic often 'succeeds.' If the shaman, the medieval witch, the psychoanalyst and the water dowser must endure frequent failure, they often profit from frequent success" (1985, 280)

There is no suggestion here, as there is in Starhawk, that magical practice could act to facilitate an occurrence that could, but would not necessarily, have occurred without such intervention.

4. Briefly, material components such as candles and oils are regarded as props, aids to concentration, which are intended to evoke certain learned symbolic associations within the practitioner. The actual spell is performed by the trained Will on the astral plane. The "astral" is thought of as a level of reality different from the material reality, but not entirely separate from it. Farrar and Farrar write,

. . . experience shows that the astral plane is a continuous spectrum. At its upper end, its images and thought forms are near-mental but belong on the astral because they are infused with emotion. At its lower end, it is sometimes called the astral counterpart of physical manifestation, in that each physical entity or object is closely associated with an astral image of itself; obviously, it is the astral counterpart of a given object or person that spell-working seeks to influence, through imagination (an astral function), concentration (mental) and willpower (something of both), as a direct path to influencing the physical. (1990, 16)

5. Archibald Lampman, "The Largest Life III," from *Lampman's Sonnets*, ed. by Margaret Coulby Whitridge. (Ottawa: Borealis Press, 1976), 117.

REFERENCES

Adler, Margot. 1986. *Drawing Down the Moon*. 2d ed. Boston: Beacon Press.

Bainbridge, William Sims, and Rodney Stark. 1985. *The Future of Religion*. Berkeley: University of California Press.

Bass, Ellen, and Laura Davis. 1988. *The Courage to Heal*. New York: Harper and Row Publishers.

Bonewits, P. E. I. [1971] 1979. *Real Magic*. Berkeley: Creative Arts Book Company.

Crowley, Vivianne. 1989. *Wicca: The Old Religion in the New Age*. Wellingborough, England: Aquarian Press.

Cunningham, Scott. 1988a. *The Truth About Witchcraft Today*. St. Paul, Minn.: Llewellyn Publications.

————. 1988b. *Wicca: A Guide for the Solitary Practitioner.* St. Paul, Minn.: Llewellyn Publications.

Cunningham, Scott, and Dick Harrington. 1987. *The Magical Household.* St. Paul, Minn.: Llewellyn Publications.

Durkheim, Emile. [1916] 1976. *The Elementary Forms of the Religious Life.* Translated by Joseph Ward Swain. London: George Allen and Unwin.

Ejerfeldt, Lennart. 1974. "Sociology of Religion and the Occult Revival." In *New Religions,* edited by Haralds Biezais, 202–214. Uppsala: Almqvist and Wiksell International.

Farrar, Janet, and Stewart Farrar. 1981. *Eight Sabbats for Witches.* London: Robert Hale Publishers.

————. 1984. *The Witches' Way: Principles, Rituals and Beliefs of Modern Witchcraft.* London: Robert Hale Publishers.

————. 1990. *Spells and How They Work.* Custer, Wash.: Phoenix Publishing.

Finney, Lynne. 1992. *Reach for the Rainbow.* New York: Putnam Publishing Group.

Fitch, Ed. 1984. *Magical Rites from the Crystal Well.* St. Paul, Minn.: Llewellyn Publications.

Green, Marian. 1983. *Magic for the Aquarian Age.* Wellingborough, Northamptonshire: Aquarian Press.

————. 1985. *Experiments in Aquarian Magic.* Wellingborough, Northamptonshire: Aquarian Press.

Johnson, Karen. 1991. *Trusting Ourselves: The Complete Guide to Emotional Well-Being for Women.* New York: The Atlantic Monthly Press.

K, Amber. 1991. *True Magick.* St. Paul, Minn.: Llewellyn Publications.

Kelly, Aidan. 1991. *Crafting the Art of Magic: Book I.* St. Paul, Minn.: Llewellyn Publications.

————, ed. 1990. *Neo-pagan Witchcraft I.* Volume in *Cults and New Religions* edited by J. Gordon Melton. New York: Garland Publishing.

Kelly, Liz. 1988. *Surviving Sexual Violence.* Minneapolis: University of Minnesota Press.

Kirkpatrick, R. G., R. Rainey, and K. Rubi. 1986. "An Empirical Study of Wiccan Religion in Postindustrial Society." *Free Inquiry in Creative Sociology* 14, no. 1 (May): 33–38.

Luhrmann, Tanya. 1985. "Persuasive Ritual: The Role of Imagination in Occult Witchcraft." *Archives de science sociales des religions* 60, no. 1 (July-September 1985): 151–170.

———. 1989. *Persuasions of the Witch's Craft: Ritual Magic in Contemporary England.* Cambridge, Mass.: Harvard University Press.

Marron, Kevin. 1989. *Witches, Pagans and Magic in the New Age.* Toronto: Seal Books.

Rabinovitch, Shelley. 1991. The Institutionalization of Wicca within Ontario through the Wiccan Church of Canada. Unpublished.

———. 1992. "An' Ye Harm None, Do What Ye Will': Neo-pagans and witches in Canada." M.A. thesis, Department of Religion, Carleton University. Unpublished.

Sandilands, Catriona A. H. 1988. "Spirituality and Praxis: Witchcraft and Neo-paganism in Canada." M.A. thesis, Department of Sociology, York University. Unpublished.

Singer, Barry, and Victor Benassi. 1989. "Occult Beliefs." In *Magic, Witchcraft, and Religion: An Anthropological Study of the Supernatural,* edited by Arthur Lehmann and James Myers, 383–392. Mountain View, Calif.: Mayfield Publishing Company.

Skelton, Robin. 1990. *The Practice of Witchcraft.* Victoria: Porcépic Books.

Starhawk [Miriam Simos]. 1979. *The Spiral Dance: A Rebirth of the Ancient Religion of the Great Goddess.* San Francisco: Harper and Row Publishers.

Truzzi, Marcello. 1974. "Definition and Dimensions of the Occult: Towards a Sociological Perspective." In *On the Margin of the Visible: Sociology, the Esoteric and the Occult,* edited by Edward Tiryakian, 243–255. New York: John Wiley and Sons.

———. 1989. "The Occult Revival as Popular Culture: Some Observations on the Old and Nouveau Witch." In *Magic, Witchcraft, and Religion: An Anthropological Study of the Supernatural,* edited by Arthur Lehmann and James Myers, 403–411. Mountain View, Calif.: Mayfield Publishing Company.

Tyrrell, Marc. 1992. "Strands of Moonlight: An Examination of the Institutionalization Process Amongst Neo-Pagan Witches in Ottawa." M.A. thesis, Institute for Canadian Studies, Carleton University. Unpublished.

Valiente, Doreen. [1975] 1985. *Natural Magic.* Custer, Wash.: Phoenix Publishing.

———. 1989. *The Rebirth of Witchcraft*. London: Robert Hale Publishers.

Warren-Clarke, Ly. 1987. *The Way of the Goddess: A Manual for Wiccan Initiation*. Lindsfield, New South Wales, Australia: Unity Press.

Whitridge, Margaret Coulby, ed. 1977. *Lampman's Sonnets*. Ottawa: Borealis Press.

Part III

History

.

8

WHITE WITCHES:
HISTORIC FACT AND ROMANTIC FANTASY

James W. Baker

AN APOLOGY TO LOUISE HUEBNER

WHEN I BECAME INTERESTED in Wicca or modern witch-craft in the early 1960s, it was Gerald Gardner's *Witchcraft Today* and Margaret Murray's *The Witch-cult in Western Europe* that formed my impression of the subject. The idea of the continuous survival in England of an ancient, universal cult until the time of the witch persecutions—or even to the present—seemed well demonstrated. By the time I was able to visit Gardner's witch museum at Castleton and meet Alex Sanders in 1970, I was fully convinced of the historical veracity of these claims.

It was at this time, while characteristically buying up every book that might shed some light on the subject, that I found *Power Through Witchcraft* (1969) by Louise Huebner, "The Official Witch of Los Angeles." It was a disappointment. A quick reading caused me to dismiss her as an ignorant practitioner of some sort of vulgar folk magic, who wasn't part of or even aware of the real witch tradition that I was so fascinated with. It was writers such as Gardner, Doreen Valiente, Justine Glass, Sybil Leek, June Johns, and Paul Huson (after a fashion) who had the real dope! Together, their books constructed what I came to call "the Witch Party Line," the foundational myth and orthodoxy of Wiccan origins.

As a historian by temperament and profession, it was my ambition to discover all of the links between contemporary Wicca (or "Wica," as Gardner invariably spelled it) and its roots in the past. This was not a search for the proof of Wiccan claims but rather a desire to know more of what had been so coyly hinted at by Gardner and other authors. Having a university library at my disposal, I diligently searched through every likely monograph and serial to find more about the early days of Witchcraft. I tracked down the majority of references cited in *Witchcraft Today*, those listed in the bibliography in *The Meaning of Witchcraft*, and any other source that might shed some light on Wicca before Gardner. Anthropology and archaeology, theological history and classical studies, everything was grist to the mill.

But the result was mostly chaff. It became clear after two years or so that there wasn't much out there to be found, if one was strictly interested in Wiccan history. All of the material quoted by Gardner and the others, with the exception of the *Book of Shadows* itself, was neither new nor directly relevant to British Wicca. There was a wealth of suggestive material from other times and other cultures, but there was no demonstrable pattern of white religious Witchcraft, as exemplified by contemporary Witchcraft.

The ritual material in the *Book of Shadows* itself was skeletal in nature and quite inadequate as theology or exegesis. I searched for evidence and examples of a unified Horned God and Goddess cult, for the religious use of pentagrams, athames, cords, and the sigils in the *Book of Shadows*, for casting Wiccan as opposed to Solomonic circles, for the application of Wiccan values, but all to no avail.

Alex was no help. He just suggested various books I already knew about or occult ones which, while tangentially related, represented quite different mind-sets from Wicca as a religion. Robert Graves' *White Goddess* for example was evocative and inspirational, but its symbols didn't really accord with Gardner at all. In addition, the "poetical truth" that Graves invoked was obviously quite a different matter from historical veracity. I had become a bit impatient with "poetical truth" by this point. I had (and have) no quarrel with Wicca as a valid faith and religious practice, but the dawning realization that I had been deceived by its historical claims was galling.

The final revelation came from Francis King's pioneering *Ritual Magic in England* (1970). As a schoolboy in 1953 he had interviewed novelist Louis Wilkinson ("Louis Marlow") about Aleister Crowley.

Wilkinson had offhandedly mentioned that Crowley had known of a coven of witches "in his youth" but had declined to join.[1] Questioned about this, Wilkinson asserted that he himself had met such a coven, possibly the same one that Gardner knew, in the late 1930s or early '40s. He described their use of protective ointments and, taken orally, the hallucinogenic fly agaric mushroom. It was his impression that " . . . there had been a fusion of an authentic surviving folk-tradition with a more middle-class occultism" (King 1970, 179). Here at last was independent testimony that there had actually been a quite different witch cult before Gardner.

Wilkinson's evidence indicated that something was there before, but what? As King said, Gardner apparently got bored with the simple ceremonies, and " . . . he consequently decided to found a more elaborate and romanticized witch-cult of his own" (1970, 179).[2] The trick was to discern what might have been added by Gardner or some other middle-class occultist (a "proto-Gardner") and identify the residue as traditional. After talking with King at the Warlock Shop in Brooklyn, N.Y., in 1973, I decided to both fulfill my curiosity and assuage my annoyance at being bamboozled by tracing not only Wicca's past but the entire history of Western occultism. It seemed reasonable that this would make it possible to separate the occult introductions and inventions from the actual folk practices in Wicca.

There is a wealth of material on the practice of folk magic in English history. Even the earliest books on Wicca, such as Gardner's works or Doreen Valiente's *Where Witchcraft Lives* (1961), contain much historical folk magic unrelated to the rituals, practices, and beliefs of Wicca. From the sources liberally referred to by Sir Keith Thomas in *Religion and the Decline of Magic* (1971), George Lyman Kittredge in *Witchcraft in Old and New England* (1929), and the many English folklore studies, it is not difficult to observe a pattern of traditional magical belief and practice. What it demonstrates, however, is that almost all of the characteristic elements of modern Witchcraft have an "occult" bookish rather than traditional origin. I came to the conclusion that there are in fact two separate "White Witchcraft" traditions in English history: one very old and fairly moribund, and another which is very active yet no older than the twentieth century. The latter is modern Wicca. The former is the tradition of the cunning men and wise women, the more or less beneficent practitioners of traditional folk magic and popular sorcery (Kelly 1991, 38). Ironically, this was just what Louise Huebner was talking about!

I eventually found that many of my observations and conclusions had been paralleled by Aidan Kelly when *Crafting the Art of Magic* was published in 1991. Another invaluable source which separates the "religious" element from the magical one with consideration of modern Paganism is Ronald Hutton, *The Pagan Religions of the Ancient British Isles* (1991). I trust that this short chapter can serve as a useful adjunct to these books by casting some additional light on the sources of the *Book of Shadows* and by providing an outline of the actual white witches of English history.

WHITE WITCHCRAFT THEN AND NOW

The criteria by which I hoped to separate the "middle-class occult" elements from the true folk traditions in Wicca was essentially the same as Kelly's. I divided the *Book of Shadows* material into three possible categories:

1. Those elements that were characteristic of known English traditions of folk magic.
2. Those that were either clearly anachronistic in conception and/or representative of book learning and intellectualized occultism. The latter would have to be easily available in published sources in the period when Gardner (or some other innovator) was working.
3. Any element that could not be found in either type of historical source might be assumed to be new or a part of an unknown tradition.

Only segments of the rituals in the *Book of Shadows* can be said to belong to the third category, and we have no reason to doubt that they are modern compositions, thanks to Aidan Kelly. I have no need to duplicate his excellent analysis of this material. However, some other sources for borrowed material which I investigated may be of interest. Omitting details of the more obvious borrowings from Freemasonry and ceremonial magic[3] in interest of space, I have chosen to show the probable sources for the following unique elements from the *Book of Shadows:* the worship of the Goddess, the more obscure chants (the "Eko, Eko" and "Bagabi lacha" passages) in the *Book of Shadows*, the use of the term "athame," "Drawing Down the Moon," the title "Book of Shadows," and the term "wicca" or "wica" itself.

The assertion of a continuous British tradition of self-conscious Goddess/Horned God worship would appear to be quite ahistorical, but I do not intend to develop that argument here. Suffice it to say that the generic goddess cult resembles the Christian notion of a single universalistic theism far more than the localized deities and "pluricultural" approach to religion of ancient times. Gardner is known to have been considerably interested in such a concept as his novels, *A Goddess Arrives* and *High Magic's Aid*, demonstrate.[4] Other potential sources of contemporary Witchcraft, from Margaret Murray's *The Witch-cult in Western Europe* (1921) and Theda Kenyon's *Witches Still Live* (1929)[5] to Jack Parson's "The Witchcraft" (ca. 1950; in Parson 1979), also lack this distinctive goddess emphasis. Even "F.P.D." ("Foy pour Devoir"— Col. C. R. F. Seymour), "The Old Religion—A Study in the Symbolism of the Moon Mysteries," (Seymour 1968), which was written in the 1930s and centers on the evocative visualization of the Celtic feminine force, bears little resemblance to the Wiccan theology.[6] Only Leland's *Aradia* (1899) approaches Wicca in tone, but it must be considered as a source rather than independent testimony. It should be noted that Leland was not blind to the possibility of *Aradia* being in part the invention of his informant Maddalena (1963, xxiv).

The "Eko, Eko Azarak, Eko, Eko Zomelak" and "Bagabi Lacha bachabe" chants which appear in *High Magic's Aid* (Gardner 1954, 291), but not in the Cardell *Book of Shadows* in 1964, actually come from two separate sources. The first originally appeared in the art magazine *Form* in 1921 in an article, "The Black Arts" by J. F. C. Fuller, apparently quoted from some Victorian source.[7] The full chant is as follows:

Eko! eko! Azarak. Eko! eko! Zomelak!
Zod-ru-kod e Zod-ru-koo
Zon-ru-koz e Goo-ru-mu!
Eo! Eo! Oo . . . Oo . . . Oo!

The "Bagabi Lacha" segment is found in Grillot de Givry, *Picture Museum of Sorcery* (first English edition 1931), as noted by Doreen Valiente (1973, 206). In the 1963 University Books reprint de Givry says that in " . . . Le Miracle de Theophile, by the celebrated thirteenth Trouvere, Rutebouef, . . . we find the sorcerer Salatin conjuring the Devil in terms not belonging to any known language: Bagabi laca Lamac cahi achababe Karrelyos Lamac Lamec

Bachalyas Cabahagy Sabalyos Barryolos Lagoz atha cabbyolas Samahac et famyolas Harrahya." Ray Buckland once speculated that this may originally have been Hebrew (or Greek?), garbled in the usual manner by the composers of grimoires, which is a better explanation than Valiente's hope that it was an indigenous French chant.

In *The Roots of Witchcraft* (1973) Michael Harrison goes to great lengths to prove that both of these passages are Basque and evidence of the antiquity of European Witchcraft. He pointedly sidesteps considering Hebrew or Greek or even English, which is best shown by his discussion of the "witch words" mentioned by Gardner (1959, 75). "It is a pity that Dr. Gardner could not have let us know the meaning of 'Halch,' 'Dwale,' 'Warrick,' 'Ganch,' etc., for I could hardly begin to trace their origins in Basque unless I know the meanings these words bear among today's witches" (p. 174). It did not stop him from tracing the other meaningless words, but there would have been no reason to try to "find" these words in Basque when they are all good if obscure English words found in the *Oxford English Dictionary*.

The use of a black-handled knife called an "athame" might be said to be a trademark of Gardnerian Witchcraft. Knives have never played as central a role in British magic as wands or swords, so the presence of such a tool with its distinctive name would seem to be an important clue. There is no record in British folk tradition of such a knife before Gardner (who loved knives in general and wrote a book on the Malay *kris*), but there is in the grimoires. As Valiente notes, an "arthana" knife can be found in a 1572 *Clavicle of Solomon* in the British Museum. De Givry uses the term "arthame" as a generic name for a magical knife with the reference to a Solomonic manuscript *Le Secrets de Secrets*[8] (which is perhaps where Clark Ashton Smith got the term which he used with this spelling in his story "The Master of the Crabs," as Kelly notes, in an issue of *Weird Tales* in 1947).

Using Valiente's clue, I would suggest that the most likely source for the athame is from C. J. S. Thompson, *The Mysteries and Secrets of Magic* (1927), which cites Sloane ms. 3847: "The Worke of Salomon the Wise called his clavicle revealed by King Ptolomeus the Egyptian, written by H. G. on April 18th, 1572." Although the symbols on the Gardnerian knives came from the Mathers edition of the Key of Solomon, Thompson discusses the "arthany" or "arthana" itself. On page 235 a row of knives is shown among which are a "cuttelus niger" or black-handled knife, a "cuttelus alba" or white-handled knife, and the "arthany" which also has a *white* handle. The latter, he notes on page 237, is used for "cutting herbs and making the pen of the Art." Apparently Gardner based his usage of the black, white, and "boleen" knives on these, and switched the name "arthame" to the more witchy black-handled knife. On the derivation of the name itself, a plausible source (rather than Harrison's Basque or Arkon-Daraul's and Robert Graves' Arabic "Al-dhamme") might be the Old French *attame*, meaning "to cut" or "to pierce," which also can be found in the *Oxford English Dictionary*.

The other reason I have for choosing Thompson as the source is that it is here that "drawing down the moon" can be found. The often reproduced drawing of two Greek women, with sword (not knife) and wand first appears in Thompson on page 79. While this is very definitely not a British tradition, it is a well-known and rather sinister Greek practice, as can be seen from the second of the *Idyls of Theocritus* (Lang 1920, 11–19), and which has survived in modern Greek folk tradition.[9]

I would agree with Valiente that Gardner got the idea for the title "Book of Shadows" (which he never used in print) from Mir Bashir's account of a "Book of Shadows" found in Bombay in 1941, which he wrote about in an article in a magazine published by Gardner's own publisher Michael Houghton in 1949. " . . . The story ran that there was an ancient manuscript written on palm leaves, some thousands of years old in Sanskrit which tells you about your whole life by measuring your shadow" (Bashir 1949–1950, 154). It is interesting that the idea of the "measure" (which is also an old British practice) is not in the first-degree rite in *High Magic's Aid*, published that same year, but can be found (without any information on how it is to be done) in the subsequent versions of the degree. (Cardell 1964, sec. 2, 3; Kelly 1991, 56, 124).

The final contribution by Gardner is the choice of term "Wica" to indicate religious Witchcraft. While it is quite correct that "wicca" is the masculine form of the Anglo-Saxon term for "witch" (which is noted in *The Meaning of Witchcraft*), it had been out of popular usage for centuries before Gardner adopted his variant spelling to denote his sect. He apparently intended to make "witchcraft" mean "the craft of the wise" (as in "wise woman") as he dropped one *c* from the correct spelling to associate it with the root form *wis*, and modified the pronunciation to a hard *c*, as in *wicka*. Later writers innocently corrected the spelling, but kept the hard *c* sound rather than adopting the correct *ch* sound, as *wicha*.

Having discarded Gardner's attempted "wise" definition, Wiccans now tell us that a root meaning "to bend" is in some favorable way relevant to the use of the word when it was used to denote illicit practitioners of magic. This is philological non-sense. "Wicca," like "strega" or "hexe" was always pejorative. Also, as Edward Peters says, "the modern word 'witch' comes from wicca, but in an etymological sense only. [The early eleventh century] certainly had no conception of the future meaning of the feminine form of wicca" (1978, 168–169). It was only from the fifteenth century on that the word witch has meant the sort of individual that we associate with the persecutions, Halloween, and Walt Disney. Back when the terms "wicca" and "wicce" were in use, they simply meant a sorcerer or magician—a Cunningman or wise woman, in fact.

Modern Wicca is not a survival of an ancient tradition, but rather the modern syncretization of a number of old and new elements that never ever co-existed, much less were united, be-fore. A good example of this syncretic tendency are the eight yearly festivals. Far from being a single "traditional" pattern, they are a combination of the Celtic festivals of Samhain, Imbolc, Beltane, and Lughnasadh; the Anglo-Saxon Yule and the Michaelmas-like September feast; the traditional Midsummers (not part of either system); and, as Hutton says, the vernal equinox (rather than Lady Day, 25 March) is added for symmetry. There is no historic recognition of the vernal equinox, nor for the orderly eight-part system itself, which is a transparent modern conceit (Hutton 1992, 337).

IF NOT WICCA, WHAT?

The wise women and cunningmen were the real "wicca," the white witches in British history. Hundreds of documented examples sur-vive from the Middle Ages to the end of the nineteenth century. Some were no more than local amateurs with a single spell or charm, while others were literate professional practitioners with a working knowledge of astrology and ceremonial magic who at-tracted clients from near and far. Although the witches shared a number of traditional practices and beliefs, true white witchcraft was never systematized. White witchcraft was never a self-conscious Pagan faith opposed to Christianity but rather an accommodation of traditional magical practices within popular religion. The Cunningfolk's magic was practical, not theoretical, "solitary" rather than group oriented (although often collegial), more a trade or calling than a faith, and simultaneously traditional and continuously mutable. A very similar situation can be found for example in the practice of Obeah in the Bahamas. There an amalgam of European and African magic has resulted in a practical profession or trade of magic. Although Obeah retains a number of religious elements, it is not an organized cult or sect, as in the case of Santeria or Candomble (McCartney 1988, 264).

Just as there is no reason to recapitulate Aidan Kelly's thorough work on Wicca in this short piece, it is unnecessary to try to reproduce the masterful picture of British folk magic in Sir Keith Thomas's *Religion and the Decline of Magic* (1971). His chapters "Magical Healing," "Cunning Men and Popular Magic," and the section "Witchcraft" more than adequately demonstrate both the extent and practice of white witchcraft in early modern England. Eric Maple's discussion of the Cunningfolk in his *Dark World of Witches* (1961), the best popular account of the real British white witch in action, carries the story into the last century. Instead I would like to outline the most characteristic of these practices to create a composite picture of historic white witchcraft to set against the Gardnerian one.[11]

While the Cunningfolk used rituals, they were not the group-oriented circles of the legendary medieval "sabbat" or modern Wicca but the practical rites of the sorcerer or the priest. Some of their practices were survivors of what country people called "the old religion," i.e., the Catholic Church; others came from the Solomonic grimoires or from various innovations by individual practitioners. The deities invoked were not Pagan gods but the Christian Trinity and the saints, the planets (occasionally visualized as spiritual beings rather than satellites of the sun), the fairies, and assorted imps or devils.

Their dress was not a skyclad minimalism and seldom the quasi-monkish robes now associated with the occult. More often than not the Cunningfolk simply wore usual styles of the time, although it was not uncommon for some to adopt "scholars' robes" that denoted the professionalism of the cleric, doctor or lawyer, or some other distinctive articles of dress to impress their clients of their status. The setting for the consultation was often staged to impress as well. Charts, books, wands, dried crocodiles, and so forth were arranged to give the impression of magical authority. There was no call for nudity (or flagellation), and the occasional use of sex was incidental rather than central to the work at hand. There is little or no indication of any "Golden Bough"-like seasonal fertility rites.

The tools of the trade were not a standard set of ritual artefacts but simply regional British variations of the paraphernalia of sorcerers the world over. Scrying crystals, the divinatory "Bible and Key," and the sieve and shears were characteristically British as were wax, cloth or clay poppets; charms written on vellum, paper, or metal; divining or "Mosaical" rods; witch bottles and swords, wands and knives (not called athames). All sorts of animals (including human) parts, as well as vegetable, cloth, glass, pottery, metal, or mineral fragments were employed in "receipts" for magical work.[12]

The Cunningfolk had no unifying Book of Shadows but they did use many books, even if only for effect when they themselves were illiterate. Manuscript grimoires, miscellaneous collections of charms, books of formulae, astrological and pseudo-astrological handbooks, and works on occult subjects were a major means of transmitting magical knowledge among English white witches. These not only passed ideas between higher and lower culture, but provided a legitimating aura of learning in the shadowy underworld of the witch and wizard.

Ritual initiations after the Wiccan, Masonic, or secret society pattern were unknown. Instead some acted as apprentices to established Cunningfolk while others were self-taught in the traditions of the countryside. In this way the independent folk tradition was successfully maintained until the end of the nineteenth century. The real death of the old tradition was not the result of a bourgeois revolution in rationalism but rather the defection of the clientele to new and more modern, exotic forms of the same practices by Mesmerists, spiritualists, quacks, and occultists.

Astrological patterns and agricultural cycles governed traditional magic rather than a system of astronomical observances. Lucky days and propitious moments identified through traditional lists of "Egyptian Days" and astrological calculations determined the time for magic. The moon's cycles were more important than annual anniversaries, although May Eve, Midsummers', and All Hallows' Eve retained their traditional importance.

Neither devotion to a god and goddess, nor the social cohesion of group activity inspired traditional magical practices. It was instead the needs and desires of clients for healing, detection of theft, treasure hunting, fortunetelling, helping the "overlooked," removing curses, or charms for luck which motivated the activities of the Cunningfolk.

Public opinion about the Cunningfolk was ambiguous, to say the least. The Puritans in fact deemed the white witches worse

than the black satanic variety, as the latter were perceptably evil
while the white witches might easily fool a Christian into a dam-
nable relationship by appearing beneficent and actually providing
a useful service. Cunning women, wise men, blessers, conjurors,
and currens (a few of the many names for the white witches) were
regularly veiled from the pulpit and secretly supported by the
populace—unless of course the white witch did something to earn
the enmity of his or her neighbors. While both sexes were represented in the trade, the most eminent of the white witches were
usually men. The women nearly always labored under a more mixed
reputation and were more liable to be suspected of (and persecuted
for) black as well as white magic.[13]

A good example of this dangerous ambiguity can be seen in
the case of Ann Bodenham in 1653. She had been a servant and
student of the notorious Dr. Lambe in the 1620s, and set up her
own practice in Fisherton Anger (near Salisbury) after he was beaten
to death by a London mob in 1628. Apparently she had acted as a
wise woman for the district for years. Edmund Bower wrote that
she taught divers young children to read, was much addicted to
Popery (or the superstition of the "Old Religion"), and lucky and
unlucky days. "She was one that would undertake to cure almost
any disease, which she did mostly by charms and spells" (1653, 1).
Her downfall occurred at age eighty when she was accused of
witchcraft by Anne Stiles, servant to Richard Goddard. Stiles had
lost a silver spoon of her master's, and went to Bodenham to detect
its whereabouts. Bodenham told Stiles that she knew why she came,
but "as the wind didn't blow, nor the sun shine nor Jupiter appear,
so she could not help her" (p. 2).

Nevertheless, when Goddard lost some gold pieces Stiles went
again. This time the wise woman demanded seven shillings. She
opened three books with pictures in them, laying a green glass on
one of the pages, and, holding the book up to the sun, asked the
maid to look into it. She thereupon saw some people doing something in her master's house. Stiles accepted a charm made from a
yellow powder made into a cross in a piece of paper for Mr. Goddard.
It was on a third visit that Bodenham used the glass and book and
some incense to conjure up some imps ("in the likeness of ragged
boys") in a magical circle. This was too much for Stiles and the
Goddards, who took her to the law, saying she had impelled the
maid to sign a "Devil's book" (held by a Mr. Withers) and be-
witched her. Bodenham was tried and hung for her magic, with
which she had attempted too effectively to impress the credulous

Stiles. It was a fine line obviously between acceptable and unacceptable magic and poor Bodenham was unfortunate enough to upset her nervous clients (Bower 1653, 2–10).

Even so, wise women, such as Hannah Green, the "Ling Bob witch" of Yeadon, Yorkshire, might have quite successful careers. She inherited her mother's practice and flourished for forty years, leaving an estate of a thousand pounds at her death on 12 May 1810. She was even able to threaten to call the law on the editor of the *Leeds Mercury*, who had prematurely announced her death on 17 May 1806, without triggering any difficulties (Smith 1889, 271).

Three Cunningmen who flourished in or after the Age of Reason—"Auld" John Wrightson of Stokesky, Yorkshire; James ("Cunning") Murrell of Hadleigh, Essex; and Big Johnnie Bracken of Barnton, Lancashire—typify the trade in both its traditional strength and its decline. There is only room for the barest outlines of their careers here, but I would encourage interested readers to search out the references for a fuller picture of these representative white witches. Their stories will provide a far more accurate impression of the real English magical tradition than any of the post-Gardnerian corpus.

The Wiseman of Stokesky (Yorkshire), John Wrightson, flourished in the second half of the eighteenth century. Rev. Atkinson quotes an anonymous writer in 1819 that the wise men " . . . are believed to possess the most extraordinary power in remedying all diseases incidental to the brute creation, as well as the human race; to discover lost or stolen property, and to fortell future events" (1891, 14). The writer was quite disparaging in the accepted rationalist manner of "Au'd Wreeghtson" as a greedy fraud, but Atkinson characterizes this as "gratuitous misrepresentation." Respected informants who had known Wrightson were impresssed by his shrewd skill and honest judgment, and as frugal North Country men, the value of his services. When one John Unthank visited Wrightson about a suffering bullock, he found the Wise Man "seated in his consulting room, dressed in some sort of long robe or gown, girded round him with a noticeable girdle, and a strange-looking head covering on. These were some of the accustomed paraphernalia of the character assumed and its pretensions—a skull, a globe, some mysterious-looking preparations, dried herbs, etc., etc." (p. 15). Before the client could get his bearings, however, the wizard further astounded him by knowing exactly what his errand was, with great detail about the byre and situation of "Tommy Frank's black beast." He then told him that nothing could be done, that the animal would die anyways, and that if they "opened" the carcass, they would find a certain abnormality. Everything occurred as the Wiseman had predicted. (p. 19).

All of this fits the traditional pattern of the wise man. His apparent prescience (or clairvoyance), his confident assessment of the situation, and the uncanny aura around him and his trade are all part of the picture. Well-remembered successes that fit the pattern of belief overshadowed the failures until the whole trade fell into disrepute, not only with the educated but with the general public, as we shall see in our last example.

"Cunning" (James) Murrell (1780–1860), a shoemaker of Hadleigh, Essex, is a particularly good example of an accomplished Cunningman both because of the breadth of his expertise and for the relative wealth of surviving information about him. Murrell's practice ranged across the whole spectrum of white witchcraft, from healing and detection to defeating the malice of black witchcraft and the evil eye. He was born in Rochford, Essex, and was fortunate enough to have some schooling which he put to good use in his occult career. He also worked for a time as a chemist's stillman in London, which was presumably useful in his work as a healer. Murrell was a competent astrologer, herbalist, charmer, restorer of lost property, and antagonist of "black witches." He was particularly famous for his iron "witch bottles" which may have been considered a technological advance on the older earthenware or glass varieties. Stories surrounding his occult reputation such as his magical powers of flight or clairvoyance in the matter of theft recapitulate the lore of the Cunningfolk from centuries before. Years after his death, his trunk of books and manuscripts was examined by Arthur Morrison, who found works on conjuration, herbalism, and astrology Murrell had copied or inherited dating back to the seventeenth century. There were as well letters from clients from as far away as London, nativities, charms, geomantic exercises, and local intelligence that might be of use in consultations. This treasure trove of documentation was tragically destroyed in 1956 (Morrison 1900; Maple 1960).[15]

In "Big Johnnie" Bracken of Rose Hill, Barnton, Lancashire, we have an example of the sort of illiterate traditional country wizard who could serve as a portrait of his contemporary, the now-notorious George Pickingill (of which more later). Where Wrightson and Murrell were luminaries in their chosen profession, poor Johnnie was not only a more modest practitioner, but he outlived the cultural viability of his trade. Consequently in his old age he suffered the ridicule and jesting of a community no longer committed to the old ways. Big Johnnie and his wife "Tuffee" (toffee) Ann, who acted as the local shopkeeper and midwife, lived a precarious existence in the 1880s. Being illiterate, Johnnie had no use for the bookish arts of astrology or geomancy. Instead he relied on an egg-shaped crystal for his insight into the future husbands of inquiring girls, the whereabouts of wandering children (or husbands), and the location of stolen objects. Because of the "witchcraft" laws concerning payment for alleged magical services, Johnnie was careful to say that he did not charge for his skill while making it perfectly clear that a suitable gratuity was unquestionably called for. Once when an ingenuous (or willfully dense) client accepted his "Aw mak no charge" at face value, Johnnie yelled after her, "Dosto y'er, no luck follow thee, withersoiver thou gooas" (Fox 1902).

Towards the end of his life, he relied on the trade of those from outside Barnton for his livelihood. A six-foot-tall shabby eccentric with notoriously big feet, he became a figure of fun with the locals. His habit of wearing a bedraggled fur cap outdoors and a dirty red skullcap at home gave him the nickname of "Owd Redcap" among the local children, which he fiercely resented. He also suffered at the pranks of the local men, who on one occasion stole his watch and hid it in his lunch. When he was unable to discern its whereabouts, it greatly diminished his local reputation. Squalid and pinched as his career had become, Johnnie nevertheless retained the pride, independence, and shrewdness of the old Cunningfolk to the last as he shuffled about leaning on a stick carved with twining serpents, like Aleister Crowley's (Fox 1902). It was men and women like him, Bodenham, Wrightson, Green, and Murrell who were the real white witches of history.

WICCA: THE NEW RELIGION

When Gardner dropped his revelatory bombshell in *Witchcraft Today* with the implication that Wicca was or had been a pervasive secret sect in the English countryside, he was a member of the Folklore Society. I was able to ask Katherine Briggs, who remembered the event, about the impact of his book and his article in *Folklore* (private communication, 29 October 1973). The members of Folklore Society apparently quickly compared notes and, as none of them had ever found any indication of such a sect with their thorough knowledge of their own various regional areas, they dismissed his assertions. Gardner, although recognized as possessing a wide if miscellaneous knowledge of anthropological literature, was notorious as a flamboyant crank who would bring imposing knives to meetings (which intimidated some people) and Miss Briggs was rather sharp about his influence on "young people." She was firm in her opinion that it was all "moonshine."

Here we come to the central paradox for the alleged "hereditary traditions." If religious Witchcraft was as old and widespread as would be necessary for even a minority of the English and American claimants to have been connected with families with such initiatory practices, then it is inconceivable that their beliefs and symbols would have no echo in the historical record which contains so many other Pagan and magical practices and symbols (Kelly 1991, xix). On the other hand, if traditional or "hereditary" Wicca was so small and secret as to escape *any* detection (and any professional historian will recognize how ephemeral, insignificant, and localized a sect would have to be to escape all notice), then it is hardly possible that it could have been of any importance before Gardner and his successors blithely laid the whole thing open to the world. Hutton and Kelly show quite convincingly that this was the case.

I agree with Aidan Kelly that Gardner (or, less likely, an anonymous "proto-Gardner") was indirectly responsible for just about all modern witch activity. Some groups such as the Gardnerians and the Alexandrians are admittedly direct derivatives from his work. Other groups, either discerning that the Old Man had (embarrassingly) feet of clay or desiring to modify his teachings, chose to disavow him as soon as they could and build independent traditions while retaining what they liked. It is revealing, for example, that no "hereditary" rivals to Gardner (as opposed to jealous occultists such as Charles Cardell)[16] publicly challenged Gardner in his lifetime.

The most exotic of these attempts to depose Gerald Gardner was an extravagant hoax which first surfaced shortly after his death in February 1964. The gist of the matter was that the real witch tradition could be traced not to Gardner but rather to an Essex Cunning Man named George Pickingill who died in 1909. I first read about the Pickingill claim in the *Wiccan* 42 (a mimeographed newsletter) in 1975. It contained a preposterous ahistorical muddle purporting to connect Pickingill to practically every major nineteenth-century occultist, and implied that Pickingill and Hargreave Jennings were responsible for forging the cipher manuscripts that formed the basis for the Golden Dawn! On getting the preceding two

issues of *Wiccan*, I found that it had begun on a slightly more
plausible note by questioning Crowley's connection with Gardner's
rituals, but then it had spun off on a similar fantasy about Pickingill
and his alleged control over nine hereditary covens that were apparently scattered over most of southern England. The writer had
had a good scheme for a plausible if fraudulent attribution of "hereditary" Wicca to an actual cunningman rather than Gardner, but
had spoiled it by overreaching.

I had read of Pickingill (or Pickingale) in Eric Maple's *Dark
World of Witches* (1961) and contacted him to see what he might
know about this (private communication, 29 December 1975). He
told me the earliest appearance of the claim was in "The News of
the World" in 1963 or 1964, but interest soon subsided. It was his
opinion that people associated with Doreen Valiente were behind
it, though I would doubt that, as she is one of the most honest of
commentators on the subject. He assured me that he had talked
with old people who remembered Pickingill and knew his reputation at first hand, and that the whole idea was preposterous.[17]
Pickingill was a real old Cunning man, one of the last of the type,
but quite illiterate and in his later years more interested in caging
beer and getting a rise out of people than anything else. He was
very much a practicing sorcerer, but the claim that he *governed*
nine covens (Eric said the number in question was nine individual
witches) was backwards. In traditional folk magic, it is one of the
regular claims of the white witch that she or he knows of and can
constrain a great number of black witches since it is a major part of
their trade to repair or prevent evil witchcraft. The idea that Pickingill
was either a witch king or a leading occultist with international
connections was out of the question. Pickingill apparently received
some local notoriety in the folklore boom at the end of the century. It was Eric's opinion that whoever invented all of this clap-
trap had gotten the idea from his book, and had expanded the
theme considerably to make an old hedge wizard into some sort of
occult *Ubermensch*.[18]

Shrewder independence movements were careful to excise those
elements which would easily connect them with Gardner (such as
scourging, the use of the titles "high priest" and "high priestess,"
the emphasis on nudity and so forth), and anything else they suspected was anachronistic. Some became more bourgeois by adopting robes and downplaying the sexual element (at least publicly)
while others swung in the opposite direction by increasing the

orgiastic elements and adding initiations with severe whippings and wooden dildos, as is shown in the Frost's School of Wicca or in Francis King's discoveries about a Midland group in *Sexuality, Magic and Perversion* (1972, 3–9, 163–168).[19]

Still others, which had began quite independently, were swept up by the sheer popular attraction of the new Goddess movement and adopted many of its practices and tenets while claiming independence. They seem to have made good use of the description of the North African Dhulqarneni cult in Arkon Daraul's *Secret Societies* (1962) with its forked staff *(stang)* and all. It is, as Valiente notes, a particularly suitable model for modern Wicca, even though there is no evidence that such a sect ever reached Britain. However, any "wiccan" group which employs the use of athames, tripartite ritual initiations, "draws down the moon," or any of the other paraphernalia of Gardnerian Wicca owes a debt to the Old Man.

Wicca is what Eric Hobsbawm calls "an invented tradition." It was formulated in response to the psychic needs of modern people cut off from older traditions by cultural repression, industrialization, education, loss of historic community (how many people still live where their great-grandparents did?), and separation from nature. It offers a constructive balance to our culture by giving the Feminine a more than equal role in its system. It also follows the romantic and Celtic revival movements in offering an alternative to both patriarchal Christianity and intellectual rationalism. While it borrows heavily from the past, it is an unprecedented synthesis of concepts particularly suited to our own times.

Wicca has no need of its past pious fictions such as "the Witch Party Line" as social legitimacy and acceptance will come from its own merits, rather than alleged historical genealogies. I find it very irritating that the old fiction asserted by so-called "hereditary" or "traditional" or "Celtic" covens that they have been practicing Wicca or something very like it since time immemorial is still current. The implied superiority to the more honest groups who recognize their debt to Gardner, as well as to the legitimate Dianic groups which owe their existence to Z. Budapest and others, is both divisive and, to a historian, dishonest. I realize that many people received the "Witch Party Line" from their original "teachers" at face value and are reluctant to let it go. Yet if Wicca is ever to achieve social acceptance, it must be prepared to relinquish myths which do little but offer Wicca's opponents an excuse by which to deny public recognition.

NOTES

1. This is supported by Jack Bracelin (or rather Idris Shah), who notes that it was while Crowley was at Oxford, in *Gerald Gardner: Witch* (1960, 174).

2. The erroneous statement in the same book that Gardner had hired Crowley to write "elaborate rituals" for his cult can be attributed to a remark by Crowley's patron Gerald Yorke, whom King had no reason to doubt.

3. Freemasonry contributed, either directly or through the various occult orders such as the Soc. Ros., the G∴D∴ & the O∴T∴O∴ (of which Gardner was a member) which were in form Masonic offshoots: the system of three initiatory degrees, the sharp point on the breast at entry, the form of the oath, "neither bound nor free," the hoodwink, the cabletow, and the terms "working tools," the "charge," the "Craft," and "the five[fold] points of fellowship." The "Oh, do not tell the Priest, &c." rhyme in the May Eve ritual is borrowed from Kipling's *Puck of Pook's Hill*, hence Gardner's odd defensive meaning of Kipling in *Witchcraft Today* (p. 47). There are a number of other borrowings from occult literature, such as Doreen Valiente's adaptation of the Charge from Leland's *Aradia*, the "Great God Karnayna [Pan], return to Earth again," from Dion Fortune's *Moon Magic* (1956, 176), or the selection beginning "Hail Aradia [Tyche]! From the Amalthean Horn . . . " which is the reworked first stanza from Aleister Crowley's poem "La Fortune" in his *Complete Works* (1905) New York: Gordon Press, 1974, vol. 3, p. 120; and other assorted quotes from Crowley, as Kelly notes.

4. In *A Goddess Arrives*, red-headed Dayonis inadvertently inspires the triumph of a cult of Astoreth in Paphos which includes ritual nudity and bloodless sacrifice. Otherwise, however, there is nothing which would presage the creation of Wicca except an ambiguous mention of a "great rite" on p. 197.

5. Kenyon's index would appear to outline a Wiccan perspective (1. Witchcraft—The Universal Faith; 2. The Nature Cult; 3. The Gospel of the Witches [Aradia]; 4. The First Witch Doctrine: Transmutation; 5. The Initiation of a Witch, etc.) but it is still fixed in the older negative beliefs on the subject.

6. Aiden Kelly does offer some possible predecessors to the New Forest/Gardnerian pattern in *Crafting the Art of Magic: Book 1* (1991, 21–25). I agree with his opinion on the Victor Anderson group and the Gundella covens which could have been easily developed independently. The Randolph material points in quite a different, less benign direction, but would appear to be a real folk tradition (perhaps borrowing from the less savory aspects of hoodoo?) in which the witch myths inspired emulation, as in the

case of Satanism where belief preceded practice. I must demur in the case of Rhea W., however. The parallels with Wicca are too great for my credulity, and the evidence too sparse.

7. *Form* 1, no. 2 (November/December 1921): 62, reprinted in *The Occult Review* (April 1926): 231. *Form* was edited by A. O. Spare, and had a number of occult articles in it.

8. Arsenal ms. no. 2350.

9. "There was an old Greek saying that 'the witch who draws down the moon finally draws it down on herself.' . . . It was generally held that of all charms one of the most dangerous was 'drawing down the moon'—so dangerous in fact that the magician deemed it wise to arm himself in advance with a protective counter-charm against the very power whom he was about to invoke." (Smith 1915, 283).

10. Incidentally, the term "skyclad" Gardner himself credits to an Indian source (1954, 149).

11. For further reading on the Cunningfolk in addition to those articles cited further on and in the references, the following are among the more useful.

Magical formulae: W. Sparrow Simpson, "On a Seventeenth Century Roll Containing Prayers and Magical Signs . . . " *Journal British Archaeological Assoc.* 40 (1884): 297–332; Moses Gaster, "English Charms of the Seventeenth Century" [Cod. Gaster, No. 1562] *Folklore* 21 (1910): 375–378; A. R. Wright, "Seventeenth Century Cures and Cures" [from John Durant, *Art and Nature Joyn Hand in Hand* . . . , 1697] *Folklore* 23 (1912): 230–236, 490–497.

British Cunningfolk: Mary L. Lewes, "The Wizards of Cwrt-Y-Cadno" [John and Henry Harries] *Occult Review* 40 (July 1924): 17–24; Christopher Marlowe, "A White Wizard" [Fiddler Fynes, the Wiseman of Louth] *Legends of the Fenland People* (London: Cecil Palmer, 1926), pp. 213–221: W. Harbutt Dawson, "Timothy Crowther of Skipton" *History of Skipton (West Riding, Yorks).* (London: Simpkin, Marshall, 1882), pp. 390–394 (also on Crowther, see John Wesley's *Journal* Standard ed. 1913 vol. 4 [July 1761], p. 472); F. J. Pope, "A Conjuror or Cunning Man of the 17th Century" *British Archivist* 1, no. 18 (Aug. 1914): 145–147; *The Severall Notorious and Lewd Cousinages of John West and Alice West, Falsely Called the King and Queene of the Fayries.* London: Edward Marchant, 1613; E. A. Rawlence, "Folklore and Superstitions Still Obtaining in Dorset" *Proc. of the Dorset Natural History and Antiquarian Field Club* 35 (1914): 81–87; *The Character of a Quack-Astrologer* . . . (London, 1673).

A treasure trove of primary documents concerning the Cunningfolk at the beginning of the nineteenth century can be found in "The Wonderful Magical Scrapbook 1450–1850" in the Harry Price Collections at Goldsmith's Library, University of London.

The transference of the traditional practices of Cunningfolk to American include the German Pietist traditions in Pennsylvania-Dutch country, the African-American traditions in Voodoo, and the traditional British practices in New England and elsewhere. Herbert Leventhal, *In the Shadow of the Enlightenment* (New York, 1976); John Demos, *Entertaining Satan* (New York: Oxford, 1982); Richard Godbeer, *The Devil's Domain: Magic and Religion in Early New England* (Cambridge: Cambridge University Press, 1992); David Hall, *Worlds of Wonder, Days of Judgement* (New York: Knopf, 1989) have early New England material. A good source for later New England Cunningfolk is John G. Whittier, *The Supernaturalism of New England*, Edward Wagenknecht, ed. (Norman: University of Oklahoma Press, 1969).

12. For example, "Kilnsey Nan," of Wharftdale, York, told the future with a pack of cards, a divining rod, and a guinea pig (Lofthouse 1976, 78).

13. Consider Nanny Morgan, the Witch of Westwood Common (near Much Wenlock, Shropshire), who was murdered at age sixty-nine on 12 September 1857. She learned her trade from gypsies and had been consulted by both servant girls and respectable women for miles around. She was often paid in jewelry, when cash was not available, and a considerable hoard was discovered after her death (Burne 1883, 161).

14. See also William Brockie, *Legends and Superstitions of the County of Durham* (Sutherland, 1886), pp. 21–25; Richard Blakeborough, *Wit, Character, Folklore and Customs of the North Riding of Yorkshire* (Saltburn by the Sea: W. Rapp and Sons, 1911), pp. 180–185.

15. Morrison wrote an interesting novel using stories about Murrell called *Cunning Murrell* (1900), which was reprinted by the Boydell Press (PO Box 24, Ipswich, Essex IP1 1JJ), in 1977.

16. Cardell published a mean-spirited exposé of Gardner, "Rex Nemorensis" (and printed the entire *Book of Shadows*) (1964b). He apparently had ambitions of creating his own witch organization.

17. Ronald Hutton made a similar survey; see 1992, 332.

18. Claims such as, "It is no exaggeration that George Pickingill's machinations materially influenced the founding of two 'Rosicrucian' orders—the Rosicrucian Society in England and the Hermetic Order of the Golden Dawn" or "Old George was acknowledged as the world's greatest living authority on Witchcraft, Satanism, and Black Magic. He was consulted by occultists of every hue and tradition [and never mentioned by any of these notoriously prolific sorts in print!]. They came by hundreds from all over England, Europe and even America," reveal the crank nature of the whole body of nonsense. The collected letters from the *Wiccan* and the *Cauldron* magazines, attributed to someone calling himself "Lugh,"

have been reprinted in booklet form in England and America, the latter edition being by Taray Publications, Charlottesville, Vir., 1984.

19. I suspect by the way that the Frosts are quite likely to have sincerely followed up on an English (or Welsh) offshoot which had diverged from Gardner in the way the anonymous coven cited by King did.

REFERENCES

Atkinson, Rev. J. C. 1891. *Forty Years in a Moorland Parish*. London: Macmillan.

Bashir, Mir. 1949–1950. "The Book of Shadows." *The Occult Observer* 1, nos. 3 and 4.

Bower, Edmund. 1653. *Dr. Lambe Revived, or Witchcraft Condemned in Ann Bodenham* . . . London: Richard Best and John Place.

Burne, Charlotte. 1883. *Shropshire Folk-lore*. London: Trubner.

Cardell. 1964a. *Book of Shadows*.

———. 1964b. *Witch*. Clarkwood, Surrey: Dumblecott Magick Productions.

Daraul, Arkon. 1962. *Secret Societies*.

Fox, Arthur W. 1902. "The Old Fortune Teller." *Papers of the Manchester Literary Club* 28: 34–56.

Gardner, Gerald. 1939. *A Goddess Arrives*. London: Arthur S. Stockwell, Ltd.

———. *High Magic's Aid*.

———. *Witchcraft Today*.

———. 1959. *The Meaning of Witchcraft*. London: Aquarian.

Graves, Robert. *White Goddess*.

Harrison, Michael. 1973. *The Roots of Witchcraft*. London: Muller.

Hutton, Ronald. 1991. *The Pagan Religions of the Ancient British Isles*. Oxford: Blackwell.

Kelly, Aidan. 1991. *Crafting the Art of Magic*.

Kenyon, Theda. 1929. *Witches Still Live*.

King, Francis. 1970. *Ritual Magic in England*. London: Neville Spearman.

———. 1972. *Sexuality, Magic and Perversion*. New York: Citadel.

Kittredge, George Lyman. 1929. *Witchcraft in Old and New England*.

Lang, Andrew, ed. 1920. *Theocritus, Bion and Moschus*. London: Macmillan.

Leland. 1899. *Aradia.*

Leland, Charles G. 1963. *Etruscan Magic and Occult Remedies.* London: New York University Books.

Lofthouse, Jessica. 1976. *North Country Folklore.* London: Robert Hale.

Maple, Eric. 1961. "Cunning Murrell." *Folklore* 71 (March 1960): 37–43.

———. 1961. *Dark World of Witches.*

McCartney, Timothy. 1988. "Obeah, Superstition and Folklore." In *Insight Guides: Bahamas.* Singapore: APA Publications.

Morrison, Arthur. 1900. "A Wizard of Yesteryear." *The Strand Magazine* 20 (October 1900): 433–442.

Murray, Margaret. 1921. *The Witch-cult in Western Europe.*

Parson, Jack. 1979. *Magick, Gnosticism and the Witchcraft.* Quebec: 93 Publishing.

Peters, Edward. 1978. *The Magician, the Witch and the Law.* Philadelphia: University of Pennsylvania.

Seymour, Col. C. R. F. 1968. "The Old Religion—A Study in the Symbolism of the Moon Mysteries." In *The New Dimensions Red Book*, edited by Basil Wilby, 47–83.

Shah, Idris. 1960. *Gerald Gardner: Witch.* London: Octagon.

Smith, Kirby Flower. 1915. "Magic (Greek and Roman)." In *Encyclopaedia of Religion and Ethics*, vol. 8, edited by James Hastings. New York: Scribner's.

Smith, William. 1889. *Old Yorkshire.* London: Longmans, Green.

Thomas, Sir Keith. 1971. *Religion and the Decline of Magic.*

Thompson, C. J. S. 1927. *The Mysteries and Secrets of Magic.*

Valiente, Doreen. 1961. *Where Witchcraft Lives.*

———. 1973. *An ABC of Witchcraft Past and Present.* New York: St. Martin's Press.

9

THE RECONSTRUCTION OF THE ÁSATRÚ AND ODINIST TRADITIONS

Jeffrey Kaplan

Cattle die, kinsmen die,
onesself dies the same;
but words of praise never die
for those of great renown.   —Hávámál 76

THE RECONSTRUCTED NORSE/GERMANIC tradition is more easily defined than differentiated. The primary sociological factor that best serves to separate the closely linked American Ásatrú and Odinist communities—the emphasis on racial mysticism and, in its most extreme manifestation, pronounced neo-Nazi sympathies—itself offers no easily demarcated borders. Yet the groups, despite their marked affinities, are not the same, and differentiation is important. What follows then, is an admittedly imperfect attempt to differentiate these groups in both theological and sociological terms. The analysis assumes with the advantage of hindsight that the inherent tensions between Odinists and Ásatrúers as defined below were present in the movement from its inception, and it is therefore possible to consider the movements, or perhaps the opposing factions of a single movement, in isolation. What follows then is an examination of the historical development of each of the contending belief structures.

ODINISM

Odinism as it is presently understood appeared first. Although its precise origins are far from clear, its inspiration may have centered in the profound social and political crises which engulfed Germany in the chaotic period of the Weimar Republic. In this time of intermingled chaos and decadence, wandering groups of displaced or simply disillusioned German youth, known collectively as the German Youth movement began, perhaps as a lark, perhaps with more serious intent, to make sacrifices to Wotan. Many of these young people would, in the Nazi era, give up their wanderings for the greater excitement of helping to build the Third Reich with Adolf Hitler's assent to power (Jung 1964, 180). A fascinating, if eccentric, literature has grown up around the mystical endeavors of leading figures in the Nazi party, of which the revival of pre-Christian religious forms was but one manifestation (see, for example, Sklar 1977 and Ravenscroft 1982).

At the same time Hitler was in the process of consolidating his early power, the occult aspects of the Third Reich were gaining the attention of mystics outside of Germany. One such, an eccentric Australian named Alexander Rud Mills, was an unabashed Nazi sympathizer and a believer in a form of racial mysticism which posited the pre-Christian Anglo-Saxon society as the golden age of the British people. Mills in the 1930s began to turn his dreams towards the reconstruction of that perfect time in this degenerate age. Mills's diagnosis held that the contemporary malady of civilization was due to the malign influence of the Jews, and as Christianity was built on the foundation of the vile Middle Eastern Abrahamic cult, it too had to be severed from the soul of the descendants of the Anglo-Saxon race as quickly and surely as one would excise a cancer. Out of this process of reasoning came Mills's first and most influential book: *The Odinist Religion: Overcoming Jewish Christianity* (1930). *The Odinist Religion* was the first of a number of writings—mostly in tract form—that Mills would turn out for the next several decades, but it is the most revealing of the gradual process through which he was able to disengage his thought from the deeply ingrained paradigms of the dominant Christian culture and assume, step by step, an idealized Pagan philosophy (see Mills 1957). In this text, however, the names Odin, Thor, and on occasion Loki are invoked merely as a literary device to anthropomorphize facets of the Christian God in the name of race and nationalism. *The Odinist Religion* is in reality a Manichaean treatise deeply wedded to a dualist world view which offers an imagined history in which Europe is the true birthplace of civilization from whence white men descended from a common ancestor (named either George or Sigge) who is posited as the culture bearer to the world and whose progeny are held to have built the Egyptian pyramids and founded empires (1930, 31). To this imagined history and theft of culture motif, Mills adds the prominent conspiracy scenarios of the day from Judaism to Freemasonry, dire warnings against usury and miscegenation, and finally, as if to add to the cultural confusion, the claim that Christ did not die on the cross (pp. 66–67).[11]

Mills would win few converts to his Anglecyn (later Anglican!) Church of Odin, but his writings would be kept alive, more as a curiosity than anything else, in the world of the right wing publishing houses.[2] It was in this milieu that Mills would be discovered by Else Christensen and her late husband in the early 1960s, during the course of reading such right wing staples as Yockey's *Imperium* and Spengler's *Decline of the West*. But it was Mills who would inspire the Christensens to form the nucleus of the organization which would, after the death of Else's husband, become in 1971 the Odinist Fellowship in Crystal River, Florida:

> When confronted with Rud Mills' ideas and the political atmosphere of the time, I suppose that I finally realized that the problems were more of a spiritual nature than political. We chose the Scandinavian mythology as, at the time, the animosity between Anglo Saxons and Teutons (aftermath of WWII) was still lingering; Scandinavian was neutral; a rational choice, not because I'm Danish. (Interview with Christensen, 27 November 1992)

Mrs. Christensen is said to have remained so enamored with Mills's work that she has obtained a complete collection of A. Rud Mills's writings and effects, and it seems clear from this research that a primary area of differentiation between Odinists and Ásatrúers is a knowledge of Mills. From the inspiration that Mills provided to the Christensens, and through the dissemination of Mills's thought in the pages of Else Christensen's publication, *The Odinist*,[3] flow other primary differentiating factors: far greater contact with the other sectors of the "White Supremacist constellation" (Barkun 1989) than the Ásatrú adherents would find palatable; a conspiratorial view of history; a pronounced warrior ethic which emphasizes the desire to one day strike back in some form at the dominant culture for its perceived injustices; a strongly racialist strain of thought which verges easily and often into racial mysticism; and perhaps most telling of all, a reductionist concentration on reviving an idealized form of the tribal ethical values of the Germanic

and Norse (read Viking) peoples in place of the long and complex
process of reconstructing these golden age religious, communal,
and magical practices in the context of the modern world (which
is in fact the ambitious task set before the Ásatrúer).[4]

The heady combination of National Socialism, the occult,
the Viking mystique, and the quest for community proved irresistible to other long-standing elements of the "white supremacist
constellation" as well. Of these, perhaps most revealing of the
processes by which these racialist adherents seek to exploit the
Norse/Germanic revival are the activities of George Dietz. Dietz
is a German immigrant and long-time figure in American neo-
Nazi circles whose primary income appears to be derived from the
sale of anti-Semitic and racist literature through his Liberty Bell
Publications (Anti-Defamation League of the B'nai B'rith 1988,
80–81). Dietz took note of the revival of Odinist groups around
the United States and, through one of his younger associates, Ron
Hand, created the Odinist Study Group, ostensibly as a front operation for his own National Socialist (NS) movement. Hand,
operating under the name Reinhold Dunkel in NS circles and under
his own in Odinist affairs, enjoyed complete autonomy as leader of
the group, although in the Byzantine world of American National
Socialism, independence is a relative term.

The extent of George Dietz's knowledge of the Odinist revival is in some doubt. He clearly knew of Else Christensen, but
whether he knew much more is questionable.[5] The original plan
appears to have been to gather a list of local Odinist groups and
to infiltrate them, turning them gradually towards National Socialism. This plan could not be carried out as George Dietz had decided to sell his mailing list, of which the Odinist Study Group
(OSG) was a part, to other groups. This had the ironic effect of
bringing the OSG to life. That life consisted of, in effect, a mail
order kindred, in which the inclusion of the OSG's address in
certain right wing lists—especially those of Joseph Dilys in Chicago—and word of mouth—brought in a number of seekers from
across the country, many of them in the prisons.[6] Now losing interest in Odinism, Hand directs letters to the OSG to Mike Murray
of the Ásatrú Alliance (conversation with Hand, 12 September 1992).[6]

ÁSATRÚ

The organizational history of the Ásatrú movement is relatively
straightforward, but the movement itself is as difficult to define as

it is to trace the complex paths which led the members of the community to embrace Ásatrú. The term Ásatrú itself is an Icelandic word which means "belief in the Æsir" (Gamlinginn 1991, 17; Flowers 1981, 279 n. 2), a fitting misnomer for a community which embraces belief in the Vanir (elemental gods) and indeed in a host of lesser *wights* (beings).

It is clear from this research that the ranks of Ásatrúers existed long before the appearance of an organized Ásatrú community. The testimonies are many, but taken together, these tend to fall in several categories. Most common are what could be called the awakening of childhood memories. In the 1950s and 1960s, storybook adaptations of Norse mythology, often beautifully illustrated, were popular gifts for young boys. Several present-day Ásatrúers report gaining an interest in the Northern Way from this source which has yet to abate. KveldúlfR Gundarsson can still recall the title of such a work was *Norse Gods and Giants* by Ingri and Edgar Parin d'Aulaire. He obtained it at the age of six for the then princely sum of $6.95 (interview with Gundarsson, January 1993). Edred Thorsson too recalls a childhood fascination with Germanic myth and folklore; an interest which soon faded, but was rekindled in the early 1970s following a stay in Germany and German-language training (interview with Thorsson, 20 September 1992). James Chisholm, the former steersman of the Ring of Troth, "developed a penchant for reading Greek mythology books" at the age of nine, and switched to Norse mythology at his father's suggestion (interview with Chisholm, 17 November 1992). Robert Stine, at the strong insistence of his mother, was given the freedom to choose his own religious path, and would discover Norse mythology at a young age in the pages of an early 1960s edition of Collier's Encyclopedia (interview with Stine, 23–24 December 1992).

A second port of entry into Ásatrú flows from the influence of pop culture or the desire to become too involved with the occult or magical community as a teenager or young adult. The prototype of such introductions is offered by the key figure in the institutionalization of Ásatrú in America, Stephen McNallen:

> I made a personal conversion to Norse heathendom after reading the historical novel *The Viking*, by Edison Marshall, which contrasted the values of Ásatrú and Christianity. (This is the novel from which the film with Kirk Douglas . . . was made in the late 1950s). More accurately, the novel sparked further research which soon led to my conversion. This study was my first significant exposure to Germanic mythology and religion (interview with McNallen, 4 January 1993)[8]

William Bainbridge, currently a member of the governing council
(High Rede) of the Ring of Troth, "first became interested in Ásatrú
through two practically simultaneous influences: an individual who
wrote a short introduction to Ásatrú in a local Pagan newsletter,
and my beginning to study runes through the work of Edred
Thorsson" (interview with Bainbridge, 24 January 1993). Taking
the arrival at Ásatrú via the magical community to its logical extreme, the current steerswoman of the Ring of Troth, Prudence
Priest, came to Ásatrú after long involvement in other Wiccan and
Neo-Pagan traditions (conversation with Priest, 22 November 1992).

Much less talked about, but important nonetheless, are the
instances of what might be called direct revelation; that is, direct
contact with a particular god/dess. These events are deeply personal experiences, but are remarkable for the character of these
meetings. For distinct from the biblical accounts of divine revelation in Judaism and Christianity, the Norse/Germanic gods appear
to their chosen without any sense of command, or indeed, hierarchy. The atmosphere appears to closely resemble the frequent contacts
which the gods had with humans in the Eddas and sagas, where
divinity and humanity met as relative equals, and loyalty was based
on reciprocity. The number of these direct contacts are small, and
with a single exception, those so favored are loath to speak of the
matter. Yet the event, when it occurs, is life changing.

Whatever the truth of these contacts, there can be no doubt
that, for a significant number of people, none of whom could be
aware of the others' existence, some influence reawakened a passionate interest in the Norse/Germanic religious tradition. This
awakening took place in widely disparate areas of the world in a
relatively short time, and within months of each other, journals
dedicated to the Northern Way began to appear.[9] The explanation
for this sudden awakening is the subject of considerable debate in
the Ásatrú community. Yet for all of these theories surrounding the
rebirth of the tradition, it is important to stress that all hold as
axiomatic that the old gods are, in one form or another, the actual
engines powering this conversion.

Who then are the adherents of Ásatrú (Ásatrúers)? It is impossible to posit with certainty the precise size of the American
Ásatrú community. Based on interviews for this research, however,
and on estimates of the circulation of primary Ásatrú journals and
organizations, 500 committed adherents would be a reasonable
estimate, with peripheral "members" perhaps swelling the number
to a maximum of 1,000. According to one well-informed, indepen-

dent Ásatrúer, the American Ásatrú community (excluding Odinists) may be divided into four primary categories: (1) members of the Ásatrú Alliance—about 20 percent; (2) members of the Ring of Troth—about 20 percent; (3) members of independent groups—about 20 percent; and (4) unaffiliated individual adherents—about 30 percent (interview with DjúpkverkR, 14 October 1992).

A breakdown of community beyond the observation that Ásatrú is overwhelmingly white, male, and comparatively young (most adherents interviewed for this research tend to cluster between thirty and forty years of age) is impossible given the dispersion of the community. For some Ásatrúers interviewed in this research, the problem of the dearth of women in Ásatrú has often necessitated contact with local Wiccan covens for the purpose of, put bluntly (but considerably less so than is usual in conversation with this group of Ásatrúers), finding women who are already in the magical community and would thus be adaptable to the Northern Way.[11] On a more optimistic note, KveldúlfR Gundarsson notes that while there is a dearth of authentic Ásatrú women—and those who are in the community are often "Wiccan[s] with the serial number filed off and replaced by a Nordic paint job," women are increasing in numbers in the Ring of Troth (letter from Gundarsson, 14 April 1993).[12]

The occupations pursued by Ásatrúers tend to reflect a mix of blue- and white-collar professions, including accountant, business executive, military officer, farmer, dental assistant, lawyer, martial arts instructor, nurse, printer, weaver, secretary, Ph.D. candidate, university professor, architect, writer, and many more. Most tend to be well educated, with at least a B.A. degree, and many, motivated by Ásatrú return to school to obtain language or other knowledge relevant to Ásatrú (interview with DjúpkverkR, 14 October 1992).[13]

THE ÁSATRÚ FREE ASSEMBLY

With so many adherents awakening to the rebirth of Ásatrú, it was only a matter of time before organizations would be formed to link these scattered believers into some form of community. Remarkably, no less than three independent groups sprang up in three countries at roughly the same time. Although this chapter centers solely on the American groups, it is important to note that Ásatrúarmenn in Iceland was formed by Svienbjörn Beinteinsson in 1973 (Flowers 1981, 282), and in the same year, the Committee for the Restoration of the Odinic Rite was founded by John Yeowell in England.[14] The first American Ásatrú organization, the Viking Brotherhood, was formed in Texas by Stephen McNallen (p. 282; Melton 1978, 296–297). It is the Viking Brotherhood, later renamed the Ásatrú Free Assembly, to which the organized Ásatrú community in America traces its roots. An early manifesto of the Viking Brotherhood sums up the philosophy of the fledgling Ásatrú movement—and of Stephen McNallen:

A Viking Manifesto

The Viking Brotherhood is an organization dedicated to preserving, promoting and practicing the Norse religion as it was epitomized during the Viking Age, and to furthering the moral and ethical values of courage, individualism, and independence which characterized the Viking way of life. (Melton 1988, 754–755)

Virtually from its inception, the Viking Brotherhood was pressured by those both within and without the organization to promote a racialist, or frankly National Socialist, agenda. Yet in one of the earliest available documents promoting the existence of the Viking Brotherhood, *Why Ásatrú?*, a good deal of attention is given to the social and religious values of the movement. The primary values of freedom and individuality, of sacrifice and of pride even before the gods, of family and of individual and collective heroism are lauded. Issues of cosmology and theodicy are addressed, as is a frank rejection of Christianity. The ideal of a loose organizational hierarchy composed of a free association of autonomous kindreds is described. But at no time is it thought necessary to expound a view of race or national origin! (McNallen 1983).

While it is impossible to pinpoint a precise date in which Odinism and Ásatrú became distinct entities, it is safe to assume that it was in this formative period of the early 1970s that the race issue became sufficiently compelling that it could no longer be ignored. Stephen McNallen's "non-discrimination" policy may be taken as the "line in the sand" which epitomized the emerging Ásatrú community's earliest break with Odinism. The differentiation process deepened with the multi-faceted explorations of the religion, mores, and magical heritage bequeathed by pre-Christian Norse/Germanic culture to its spiritual, if not always genetic descendants[15] which is to this day more typical of Ásatrúers than of Odinists. It cannot be overemphasized, however, that the Odinist/Ásatrú break offers no clear lines of differentiation. There remained

in the Viking Brotherhood, and its immediate successor organization the Ásatrú Free Assembly, strongly racialist and even National
Socialist adherents, although the latter were decidedly in the minority. The most notable of these was Michael Murray, a self-
professed follower of George Lincoln Rockwell's American Nazi
Party (conversation with Phil Nearing, 25 July 1992).[16]

Michael Murray is an interesting case in point of the difficulty inherent in drawing absolute boundaries between Odinism
and Ásatrú, as well as illustrating the tensions inherent in the
movement from its inception to the present day. An early member
of the Ásatrú Free Assembly (AFA), he brought to the movement
undeniable energy and dedication. He in fact remains the key figure today behind one of the AFA's successor groups, the Ásatrú
Alliance, and he remains a force in the important Arizona Kindred.
To a friend:

> . . . Ásatrú is the primary interest in Murray's life, and he has to
> some extent sacrificed his career prospects and his family life to it.
> He is absolutely dedicated to the religion, and will never abandon it
> or voluntarily withdraw from involvement in it. He is also absolutely
> convinced that Ásatrú is exclusively a religion for those of Northern
> European descent, i.e., a white person's religion, and he will resist
> any movement to open the religion to non-whites. To Murray, the
> religion and an ethnocentric view of culture and spirituality are
> inseparable, and he cannot conceive of one without the other. On
> the other hand, he has actively and consistently resisted the
> politicization of Ásatrú, and has worked to expel practicing Nazis
> from the Arizona Kindred and to exclude them from the Ásatrú
> Alliance. He appears convinced that the revitalization and resur-
> gence of the Northern European peoples, to which he is committed,
> must be brought about by religion, and specifically, non-Judeo-Christian
> religion, and that it will be harmed by the activities of politically
> oriented groups such as white supremacists. (Interview with William
> Bainbridge, 24 January 1993).

It is not atypical of small, fledgling religious communities
that relatively marginal issues can often become divisive far out of
proportion to their centrality to the religion itself. So it is with
race and Ásatrú. Where self-identified Odinists are often drawn to
the belief system by pre-existing racialist beliefs, Ásatrúers are a
considerably more diverse community for whom racial pride, while
important, is in most instances of decidedly secondary importance
to the greater considerations of spirituality and the "remagicalization"
of the world (Berger 1967). Yet in the small world of Ásatrú, race

has become a searing issue, and on which increasingly has become the primary source of division in the movement.

This tension over the issue of race and qualifications for membership would arguably have been manageable had it not been for several organizational features of the early Ásatrú Free Assembly. The primary values of individualism and independence precluded the AFA from acting as anything more than an advisory board to those who chose to seek their council. In Steve McNallen's words: "There is no 'Ásapope,' and that's the way we like it" (interview with McNallen, 4 January 1993). Individual kindreds were entirely autonomous, bound to the national organization by ties of *troth* and by the submission of dues which brought with it a subscription to the AFA's publication, *Runestone*.[17] The AFA (read McNallen) could and did publish their views through this vehicle, but the idealized Viking notion of equality even before the gods hardly provided much institutional support for the national leaders seeking to enforce their views, even if they were so inclined (and in any case, they were not interested in doing anything of the sort).

Adding to the AFA's instability were two additional factors: the somewhat eccentric vehicles through which the AFA advertised its existence, and the concentration of responsibility on the shoulders of Steve McNallen and his wife Maddy Hutter. In his effort to publicize the fledgling movement, McNallen advertised in everything from a "national magazine dealing with metaphysics and Fortean phenomena" (interview with McNallen, 14 January 1993) to that bible of armchair mercenaries (and occasional contract killers) *Soldier of Fortune* (Adler 1986, 279; conversation with Nearing 12 December 1992).[18] This eclecticism could not but bring together an unusual (and somewhat incompatible) mix of people.

Given this egalitarian organizational ethos, McNallen was left with vast work responsibilities and great prestige, yet little effective power. Modern Pagan groups are notorious for cannibalizing leaders through rumor, innuendo, just plain jealousy or simple indifference, rendering any style of leadership virtually ineffective, and all but guaranteeing that any controversy carries within it the seeds of fragmentation—an event that could occur at any time when the leader simply tires of the workload and the conflict (Dauster 1992). McNallen describes this succinctly:

> The AFA foundered for several reasons. For one thing, Maddy and I just burned out. We were each putting in about sixty hours a week on the cause, in addition to my full-time job and Maddy's part-time

employment. The interpersonal hassles contributed as well. (Interview with McNallen 4 January 1993)

McNallen could have turned for help to others in the organization, but there were at the time factional schisms and simple personality clashes that would have rendered such an option largely ineffective, even had he chosen to go this route. Robert Stine recalls the twilight of the AFA:

> We, Stephen McNallen, his wife Maddy Hutter, Kelly LaZatte, my wife, and yours truly, made the AFA too large of a monster for us to control, it thus broke free and devoured us . . . I went to the first Texas Althing, and had a great time, the second Texas Althing I attended I stayed there . . . We moved the AFA headquarters from Steve's house into an office/storefront in downtown, in Brekenridge, Texas. All was going well, I guess the sign I painted for the storefront is still there. Then the Texas economy went bust, I lost my job, in short order Steve lost his job. Kelly and I lived on what she could make doing laundry in an old folks home, Steve and Maddy lived on savings, we held on trying to make it, the AFA could not make enough to support us . . . (Interview with Stine, 22–24 December 1992)

Yet it is clear in retrospect that even had these problems of organization and leadership been solved, the doom of the AFA was probably inevitable, and once again, race played a role in the group's demise. For the AFA was no mere mail order church. Rather, the emotional heart of Ásatrú is community, and numerous local and regional gatherings for seasonal religious ceremonies *(blot)*, for *sumbels* (religious ceremonies characterized by ritual drinking behavior), and for folk moots (general gatherings for primarily social purposes) are in fact celebrations of this communal spirit. At the apex of these gatherings, however, is the Althing, a national assembly of kindreds gathered for religious ceremony, competitive games, and, unlike other Ásatrú gatherings, to discuss organizational policies. These Althings are free gatherings of equals, and the parameters of debate are virtually unlimited. The Althings brought the inherent tensions and contradictions of the AFA to a head. One incident at the AFA's second Althing is indicative of these dangers:

> . . . The second Althing I was at Mike [Murray] was downright scary. He arrived late in the evening in a van with three other fellows. Steve [McNallen] greeted them and they stood around the van talking and drinking beer for half an hour or so, then suddenly Mike went off in a very angry tone, and I heard him say, "Why don't we just kill the fucking faggot" and he rummaged in the van for a few

seconds and produced a MAC-10. At this, I returned to my tent, for I knew what was going on. I had already been at the Althing site for several days, and two days before a postman from San Francisco had arrived at the Thing. A young fellow, tall, blond, well made, and gay. Kelly and I had entertained him for the past couple of days waiting for others to arrive; he was a delightful fellow that I liked very much, but I was soon to learn that Homosexuality and Ásatrú do not mix. This poor fellow was shunned, publicly humiliated, and made to swear that he would change his sexual preference, or leave Ásatrú . . . this is when the custom of everyone having his own personal drinking horn came into vogue, the rightwingers were afraid to drink after a "cocksucker," their words, not mine. (Interview with Stine, 22–24 December 1992)

More will be heard of Mike Murray later, however, lest these quotes leave an entirely one-sided picture of the man, it is important to note that even his detractors—and he has a remarkable quantity of these—do not hesitate to point out that Murray cares deeply about the religion, and that he is genuinely committed to the spirit of open dialogue and equality which is the heart of the troth relationship.

At the same time, the presence of racialist and National Socialist adherents at Althings, and within the AFA, was a problem which could no longer be ignored. The struggle for the soul of the movement which continues to this day was being waged in earnest, and the pressures on Stephen McNallen were formidable. McNallen was in an increasingly difficult position. His own politics would appear to fit comfortably into the right wing of the political spectrum.[20] In the combined Ásatrú and Odinist communities, however, that political spectrum changes considerably, and McNallen suddenly becomes very much the man of the center—and thus a legitimate target for both sides (conversation with Stine, 1 April 1993).[21]

As Althing 7 in 1987, the last year of the AFA's existence, approached, it was clear that the leadership of the group, exhausted, frustrated and bankrupt, simply would not be able to organize the event (interview with Stine 23–24 December 1992).[22] In desperation, McNallen tried at the eleventh hour to delegate responsibility for the AFA to a committee consisting of such core members as Steve McNallen and Maddy Hutter, Mike Murray, Alice Karlsdóttir, Robert Stine, Ariel Bentley, John Parmenger, and a few others. The committee, styling itself the Southern Heathen Leadership Conference, met once and issued a single document which in effect divided the responsibility for various AFA functions between committee members, froze applications for new membership, and announced that McNallen and Hutter would be taking a much deserved and long overdue vacation.[23] It was a futile effort as McNallen would have remained saddled with the continued responsibility of editing and publishing *Runestone*. In the end, McNallen went off to California, the committee drifted apart, *Runestone* was folded, and the Ásatrú Free Assembly, formerly the Viking Brotherhood, was dead. Even as the AFA was in its death throes however, two very different successor organizations were poised to take up the Raven Banner.

These groups, the Ásatrú Alliance and the Ring of Troth, came to represent the contentions surrounding the central dichotomy of the AFA: the more politicized, racialist majority of the AFA, and those for whom the magical and scholarly potential of the movement were at the forefront of the reconstruction of the Norse/Germanic religion, and for whom race was either of little interest or for whom racialist thought was anathema. Before taking up the cases of these still extant groups, however, Steve McNallen's retrospective analysis of the lessons of the AFA's demise deserve careful consideration for their echo of the experience of others:

> One of the hardest-learned lessons from the old AFA . . . was this: the time has not come for widespread public acceptance of Ásatrú. At one point we exposed a million or so readers to our beliefs in a newspaper article that was published coast-to-coast. The piece in question presented the AFA fairly and in some detail. Nevertheless, we received exactly *two* inquiries as a result. . . . We must be content, for now, to grow slowly. We must seek quality rather than quantity . . .
>
> The Wiccans did this for years (or centuries, if you believe modern Wiccan claims to an unbroken, ancient lineage). Do any of you remember the early 1960s, before the incredible cultural upheavals that came with the second half of that decade? "Witchcraft," as it was called then, was a genuine underground phenomenon. You just didn't breeze into a local coven, get initiated shortly thereafter, and start dancing naked around a cauldron in someone's apartment. Applicants were carefully screened and underwent a more or less rigorous education before being accepted by the group. By being selective, covens were able to sink their roots deeply and develop depth—depth of vision, depth of commitment, and depth of knowledge. . . .
>
> On the other hand, Asafolk should support any efforts that will educate the public about our Gods or the society with which

they are most identified, namely, the Vikings. One reason that the
time is not right for mass conversions to Ásatrú is that the average
person has no knowledge of history; he or she has no conceptual
context into which Ásatrú could fit. For this reason, we should boost
Leif Erikson Day, wear T-shirts with a Viking theme, join the Sons
of Norway, get the local library to purchase books on Norse
history . . .

The result is a two-pronged approach: one underground and
one above ground. Each compliments the other . . . (1990, 7–8)

THE ÁSATRÚ ALLIANCE

McNallen's advice was offered in 1990 to the Ásatrú Alliance (AA)—
a fitting enough venue as the AA is the heir to as much of the
original Ásatrú Free Assembly's form and spirit as can be said to
survive today. The AA emerged quickly from the ashes of the AFA,
thanks largely to the energy of Mike Murray and to the resources
of the Arizona Kindred, centered in Payson, Arizona. So swift was
the AA's emergence that Althing 8 was organized and held in Arizona in June, 1988. In short order, the Arizona Kindred's own
house organ, *Vor Trú*, edited by Arizona Kindred president,
Thorsteinn Thorarinsson, was expanded to serve as the national
voice of the Ásatrú Alliance (Murray 1988, 9).[24] With control of
the only organ of communication between the constituent kindreds
and the national organization, and with the Arizona Kindred's Mike
Murray acting as Lawspeaker (effectively, the president), the Arizona Kindred in practice controlled the organization.

At Althing 8, a group of delegates drawn from member kindreds
was selected to write the bylaws of the fledgling Ásatrú Alliance.
The bylaws would be amended with every Althing, but the basic
thrust of the bylaws set at Althing 8 have endured with few major
changes to this day. The decisions taken were structured into the
four categories: general tenets, kindred definition and rules for
membership, individual membership requirements, and Althing voting
procedures.

Of the seven general tenets adopted on 18 June 1988, several
prominent themes emerge. The Alliance is described as a free association of kindreds and individuals organized along tribal/demo-
cratic lines (neither term is defined); but of greater import, the AA
is to be "apolitical; it is not a front for, nor shall it promote any
political views of the 'Right' or 'Left.'" The Alliance (unlike the
Ring of Troth) was to have no established priesthood, and would
promote itself through publications and regional moots and things.

The publishing, however, would be the exclusive preserve of the Arizona Kindred. Finally, a spokesperson would be elected and would be empowered to represent the AA between Althings in all its affairs, and this leader would not be allowed to stand for re-election.[25]

While the near total control of the Alliance by the Arizona Kindred appeared at first to portend the accession of the racialist views of Mike Murray, in practice, the middle-ground policies of Steven McNallen's leadership of the AFA won the day. The explanation for this turn of events probably lies in Murray's genuine dedication to the movement and his determination, whatever his personal view, to serve the bylaws' mandate that the AA be a non-political religious organization. More, in the AFA Murray had the luxury of radicalism, knowing that McNallen could and would act to prevent serious damage to the organization. He in effect could play Loki to McNallen's Odin—the gadfly who would let pass no opportunity for mischief, but who in the end would bend to the will of the gods and bring benefit to all. Now, with the mantle of leadership on his own shoulders, Murray would be forced to act with prudence in the interest of protecting the organization. Thus, when Murray faced his first challenge from National Socialist ranks, he reacted in precisely the way McNallen had in 1978 when he held a press conference in San Francisco which denounced a local NS group for billing themselves as Odinist in order to gain access to public meeting space (Flowers 1981, 280 n. 2; McNallen 1978, 13–14).

The occasion for this event was a 1988 issue of *Speaking Out*, an eccentric National Socialist publication of the New Dawn, an organization whose leader (and only known member) is Michael Merritt of Burbank, California.[26] Following long-standing practice in racialist right wing circles and apparently having in his possession an issue of *Vor Trú* (which lists the names and addresses of all AA member kindreds), Merritt published this information, implying that these kindreds were in agreement with National Socialist ideals. This publicity clearly displeased some of the effected kindreds, and Murray was left with the task of contacting Merritt and insisting that Murray's letter of protest be published in the next issue of *Speaking Out*, and that Merritt cease to publish this directory in the future. The key section of Murray's letter read:

> The Alliance does not advocate any type of political or racial extremist views or affiliations. We do not support the *New Dawn* nor share its views.[27]

In introducing Michael Merritt's reply to the *Vor Trú* reader-
ship, Murray, whose own past NS connections give his words a
ring of expertise on the subject of wannabe storm troopers, states
that Merritt "betrays his apparent lack of maturity by slandering
the Alliance with typical drugstore Nazi epithets."[28]

A number of issues would roil the pages of *Vor Trú* in the
years between Althing 8 in 1988 and Althing 12 in 1992 (both in
Arizona), but none would be as divisive as that of race. Mike Murray,
like Steve McNallen before him, was in the unenviable position of
occupying a middle ground in which all views could be accommo-
dated within the Alliance, but the organization itself would of necessity
be kept clear of violating its bylaws by taking an official position.
This pressure was played out in the pages of *Vor Trú*, and more
devastatingly, at Althing 9. Most revealing of the irrevocability of
the split between Odinists and Ásatrúers however—and of Murray's
own disagreeable task—are a series of letters published in the open
forum of *Vor Trú*.

A key front in the contest between Odinism and Ásatrú as they
are defined here is found in the prisons. Throughout the 1980s,
Odinist centers have conducted—invariably at the request of the
inmates themselves—an important outreach ministry in the prisons
of America.[29] There, Odinism competes with Christian Identity for
the allegiance of white racialist prisoners.[30] Ásatrú, however, is rarely
mentioned in the prison context, and if truth be told, most Ásatrúers
would not have it any other way. It was therefore something of a
surprise when Murray published in the pages of *Vor Trú* a letter
from Kevin Hunt, a prisoner in the Nebraska prison system. The
letter itself was remarkable for having eschewed any but the most
elliptical reference to race, concentrating instead on an emotional
paean to the gods, and centered on the declaration that life in prison
is "a constant battle, filled with pain and anger, sorrow and bitter-
ness, but from the bonding of each brother of our kindred and the
help from Ásatrú folk in the free world, we can find sanctuary from
all this." Murray's reply is instructive of the strongly negative feelings aroused by prisoners among most Ásatrúers (as indicated in an
interview with Djúpkerkr, 30 December 1992):[31]

> These fellows are not a bunch of racist punks. They are sincerely
> trying to practice their ancestral faith within the walls of the prison.
> They hold regular gatherings where their families join them from
> the outside and hope to join the mainstream of the Ásatrú commu-
> nity after they have paid their debt to society. I believe they are
> worthy of our support and encouragement.[32]

If Kevin Hunt is no racist punk, the same could not be said for Dane, the self-styled spokesman for the Ram's Horn Kindred, the Tyr's Song Kindred, the Kindred Motorcycle Club, and the New York State Odinist Prisoners Alliance. Responding to an essay from Australian Kim Peart which stated that Viking society was in no sense racist, and that the Ásatrú Community too should be open to any race or previous faith, Dane presents a succinct encapsulation of the Odinism of the Order's Robert Mathews and of the most strongly racialist members of white Odinist prison groups. Of more immediate import, his letter points out in graphic terms how little middle ground there would be between the more strongly racialist Odinists and even the most right wing strain of Ásatrú. The very fact that Kim Peart's offending letter was published in *Vor Trú*, which is seen with some justice as being heavily tied to the Arizona Kindred, is posited by Dane as evidence that the Alliance in general, and the Arizona Kindred in particular, are race traitors and, if it were possible, would be subject to a war of reprisal.

> . . . our community has determined that our people have once again been misled and that the Arizona Kindred is promoting the corruption of our folk through bastardization, mongrelization and assimilation which is not only suicide but genocide; and that our communities must not only distance ourselves from the Alliance, but demand a Holy war, so to speak, so that the Alliance will remove the corruptors or discontinue referring to itself as Odinist . . . heed the words of the High One—life is struggle, not fun and games. Awaken or perish. We serve Asgard.[33]

While Mike Murray's balancing act between the extremes of racialist and non-racialist Ásatrú opinion could be maintained indefinitely in the pages of *Vor Trú*, the annual Althings were a different story. Here, the question of race could not be dealt with as an issue of abstract policy. Rather, the subject quickly became enmeshed in emotional ties of friendship, sworn brotherhood, and in the end, of perceived betrayal. Such was the case of Althing 9, held in Arizona in 1989.

There exist in Alliance circles a number of versions of events at Althing 9, but what is most striking is the remarkable consistency of accounts regarding the event. More remarkable still, and largely unknown to the Ásatrú community, there exists a two-hour tape recording of the central confrontation at the Althing 9 Council which has been made available to this research. What follows then is pieced together from interviews with participants from both camps, supplemented with material from the cassette record. It is important to keep in mind, however, that while the underlying issue was racialism in the Alliance, at no time does the subject appear to have been addressed directly. Rather, the battle was waged by proxy over the interpretation of the Alliance bylaws, and more centrally, over the meaning of a flag, over the ties of troth and blood brotherhood, and, in the minds of some, over the soul of the movement. Interestingly enough, at the time the subject was raised by the Old Northwest Kindred, the deliberations of the council were engrossed in the damage to the movement which Edred Thorsson's involvement in the Temple of Set had brought about. The sudden change of subject caught the council completely by surprise (cassette recording; conversation with Phil Nearing, 4 April 1993).

The Old Northwest Kindred, at the time centered in Chicago with about a dozen members, arrived at the Althing site early and were guests in the home of Mike Murray in Payson, Arizona. Four members had made the trip, Phil Nearing (who was to be elected to replace Mike Murray as speaker of the Alliance), Robert Stine, another long-time Ásatrúer who was the head of the Brewers' Gild,[34] and Scott Enslin (aka Bagelwolf). All drove to Arizona in the same car, although nothing was planned or said about provoking a confrontation at the Althing.

This is not to say that the issue was far from their minds. Some aspects of Althing 8 had left a bad aftertaste among members of this group. There were a cadre of National Socialists at the earlier event, although they tended to be relegated to the periphery. One incident did occur, although few at the time seemed aware of it. One kindred from the Washington State area attended, bringing in tow the Wiccan/Jewish wife of one of the members. This became known, and some objections were raised to her presence, apparently by California adherent Dan West (aka Redbeard, King of the Thor's Hammer Kindred) (conversation with Nearing, 4 April 1993).[35] Most however, followed the lead of the women from the Arizona Kindred and went out of their way to make her feel welcome. The racialism that was present at Althing 8, however, had a particularly negative effect on the head of the Brewers' Gild, who pointed out that if the racists in AA were left unchallenged, they would simply bring in their friends and subvert the movement, and Scott Enslin, whose mother was Jewish (leaving him with an obvious distaste for expressions of anti-Semitism).[36]

The determination to make a stand on the race issue may have crystalized during the Old Northwest Kindred's stay in Murray's house. In conversation, Murray appears to have made an anti-Semitic remark to which Enslin took exception. Although he said nothing at the time, that ended his relationship with Murray (conversation with Nearing, 4 April 1993). However, while Althing 8 and Murray's occasional tendency to speak faster than he thinks provides the context for Northwest's actions, the precipitating cause was the presence of the eccentric leader of the New York/New Jersey based Ocean Kindred, Paal-Erik Filssennu. Filssennu's primary claim to fame is his quixotic quest to reclaim Greenland as something of an ethnic homeland, his invention of a language for this putative mini-state (contemptuously referred to by some as mock-Icelandic), and for his leadership of the National Socialist oriented Amerist Folk Bund.[37] At Althing 9, Filssennu set up a table next to Old Northwest's campsite containing literature from his Amerist Folk Bund, in which Enslin (Bagelwolf) took an immediate interest. So much so, in fact, that he pulled up a lawn chair, took each of the many pieces of literature, one at a time, read it thoroughly, and quietly tossed the item back on the table before taking the next item for inspection. It was in the course of this meditation on Folk Bundism that Enslin noticed that the flag of the future Amerist Folk Republic was in fact flying over the central "sacred space" of the campground—the very area where *blots* and *sumbels* were held, and where oaths were sworn and the gods propitiated. Clearly, in his view, the banner was being used as a political symbol, and as such, was in clear violation of the bylaws forbidding political stands by the organization. It had to come down immediately, and Enslin had little difficulty in winning the Old Northwest Kindred to this position (conversation with Stine, 4 April 1993).

Complicating the matter was Mike Murray's insistence that the flag was his personal banner, and under it a member of Old Northwest had once sworn a warrior's oath of eternal troth to Murray when both were members of the Warrior's Gild (conversation with Bainbridge, 3 April 1993).[38] The Old Northwest demand that the flag be lowered was thus not only a shock, but in Murray's eyes, an act of betrayal. There was, in the memory of all participants interviewed for this research, a strong belief that at the time, violence appeared to be a likely outcome of the confrontation. Although no Ásatrú gathering has ever resulted in violence, the combination of emotional argument, large amounts of alcohol, and the presence of guns at these events always offers the possibility of, at minimum, an unfortunate accident.

With this possibility in mind, the Old Northwest Kindred formulated a plan by which, if a battle ensued, they would be ready. Armed with a single 9mm pistol and an assortment of edged weapons, the original plan assigned each member a designated target (with Mike Murray being the first to go), and having neutralized the primary targets, called for the anonymous "Brewer" and Phil Nearing to retreat to the car with Stine and Enslin to provide cover for their retreat. The point appears to have been to assure that when the authorities were apprized of the battle, at least the Old Northwest version of events would be available to counter that of what, at the time, they believed would be a united front put up by the Arizona Kindred and its supporters.[39] Nearing, however, a martial arts teacher of the *Wing Chun* school, wouldn't hear of leaving. The Brewer's respiratory problems made him an obvious choice to go, but the loss of the kindred's best fighter made little sense. Thus, Enslin was chosen to replace Nearing in the car, leaving Stine and Nearing to fight a rear-guard action to allow for their escape (conversation with Stine, 4 April 1993).

In the end, following hours of emotional but non-violent debate, Murray's position that the banner was his personal, and thus apolitical, symbol did not prevail (cassette recording). Indeed, in a most unViking act, Murray left the argument in defeat with several mead horns in tow, and sat and wept under his doomed banner. The Old Northwest carried the day, Phil Nearing was elected thingspeaker as planned, and Althing 10 was confirmed for the Ohio home of Robert Stine. But the cost was high. Old Northwest determined that, after Althing 10, they would leave the Alliance, and now evince some disgust that they had not done so earlier. Both the Brewer and Scott Enslin have less active participation in organized Ásatrú (cassette recording; conversation with Nearing, 4 April 1993). The Alliance soon returned to what it always was—a group which is very much an extension of Mike Murray and the Arizona Kindred—with a majority of racialist kindreds, but with an increased determination to keep the Alliance on a non-political footing (conversation with Stine, 4 April 1993; interview with Bainbridge, 24 Janaury 1993).[40]

Althing 10 was held without incident in Ohio, and it returned to the pattern of previous events. Religious ceremonies, contests, ritual drinking and boasting, and a council meeting most notable for inconsequential discussions. A good part of the credit for diffusing the lingering tensions from Althing 9 may be credited to

Robert Stine who, as host, elected to move the event grounds from the usual easily accessible public park to a beautiful lake shore in a distant, hidden valley whose primary attraction beyond the scenery was the utter impossibility of getting in or out without a local guide. It is perhaps unremarkable that, being thrust into an area which, in Bob Stine's words was like returning to the tenth century, served to focus the collective mind on cooperative and non-confrontational pursuits!

THE RING OF TROTH

Very much the brainchild of Edred Thorsson, the Ring of Troth emerged on 20 December 1987, almost contemporaneously with the Ásatrú Alliance, from the wreckage of the Ásatrú Free Assembly (interview with Thorsson, 20 September 1992). Thorsson had previously established a specialized organization, the Rune Gild, in January 1980. The Gild today functions primarily through the mails to spread knowledge of the religious, magical, and divinatory aspects of the Futhark, or runic alphabets. The primary difference between the two organizations according to James Chisholm, the former steersman of the Ring of Troth and a member of the Rune Gild from 1985, is that the Rune Gild is an expressly magical and initiatory organization while the Ring of Troth is not primarily magical in nature (interview, 17 November 1992).

For reasons of his own, Thorsson is somewhat cautious today about taking too much credit (or responsibility) for the Ring of Troth; however, it was Thorsson who most clearly saw the need for an organization to take up the fallen standard of the AFA, but at the same time, to learn from Steve McNallen's mistakes:

> . . . on Mother Night, December 20, 1987CE [I] founded together with James A. Chisholm the Ring of Troth. Different from the AFA, the RoT was never a "one man show." I was *never* the leader of the organization—I was its Father but have always been apart from the actual running of the organization . . . I never wanted to be the leader of a religious group within the greater Troth,[42] although between the years of 1988 and 1992 much of my personal effort was directed toward steering the newly raised ship of Troth. (Interview with Throsson, 20 September 1992)

While it can be argued with some justice that no organization fathered by so mercurial a figure as Edred Thorsson could be expected to function smoothly, the path of the Ring of Troth has been particularly different. In theory, however, the Ring of Troth as originally posited did fill a void in the Ásatrú community in that it suggested possibilities far beyond what the Ásatrú Free Assembly or the Ásatrú Alliance could have hoped to create; that is, a functioning religious institution upon which the reconstruction of the Norse/Germanic religious heritage could be accomplished in a relatively short time and fully within the exigencies of modernity.[43] To do this, the RoT would focus its primary energy on the formation of individuals rather than the kindreds which are the passion of Mike Murray and the Ásatrú Alliance.

The Ring of Troth's emergence was bitterly resented in some Ásatrú Alliance quarters, both as a rival for membership and influence and, of greater import, as a manifestation of the all too apparent fact that the divisive pressures which sundered the AFA would not soon be breached by the Alliance. At the time of Althing 9 in 1989, Murray's resentment against the Ring of Troth boiled over in *Vor Trú*, and the tenor of Murray's diatribe provides a telling illustration of the gulf which separates the Alliance from the Ring of Troth. In a single emotional outburst, Murray speaks from his heart rather than from his office as thingspeaker of the Alliance, and what emerges is a classic rendition of grievances, Manichaean suspicions, and paranoid fears which are the common coin of the literature of the white supremacist constellation. For here is a call to arms—issued (as is the custom in this milieu) in the name of an organization which has never dared to commit an act of violence—and a call for racial survival:

> . . . They rage at us because in their stupidity they feel that Ásatrú should be the religion of a chosen cult of 'thinkers and solitary priests,' they call us rabble because we accept ALL worthy men and women of the Folk into our fold. Not just philosophers with Phd [*sic*] behind their name. They talk in holy platitudes of 500 year cycles, doing nothing for the Folk today. Do they honestly think that our children will still be around in 500 years if we fail to act today? Wake up! We're headed for extinction in a hurry! And the Holy Faith of Ásatrú is the only thing that can halt this rapid slide into genetic oblivion. We are in a very real war for survival. Wars aren't fought by philosophers, they're fought by men and women of conviction and courage . . . People who would talk to all who would listen about our Holy Mission. People that work every day, day in day out for the Folk. People who openly stand up to the system and defy it for the christian dominated shore it is.[44] A system that would grind us up and cremate the remains if they could get away with it. (Murray, 1989, 20)

The organizational blueprint for the RoT was set out in Thorsson's *A Book of Troth*, which "is the official, basic document of the organization known simply as 'The Ring of Troth'" (1992, xii). The organizational plan outlined for the Ring of Troth was audacious; so much so that it is difficult to understand at this remove how Thorsson could have overlooked (or simply ignored) its obvious contradictions. To illustrate the current straits of the Ring of Troth then, it is useful to explore the elaborate theoretical structure outlined in *A Book of Troth*, and to compare this with the somewhat less grandiose reality at the RoT's headquarters in Austin.

A Book of Troth (1992) provides the organizational framework for the Ring of Troth which is in all essentials followed to this day. At the apex of the organization sits the High Rede, which Thorsson describes as the "board of directors" for the organization (p. 203).[45] The High Rede was to take responsibility for three major tasks: (1) creation of a training curriculum for Elders of the Troth; (2) ordination of Elders of the Troth; and (3) the licensing of the Elders of the Troth (empowering them to set up a *hof* or "church") (p. 204). In other words, the High Rede was conceived as essentially an ecclesiastical bureaucracy (as loath as Ásatrúers would be to employ a terminology so colored by Christian concepts). These Troth Elders, under the direction of the High Rede, would continue an ongoing course of study and training and the High Rede would record their spiritual and magical progress as well as their ethical standards, all of which would be a matter of public record. "In short, the Ring of Troth exists to re-establish a true 'priesthood' within our folk" (p. 204).

Thorsson's conception of a High Rede providing the training to an embryonic cadre of priests and priestesses (*godhi* and *gydhja* respectively) is brilliant, save for one practical flaw: Where in this day and age can a ready-made Council of Elders be found who would be learned and respected enough to take charge of a program of priestly training (and licensing), and for that matter, where would the novices be found who would undertake this arduous (and poorly remunerated) spiritual path? Indeed, given the small size and broad geographic dispersion of the Ásatrú community, where would these newly minted religious be sent (and supported on the local level, according to the Ring of Troth's vision)?[46]

The answer to all three of these questions is the same: it could not be done. It was simply not possible to create a circle of qualified Elders, a capable and motivated core of novices, a widely respected High Rede, or, indeed, a self-supporting "mission field"

by an act of administrative fiat. Thus, from the beginning the High
Rede simply could not produce the mandated group of Troth Elders. Only Thorsson could have qualified from the organization's
inception, and currently, KveldúlfR Gundarsson meets the rigorous Eldership standards.[47] Others were appointed in recognition of
their work for the Troth, and yet others for reasons known only to
Thorsson. The condition of the Elder Training Program, a responsibility which soon fell to KveldúlfR Gundarsson, has not fared
greatly better.[48]

    With so demanding a program expected of Troth Elders, and
with the dearth of members of the High Rede who are remotely
qualified to assume the title of Elder which is based on these criteria, it is little wonder that the High Rede of the Ring of Troth
has been from its inception a fractious group. This was of less
concern when the core of the Ring of Troth was centered in a
closely knit group of friends in Texas. There, the core group consisted of James Chisholm as steersman, Dianne Ross as editor of
Idunna (and responsible for nearly every other imaginable administrative task), John Gyori, and eventually KveldúlfR Gundarsson.[49]
Edred Thorsson was never far from the action, but he claimed no
official role in the RoT beyond paternity.[50] When this group expanded, however, a delicate situation became untenable, with problems
arising from two directions: Edred Thorsson's increasingly public
explorations of the dark side of Odin and the increasing gap between the organization's ambitions and its less grandiose realities.
These strands of history flow together, but before leaving the subject of the High Rede, a postscript is in order.

    As originally envisioned in *A Book of Troth*, The High Rede
was to have eight sitting members plus a ninth member who would
coordinate and lead the Rede (p. 205). Currently, there are eight
members including Steerswoman Prudence Priest. Of these, only
four are Elders of the Troth, KveldúlfR Gundarsson, Gert Æscbeam
McQueen, Prudence Priest, and Dianne Luark Ross. Of these, only
Gundarsson meets the requirements for Eldership, while the other
three, generously, have some work to do. It is small wonder then,
that in private conversations with various members of the High
Rede, there is scarcely a kind word to be heard about the High
Rede as a group, and very few encouraging words to be heard of
the Rede members as individuals.[51] However, lest the reader be left
with a totally negative portrait of the Elder Training Program, and
indeed, of the High Rede, the ever diplomatic William Bainbridge,
himself a member of the High Rede since 1992 (an Edred Thorsson

choice), should be accorded the last word on the subject. Noting that the Eldership Training Program has been under Gundarsson's full control only since March, 1992, "it is simply unreasonable to expect to see concrete results at the present time" (interview, 24 January 1993).

Bainbridge makes a key point in his analysis of the Ring of Troth when he stresses the contention that the RoT has existed in its current form only since March 1992. Until then, the organization, like the ambitious Elder Training Program, was in chaos, buffeted on all sides with controversies of its own making. Fittingly for a movement which debates the tripartite theories of Georges Dumézil (1973) with some passion,[52] three (probably) unrelated revelations swept through the Ásatrú community in the first year of the RoT's existence: Edred Thorsson's (and later, James Chisholm's) connection to the Temple of Set, the same cast of characters' involvement in sadomasochistic activity, and finally, the case of Rob Meek (a rising star of the RoT who exposed in particularly bad terms Thorsson's Temple of Set activities). Meek, as the controversy over the Temple of Set was reaching its peak, was arrested in Dallas, Texas, accused and later convicted of the murder of his wife. Given this triple shock, it is a testament to the viability of the Ring of Troth (or to the protection of the gods) that the organization survived at all.

Edred Thorsson made no secret of his connection to the Temple of Set, and its Order of the Trapezoid. Thorsson argues, with considerable justification, that his connection with Satanism, and with both the Church of Satan and the Temple of Set, was known to many within the Ásatrú community from the days of the AFA. However, there is considerably less documentation for Thorsson's belief that McNallen (or any other Ásatrú figure) understood the left-hand path that he had chosen, much less that McNallen had approved of it.[53]

The sources interviewed for this research are unanimous in their recollection that Rob Meek was in fact the one who went to considerable lengths to publicize the "Satanist infilgration" of Ásatrú. Chisholm claims Meek seems to have been motivated·by "repeated viewings of Geraldo's Satanism specials" (interview 17 November 1992). Meek apparently learned about Thorsson's Temple of Set (ToS) affiliation through a young female Setian who boasted at a Dallas occult bookstore of knowing Edred Thorsson through her connection with the ToS. The local occult community being as small and interconnected as it is, it took little time for this news

to get to Rob Meek. According to Edred Thorsson's recollection,
Meek had held a grudge for some time because Thorsson had not
deigned to communicate with Meek as his star was rising with the
Ring of Troth. Add to this that in the course of the Temple of Set
controversy when four or five letters were exchanged between the
two, Thorsson apparently refused to rise to Meek's support of the
Vanir against the Æsir, and the break was irreparable (interview
with Thorsson, 15 April 1993).[54]

The backlash against Thorsson was indeed strong, and began
with the reception of his and James Chisholm's letters at Althing
9. There, a statement was adopted declaring that there could be no
connection between Ásatrú and Satanism. In particular, the Alliance went on record as opposing:

> any connection between Ásatrú and the "prince of darkness" or any
> other alien deities . . . [in particular with] outlandish . . .
> Mediterranean archetypes, deities, philosophies and ideas into our
> pure faith . . . We shall have no part in any attempted rehabilita-
> tion of Nazi occultism [because] the Nazis did more damage to our
> Folk and to Germanic spirituality in two decades than any group
> since our forced conversion to Christianity[55] . . . Regarding Edred
> Thorsson, we recognize his unique and irreplaceable contribution to
> our rediscovery of our spiritual and magical heritage . . . because
> of the great respect we all felt for Thorsson and his work, we have
> been all the more hurt and dismayed to learn of his recent and
> extensive connection with Satanism . . . In secretly associating himself
> with satanic organizations, and insinuating satanic teachings into his
> work, particularly in the Rune Gild, Edred has let us down, and if,
> as rumored, he has regarded us as sheep to be manipulated and led
> about without explaining the origin of his teachings or the direction
> of his leadership, then he has unforgivably insulted us as well. However,
> the Alliance has no intention of leading inquisitions or pronouncing
> anathemas. The All Father [Odin] has always been a stirrer of strife,
> and, as his children, we do not fear the free competition of
> ideas . . . (cassette recording of Althing 9, June 1989)[56]

Over the following year, the attack escalated in the pages of
Ásatrú publications in the United States and England. Struck by the
unremitting hostility towards the Ring of Troth in the letters arriv-
ing at *Vor Trú* for its fall 1990 issue, William Bainbridge felt constrained to come to the defense of the organization and its leaders:

> . . . insofar as I am aware, the Troth is neither satanic nor in any
> way sympathetic to nazism *[sic]*. It also seems not to be racist, which
> is far more to my taste than the Alliance's apparent ambivalence in
> that respect. (Bainbridge 1990, 24–25)

More, ever the lawyer, Bainbridge suggests the sacralization of the American Constitution:

> To my mind, the First Amendment represents one of the very greatest achievements of the English-speaking peoples, and contains at least as much of the wisdom of Odin and Tyr as anything that has ever appeared in an Ásatrú journal.

Meanwhile, the Ring of Troth in Texas was hardly a passive observer to all this. Fighting attacks from Rob Meek on one front, and fending off attacks from the Alliance and other Ásatrú sources on the other, Dianne Ross, the ever loyal editor of *Idunna*, opened a line of defense in the form of a most unusual two-page letter addressed individually to *Idunna* subscribers and Ring of Troth members:

> . . . it seems perhaps timely to touch briefly on the allegations made regarding possible "Satanic" influences on the Troth. I have been a member of the Ring of Troth for eight months and . . . I have seen absolutely no "Satanic" influences within the Troth and certainly in no way is the Troth seen as a recruitment ground for the Temple of Set . . .
>
> Edred Thorsson and James Chisholm . . . both spend between twenty and thirty hours a week in their dedication to this religion, in addition to their full time jobs . . . Really, they have given all their adult lives . . . I would not have even known of any of this business if it had not been for Rob Meek in Arlington [Texas] and it seems to me that everything has been blown completely out of proportion. In the eyes of the Christians we are all Satanic. What Troth members do in their free time, in their private lives, as long as it's legal, should be respected . . . If we cannot be flexible enough to allow for an understanding of all of Odhinn's aspects and other explorations of a personal transformative nature, what will happen when the time comes to confront our real opponents when they come to understand our aim? . . . If Rob Meek would spend his time writing on the Vanic Gods and Goddesses and their mysteries we would all be the better for it. He despises Odhinn and is so frustrated that the good books written in recent times have all been by written by Odians. Rather than find out if he can produce a major writing of quality from a Vanic perspective it seems he finds a perverse satisfaction in causing strife and dissension . . . (29 July 1989).

This letter is rich in allusions to several of the central religious motifs attendant to the current reconstruction of Ásatrú in the modern world, and Rob Meek's rebellion (or betrayal) is posited here as arising from this ethos. Whether this is true or not, the letter deserves some analytical attention—particularly in light of the tragic denouement to Rob Meek's story.

Most striking perhaps, is the assertion—correct in the view of fundamentalists—that Christians consider Neo-Pagans satanic in any case. Ásatrú, like Odinism, is an explicitly anti-Christian belief system. This may be expressed with varying degrees of intensity, ranging from the contemptuous "White-Krist" of Edred Thorsson to the simple refusal to capitalize "christian" in the work of KveldúlfR Gundarsson. However it is expressed, it is based on the belief that Christianity displaced the old religion and its native values, replacing it with an alien, Mediterranean cult which had the effect of devastating the culture of the Norse/Germanic peoples. It was in this view a historical disaster, the remediation of which is one of the central goals of Ásatrú today. Thus, the cryptic caution, "What will happen when the time comes to confront our real opponents when they come to understand our aim?" This is seen by most Ásatrúers as inevitable, given the pronounced intolerance they see as inherent in Christianity.

Yet while Christian "intolerance" is seen as the context for Meek's actions, the proximate causes could well have been drawn from the Eddas themselves: Odin as strife-stirrer, the war between the Vanes and Æsir, jealousy and revenge.

Shortly after Meek's campaign against satanic influences in the Troth, however, he found himself facing other, more serious problems. It might be well then, to look briefly at Meek's career in Ásatrú, for it was with his fall that the Ring of Troth, at the height of the Satanism controversy which simply refused to abate, was faced with a second crisis—this one not of its own making.

Rob Meek came to Ásatrú in 1985 in the course of a spiritual quest which he undertook at the urging of his mother, then dying of lymphatic cancer in his native San Antonio, Texas. Born in 1963 into a religious Episcopalian family and educated in the local Christian school system from 1976 to 1979, Meek investigated Islam, Eastern religions, and a number of other religious ports of call before finding his way to the then-headquarters of the Ásatrú Free Alliance, the Northern European Heritage Center in Breckenridge, Texas, manned by Steve McNallen and Robert Stine.[57] He adopted the AFA philosophy and returned to Arlington, Texas, where he founded a small kindred that disbanded with the dissolution of the AFA.

In 1987 he married Anne Harrington, who was to become a force in Ásatrú as the founding editor of the journal *Northways*. Coming into contact with Mike Murray and the Ásatrú Alliance in that year, Meek, now more commonly known by his magical name of Ingvar Solve Ingvisson, re-established a kindred in Arlington in 1988. Learning of the Ring of Troth, he quickly joined, working his way within a year to membership on the initial High Reed, while returning to the University of Texas at Arlington to pursue a B.A. in General Studies.[58]

A literal dark shadow cast a pall over the career of Ingvisson/ Meek, however. He had been diagnosed with a brain tumor, which in time would grow and, some recall, take on a kind of personality for Meek who gave it a name, would refer to it at times as a friend, and would on occasion converse with it. He was, in fact, becoming increasingly unstable, and his dramatic denunciation of Edred Thorsson for "satanic activities" should in retrospect probably be seen as but another spiritual way station which would by some accounts lead him out of Ásatrú even as the RoT was still reeling from the Satanism controversy.

The story would not end there. On the evening of 18 February 1991, Rob Meek murdered his wife, Anne Harrington, reportedly in her sleep, and buried her body at a landfill near the Dallas Airport. Following his arrest, he was ritually cursed throughout the Ásatrú community.[59] For the Ring of Troth, however, the event— with which they had nothing to do save by association—was a second disaster. Meek was simply too deeply involved in the conflict with Thorsson and the RoT over Satanism for disclaimers pointing out that he was no longer an adherent of Ásatrú at the time of the crime to make much difference.[60] In the minds of many, Satanism and murder were of a piece, and the Ring of Troth was twice cursed. But the disaster would not be properly Dumézilian if it did not come in threes, and the expectant Ásatrú community was not to be disappointed.

It was at about this time that Edred Thorsson's connections to sadomasochistic practices became the gossip of the Ásatrú community. Thorsson for his part hardly made any secret of this, but as with all of his activities, there was a religious dimension to the newest scandal which few Ásatrúers were ready to accept or understand. For Thorsson, it is through extremes, the polarity of pain and pleasure, for example, that one achieves transcendence, and transcendence is the very essence of the Odinic archetype. More, Odin in one of his aspects is known as the god of fetters.

The idea for the actualization of this form of sexuality in a ritual context appears to have been drawn from the novel, *Story of O* (Réage, 1965), although according to Thorsson two traditional cultures, northern European and Japanese, utilize these practices in a religious context (interview with Thorsson, 15 April 1993). However this news first became public, the Ásatrú community was soon fascinated to be apprised of the accoutrements of Edred Thorsson's shamanic journeys into the dark side of Odin. Unkind jokes about the "Roissy Kindred" aside, Thorsson had once again made little secret of his practice of various forms of shamanic sex magic, and even in his popular-market books, had given broad hints about the magical use of sadomasochistic practices. Borrowing loosely from Eliade, he offers this description, for example, of the use of seith (shamanic trance) magic:

> To work seith . . . you must first achieve an altered state of consciousness. Traditionally, this was done with a variety or combination of techniques, including drugs, sleep deprivation, fasting, sensory overload, and even physical tortures, which might be combined with chanting, dancing, and perhaps the playing of some rhythmic instrument. (1993, 161)

It would be atypical for Edred Thorsson to actuate any practice without making an organization and/or a religion out of it, and so was born the Order of the Triskelion. The Triskelion refers to the three-pronged (Dumézil redux) signet ring worn by the habitués of Roissy, the domicile in which O is introduced to the polarities of pain and pleasure. There are two Triskelion suborders, the Roissy Society for male dominants and female submissives, and the Onyx Circle for female dominants and male submissives. Advancement in the group, as in the Temple of Set and Rune Gild, is by initiation, and membership is by invitation (interview with Thorsson, 15 April 1993).[61]

Clearly, Edred Thorsson—and James Chisholm as well—were simply too controversial to remain associated with the Ring of Troth if that organization was to survive. Thus, by 1991, the search was on for a new steersman, one who would be free of damaging associations from the RoT's turbulent past. There was some urgency to this search, for with the RoT seen as in disarray, there was talk throughout Ásatrú circles of forming a new, non-racialist grouping separate from the Ásatrú Alliance, but free as well from the taint of the RoT's current difficulties (interview with Bainbridge, 24 January 1993). Eventually, the choice fell on the disgruntled former thingspeaker of the Ásatrú Alliance, Phil Nearing of the Old Northwest Kindred.

Phil Nearing had by this time severed his relationship with the Alliance. Before quitting the AA however, Nearing was a member of the Rune Gild, and thus was known to Thorsson, and he had met James Chisholm at Althing 8 (interview with Nearing, 9 April 1993). Shortly after this, Nearing, by now increasingly disgusted with the racialism in the AA, wrote a letter to the RoT stating that he was not an enemy of the organization, but in fact, something of an ally, and this opened a considerable correspondence. At this time, however, Nearing first got wind of the Harrington murder, and this was confirmed by James Chisholm over the phone, although the latter expressed some surprise that he had heard about it so soon. With these scandals, Nearing was convinced privately that he would have nothing to do with leading the organization.[63] Still, when he was invited in July, 1991, to meet with Edred Thorsson and James Chisholm in Austin to discuss Nearing's accepting the steersmanship, the chance to meet Thorsson and assess the situation firsthand was simply too inviting to pass up. From the perspective of the Austin group, primarily composed at this point of Thorsson, Chisholm, and the new *Idunna* editor, Ed Van Cura, the very fact that Nearing and company would take the trouble to fly down to Texas was evidence that "something was going to happen," even if no assurances or commitments had been made in advance. During the event, however, they "acted like a bunch of tourists," according to Thorsson (interview 15 April 1993).[64]

In fact, this is precisely what the putative candidates were. Tales of the macabre doings in Austin were sufficiently lurid as to make the invitation irresistible. Still, Nearing deemed it advisable to bring trusted friends with him, and thus he asked William Bainbridge and one other well-known independent Ásatrúer to attend (interview with Nearing, 9 April 1993). Of course, the transfer of power never took place—although each of the three visitors had the opportunity to individually turn down the large Thor's hammer necklace which is the symbol of the steersman's office (Dumézil yet again). Eventually, the office was bestowed with due ceremony on Prudence Priest in San Francisco in March 1992.[65]

With the transfer of the steersmanship to Prudence Priest, the first phase of the Ring of Troth, the era of Edred Thorsson, came to a close. William Bainbridge is correct in his assertion, offered as a plea for patience, that the current RoT is in fact a new creation, at this writing only a year old. And at this writing as well, the Ásatrú Alliance under Mike Murray continues much as it was before. What then, can be said about the future of these Ásatrú organizations, and indeed, about the Ásatrú community as a whole?

CONCLUSION

The Ring of Troth is in a very real sense the most "accessible face of the Odinist/Ásatrú community." Its diversity appears to be an important factor in its viability. It is the Ásatrú group that, for better or worse, "looks most like America," to borrow a contemporary cultural catchphrase. Indeed, individuals within the Ring of Troth reflect an often astonishing diversity, including members with interracial marriages, and members whose kindreds boast Jewish, black, and homosexual membership. One kindred even includes a trans-sexual Ásatrúer!

Not the least of this diversity is a scholarly core group, a tradition begun by Edred Thorsson, and carried on today by KveldúlfR Gundarsson. While it may be argued with some justice that the RoT's original mission—the creation of a trained, professional Ásatrú priesthood—is far from realization, and that, indeed, the serious scholarly ideal upon which the organization was founded is in danger of being left by the wayside, nonetheless, the organization is by far the greatest source of research on the revitalization of the tradition on the basis of the historical record. More, the leadership of the Ring of Troth has been the most outspoken in their opposition to racialism and in their quest to form a community of believers which would be congenial to the establishment of stable families, and would thus hold out the greatest potential for establishing Ásatrú as a viable, minority religious community in the American context.

More, in Weberian terms as these have been adapted to the academic study of new religious movements, it is the Ring of Troth, with all of its turbulent history, rather than the Ásatrú Alliance which most fits the profile of a movement destined to succeed. Its original charismatic founder, Edred Thorsson, a true visionary but a hopeless administrator, routinized his own (and thus the organization's) charisma by investing it in a governing board, the High Rede, and left much of the decision making to that body. Conversely, in the Ásatrú Alliance, no obvious successor to Mike Murray has emerged. In theoretical terms, this does not bode well for the post-Murray future of the Alliance (Melton 1990; Wilson 1987, 33).

Where Odinism has found a comfortable niche in the white supremacist constellation (and thus, off the map of contemporary cultural discourse), individual Odinists, primarily in the pages of *Vor Trú* and at the Ásatrú Alliance Althings, do interact with the

Ásatrú community. Yet unlike the Ring of Troth—and a number of independents who find the RoT philosophy more attractive than that of the AA—the Alliance, with the sole exception of at Althing 9, has evinced little interest in finding a place in the dominant cultural ethos of America. It is in its compatibility with both the magical community and the dominant culture that the Ring of Troth most clearly stands apart from the Ásatrú Alliance, and it is precisely this factor which appears destined, unless steps are taken relatively soon to heal the growing breach, to render the organizations as distinct—and as incompatible—as the Ring of Troth is from, say, Else Christensen's Odinist Fellowship.

While this observation is meant as neither final nor inevitable, it is clear that some action must be taken relatively soon to bring a unified direction to the Ásatrú community. For while most Neo-Pagan reconstructed traditions are accorded the space and time for development, Ásatrú simply does not have this luxury. The danger facing Ásatrú is, unfortunately, inherent in its current location in America's religious mosaic. The Northern Way stands at the gateway to that most feared and despised of American belief systems; white supremacy. Beyond the walls that they have elected to ward lie the demons who lurk at the frayed edges of the modern American consciousness: Nazis and Klansmen, Christian Identity and the Church of the Creator, and so many more. If many of these groups are, shorn of their popular media mystique, considerably less than a threat to the continued existence of the republic, it remains true nonetheless that the very invocation of these names generates fear within the dominant culture, and thus carries the ultimate threat of suppression. And it is the compatibility of some elements of this contemporary cultural demonology with some elements of the Northern Way which may awaken forces capable of dislodging the movement from its border redoubt and into the wilderness inhabited by the white supremacist constellation. (Kaplan 1993a). Whether Ásatrúers will find it within themselves to unify the movement, and to realistically confront its own internal demons, will ultimately determine Ásatrú's survival.

NOTES

1. Mills here seems not to have been aware of the similar "passion" of Odin who in effect suffered crucifixion in one myth cycle as a shamanic wisdom quest! In the poem *Hávamál* from the Poetic Edda, Odin is depicted as hanging for nine days on the world tree, Yggdrasil, and like

Christ, his side was said to have been pierced by a spear. Yet Odin's quest was shamanic, not sacrificial, and the prize was knowledge of the runes. See Davidson (1964, 143–145). On the paradigm of Germanic shamanism reflected by this myth, see Eliade (1964, 379–387).

2. What remains in print can be purchased from James Warner's mail order catalogue in Metaire, Louisiana. Warner, a long time Christian Identity figure, is believed to have some Odinist sympathies (as did Ku Klux Klan Grand Dragon Robert Miles), although the persistent rumor in right wing circles that Warner had become an Odinist is unlikely to be true.

3. Ásatrúers were belatedly treated to a discussion of Mills in the Ásatrú Alliance organ, *Vor Trú* (vol. 45, Summer 1992).

4. *The Odinist* has over the years strongly reflected all of these points. Indeed, writings on the gods or exegesis on the Eddas and sagas are few and far between, while commentaries on right wing texts, the news of the day, warrior ethics, and even at times essays that verge on, if not explicitly endorse, standard anti-Semitic themes are regular fare. See for example, "The Racial Mysticism of Alfred Rosenberg," *The Odinist* 51 (1980): 1; or "Philosophers and the Jewish Problem," *The Odinist* 58 (1981): 1.

5. A primary research difficulty is that Dietz's leadership style is such that he never explicitly gave an order. Rather, he employed hints and subtle manipulation to effect his will among his young subordinates. Failing this, the subordinate would be offered the chance to publish his views in one of Dietz's Liberty Bell Publications, and Dietz would simply change the text to faithfully reflect his own viewpoint (Anti-Defamation League of the B'nai B'rith 1988, 80–81).

6. Ron Hand himself, a graduate of the Methodist Theological School in Delaware, Ohio, was once a United Methodist pastor in Newell, West Virginia, from 1975 to 1978, and was for several years an assistant prison chaplain in West Virginia as well (letters from Ron Hand dated 9 September 1991 and 5 November 1991).

7. Chisholm's primary current claim to fame is in his self-proclaimed role as our greatest living authority on troll lore.

8. Cf. "What About the Vikings?" *The Runestone* 1 (Fall 1992): 8–11. This edition of the *Runestone*, the first to be published by Steve McNallen and Maddy Hutter since the original eponymous journal folded in 1987, confirms the influence of the Edison novel and film, and argues that despite the recent trends toward scholarship and esoteric magical explorations among many current Ásatrúers, the Vikings remain in his view the primary golden age model for emulation for the Ásatrú community.

9. Stephen McNallen recalls of this time (c. 1972):

Else [Christensen] began publishing within a few months of the time the first *Runestone* appeared, and *Raven Banner* made its debut in England, courtesy of the Odinic Committee. These happenings weren't quite simultaneous, but darned near so, and with utterly no contact among us until much later. I consider this to be a significant synchronistic event. (Interview with McNallen, 4 January 1993)

10. These numbers are in general accord with the best estimate of DjúpkverkR and other observers of the movement (conversation with DjúpkverkR, 3 April 1993).

11. As low as this percentage is in the United States, the situation in Britain appears even more dire, with the Odinic Rite appearing to be 100 percent male at this time (letter from Gundarsson, 14 April 1993).

The names of these Ásatrúers associating with the Wiccan covens are withheld by demand. Other Ásatrúers note in less earthy terms that Ásatrú women are so few and far between that it is common to marry either a Wiccan, a woman willing to convert, or as a last resort, a tolerant agnostic (interview with Robert Stine, 23–24 December 1992). Odinists face an even more serious problem in terms of attempting to create viable belief communities with a workable balance of the sexes. Odinism in fact is overwhelmingly male. In fact, Else Christensen is the only female Odinist leader of which this research is aware. Mrs. Christensen provides some valuable insight into the contradictions inherent in female involvement in what is at root a warrior religion:

> Funny enough, I've more been "one of the boys" than represented the female aspect. However, maybe that actually accentuate[s] the equality of male and female; but I've been told that I think like a man; it was meant as a compliment, I don't know if it is (my husband trained me well/cut the bull!), but it may be the reason that I somehow became the director of a warrior religion . . .
>
> Maybe the male ego in some cases has been an obstacle; women (some) may be more willing to negotiate. As we are dealing with spiritual matters, I receive many letters from men (mostly prison inmates) who need some handle on their religious beliefs in tune with their inner convictions which nobody gave them before. "If I had known what you have explained to me now, I wouldn't be where I am today." I am aware that to some degree I am a mother or older sister figure. (Interview with Christensen, 27 November 1992)

12. Gundarsson notes that the attraction of Wiccan women reflect deeper considerations than simple numbers and availability. They are, in keeping with the general philosophy of Neo-Pagandom, tolerant of Viking eccentricities: "I worship the goddess because I am a woman, being a Viking is a boy thing, and that's okay too."

13. It might be added that Ásatrúers, like many Neo-Pagans, are voracious readers as well.

14. Beinteinsson remains something of an icon for Odinists as well. *The Odinist* carries the remarkable story of one young American Odinist who made the journey to see Beinteinsson, only to find the language barrier impassable. The reader is reminded of religious seekers of an earlier day who would make pilgrimages to distant holy men only to discover that they were equipped linguistically and culturally to do little more than stare at the radiant countenance of the learned one, and to write moving accounts to the effect that the worthy's beatific smile changed the seeker's life. For just such a touching account, see *The Odinist* 49 (1989): 9.

15. It has always been something of an inside joke in Ásatrú circles that many of the best-known leaders of the movement, including Stephen McNallen and Mike Murray, are Irish rather than German or Scandinavian. This however is not seen as a negation of the claim to Viking descent, thanks to the Vikings' notable success in expanding the Nordic gene pool in the normal course of interaction with the female inhabitants of any land playing reluctant host to a Viking war band.

16. Many others have made this point as well, but they prefer to remain anonymous.

17. *Troth* is an important concept which defies simple translation. Technically, the word may be rendered as "truth" in the sense of loyalty or pledged faithfulness (see Gamlinginn 217). But the term has far deeper connotations to the Ásatrúer, signifying a totalistic way of life reconstructed along the lines of the movement's golden age progenitors. For the best treatment of the concept of troth, see Thorsson 1992.

18. Robert Stine who would become a core AFA member, discovered the group through *Soldier of Fortune* (interview with Robert Stine, 22–24 December 1992).

19. Bob Stine is himself an interesting illustration of the contradictions—and possibilities—inherent in Ásatrú. As a young man, he was loosely involved in Ku Klux Klan and Nazi party activities, but following a stint in the army, turned away from these groups, and today along with Phil Nearing, is one of the strongest opponents of racialism or prejudice in Ásatrú.

20. A good illustration of this point is contained in a 31 December 1992 letter commenting on an article which noted the irony of Christian fundamentalists targeting Ásatrúers as "enemies" given certain affinities between Stephen McNallen's political philosophy and those of mainstream Protestant fundamentalists:

> I think that it's fairer to say that we share *certain* values with Fundamentalists . . . My biggest reservation, the one that prompts

my comment, is on the matter of tolerance. I think most Asafolk [Ásatrúers] are more tolerant than most fundamentalists, in general.
  Still, as noted and quoted, we do have some opinions in common—family, less government intervention, and the like. (Letter from Stephen McNallen, 31 December 1992).
  Cf. Kaplan 1993a.

  21. Stine recalls McNallen saying several times that he was a racist, but the race issue was simply not important enough to risk the survival of the movement—and its tax-free status—in a pointless political crusade. McNallen would often follow the declaration with the rhetorical question, "who among you do not feel your family is the best and most deserving?" (interview with Robert Stine, 23–24 December 1992).

  22. Ironically, while the AFA's leaders were in dire straights, the organization remained fiscally sound.

  23. Letter addressed to all AFA members from the Southern Heathen Leadership Conference, May/June 1987.

  24. *Vor Trú* emphasizes ness from the various AA kindreds, and presents lively policy discussions and arguments over a range of issues. It publishes historical and religious essays as well, but here the quality is, at best, uneven. The Ring of Troth's *Idunna* features far stronger scholar articles as well as imaginative rituals and compelling debates on questions of greater interest to scholars and graduate students than to the general population of Ásatrúers. A common lament in the Ásatrú community in fact is that *Idunna* too often reads like a term paper. Of the national journals, the ideal compromise appears to be *Mountain Thunder. Mountain Thunder*, edited by Wilfred von Dauster in Colorado, is a lively middle way between the "bulletin board" which is *Vor Trú* and the graduate seminar which is *Idunna;* lively, well written, and featuring a mix of scholarship, ritual, art and poetry—as well as some astonishingly liberal (for Ásatrú standards) polemics. Significantly, *Mountain Thunder* is independent of any national organization or local kindred, and thus need answer only to its editor and his subscribers (on *Mountain Thunder*, interview with Wilfred von Dauster, 31 March 1993). A number of other Ásatrú publications exist as well, most produced by local kindreds, and a few represent distinct subgroups or guilds within Ásatrú. The most colorful of these may have been *The Frothing Vat*, the organ of the Brewer's Gild, a selfless band of Ásatrúers fanatically dedicated to the creation of the ultimate mead!

  25. *Vor Trú* 30 (Haust/Fall 2238 R.E./1988), p. 17. Race is implicit here, but is not mentioned explicitly.

  26. New Dawn promotes the idea that National Socialism and Hitler cultists in general are perceived in such negative terms by the American public that the ideals of National Socialism will never be implemented unless the name and rhetoric are radically revised. Merritt's mission in

essence is to put old wine in new bottles by marketing National Socialism as the New Philosophy and American Socialism. (See Anti-Defamation League of the B'nai B'rith 1988, 48.)

27. Letter dated 11 August 1988 published in *Vor Trú* 30 (Haust/Fall 2238 R.E./1988): 12. *The New Dawn* was another of the several interchangeable publications issued by New Dawn.

28. *Vor Trú* 30: 13.

29. Else Christensen continues to conduct such a ministry, where she councils non-violence and, in recent years, a process of cooperation with, and in fact, learning from, Nation of Islam prisoners. (interview with Else Christensen, 27 November 1992). Cf. "Kwanza," *The Odinist* 137 (1991): 1. The Odinist Study Group in Indiana, too, until recently, conducted a significant prison ministry.

30. For a microcosmic look at this contest, see the Aryan Nations' prison outreach, "Letters," *The Way* (June 1987): 6. This is noted as well in Kaplan 1993b.

31. Gert McQueen, a member of the High Rede of the Ring of Troth, has considered a prison ministry, but the idea died for lack of support (letter from Gert McQueen, 14 December 1992).

32. Kevin Hunt, "An Open Letter to the Ásatrú Community," *Vor Trú* 33 (Midyear/Summer 2239/1989): 19; and Mike Murray's reply to Kevin Hunt, p. 19.

33. "Letters to the Editor," *Vor Trú* 37 (Summer 2240/1990): 24–26; and "Letter to Ed," *Vor Trú* 38 (Fall 2240/1990): 26. Note as well that this response appears to be heavily influenced by the sort of militant imitations of Middle Eastern Islamist rhetoric which are common among black Nation of Islam prisoners.

34. This adherent has since left active participation in Ásatrú and is pursuing Ph.D. studies at a university in the Midwest. For this reason, his name will be withheld.

35. Thor's Hammer Kindred is remembered as one of the most extreme proponents of racialism in the AA. Also known as the Troll Kindred for the remarkable physical ugliness of the members of the group, Thor's Hammer Kindred won a measure of renown when, in the latter days of the AFA, the group demonstrated its disgust with McNallen's failure to adopt an openly racialist position and for his having ended the practice of chartering kindreds by returning its charter document with a .44 caliber bullet hole in it. Some, speaking on condition of anonymity, interpreted this as a death threat, and note that McNallen may have received several of these in this period. Others, however, were simply amused— and somewhat critical of Redbeard's marksmanship.

36. In strictly not-for-attribution conversations with Ásatrúers, it is apparent that some adherents do have Jewish family members, while the kindred headed by current Ring of Troth Steerswoman, Prudence Priest, contains one Jewish convert to Ásatrú, memorably named Thor Bernstein (conversation with Priest, 22 November 1992; see also *Yggdrasil* 9, no. 3 (Freyfaxi 1992): 1.

37. Conversations with Nearing, 4 April 1993; with Bainbridge, 3 April 1993; and with Stine, 4 April 1993. In something of a remarkable *volte face*, this same Filssennu who in 1989 would posit a strong racialist stand as the key to Ásatrú's survival, would only two years later decry the entry of Christian Identity and other far rightists into Odinism, which purged of its most virulently racialist elements, should be reunited with Ásatrú! See "Ocean Kindred of New York News," *Vor Trú* 35 (Yule 2239/ 1989): 28; and "Letters," *Vor Trú* 39 (Winter 2241/1991): 26–27.

38. It is important to note that the flag itself was not the same as the Warrior Gild flag.

39. In the event, the Arizona Kindred were by no means the mono-lith that Old Northwest had expected. It was arguably the wide spectrum of opinion within Arizona Kindred ranks which was a key to diffusing the situation. Indeed, in the end, William Bainbridge opened negotiations aimed at a compromise with Old Northwest (conversation with Stine, 4 April 1993). Bainbridge's legalistic diplomacy, technicalities and all, is captured on the cassette recording of Althing 9, June 1989.

40. One significant change which did take place with the AA in the wake of Althing 9 was the adoption of a new addition to the bylaws: "All major additions or changes to the Alliance By-Laws should when possible be submit-ted in advance to each Kindred, either in writing or by phone." No more surprises, please! ("By-Laws of the Ásatrú Alliance As Approved at Althing— July 6, 2241 Runic Era [1991]," *Vor Trú* 41 [Summer 2241/1991]: 24).

41. Mother Night refers to the first of the twelve nights of the Yule celebration. For the meaning and ritual content of the holiday, see the forthcoming KveldúlfR Gundarsson, *Teutonic Religion*. The ceremony itself was a simple one. Only Thorsson and Chisholm were present at the cer-emonial site, a stone altar behind Thorsson's house in Austin. Thorsson "invested" Chisholm with the steersmanship of the RoT by transferring to him with "appropriate words" several symbols of the foundation of the religion: a Thor's hammer which Thorsson had worn to the first Ásatrú Free Assembly Althing in 1979, a stone from the Assembly Rock in Ice-land, and a twig from an ash tree taken from the site of the last function-ing temple of the Old religion at Uppsala, Sweden. This ended with "the declaration that the Ring of Troth was hereby founded with the aim of reestablishing the ancestral faith of the Germanic peoples" (interview with Thorsson, 15 April 1993).

42. This is a point upon which Thorsson is adamant. He felt the need, as the movement's only widely published author at the time and as one of its best known figures, to avoid at all costs the formation of a cult of personality centered on a single charismatic leader. The Temple of Set embroglio demonstrated the wisdom of such a course in graphic terms. (Interview with Thorsson, 15 April 1993.)

43. Or indeed, postmodernity, for as Edred Thorsson would have it, the "Troth is on the vanguard of that cultural movement" (interview, 20 September 1992).

44. Murray here follows the common Odinist/Ásatrú convention of spelling Christian with a lowercase c.

45. A Book of Troth was published in 1989, a full three years before Timothy Miller's collection on the post-charismatic phase of new religions in which Gordon Melton made exactly this observation: that those new religious movements which thrive after the founder's death are those in which the original charismatic visionary during his or her lifetime had the foresight to transfer effective authority over the day-to-day affairs of the movement to a board of directors modeled on the governing board of a corporation (Melton 1990, 10).

46. If all of this recalls the earliest days of Christianity in which the Apostles scattered to preach and write and cajole the tiny Christian communities into a spiritual force would be destined to wrest to itself the mantle of empire, one perhaps could get a glimpse of Edred Thorsson's true model for the Ring of Troth—i.e., the early Church! Such a vision would be very much in keeping with his own view of Christianity, and would do much to explain his seemingly incongruous attraction to the dualistic Christian concept of Satanism as well. Indeed, confronted with this question directly, Thorsson has no hesitation in claiming that the early Church is indeed an attractive model for the fledgling Troth. The key point is that the Christian model worked, and while it would be desirable to have the tradition passed from father to son as it was before Christianity, the lack of knowledge of the Old Ways in families now necessitates an ecclesiastical structure. The situation facing Ásatrú's current endeavor to paganize the Folk is precisely analogous to Christianity's task in the Pagan era of evangelizing the Folk. (Interview with Thorsson, 15 April 1993.)

47. Thorsson today asserts that the High Rede was never intended to be composed exclusively of Troth Elders, but rather, of the functional equivalent of ecclesiastical bureaucrats (interview with Thorsson, 15 April 1993). While this may be feasible in an established institution (as, say, the medieval Church), how a group such as this could carry out the function of overseeing a cadre of Elders and Elders-in-training without the latter rejecting their authority is hard to envision.

48. Indeed, in his forthcoming book, *Teutonic Religion*, Gundarsson, the Lore Warden and Master of the Elder Training Program for the Ring of Troth, makes the incredible statement: "At present, no real 'training program' has been created for godwo/men, nor is there any sort of certification or initiatory program such as exists in other religions." Not exactly a ringing vote of confidence! Privately, Gundarsson notes that there are twenty-one persons currently enrolled in the program, of whom four are women. However, he has only certified one as an Elder, and this certification was provisional so that the individual could have a title with which to pursue essentially political and public relations tasks. Although Gundarsson takes care not to name this individual, the reference is clearly to Gert McQueen. (Letter from KveldúlfR Gundarsson, 14 April 1993.)

49. Dianne Ross lived at the time in San Antonio, Texas, putting in eight or more hours a day, five days a week, handling RoT administrative duties, and driving in to Austin for magical and ceremonial workings once or twice per week (interview with Chisholm, 17 November 1992).

50. Or, as he reflects today, his role in the RoT was analogous to that of God and the universe, as conceptualized by a Deist (interview with Thorsson, 15 April 1993).

51. KveldúlfR Gundarsson is the sole exception to these remarkably poisonous relations. While all agree that Gundarsson is yet very young, he appears to be the hope of the RoT's future in everyone's eyes. It is also of some benefit to Gundarsson that he spends a great deal of his time abroad and thus, despite the wonders of E-mail, at some remove from the conflicts which rend the High Rede.

52. Arguing for Dumézil's view is Stephen A. McNallen, "Magic, Asafolk and Spiritual Development," *Mountain Thunder* 4 (1992): 5–6. Arguing the countercase is KveldúlfR Hagan Gundarsson, "Wisdom, Might and Fruitfulness: Dumézil's Theory in the Germanic Rebirth," *Mountain Thunder* 6 (1992): 5–9.

53. McNallen for his part now holds that he knew little about Thorsson's Satanism until the end of the AFA, and in any case, finds "that Ásatrú and Satanism are incompatible belief systems for one person to hold, just as Ásatrú and Christianity would also be incompatible" (interview with McNallen, 4 January 1993). Thorsson counters that he discussed LeVey's *The Satanic Bible* with McNallen, and recalls McNallen asserting that he had read the book and stated "I found nothing in the book I can disagree with" (letter from Thorsson, 13 May 1993).

54. Thorsson in fact felt that with a renewal of hostilities between the Vanes and the Æsir, all was right with the universe.

55. The "rehabilitation of Nazi occultism" charge, carrying with it the implication that Thorsson subscribes in some way to subtly packaged

National Socialist doctrine, is clearly a sore point with Thorsson. In an article that decries racialism as a "nineteenth century dualist construct," Thorsson fails to address the issue of how the Order of the Trapezoid (which goes unmentioned) can claim to have done precisely this (Thorsson 1989). Even today, Thorsson remains incredulous that Mike Murray of all people would criticize anyone on the basis of neo-Nazi ideology (interview with Thorsson, 15 April 1993).

56. The statement went on to condemn James Chisholm, but otherwise declined to become entangled in the chaotic situation that was then unfolding in Texas, or to take sides in the Rob Meek/Edred Thorsson feud.

57. Meek was at the time a member of the Society for Creative Anachronism, and this group had been invited by McNallen to put on a demonstration of medieval costumes and jousting for the Heritage Center's grand opening. Meek stayed on to learn more of the Northern Way. (Interview with Stine, 1 April 1993.)

58. Rob Meek's biography was printed in *Idunna* before his fall from grace. He is held up as a model for all to emulate. (See "Announcements," *Idunna* 1, no. 4 (February 1989): 34–35.

59. See "Letters to Editor," *Vor Trú* 41 (Summer 2241/1991): 30.

60. Indeed, some still believe that Meek's fall was engineered magically by Edred Thorsson in his role as a Satanist. Thorsson denies this, saying that the Temple of Set—unlike the Church of Satan—does not use magical means to deal with mundane attacks. He was confident from the beginning that Meek would ultimately be destroyed, but by the gods, not by a magical working. (Interview with Edred Thorsson, 15 April 1993.)

61. See also "Order of the Triskelion," unpublished, privately circulated form letters which outline the general tenets of the Order, n.d.

62. Nearing recalls that at Althing 8, Chisholm had brought a copy of the manuscript for *A Book of Troth*, which he found interesting. Nearing's interest must have made an impact on Chisholm, who was struck by the indifference of all but a "few thoughtful individuals" to the manuscript. (Interview with Chisholm, 17 November 1992.)

63. "Satanism, murder and S&M just ain't going to make it for a religion that wants to grow . . . " (interview with Nearing, 9 April 1993).

64. On further reflection, Thorsson notes that "these tourists . . . hardly got their money's worth: If they had asked the right questions they might have had some real stories to tell back home" (Letter from Edred Thorsson, 13 May 1993).

65. Interview with independent Ásatrúer (name withheld), 14 October 1992. Edred Thorsson adds that Prudence Priest, with whom he had

once considered co-authoring a book, was a Bainbridge choice, and one upon which he prefers today to reserve comment, noting that of the potential candidates, "she doesn't have anything that is terribly bad, and people like her" (interview with Thorsson, 15 April 1993).

REFERENCES

Adler, Margot. 1986. *Drawing Down the Moon.* 2d ed. Boston: Beacon Press.

Anti-Defamation League of the B'nai B'rith. 1988. *Extremism on the Right: A Handbook.* New York: ADL.

Bainbridge, William. 1990. "Letter to the Editor." *Vor Trú* 38 (Fall 2240/ 1990): 24–25.

Barkun, Michael. 1989. "Millenarian Aspects of 'White Supremacist' Movements." *Terrorism and Political Violence* 4 (October 1989): 409–434.

Berger, Peter. 1967. *The Sacred Canopy.* New York: Doubleday.

Dauster, Wilfred von. 1992. "The Perils of Pagan Leadership." *Mountain Thunder* 5: 21–23.

Davidson, H. R. Ellis. 1964. *Gods and Myths of Northern Europe.* Middlesex, England: Penguin.

Dumézil, Georges. 1973. *Gods of the Ancient Northmen,* edited by Einar Haugen. Berkeley: University of California Press.

Eliade, Mircea. 1964. *Shamanism: Archaic Techniques of Ecstasy,* translated by Willard R. Trask. Bollingen Series LXXVI. New York: Pantheon.

Flowers, Stephen E. 1981. "Revival of Germanic Religion in Contemporary Anglo-American Culture." *Mankind Quarterly* 21 (Spring 1981): 279.

Gamlinginn. 1991. *The Ordasafn of Gamlinginn.* Albuerque, N.M.: Hrafnahús.

Gundarsson, KveldúlfR. Forthcoming. *Teutonic Religion.*

Jung, C. G. 1964. "Wotan." In *The Collected Works,* by C. G. Jung, vol. 10. Bollingen Series XX. New York: Pantheon.

Kaplan, Jeffrey. 1993a. "The Anti-Cult Movement in America: An History of Culture Perspective." *Syzygy* 2 (Summer 1993).

———. 1993b. "The Context of American Millenarian Revolutionary Theology: The Case of the 'Identity Christian' Church of Israel." *Journal of Terrorism and Political Violence* 5 (Spring 1993).

McNallen, Stephen. 1978. "Nazi Exploitation Blocked!" *Runestone* 25: 13–14.

———. 1983. "Why Ásatrú?" In *Selections from Runestone: An Odinist Anthology*. Grass Valley, Calif.: Ásatrú Free Assembly.

———. 1990. "On the Growth of Ásatrú." *Vor Trú* 38 (Fall 2240/1990): 7–8.

Melton, J. Gordon. 1978. *The Encyclopedia of American Religions*, vol. 2. Wilmington, N.C.: McGrath Publishing.

———. 1988. *The Encyclopedia of American Religions: Religious Creeds*. 1st ed. Detroit, Mich.: Gale Research Co.

———. 1990. "Introduction: When Prophets Die: The Succession Crisis in New Religions." In *When Prophets Die: The Postcharismatic Fate of New Religions*, edited by Timothy Miller.

Mills, A. Rud. c. 1930. *The Odinist Religion: Overcoming Jewish Christianity*. Melbourne, Australia: self-published.

———. 1957. *The Call of Our Ancient Nordic Religion*. Melbourne, Australia: self-published.

Murray, Mike. 1988. "Ancestral Faith vs. Vor Trú?" *Vor Trú* 30 (Haust/Fall 2238 R.E./1988).

———. 1989. "The State of the Alliance Part Three." *Vor Trú* 33 (Midyear/Summer 2239/1989): 20.

Ravenscroft, Trevor. 1982. *The Spear of Destiny*. York Beach, Minn.: Samuel Weiser.

Reáge, Pauline. 1965. *Story of O*. New York: Ballantine.

Sklar, Dusty. 1977. *Gods and Beasts: The Nazis and the Occult*. New York: Thomas Y. Crowell Co.

Thorsson, Edred. 1989. "Who Will Build the Hearths of the Troth: Are Racial Considerations Appropriate?" *Idunna* 1, no. 2 (July 1989): 16–24.

———. 1992. *A Book of Troth*. St. Paul, Minn.: Llewellyn.

———. 1993. *Northern Magic*.

Wilson, Bryan R. 1987. "Factors in the Failure of the New Religious Movements." In *The Future of New Religious Movements*, edited by David G. Bromley and Phillip E. Hammond. Macon, Ga.: Mercer Press.

10

THE RESURGENCE OF MAGICAL RELIGION AS A RESPONSE TO THE CRISIS OF MODERNITY: A POSTMODERN DEPTH PSYCHOLOGICAL PERSPECTIVE

Adrian Ivakhiv

INTRODUCTION

THE LAST FEW DECADES HAVE SEEN a resurgence of Western magical, hermetic, and occult thought and practice in North America and Europe. This development is in many ways analogous to previous surfacings of the magical and occult "underground" (such as in the last decades of the nineteenth and beginning of the twentieth centuries). Each such resurgence, however, responds to different historical circumstances and needs.

In this chapter I argue that this heritage of magical thought and practice has recently been contributing to the development of a postmodern worldview of environmental and psychic relatedness, a re-enchanted cosmology of meaningful correspondences that would offer itself as a response to what is sometimes called the crisis of modernity. I draw on archetypal depth psychology, and the writings of certain anthropologists and cultural and religious historians, to propose a "communication model" of human "psychic ecology." The territory I explore here is that in which the discourse of *ecology*—that concerned with our interrelationships with the living world around us—intersects with that of the *sacred*—that is, myth, ritual, and religion, the methods and symbols by which we cultivate, both individually and collectively, a sense of meaningful relationship with the world.

Religion, conventionally, is taken to mean a set of beliefs or a system of values and practices that relate to some kind of "ultimate meaning." In a secular society, religion is partly substituted by ethics, the discourse about what it is to live a good and decent life. The problem with the ethical is that it assumes a modern, rational subject, one who is capable of choosing and acting on decisions based on moral and intellectual considerations. Psychoanalysis and depth psychology, together with the cumulative impact of the events of the twentieth century (two world wars, Auschwitz, Hiroshima, the Gulag, etc.), have convinced many that this model is flawed: that there is a realm of the psyche—the unconscious, in psychoanalytic terms—that is beyond the control of the rational individual self.

The magical traditions, at least as they have been reinterpreted in our time, suggest that we can communicate with this "other realm" through dream, myth, story, ritual, and the body. This would be a hit-and-miss form of communication, were it not for the existence of cultural "maps"—symbologies and traditions of practice that mediate across this gap. Some of these traditional "maps" that have resurfaced in recent years include tarot, astrology, Kabbalah, ritual magic, alchemy, Celtic and native lore, runes, and other forms. According to the magical traditions, some of the most novel and interesting phenomena in European cultural history have in fact been attempts (whether conscious or unconscious) to mediate across this "gap" in order to redress imbalances within the "psychic economy" of Europe, through the application of magical symbol systems, images, and practices. The appearance of the Arthurian cycle and the Grail legends, for instance, and the troubadour love poetry of the twelve and thirteenth centuries, can be seen as attempts to redirect the warrior-like energy of knightly chivalry toward more positive, spiritual ends. The undercurrent of Marian worship in Catholic Christianity, whose widespread popular emergence toward the end of the Middle Ages followed these earlier developments, can be seen as an injection (or unconscious re-emergence) of Goddess worship into patriarchal Christianity. On the other hand, it could also be seen as a "co-optation" by the Roman Catholic Church of troubadour romanticism and of other heretical movements of the time, such as Catharism and the

Albigensian heresies.[1] The cults of saints, angels and archangels, in both Catholicism and Islam, can also be interpreted as veiled re-appearances of the popular desire to worship the full, polytheistic diversity of divinity's possible manifestation.

In our time, the issue of ecology and the problematic rela-tionship between human society and the natural world has perhaps become *the* pressing concern, to which religious and spiritual movements have had to respond. Related to the ecological issue is the re-imagination of the sacred, and particularly its genderized representation. Magical, Neo-Pagan, and Goddess spirituality, I will argue, have all responded to this need for an ecological and gender rebalancing in the mythical imaginary of contemporary Western society.[2]

A COMMUNICATION MODEL OF "PSYCHIC ECOLOGY"

Any human society is held together, consciously or otherwise, by more or less common assumptions and ideas. Invisible boundaries or margins separate the society from what does not belong to it; similar invisible forces maintain a tension between the core of that society—its mainstream—and its peripheries.

German anthropologist Hans Peter Duerr, in his book *Dreamtime* (1985), posits a boundary that separates wilderness from civilization, a boundary that since time immemorial, or at least since the emergence of human societies, has been straddled, bridged, and crossed (temporarily and periodically) by certain people; these have usually been specialists—shamans, sorcerors, witches, and the like—though sometimes their numbers have included a wider cross section of a given society, in individual "vision quests" and rites of passage or in collective ritual activities.

In a healthy society, this boundary is usually found some-where toward the peripheries, but still within the reaches, of the society itself. When it gets shifted out *beyond* the society's margins, however—as it did during the Christian inquisition—these special-ists become social outcasts, and the guardians of the status quo project "evil" traits onto them. In times like these, the society reveals an inability or unwillingness to speak to the "wilderness"; its members are afraid of the "dark" side of human nature, of its "evilness" and bestiality, and they cannot accept the half-human, half-animal. When the lines of communication are cut between our selves—or our self-images, rather—and "others" (for instance, between Nazis and Jews, or straights and queers, and concomitantly, between Nazis *as they see themselves* and the purportedly "Jewish" aspects of their own nature), these unconscious projections initiate a vicious circle of aggressiveness and destruction.

The process of "disconnection," then, can be thought of as occurring in stages: the lines of communication are cut; we lose the ability to "talk to" certain parts of our own selves, potentials present within our psychic natures; we project what we see as the "evil" in these aspects onto others. The ecology of our psyches, the ecology of story, myth, archetype, that relates us to the world, with its diversity of balances and interrelationships, is broken.

The way to regain this balance is by learning to *address* the diversity of manifestation, the archetypal pantheon of images and possibilities present within ourselves and in the world around us. We address it by speaking to it and identifying with it—through the conscious use of our imagination, our feelings, and our will. This is precisely the meaning of the word "magic" as it is used by certain practitioners of the Western magical or occult tradition. In traditional societies, myth, storytelling, and ritual activities performed a similar function, and served to maintain a sustainable relationship between the different structural elements of the cosmos: human society and the gods, conscious ego and unconscious underworld.

This model of psychic ecology can be rephrased by postulating the following points:

1. Like all animals, we naturally perceive the world around us in terms analogous to how we perceive ourselves: we "morphize" the world, personify and personalize it; we give it a body, and do the same for all of its diverse expressions, providing them with forms with which we can relate and communicate. Specifically, we humans *anthropomorphize* the world.

2. Because of our linguistic capabilities, we communicate not merely through unrelated images, but by telling *stories*, weaving complex narratives out of the images, metaphors, and "morphisms" we perceive.

3. From a depth-psychological point of view, the myths, dreams, and stories that make up a social group's more or less common imaginary reality—the inner worlds, "dreamtimes," "otherworlds," and "underworlds" of the imagination, with their anthropomorphized or otherwise-morphized inhabitants (beasts and half-beasts, giants and dwarves, elves and angels, heroes and mentors, attrac-

tive and repulsive mythic personages), as well as the various experiences they undergo (heroic journeys, battles, quests, and so on)—are compensatory functions of the human biopsychic organism interacting with its environment (including its social and cultural environment). The human organism, writes Jungian analyst Anthony Stevens, contains an "archetypal endowment" that presupposes

> the natural life-cycle of our species—being mothered, exploring the environment, playing in the peer group, adolescence, being initiated, establishing a place in the social hierarchy, courting, marrying, childrearing, hunting, gathering, fighting, participating in religious rituals, assuming the social responsibilities of advanced maturity, and preparation for death. (1982, 91)

There is, in other words, an ecology of symbols, an ecology of culture (revealing itself in the myths, beliefs, stories, and rituals of a given sociocultural group) that corresponds to the psychodynamic ecology of the human person, as well as to the bioecology of the environment within which the cultural group lives. The correspondence is never precise (nor can it be); however, it may be useful to conceive of it in terms of a continuum along which societies can be located, ranging from the well adapted or "healthy" at one end, to the maladapted or "diseased" at the other. Anthropologist Roy Rappaport makes the point that humans are as much at the service of the conceptions and meanings they or their ancestors have constructed, as those conceptions are parts of their adaptations to their environment. In other words, culture "possesses" the human species: "The symbolic capacity that is central to human adaptation produces concepts that come to possess those who thought them into being." He continues:

> When the world is constructed, in part, out of symbols, enormous variation becomes possible. This makes for adaptive flexibility, but at the same time multiplies possibilities for disorder. It becomes necessary for every society, therefore, to canonize or sanctify certain versions of order, and to deny, reject, forbid, or anathematize conceivable alternatives . . . *In all societies* such arbitrary orders have become sacred. They become unquestionable by being established on religious grounds although they're neither verifiable nor falsifiable. Ultimate sacred postulates, postulates about gods and the like, are the ground upon which human social and cultural orders have always been built. (1988, 31)[3]

In modern times, however, we have seen the emergence of a science that attempts to liberate us from the constraints of religion.

> [T]he epistemologies through which modern science discovers physical law are inimical to the symbolic processes through which humanity constructs its guided meanings. The concept of the sacred is, as a consequence, in deep trouble and we as yet have nothing adequate with which to replace it as a ground for social life. (Rappaport 1988, 33)

This is the dilemma in which contemporary Euro-American society finds itself: as a culture, we have lost the sense of sacredness in our relationship with the world about us. The world we live in is a disenchanted one, made up of discrete, disconnected (or at least, not *meaningfully* connected) objects, amongst which we are free to do what we please; but we don't know what it is we should do or what our rightful place amidst it all is meant to be. I find myself in agreement with those, like Rappaport, Morris Berman, and Gregory Bateson, who see this as a gap that needs to be filled, but at the same time are aware of the dangers of attempting to plainly and uncritically fill it by reverting to older, once-"enchanted" cosmologies.[4]

The solution we seek is a paradoxical one: on the one hand, to maintain our self-consciousness, our critical distance; on the other, to regain our intimate involvement with the world, our participatory relatedness, wonder, and innocence in the midst of the world. The paradox, however, is perhaps at the very root of our human nature: like our bihemispheric neocortical brain structure, one half of which apparently specializes in logical and analytic functioning, while the other perceives holistically, imagistically, synthetically and intuitively, we need to conceive of ourselves as a unified body with a complementary set of "hands"—one for intuition, empathy and faith; the other for skepticism and critical reasoning.

THE SEPARATION: MECHANISM VS. ORGANISM

The past couple of millennia of Western civilization have been accompanied by an undercurrent of magical, hermetic, and occult thought and practice that has occasionally surfaced in broad movements, but for the most part has remained hidden and esoteric (except to the degree that it fits into the dominant ideology, e.g., medieval Christianity). This occult heritage includes the Greco-Roman mystery schools, the various Gnostic sects and movements, Sufis, medieval and Renaissance alchemists and magicians, Kabbalistic mystics, Neoplatonists, Freemasons, Rosicrucians, and various occult revivalists of the nineteenth century. In our own time there has been a tremendous upsurge of interest in Native spirituality and shamanism, Neo-Paganism and Goddess religion, several varieties of occultist magic, astrology, Eastern philosophies, and so on.

In the more distant past, however, the magical usually went hand-in-hand with the rational. It was only around the early seventeenth century, according to a number of writers (including Berman and Bateson) that the Western world's dominant intellectual focus shifted from a more-or-less organicist, relational view to a mechanistic, instrumental view. The Batesons single out Descartes' dualist separation of "mind" from "matter" as establishing bad, "perhaps ultimately lethal premises" for the epistemology of science (Bateson and Bateson, 1988).[5] Michel Foucault (1973) similarly sees a change occurring around this time, from a pre-classical world in which meaning is seen to be embedded in the "resemblance" structures of the world, to a classical age, an age of representation, in which the world has been separated from the language describing it (this separation ultimately leads into the modern age). The shift can be noticed, retrospectively, in writings of the time: one can see a kind of tug of war going on between the "mechanists" (Descartes, Kepler, the later Newton, et al.) and the "organicists" (Robert Fludd, Athanasius Kircher, the Cambridge Platonists, and others), almost all of whom, however, either were firm religious believers or actually studied and practiced the occult arts, such as astrology and alchemy.[6] Out of the clash between the two worldviews, influenced by political and other processes of the day, mechanistic science emerged victorious, while the magical, organic, resemblance- and correspondence-based view of the world was largely left behind.

What can be said about the magical worldview that had its last major stand in this formative era at the beginnings of modernity?

MAGIC: THE WESTERN TRADITION

Contemporary practitioners of occultist magic define the term to mean something like "the science and art of the human imagination" (Gareth Knight 1978, 9), "a set of methods arranging consciousness to patterns" (R. J. Stewart 1987, 1), or "the Science and Art of causing change to occur in conformity with Will" (Aleister Crowley in Adler 1986, 82).[7] Francis King distinguishes between the magic of the stage illusionist (which the others don't consider "magic" at all), the magic of the anthropologist (superstition, fertility rites, etc.), black magic, and the magic of the Western occultist, "a highly sophisticated system whose origins are to be sought . . . in the Hermetica and the Gnostic literature of the Roman Empire" (1975, 8). (Most others would likely concur that it is this latter magic that is the relevant one, though perhaps its origins go farther back and, in fact, blend into the "primitive," anthropological variant.)

Whichever definition one favors, it is clear that magic has something to do with *imagination* (a word that shares etymological roots with "magic"), with *patterns* (of images, symbols, correspondences between the human, natural, and macrocosmic worlds), and with some sort of *efficacy*. Contemporary witch Starhawk writes,

> Magical systems are highly elaborate metaphors, not truths. When we say 'There are twelve signs in the zodiac,' what we really mean is 'we will view the infinite variety of human characteristics through this mental screen, because with it we can gain insights' . . . The value of magical metaphors is that through them we identify ourselves and connect with larger forces; we partake of the elements, the cosmic process, the movements of the stars. (1979, 192)

The traditional magical worldview reflects a cosmology of pre-Enlightenment Europe: the theory of the *four elements* (earth, air, fire, and water, with their corresponding humors, and so on); the *geocentric cosmos* with several (frequently seven) planes corresponding to the planets, each of which corresponds further to certain qualities, colors, etc.; the *twelve zodiacal signs;* hierarchies of entities or energies including elementals, angels, demons, gods, and the like. Unifying all of this was a doctrine—or, rather, an underlying, unquestioned assumption—of *correspondence*, the recognition of resemblances.

> The world was seen as a vast assemblage of correspondences. All things have relationships with all other things, and these relations are ones of sympathy and antipathy . . . Things are also analogous to man in the famous alchemical concept of the microcosm and the macrocosm: the rocks of the earth are its bones, the rivers its veins, the forests its hair and the cicadas its dandruff. The world duplicates and reflects itself in an endless network of similarity and dissimilarity. (Berman 1981, 62)

This body analogy is often found among non-literate or so-called "primitive" peoples. In the Ecuadorian and Peruvian Andes, for instance, as Joseph Bastien documents in *The Mountain of the Condor,* the mountains are thought of as being human bodies—the upper-most level makes up the head, the mid-section is the belly, the rivers are legs; through their ritual and ceremonial activities the Indian communities of each of three distinct altitude-levels maintain the mountain's body in harmony, socially (e.g., through intergroup marriage), economically (e.g., the agriculturalists in the valleys exchange goods with the herding communities in the highlands), and spiritually (relating themselves mythically to the mountain) (1985).[8]

Along with the recognition of universal correspondences, the European magical worldview encompassed a "doctrine of signatures," illustrated by the Renaissance magician Agrippa:

> All stars have their peculiar natures, properties, and conditions, the Seals and Characters whereof they produce, through their rays, even in these inferior things, viz., in elements, in stones, in plants, in animals, and their members; whence every natural thing receives, from a harmonious disposition and from its star shining upon it, some particular Seal, or character, stamped upon it; which seal or character is the significator of that star, or harmonious disposition, containing within it a peculiar Virtue, differing from other virtues of the same matter, both generically, specifically, and numerically. Every thing, therefore, hath its character pressed upon it by its star for some particular effect, especially by that star which doth principally govern it. (Berman 1981, 63).

These signatures or signs could be deciphered through *divination*, which Berman takes to mean "finding the Divine, participating in the Mind that stands behind the appearances." Thus, coupled with a seemingly static view of the cosmos is the idea that one could come into greater "sympathy" with things, learn to read the signs and, in a Taoist manner, to "flow" better with the energies of the universe, or—and here the instrumentalism enters in, which later takes over in the scientific enterprise—to manipulate these signs for one's own or others' advantage (or disadvantage).

It has become commonplace to distinguish between "black magic" and "white magic"; one could say that to the extent that magic is meant to extend the "profane" realm of instrumental control over things for one's personal (egoic) benefit or at the expense of others, it can be considered "black magic," while to the extent that it attempts to bring the practitioner into alignment or sympathy with a larger, Divine or cosmic will, or to encounter in an "I-Thou" relationship that which is around oneself, it is "white magic." In reality, though, magic is perhaps best considered a neutral collection of techniques meant to facilitate the apparent gap between mind and matter, and, psychologically speaking, between conscious and unconscious.

There is, in any case, a distinctly organicist, developmental, process-oriented current in the magical worldview that manifests clearly in alchemical philosophy; this is the idea that human beings are "incomplete," "unfinished" creations, and that, like the trans-mutation of base metals into gold that alchemists attempted to effect, so the human individuality can undergo such a transmuta-tion and refinement. The alchemists saw the metals gold and silver as the "earthly reflections of sun and moon, and thus of all the realities of spirit and soul which are related to the heavenly pair" (Burckhardt 1960, 11).[9]

This "self-developmental" thread within the magical cosmol-ogy, together with the holistic worldview of correspondences of elements and qualities, is characteristic of the entire European magical subculture—an underground current that included such special-ized phenomena as Kabbalism (Jewish and Christian and other variants), alchemy, and Neoplatonism, but also popular phenom-ena like the Arthurian cycle of myths and legends, and the use of card decks, such as the tarot, for divination. All of these reveal a reaching out from within the boundaries of conventional, institu-tionalized worldviews (nominally Christian or Judaic) towards "psychic ecologies" of greater diversity, mystery, and richness.

A brief consideration of the Kabbalah and the tarot can be used to illustrate this. The "Kabbalah" (also spelled "Cabala" and "Qabalah"), refers to the "received teaching" of Judaic mysticism. Though its roots go much further back, a widespread movement of Kabbalistic speculation and mysticism emerged around the twelfth and thirteenth centuries in Spain and Italy. Its influence spread throughout the European world, becoming an important compo-nent within the general Christian-Hermetic philosophy of the Renaissance (as found, for instance, in Agrippa, Pico della Mirandola, Edmund Spenser, John Dee, and later echoing through the Rosicrucian movement and even Shakespeare [Yates 1964]). The central symbol of Kabbalism is a system of correspondences repre-sented as the Tree of Life, a portrayal of the (variously interpreted) emanations of the Godhead, or states of being, traditionally called the *sephiroth*, all of which correspond to certain divine names and attributes, angels and archangels, spiritual experiences, virtues (and vices), colors, symbols, precious stones, plants, animals, perfumes, and so on. The Tree of Life, furthermore, contains within itself twenty-two "paths" connecting the ten *sephiroth*, which themselves correspond to the twenty-two letters of the Hebrew alphabet (and which were correlated by later occultists to the twenty-two trumps of the traditional tarot deck). The goal of the Kabbalistic magician was to "ascend" up the "ladder" of *sephiroth*, by coming to incorporate the divine energies within himself, through an inner understanding of and/or identification with them.[10]

In the case of the tarot, the twenty-two trumps represent stages or experiences on the "path of life" (or the more esoterically understood path of spiritual development). A standard deck contains cards such as the Fool (or Trickster), the Magician, the Lovers, the Sun, the Moon, Justice, the Hermit, the Wheel of Fortune, the Hanged Man, Death, the Devil, the Tower, and Judgment. The Minor Arcana includes the court cards (usually four per suit) and ten numbered cards (corresponding to the ten *sephiroth*) of each of four suits; the suits themselves correspond to the four elements of the traditional medieval worldview (air = swords; fire = wands or rods; water = cups; earth = disks, pentacles, or shields). Thus, we have a complete, systematic representation of the known (and unknown) universe. Both the Kabbalistic Tree of Life and the tarot Major Arcana (the trumps) constitute schematic diagrams of what Carl Jung would call the path of individuation—the process of becoming an "undivided" (in-dividual), self-actualized, integrated, whole person, in whom the various parts of the self are harmoniously interrelated. At the same time, both of these conplementary "diagrams" are contained within (and contain within themselves) the worldview of correspondences that is integral to the magical cosmology of the Middle Ages and Renaissance.[11]

Seeking the roots of the Renaissance magical cosmology one is inevitably led back to the classical world of the Pagan Greeks and Romans. These, together with the civilizations of the Middle East, are nominally considered to be located at the sources of "Western civilization." However, it is only in our century that an increasing number of scholars have been studying the roots of these civilizations, in turn, in such earlier cultures as that of pre-Hellenic Minoan Crete and—much earlier still—in the "Old European civilization" of the seventh to fourth millenia B.C.E. The mythologies of these two cultures exhibited a very prominent recognition of female goddess figures, related to fertility, and of various animal and nature figures (cow, bull, snake, moon).[12] Classical Greek culture can be seen as a "humanized" development from these earlier, more nature-embedded cultures. Many of the classical Greek gods had originally been represented as animal or as part-human, part-animal figures (LaChapelle 1988, 120).[13] Egyptian gods and goddesses were usually portrayed as being part-animals (hawk-headed

Horus, dog-headed Anubis, jackal-headed Set, ibis-headed Thoth).
The polytheistic mythologies at the sources of Western culture can
thus be seen to have developed from beginnings not too different
from the nature-embedded shamanism and animism of indigenous
cultures the world over. Druidic practices among the Celts have
been traced back to shamanic roots that resemble some of the
shamanistic practices of North American Indians, with their to-
temic animals and "animal helpers."[14] Robert Graves, in his "historical grammar of poetic myth," *The White Goddess* ([1948] 1966),
argued that at the roots of much of European culture is a poetic,
intimate familiarity with the vegetable and animal worlds; and Sir
James George Frazer's *The Golden Bough* ([1922] 1978), an encyclopedic, twelve-volume study of seasonal rites and festivals of European peoples (which still existed as late as the turn of the century,
in "fossilized" form perhaps, in peasant culture throughout Europe), documented the many rites associated with fertility, the
movements of the sun and moon, the passing of the seasons, and
the yearly agricultural cycle.

I have listed these points, almost at random, in order to suggest that there is, underlying Western culture, a stratum of nature-
embedded magical thinking that sees the world as an ecology of
fertile diversity and correspondence, and that this stratum is not as
far away from us as we moderns might think. The correspondences
between the various "elements" and "qualities" that make up the
natural world need not be abstract; our understanding of them can
be rooted in a sense of wonder and empathy with the powers of
nature.

A number of contemporary depth psychologists, including James
Hillman and David Miller, taking their cue from Carl Jung, have
been calling for a "polytheistic psychology" that would revive the
plurality and diversity of "gods" within us, as an antidote to the
"disenchantment" brought on by centuries of a rigid and "mythically poor" monotheism and by (still "poorer," perhaps) utilitarian
scientific rationalism. The depth-psychological processes they propose are analogous to the processes undergone by initiates of the
classical-era Mysteries: descents into the "Underworld" (of the
unconscious), the death of the ego (the personality-construct we
imagine into existence for the purposes of differentiating ourselves
from whatever is "other"), confrontation with the "shadow," meetings with various gods, rebirth of the Self, and so on. (I am mixing
terminology here—Jungian psychological concepts with traditional
mythological terms—to highlight their interchangeability.)[15] The

"journeys" undertaken by shamans are more or less analogous: they are attempts to address the diversity of powers, spirits, inner potentialities within and outside of ourselves, in order to keep alive the proper relationship between the human and natural worlds.

On the nature of these powers, Hillman writes: "Polytheistic psychology obliges consciousness to circulate among a field of powers. Each God has his due as each complex deserves its respect in its own right" (1981, 115). The gods or "Powers," as Miller refers to them, "are the potency in each of us, in societies, and in nature. Their stories are the stories of the coming and going, the birth and death of this potency as it is experienced" (1981, 77). Polytheistic depth psychology proposes an "imaginal" practice that re-envisions the world as a personified cosmos. Before exploring the implications of this conception of magic as an imaginal practice of personifying the world, however, it would be worth retracing the contemporary magical revival to one of its immediate sources.

A MODERN REVIVAL: THE GOLDEN DAWN

The latter decades of the nineteenth century saw a dramatic upsurge of interest in occultism and spiritual esoterica. One of the movements that emerged at this time—an occult fraternity called the Order of the Golden Dawn—merits our attention as a full-fledged modern attempt to revive magical thinking.[16]

Founded in the 1880s in England, the Golden Dawn synthesized a system of magical practice that combined knowledge of the four elements, alchemical symbology, astrology, Masonic and Rosicrucian initiatory symbolism, ideas and practices from the Greco-Roman mystery schools, and ancient Egyptian magic, and wove them all into a functional and practical cosmology; an initiate's task was to follow a gradated series of studies and experiences, working his or her way through the paths and "worlds" (levels) of the Kabbalistic Tree of Life, leading, theoretically, to mastership or adepthood.

Through visualization and ceremonial ritual, the occultist of the Golden Dawn utilized all of the senses—sight (colors, symbols, ritual robes, actions, and implements), sound (the chanting or "vibration" of mantras and "god-names"), taste (sacramental foods), smell (incenses and perfumes), and the kinesthetic sense (through "astral travelling" or "skrying," i.e., the movement of the imaginal or "soul body" while in a trance state)—in order to experience certain states of awareness. The way towards these experiences had been prepared for by much prior meditation and contemplation, as well as exercises in concentration and mental skills. Through visualized encounters with various archetypal "god-forms" the magician learned to identify with the various energies or states represented by these personae. To give an example, a magical rite might be conducted to invoke the powers of Mars, the martial virtues of bravery, loyalty, discipline, justice, etc. According to the laws of correspondence, red robes would be worn, a ruby placed on one's finger, incense corresponding to Mars would be burned (perhaps pepper or tobacco), the number of Mars (five, in the Tree of Life system) would surround the magician (five lights illuminating a five-sided altar standing in the center of a five-pointed star), the corresponding prayers or invocations would be spoken, and so on. When the ritualist's mind was sufficiently concentrated on these activities and their meanings he would become capable of participating in the essence of the qualities of, in this case, "Mars" (or whatever that may represent).

The Golden Dawn system, in effect, constituted a training program for expanding the capacity to identify with and channel universal energies and archetypes. The "gods" or "angels" or other beings invoked were considered to be, at one and the same time, representations of energies or internal states of mind, and "real" beings in their own right. In practice, the Golden Dawn failed, however (as an organization)—for very predictable reasons: its most prominent individuals were "all too human," and not necessarily wise enough to control the energies they were invoking. "As it turned out," writes Nevill Drury, "losing one's ego was not the simple task it appeared, and some magicians, including Mathers, found themselves behaving like 'gods' without having first gained the complete spiritual awakening [necessary for this]" (1985, 97). Ego clashes and infighting, exacerbated by the scandalous, for its time, activity of a few of its members, precipitated the organization's ultimate demise.

In retrospect, however, the Golden Dawn's imprint lies on the face of much of the magical and occult activity of our time (include Earth-centered Witchcraft, Neo-Paganism and "Goddess spirituality," as well as more traditional magical lodges), and some of its members, such as Dion Fortune, W. B. Yeats, and, despite his notoriety, Aleister Crowley, have left behind a legacy that is very much alive. Occult historian Francis King claims, with considerable justification, that the synthetic genius of the Golden Dawn "was largely responsible for the survival and revival of the Western magical tradition" (1975, 24).[17]

In examining all of this, it becomes clear that one of the main insights of the magical philosophy is the understanding that religious or magical symbols are metaphors expressing experiential realities. They are not objects of belief outside of ourselves, as religious symbols tend to become within the dominant culture. Magic, as an experiential praxis, involves the practical, phenomenologically based experience of the symbols and archetypes that are the content of its rites and practices. The symbol systems of magical traditions constitute metaphoric ecologies of the "inner" and "outer" world, maps of territories meant to be traversed by human consciousness. To the extent that they are lived realities, constantly being worked at and re-adapted to changing circumstances, these "maps" are balanced and "healthy." Over time, certain symbols and archetypes arise into greater prominence, while others recede into the background. An unbalanced society, on the other hand, whose magic is largely unconscious (i.e., the channelling of imagination and desire through advertising, the mass media, popular sports and entertainment, the entire "fantasy industry"—all forms of neither "white" nor "black," but rather a muddy "grey" magic), neglects certain archetypes at its own risk; these inevitably reappear of their own accord—either in a healthy, conscious manner (like the re-emergence of the Goddess archetype today), or in a destructive, "demonic" form resulting from having been actively suppressed and projected onto others (like the Nazi purification of the "dark" and "evil" races). Deliberate and tradition-based magical practice thus offers a way of consciously attuning oneself to the energies and archetypal forces that dwell deep within our "souls" whether we acknowledge them or not.

THE GODDESS, NEO-PAGANISM, AND ECOLOGICAL POLYTHEISM

The recent emergence of Goddess imagery constitutes one of the more dramatic developments in the religious imagination of our day. The dominant Western religious symbology of the past two millenia has stressed a divinity composed of "Father," "Son," and "Holy Spirit," with no explicitly feminine element (except to the extent that the Virgin Mary represented a Goddess). In the twelfth and thirteenth centuries, as mentioned earlier, the Christian Marian cult arose in southern Europe to modify this unbalanced pantheon. Today, when Mother Earth is perceived as being under attack by an industrial order, the archetype of the Goddess is reappearing both in pop-environmentalist imagery, and in the more esoteric practices of Goddess-worshippers, witches, Neo-Pagans, aspiring shamans, and others that make up a broad movement of Gaian, "Earth-centered" or "creation-centered" spirituality. The common thread weaving its way through this movement is a dedication to the Earth and to the "God(dess)" who is not somewhere "out there," transcendent and separated from the Earth and its life, but who is immanent, dwelling within the life around us and within ourselves.[18]

Neo-Paganism of the feminist or goddess-oriented variety has emerged out of a broader movement that seeks to articulate a "women's spirituality." Probably the best-known modern witch, Starhawk, has been one of the leading spokespersons in the feminist spirituality movement. She has taught at the Institute in Culture and Creation Spirituality (of Holy Names College in Oakland), founded and directed by renegade Catholic "creation theologian" Matthew Fox. In her books *The Spiral Dance* (1979), *Dreaming the Dark: Magic, Sex, and Politics* (1982), and *Truth or Dare: Encounters with Power, Authority, and Mystery* (1987), Starhawk has dealt with the political implications of theologies of *transcendence* as against theologies of *immanence* (i.e., God as being outside the world vs. God[dess] as within the world). She has articulated carefully worked out notions of "power-over" (authoritarian, hierarchic, abstract power and control), "power-from-within" (personal ability and spiritual integrity), and "power-with" (the power of influence and of collective action). Her response to the crisis of modernity can perhaps be summed up in the following passage from *Truth or Dare:*

> The mysteries are what is wild in us, what cannot be quantified or contained. But the mysteries are also what is common to us all: blood, breath, heartbeat, the sprouting of seed, the waxing and waning of the moon, the turning of the earth around the sun, birth, growth, death, and renewal. . . . Yet somehow we human beings, made of the same materials as the stars, the eucalyptus, the jaguar and the rose, we who inherit four billion years of survival have managed to create a culture in which the power of the mysteries has been denied and power itself has been redefined as power-over, as domination and control. (1987, 6)

Starhawk explains the potency of Goddess imagery in the following terms:

Earth-based spirituality values diversity, imposes no dogma, no single name for the sacred, no one path to the center. But at this moment in history, the mythology and imagery of the Goddess carry special liberating power. They free us from the domination of the all-male God who has so strongly legitimized male rule, and by extension, all systems of domination. The Goddess represents the sacredness of life made manifest. All of the symbols and practices associated with her reaffirm her presence in this world, in nature and culture, in life and death. . . . The mystery, the paradox, is that the Goddess is not "she" or "he"—or she is both—but we call her "she" because to name is not to limit or describe but to invoke. We call her in and a power comes who is different from what comes when we say "he" or "it." Something happens, something arises that challenges the ways in which our minds have been shaped in images of male control. The hum of bees drowns the sound of helicopters. (p. 21)

It is those images of male control that feminist Goddess spirituality, in particular, sees at the root of both the environmental crisis and patriarchal traditions in general.

Personification of the nonhuman other, in the sense that Starhawk is describing it here, is, as we have seen, also a feature of the archetypal polytheistic psychology of James Hillman. Hillman calls personification an "epistemology of the heart, a thought mode of feeling" (1975, 15). Only a thoroughly depersonalized world, according to his view, can be ransacked for its "natural resources" and left to rot. Depersonalization, for Hillman, has stultified our imaginations; Hillman's cure is to recover the image- and meaning-bearing quality he calls *soul*, the reflective and mediating moment (not a substance) which "makes meaning possible" and "turns events into experiences." "Soul-making," he continues, "depends on the ability to personify" (p. 3). Personification allows subjectivity, intentionality, and passionate identification back into the world—a world that can then become a "polytheistically" ensouled, animated community once again.

In Hillman's view, however, it is not *we* who personify; rather, imaginal persons

are given with the imagination and are its data. Where imagination reigns, personifying happens. We experience it nightly, spontaneously, in dreams. Just as we do not create our dreams, but they *happen* to us, so we do not invent the persons of myth and religion; they, too, happen to us. (1975, 17)

Roberts Avens (1984), who draws some fascinating connections between Martin Heidegger's philosophical phenomenology and

Hillman's "angelology," interprets Hillman's "soul" as being essentially equivalent to Heidegger's notion of "Being" or *Dasein* (the
Being that is between and that precedes subject and object, the
"pre-conceptual togetherness of man and world"). Hillman suggests that the notion of "psyche" or "soul" is more embracing than
the notion of "man," the universalized Cartesian subject, for

> Soul enters into all of man *[sic]* and is in everything human. . . . Man
> exists in the midst of psyche; it is not the other way around. There-
> fore, soul is not confined by man, and there is much of psyche that
> extends beyond the nature of man. (1975, 173)

Both Heidegger's phenomenology of Being and Hillman's
angelology of soul represent attempts to blur the radical Cartesian
dichotomy of "inner" and "outer," subjective (human) self and
objective (nonhuman) world. The soul or psyche, explains Avens,
dwells in the "soul of the world," the *Anima mundi*. It works with
images, archetypes, fantasies, personifications, angels, gods. The
psyche, as the world itself, reveals itself as a multiplicity: it is *not*
merely the egocentric self, "that capital 'I' appearing the monotheism of consciousness . . . , in monotheistic science and metaphysics," whose fantasy of a "unity of self" has proven so dangerous to
the world (Hillman 1975, 41). Rather than trying to cure the "pathological fragmentation" wherever it appears, archetypal psychology
appears to the pluralistic diversity of the imaginal world to "cure
consciousness of its obsession with unity" (p. 41).

> For the house the psyche actually inhabits is a compound of con-
> necting corridors, multi-leveled, with windows everywhere and with
> large ongoing extensions "under construction," and sudden dead ends
> and holes in the floorboards; and this house is filled already with
> occupants, other voices in other rooms, reflecting nature alive, echoing
> again the Great God Pan alive, a pantheism rekindled by the psyche's
> belief in its personified images. (p. 42)

In treating these images as real, however, it is not that we are
schizophrenically dissociating ourselves from them, since they *are*
our selves. Neither are we reducing the genuine others in the world
about us into mere images of our fantasy; we are, in fact, admitting
that our perceptions of these others are *our* images, our imaginal
personifications of others that ultimately (contra Descartes) remain elusive and unknowable. Both self and other create—and are
created by—the world of our interactions in this process of imaginal co-constitution. Thus, the rigid, individualistic ego, the ahistorical,

rational subject of Cartesian modernity, begins to blur into the ongoing, imaginal "soul-making" of the world.[19]

A number of environmental philosophers and "deep ecologists" have developed this idea of "transpersonal boundary blurring" to the task of expanding our sense of *identification* with the natural environment. Ecophilosopher Warwick Fox, in his book *Toward a Transpersonal Ecology: Developing New Foundations for Environmentalism*, for instance, encourages the practice of extending the "sense of self" beyond one's "egoic, biographical, or personal sense of self," so as to develop "a wider 'circle of identifications' that would include progressively more and more of the natural world" (1990, 202 and 197).

One might see a danger in Fox's, and some transpersonal psychologists,' idea of "expanding the self." An expanded self could easily subsume other parts of the world into itself, as it were, on its own terms. Presuppositions, unconscious desires, and imaginative fantasy are always at work, however, and this needs to be recognized.[20] Hillman's archetypal psychology and some of the revisionings of divinity found in Neo-Paganism recognize more explicitly this role of the imagination in the representation and construction of "selves" as well as "others." The magical worldview that is emerging in many of these movements recognizes the *creative* element in postmodern and post-Christian revisionings of religion. Given the postmodern temper, it seems to be more willing to accept that myth, story, and creative imagination[21] *mediate* between the rational self and a polytheistic diversity of Others— who may be called God(s) or Goddess(es), may even be called Nature or the unconscious, but which are ultimately ungraspable and beyond all names.[22]

In this chapter, I have tried to show that the contemporary resurgence of magic, when placed in the perspective of a polytheistic, archetypal depth psychology, can be seen as a postmodern response to the disenchanted and depersonalized worldview of modernity. Locating the source of the crisis within the Cartesian vision of a radical separation between self and world, humans and nature, conscious and unconscious, the resurgent magical tradition is thus a response to the present ecological crisis. In contrast to the Cartesian self-other disjunction, an explicitly *postmodern* imaginal/ magical praxis affirms the ceaseless interplay between "self" and "other"—that is, between a *self* that is not a thing but a process (dynamic, mediative, reflective, and multiplicitous)—and a variety of *others* that are ultimately ungraspable, uncontrollable, even unknowable, but that appear to us in an endless diversity of guises. What occurs in that *interplay* is the ongoing play of imagination, desire, dialogue—the psychic and cultural (re)production of identities and differences, of images and personifications.

The contemporary resurgence of magical religion can be seen, then, as an attempt to enrich the "psychic ecology" of contemporary culture by remythicizing and re-"story-ing" our world and the living beings that make it up. It is part of a collective effort whose ultimate goal is to end the divorce between conscious and unconscious, psyche and techne, culture and nature, empathetic identification and critical distance, faith and skepsis.

NOTES

1. This view is well presented in Morris Berman, 1989.

2. For reasons of ease of use, I will make use of the rhetorical "we" in this chapter, sometimes as a stand-in for humanity as a whole, at other times as representing Euro-American society specifically, and occasionally as a scholarly authorial convention. There are dangers associated with such a conflation: it frequently assumes the privileged perspective offered by the colonial legacy of European modernity. The magical traditions of which I write, however, themselves tend to make this conflation, but at the same time submit the "we" of Euro-American modernity to a kind of depth-psychological "deconstruction." I will follow this practice, while recognizing its risks.

3. See also Rappaport 1978, and, especially, 1979. Rappaport calls ritual "*the* basic social act," whose very structure contains inherent meanings and effects. Ritual and liturgical orders, according to Rappaport, perform a multitude of functions: they demarcate distinctions, but also join them into significant wholes; they give form to inchoate matter; they bind together, unite and reunite the psychic, social, natural, and cosmic orders which language (by making distinctions) and the exigencies of life pull apart; they provide the quality of "sanctity," "unquestionableness," "the sacred," the "numinous," as well as moral norms, to which the performer publicly binds himself. "The unfalsifiable supported by the undeniable yields the unquestionable, which transforms the dubious, the arbitrary, and the conventional into the correct, the necessary, and the natural."

4. See Morris Berman's classic *The Reenchantment of the World* (1981), and his *Coming to Our Senses: Mind and Body in the History of Western Culture* (1989); also, Gregory Bateson, *Mind and Nature: A Necessary Unity* (1980), and Gregory and Mary Catherine Bateson, *Angels Fear: Towards an Epistemology of the Sacred* (1988). Both Berman and Bateson attempt to lay

the epistemological foundations for an alternative, empathetic, and participatory science.

Berman's *Coming to Our Senses* explores Western culture's "somatic history," tracing a heretical or "countercultural" semi-underground tradition that is rooted in bodily experience, and that aims at undoing the alienation that has been with us since the emergence of "ego-consciousness" and especially since the development of an agriculturally based "binary logic" (wild vs. tame, self vs. other). He carefully analyzes four historical "breakthroughs to interiority," as he calls them, along with their ultimate outcomes: (1) the rich cultural diversity of the Mediterranean basin at the beginnings of the Christian era (Greek philosophy, Jewish ethics and magic, oriental Gnostic practices, etc.) from which emerged a victorious, ultimately monolithic world religion—Christianity; (2) heretical religious movements in southern France, Spain, and Italy (Cathars, Albigensians, etc.) in the eleventh to thirteenth centuries, which eventually resulted in the co-optation of romantic love by the Catholic Church into the Marian cult, in a secular, more acceptable form in the courtly love tradition, and ultimately in the institutionalization of "thought crime" and the administrative persecution of it via the Inquisition; (3) the rejection of Church Aristotelianism and academic Scholasticism in the sixteenth and seventeenth centuries, resulting in the creation of a new *Weltanschauung* that institutionalized the experience of magical "ascent" into the purely exterior, abstract, mechanized form of modern science; (4) finally, the Nazi phenomenon, representing the re-emergence of the same "energy" (towards transcendence and the eradication of the split or "basic fault" in consciousness) into a new form combining a paranoid, dualist, racist cosmology with a nationalist political program to accomplish racial purity.

Berman sees in today's "New Age" phenomenon a movement in danger of being co-opted into a "cybernetic holism" by the present-day "Church"—the scientific, industrial, corporate establishment. His solution is that we, once and for all, reject the "binary mode" with its concomitant need for "redemption" from some "evil" world, and substitute it with a "kaleidoscopic" mode (closer to the worldview of hunter-gatherers than to "binary" agriculturalists), a meeting of the world "in a spirit of aliveness and curiosity rather than one of need or desperation." We need to cultivate balance and "reflexivity"—the capacity to see *ourselves* in a state of need or commitment; we need to develop a new code that is itself about coding.

5. The Bateson's attempt to establish an alternative epistemology draws on Carl Jung's distinction between *Pleroma* ("the unliving world described by physics which in itself contains and makes no distinctions") and *Creatura* ("that world of explanation in which the very phenomena to be described are among themselves governed and determined by difference, distinction, and information"). The book explores those activities—art, poetry, and the sacred—which take place at the interface between *Creatura* and *Pleroma*, activities that necessarily involve metaphor

("the main characteristic and organizing glue of this world of mental process").

An excellent account of the fall of the organicist worldview and its replacement by a patriarchal, mechanicist model of nature is Carolyn Merchant's *The Death of Nature: Women, Ecology, and the Scientific Revolution* (1990).

6. Historian Frances Yates has carefully documented the important role played by occult and magical thinking during the Renaissance, a role that had been significantly underplayed in previous Renaissance historiography. See her *Giordano Bruno and the Hermetic Tradition* (1964), *The Rosicrucian Enlightenment* (1972), and *The Occult Philosophy in the Elizabethan Era* (1979).

7. Useful introductions to the history of magic include Francis King, *Magic: The Western Tradition* (1975), Caitlin and John Matthews, *The Western Way* (volumes 1 and 2, 1985–1986, and Manly Palmer Hall, *The Secret Teachings of All Ages: An Encyclopedic Outline of Masonic, Hermetic, Qabbalistic and Rosicrucian Symbolical Philosophy* ([1928] 1977).

8. For "primitive" peoples' mythology and worldviews in general, see Sam Gill, *Beyond "the Primitive": The Religions of Nonliterate Peoples* (1982).

9. Burckhardt, unlike most medieval historians, sees alchemy as a genuine spiritual tradition, with an organic and consistent doctrine of teachings and practices, based on the reciprocal correspondence of the universe and man (i.e., the Hermetic axiom, "As above, so below"). For two other views on the subject, see Carl Jung's *Psychology and Alchemy* (*Collected Works*, volume 12, 1968); and Richard Grossinger's *The Alchemical Tradition* (1983).

10. Gershom Scholem is usually considered to be the foremost historical authority on Kabbalistic mysticism; see his *Kabbalah* (1974a) and *Major Trends in Jewish Mysticism* ([1941] 1974b). Z'ev ben Shimon Halevi, *Kabbalah: Tradition of Hidden Knowledge* (1979), is a useful introduction. The most highly touted manuals of practical "Qabalism" (the preferred modern spelling) among contemporary occultists are Dion Fortune, *The Mystical Qabalah* ([1935] 1979) and Gareth Knight, *A Practical Guide to Qabalistic Symbolism* (one-volume ed., 1978). These authors present the Qabalistic system as a workable "yoga of the West."

11. Richard Cavendish, *The Tarot* (1975) is an excellent general introduction to the tarot cards, their history, symbolism, and usage (for divination and for meditation), and their relationship to the Cabala. Sallie Nichols, *Jung and Tarot: An Archetypal Journey* (1980) is a Jungian analysis of the twenty-two trumps of the Greater Arcana.

12. The foremost archaeologist of the "Old European civilization" is Marija Gimbutas; see her *The Goddesses and Gods of Old Europe, 6500–*

3500 B.C.: Myths and Cult Images (1982) and *The Language of the Goddess* (1989). On Goddess and animal imagery in ancient myth in general, see Buffie Johnson, *Lady of the Beasts: Ancient Images of the Goddess and Her Sacred Animals* (1988), Elinor Gadon's *The Once and Future Goddess* (1990), and Ann Baring's comprehensive *The Myth of the Goddess: The Evolution of an Image* (1991).

13. Incidentally, this book by "deep ecologist" and "eco-ritualist" LaChapelle is probably one of the most important, broad overviews of how human society has been "uprooted" from the natural world and how it can be *re-rooted:* she discusses ethology, the relationship between people and animals, archetypal depth psychology, primitive cultures, Taoism, the psychology of perception, the role of ritual and of "the sacred," and finally offers a manual of activities, ranging from childrens' play rituals, rites of passage, land rituals, seasonal ceremonies, and the usage (as close to universal as anything can be) of such elements as chanting, drumming, the gourd, the burning of sage, dance, etc. See also her *Earth Festivals* (1976) and *Earth Wisdom* (1978).

14. See, for instance, Ward Rutherford, *The Druids: Magicians of the West* (1978). A recent book that persuasively traces the historical roots of Witchcraft and Goddess religion to age-old shamanistic traditions, is Carlo Ginzburg's *Ecstasies: Deciphering the Witch's Sabbath* (1991). Ginsburg's thesis connects the various European accounts and popular myths related to witches and their persecution (as well as the persecution of Jews, lepers, and Muslims) with a hidden shamanistic culture whose traces can be found throughout the distant and recent past (including in the subculture of Italian *Benandanti* which Ginzburg thoroughly documented in his earlier *The Night Battles*). This argument bears superficial resemblance to one that, in a much grosser form, was once put forward by Margaret Murray, and later, for the most part, discredited. Ginzburg, however, as one of the leading historians of Renaissance Europe, presents a thoroughly researched and sophisticated analysis that is convincing in at least some of its major assertions.

15. On archetypal psychology, see James Hillman, ed., *Facing the Gods* (1980), *The Myth of Analysis* (1972), and *Re-Visioning Psychology* (1975); David Miller, *The New Polytheism* (1981); Peter Lemesurier, *The Healing of the Gods: The Magic of Symbols and the Practice of Theotherapy* (1988); Robert Avens, *The New Gnosis: Heidegger, Hillman, and Angels* (1984); and of course, the writings of Carl Jung, e.g., *Collected Works* vol. 9, pt. 1: "The Archetypes and the Collective Unconscious," and vol. 12, pt. 2: "Aion: Researches into the Phenomenology of the Self" or Jung, et al., *Man and His Symbols* (1965).

16. Ellic Howe, *The Magicians of the Golden Dawn* (1972) is a good historical overview of the Golden Dawn; Israel Regardie, *The Complete*

Golden Dawn System of Magic (1984) presents the bulk of its practices. See also: Francis King, *Magic: The Western Tradition* (1975); S. L. MacGregor Mathers, *Astral Projection, Ritual Magic, and Alchemy* (1972); Israel Regardie, *The Golden Dawn* (1937) and *The Tree of Life* (1969); and Nevill Drury, *Don Juan, Mescalito, and Modern Magic: The Mythology of Inner Space* (1985). Ithell Colquhoun's *Sword of Wisdom: MacGregor Mathers and the Golden Dawn* (1975) is a rather more biased, if informative, account.

17. See also King's *Rites of Modern Occult Magic* (1971). One of the most interesting currents to develop out of Golden Dawn related sources ("genetically" related to the Golden Dawn mainly via Dion Fortune) is a school of writers allied around the idea of a "Western," and specifically "British Mystery Tradition"—a fusion of "native" lore (e.g., Arthurian and Grail cycles, the Welsh *Mabinogion*, Irish sagas, fairy lore, and general Celtic myths, folksongs, etc.) and the more abstract, Hermetic traditions of esoteric occultism, alchemy, ritual, and ceremonial magic. Their work is paving the way to a broader appreciation of the experiential dimensions of story and myth, and their relation to the geographical-ecological environment. See John and Caitlin Matthews, *The Western Way* (volumes 1 and 2, 1985–1986), John Matthews, ed., *At the Table of the Grail: Magic and the Use of the Imagination* (1987), Caitlin Matthews, *Mabon and the Mysteries of Britain: An Exploration of the Mabinogion* (1987); Robert J. Stewart, *The UnderWorld Initiation* (1985), *The Mystic Life of Merlin* and *The Prophetic Vision of Merlin* (both 1986); and Gareth Knight, *The Secret Tradition in Arthurian Legend* (1984).

18. The definitive survey of Neo-Paganism and Earth spirituality remains Margot Adler's excellent *Drawing Down the Moon: Witches, Druids, Goddess-Worshippers, and Other Pagans in America Today* (1986). See also Jungian analyst Edward C. Whitmont's *Return of the Goddess* (1987), Charlene Spretnak's collection of feminist writings *The Politics of Women's Spirituality: Essays on the Rise of Spiritual Power Within the Feminist Movement* (1982), and the collection *Weaving the Visions: New Patterns in Feminist Spirituality*, edited by Judith Plaskow and Carol Christ (1989).

A very interesting anthropological account of ritual magic groups in contemporary England is T. M. Luhrmann, *Persuasions of the Witch's Craft* (1989). On neo-shamanism, see, for instance, anthropologist Michael Harner's venture into popular writing, *The Way of the Shaman* (1980), or Shirley Nicholson's (ed.) *Shamanism: An Expanded View of Reality* (1987). Journals such as *Shaman's Drum: A Journal of Experiential Shamanism* (Cross-Cultural Shamanism Network, P.O. Box 430, Willits, Calif., 95490), *Gnosis: A Journal of the Western Inner Traditions* (P.O. Box 14217, San Francisco, Calif., 94114), and *Woman of Power: A Magazine of Feminism, Spirituality, and Politics* (P.O. Box 2785, Orleans, Mass. 02653) are ongoing sources of information in these areas.

19. An attempt to link archetypal psychology with Alfred North Whitehead's process philosophy, in the context of an explicitly "postmodern"

metaphysics, is David Ray Griffin's (ed.) *Archetypal Process: Self and Divine in Whitehead, Jung, and Hillman* (1989).

20. In the deconstructive parlance of Jacques Derrida, one could say that the dispersive effects of *différance* are "always already" at work in everything. I would emphasize, however, that this *différance* is not just a textual, linguistic effect, but a psychic and *imaginal* one (where "image(ry)" includes not only the visual, but the bodily and multi-sensorial).

21. Interesting approaches to the experiential use of story and myth are found in the popular and transpersonal-psychological writings of Jean Houston, Jean Shinoda Bolen, Stephen Larsen, and occultist Dolores Ashcroft-Nowicki, among others (see, e.g., Houston, *The Search for the Beloved: Journeys in Mythology and Sacred Psychology* [1987]; Feinman and Krippner, *Personal Mythology* [1988]).

22. This ultimate elusiveness of the Other is emphasized in post-Derridean, deconstructive religious and ethical philosophy. Derrida's method of deconstruction has been compared to the apophatic tradition of "negative theology," and has been called a "philosophy of the limit," which, in exposing "the quasi-transcendental conditions that establish any system" of thought, "demonstrates how the very establishment of the system as a system implies a *beyond* to it" (Cornell 1992, 1). For various versions of an ethical philosophy of alterity and *différance*, see the work of Mark Taylor (*Erring: A Postmodern A/theology*, 1984; *Altarity*, 1988); John Caputo (*Against Ethics*, 1993); Edith Wyschogrod (*Saints and Postmodernism: Revisioning Moral Philosophy*, 1990); Drucilla Cornell (*The Philosophy of the Limit*, 1992), as well as Coward and Foshay, eds., *Derrida and Negative Theology* (1992), and Berry and Wernick, eds., *Shadow of Spirit: Postmodernism and Religion* (1992). This recognition of the elusiveness and ungraspability of the religiously encountered Other provides a useful counterpoint to the more "essentialist" interpretations of Goddess religion and other variants of contemporary magic.

REFERENCES

Adler, Margot. 1986. *Drawing Down the Moon: Witches, Druids, Goddess-Worshippers, and Other Pagans in America Today*. Boston: Beacon Press.

Avens, Robert. 1984. *The New Gnosis: Heidegger, Hillman, and Angels*. Dallas: Spring.

Baring, Ann. 1991. *The Myth of the Goddess: The Evolution of an Image*. San Francisco: Harper and Row.

Bastien, Joseph. 1985. *Mountain of the Condor: Metaphor and Ritual in an Andean Ayllu*. St. Paul: West.

Bateson, Gregory. 1980. *Mind and Nature: A Necessary Unity*. New York: Bantam.

Bateson, Gregory, and Mary Catherine Bateson. 1988. *Angels Fear: Towards an Epistemology of the Sacred.* New York: Bantam.

Berman, Morris. 1981. *The Reenchantment of the World.* Ithaca: Cornell University Press.

———. 1989. *Coming to Our Senses: Mind and Body in the History of Western Culture.* New York: Simon and Schuster.

Berry and Wernick, eds. 1992. *Shadow of Spirit: Postmodernism and Religion.* New York: Routledge.

Burckhardt, Titus. 1960. *Alchemy: Science of the Cosmos, Science of the Soul.* Baltimore: Penguin.

Caputo, John. 1993. *Against Ethics.* Bloomington: Indiana University Press.

Cavendish, Richard. 1975. *The Tarot.* New York: Crescent.

Colquhoun, Ithell. 1975. *Sword of Wisdom: MacGregor Mathers and the Golden Dawn.* London: Neville Spearman.

Cornell, Drucilla. 1992. *The Philosophy of the Limit.*

Coward and Foshay, eds. 1992. *Derrida and Negative Theology.* Albany: SUNY Press.

Drury, Nevill. 1985. *Don Juan, Mescalito, and Modern Magic: The Mythology of Inner Space.* London: Arkana.

Duerr, Hans Peter. 1985. *Dreamtime: Concerning the Boundary Between Wilderness and Civilization.* Translated by F. Goodman. New York: Basil Blackwell.

Feinman and Krippner. 1988. *Personal Mythology.* Los Angeles: Tarcher.

Fortune, Dion. [1935] 1979. *The Mystical Qabalah.* Reprint, New York: Ibis.

Foucault, Michel. 1973. *The Order of Things.* New York: Pantheon.

Fox, Warwick. 1990. *Toward a Transpersonal Ecology: Developing New Foundations for Environmentalism.* Boston: Shambhala.

Frazer, James G. [1922] 1978. *The Golden Bough.* Abridged ed. London: Macmillan.

Gadon, Elinor. 1990. *The Once and Future Goddess.* San Francisco: Harper and Row.

Gill, Sam. 1982. *Beyond "the Primitive": The Religions of Nonliterate Peoples.* Englewood Cliffs, N.J.: Prentice-Hall.

Gimbutas, Marija. 1982. *The Goddesses and Gods of Old Europe, 6500–3500 B.C.: Myths and Cult Images.* Berkeley: University of California Press.

———. 1989. *The Language of the Goddess*. New York: Harper and Row.

Ginzburg, Carlo. 1991. *Ecstasies: Deciphering the Witch's Sabbath*. New York: Random House/Pantheon.

Graves, Robert. [1948] 1966. *The White Goddess: A Historical Grammar of Poetic Myth*. Reprint, New York: Farrar, Straus and Giroux.

Griffin, David Ray, ed. 1989. *Archetypal Process: Self and Divine in Whitehead, Jung, and Hillman*. Evanston: Northwestern University Press.

Grossinger, Richard. 1983. *The Alchemical Tradition*. Berkeley: North Atlantic.

Halevi, Z'ev ben Shimon. 1979. *Kabbalah: Tradition of Hidden Knowledge*. London: Thames and Hudson.

Hall, Manley Palmer. [1928] 1977. *The Secret Teachings of All Ages: An Encyclopedic Outline of Masonic, Hermetic, Qabbalistic and Rosicrucian Symbolical Philosophy*. Reprint, Los Angeles: Philosophical Research Society.

Harner, Michael. 1980. *The Way of the Shaman*. New York: Harper and Row.

Hillman, James. 1972. *The Myth of Analysis*. Evanston: Northwestern University Press.

———. 1975. *Re-Visioning Psychology*. New York: Harper and Row.

———. 1981. "Psychology, Monotheistic or Polytheistic." In *The New Polytheism: Rebirth of the Gods and Goddesses*, edited by David Miller. Dallas: Spring.

———, ed. 1980. *Facing the Gods*. Dallas: Spring.

Houston, Jean. 1987. *The Search for the Beloved: Journeys in Mythology and Sacred Psychology*. Los Angeles: Tarcher.

Howe, Ellic. 1972. *The Magicians of the Golden Dawn*. London: Routledge and Kegan Paul.

Johnson, Buffie. 1988. *Lady of the Beasts: Ancient Images of the Goddess and Her Sacred Animals*. San Francisco: Harper and Row.

Jung, Carl. 1968. *Collected Works*. Princeton: Princeton University Press.

Jung, Carl, et al. 1965. *Man and His Symbols*. New York: Dell.

King, Francis. 1971. *Rites of Modern Occult Magic*. New York: Macmillan.

———. 1975. *Magic: The Western Tradition*. London: Thames and Hudson.

Knight, Gareth. 1978. *A Practical Guide to Qabalistic Symbolism*. York Beach, Me.: Samuel Weiser.

———. 1984. *The Secret Tradition in Arthurian Legend.* Wellingborough: Aquarian.

———. 1989. *A History of White Magic.* New York: Samuel Weiser.

LaChappelle, Dolores. 1976. *Earth Festivals.* Silverton, Colo.: Finn Hill Arts.

———. 1978. *Earth Wisdom.* Silverton, Colo.: Finn Hill Arts.

———. 1988. *Sacred Land, Sacred Sex, Rapture of the Deep: Concerning Deep Ecology and Celebrating Life.* Silverton, Colo.: Finn Hill Arts.

Lemesurier, Peter. 1988. *The Healing of the Gods: The Magic of Symbols and the Practice of Theotherapy.* Longmead, U.K.: Element.

Luhrmann, T. M. 1989. *Persuasions of the Witch's Craft.* Cambridge: Harvard University Press.

MacGregor Mathers, S. L. 1972. *Astral Projection, Ritual Magic, and Alchemy.* London: Spearman.

Matthews, Caitlin. 1987. *Mabon and the Mysteries of Britain: An Exploration of the Mabinogion.* London: Arkana.

Matthews, Caitlin, and John Matthews. 1985–1986. *The Western Way,* vol. 1 and 2. London: Arkana.

Matthews, John, ed. 1987. *At the Table of the Grail: Magic and the Use of the Imagination.* London: Arkana.

Merchant, Carolyn. 1990. *The Death of Nature: Women, Ecology, and the Scientific Revolution.* San Francisco: Harper and Row.

Miller, David. 1981. *The New Polytheism: Rebirth of the Gods and Goddesses.* Dallas: Spring.

Nichols, Sallie. 1980. *Jung and Tarot: An Archetypal Journey.* York Beach, Me.: Samuel Weiser.

Nicholson, Shirley, ed. 1987. *Shamanism: An Expanded View of Reality.* Wheaton, Ill.: Theosophical Publishing House.

Plaskow, Judith, and Carol Christ, eds. 1989. *Weaving the Visions: New Patterns in Feminist Spirituality.* San Francisco: Harper and Row.

Rappaport, Roy. 1978. "Sanctity and Adaptation." In *Ecology and Consciousness,* edited by Richard Grossinger. Richmond, Calif.: North Atlantic.

———. 1979. *Ecology, Meaning, and Religion.* Richmond, Calif.: North Atlantic.

———. 1988. Interview. *Whole Earth Review* no. 61 (Winter 1988).

Regardie, Israel. 1937. *The Golden Dawn.* Chicago: Aries.

————. 1969. *The Tree of Life.* New York: Samuel Weiser.

————. 1984. *The Complete Golden Dawn System of Magic.* Phoenix: Falcon.

Rutherford, Ward. 1978. *The Druids: Magicians of the West.* Wellingborough, U.K.: Aquarian.

Scholem, Gershom. 1974a. *Kabbalah.* New York: NAL/Mentor.

————. [1941] 1974b. *Major Trends in Jewish Mysticism.* New York: Schocken.

Spretnak, Charlene. 1982. *The Politics of Women's Spirituality: Essays on the Rise of Spiritual Power Within the Feminist Movement.* Garden City: Anchor/Doubleday.

Starhawk [Miriam Simos]. 1979. *The Spiral Dance: A Rebirth of the Ancient Religion of the Great Goddess.* San Francisco: Harper and Row.

————. 1982. *Dreaming the Dark.* San Francisco: Harper and Row.

————. 1987. *Truth or Dare: Encounters with Power, Authority, and Mystery.* San Francisco: Harper and Row.

Stevens, Anthony. 1982. *Archetypes: A Natural History of the Self.* New York: William Morrow.

Stewart, Robert J. 1985. *The UnderWorld Initiation.* Wellingborough, U.K.: Aquarian Press.

————. 1986a. *The Mystic Life of Merlin.* London: Routledge and Kegan Paul.

————. 1986b. *The Prophetic Vision of Merlin.* London: Routledge and Kegan Paul.

————. 1987. *Living Magical Arts.* Poole, U.K.: Blandford Press.

Taylor, Mark. 1984. *Erring: A Postmodern A/theology.* Chicago: University of Chicago Press.

————. 1988. *Alarity.* Chicago: University of Chicago Press.

Whitmont, Edward C. 1987. *Return of the Goddess.* London: Arkana.

Wyschogrod, Edith. 1990. *Saints and Postmodernism: Revisioning Moral Philosophy.* Chicago: University of Chicago Press.

Yates, Frances. 1964. *Giordano Bruno and the Hermetic Tradition.* New York: Random House.

————. 1972. *The Rosicrucian Enlightenment.* Routledge and Kegan Paul.

————. 1979. *The Occult Philosophy in the Elizabethan Era.* Routledge and Kegan Paul.

Part IV

Ethics

11

WHAT HAS ALEXANDRIA TO DO WITH BOSTON? SOME SOURCES OF MODERN PAGAN ETHICS

Chas S. Clifton

RELIGION AND ETHICS ARE COMMONLY HELD to be intertwined, but in the case of Neo-Paganism, some of the typical ingredients are missing. This new religion has no sage and no scripture, no commonly agreed upon source of revelation. It is non-scriptural but not truly "oral," for its adherents produce masses of writing—books, journals, newsletters. And while it is officially polytheistic, some of its ethical formulations sound curiously like American Buddhism—or perhaps, to use Alan Watts's old formula, like "Beat Zen." (Perhaps this is because both American Buddhism and American Neo-Paganism are nourished by a common nineteenth-century tradition of Emersonian and Thoreauvian idealism.

In other words, although modern Neo-Pagans, particularly witches (or "Wiccans"), see themselves as following a (sometimes antinomian) Western magical tradition with chiefly European roots, they may well have also absorbed as Americans that tradition called "nature religion" by Catherine Albanese (1990). These two paths—one starting in Alexandria and one (for symmetry's sake) starting in Boston—frequently come out of the woods at the same meadow.

Let us deal with the former first, the "Alexandrian," esoteric, magical path. The story has frequently been told how the modern

Witchcraft revival was signaled by the publication in 1954 of *Witchcraft Today* by Gerald Brousseau Gardner (1884–1964), a British civil servant retired to his home country after a career in the Far East (see, for example, Clifton 1992, 21–38). Here, the origin myth continues, he encountered a coven of witches whose tradition stretched back centuries, was initiated, and later received permission to write about them—much of *Witchcraft Today* has a quasi-anthropological tone, speaking of "they" rather than "we."

This disingenuous pronoun-switching masks an important fact, according to one revisionist historian of Wicca, Aidan Kelly (himself a follower of this tradition). In Kelly's reading of the story, Gardner and his associates wanted to *create* the "Old Religion" (yet another synonym for Wicca), but had only a mish-mash of folk practices and the essentially Judeo-Christian ceremonial magical tradition to draw upon, plus Freemasonry and the general ideas about classical Paganism they had acquired in school. Consequently they were innovators disguising themselves as reformers: "Gardner [and, I would add, his fellow coveners and initiates] . . . did in fact think that what he was doing was reforming an older religion—because founders of new religions usually seem to think that they are putting an old religion on a firmer foundation by introducing a few new elements into it" (Kelly 1991, 182).

Within the self-recognized Western occult tradition in which Neo-Pagan Witchcraft places itself, one key idea has appeared in several guises. In Wicca, it frequently appears in the mock-Elizabethan language favored by Gardner and others (which gives their creations an antique appearance): "An it harm none, do what thou wilt." Of course, since many modern English speakers are not accustomed to "an" meaning "if" or "and if," they tend to write it as a shortened conjunction, leaving any outsider wondering "*What* and it . . . ?" Others face the facts and write or say, "If it harms no one, do what you will."

To maintain the mock-archaic tone (nothing new in organized religion since the days of ancient Babylon), this saying frequently is referred to as the Wiccan Rede, "rede" being Old and Middle English for "advice" or "counsel."[1]

Gardner and some of his contemporaries in British occult circles were acquainted with the flamboyant Edwardian ceremonial magician Aleister Crowley, whose chief dictum was "Do what thou wilt shall be the whole the Law." They may have recognized the phrase's longer lineage, its Rabelaisian connection, and even the version promulgated by Augustine of Hippo: "Love [God] and do what you will." The dependent clause may have served to soften the phrase's apparent self-centeredness, but our attention should focus on "Do what you will," which can be better understood in terms of another of Crowley's teachings: "Every man and every woman is a star" (in the astronomical rather than the cinematic sense). In other words, if a woman or man follows the life path that is her or his "true will," conflicts between them will evaporate, even as stars maintain their places in the galaxy and rarely collide with one another.

Thus, "Do what you will" in all its variants is not a license to self-indulgence but a challenge: find out what your destiny is and fulfill it. Stewart Farrar, a British novelist and Gardnerian initiate,[2] who became one of the most prolific Wiccan writers of the 1970s and 1980s, notes in his own discussion of Crowley's influence on the Wiccan Rede that "Unlike some other religions, Wicca seems reluctant to lay down in codified detail what is 'sinful.' This reluctance is certainly not indifference to moral issues." In the next paragraph Farrar quotes his own Craft teacher, Alex Sanders, as saying, "Wicca teachers power and free will to use it, once you understand *how* to use it" (1971, 49).

The result of applying this moral stance, says Judith Harrow, a Wiccan priestess and psychotherapist in Manhattan, is a "high-choice ethic." Discussing Paganism and conscientious objection to military service, Harrow cites a statement issued by the Covenant of the Goddess (a national network of Wiccan groups of which she has been an officer) during the 1991 Gulf War:

> It is [Covenant of the Goddess's] policy to support individual matters of conscience. We understand that devotion to the Goddess may either direct individual members to participate in war, or to conscientiously object to participating in a war. We pray that the wisdom of the Goddess guide all members of our faith who face such a decision. So, conscientious Pagans handle the question of violence just as we handle any other truly important issue. We find out as much as we can about any given situation, apply our values as well as we can, choose on a case-by-case basis, and accept the consequences of our choices. In legal terms, this is called the "selective Conscientious Objector" position, and it is not recognized as a valid legal option. The "all-or-nothing" standard of the draft laws infringes on Pagan religious teachings, which insist on our right and responsibility to choose. By so doing, it also violates the American Constitution and the freedom the American military purports to defend. (1995, 144)

Harrow's discussion of conscientious objection, however, comes in the context of her interviews with a group of Pagan military veterans. (Admittedly, she adds, "For Pagan youth, trained to a high-choice ethic, the military emphasis on taking orders will be especially challenging" [p. 145].) Although the Wiccan Rede could be used to justify pacifism, it usually is not so used; instead, Neo-Pagans are more likely to espouse a philosophy of self-defense (on the personal, community, and national levels) based more on natural law. "You'll never convince me that it would be unethical to take physical action to stop a rape to which I was a witness, and I don't see that it can be unethical to do magically anything that it is ethical to do physically," as one recent correspondent put it (personal communication with Michele Cox 26 July 1993).

Also accompanying the Wiccan Rede in common Pagan parlance is the so-called "Law of Threefold Return" or "Law of Three." This law simply restates the maxim "As you sow, so shall ye reap."[3] Its "threeness" could well derive from a line in the Gardnerian second-degree initiation ritual: "Learn, in witchcraft, you must ever give as you receive, but ever triple" (Farrar 1971, 91). From this line derives the concept that whatever good one does—or evil—returns in triplicate. (And of course Americans have the popular saying that bad things, at least, come in threes.)

In preparing this chapter, I deliberately opened a "thread" (series of linked electronic messages) on CompuServe, a national electronic data service with two Pagan-oriented sections, on what constituted Pagan ethics. A typical response came from Carole K. Bede: " 'Pagan ethics' depend a great deal on the particular Pagan you are talking to. . . . The baseline seems to be the Law of Three since even the concept of 'harming none' is open to interpretation" (personal communication, 25 July 1993). Indeed, one frequent discussion I have participated in at other times revolves around the question of whether "harming none" also applies to one's self (e.g., drug use, suicide) or whether the individual is free to do anything to himself or herself under the concept of "true will." In addition, several respondents' electronic messages repeated the idea that "divine revelation is not relevant to Pagan ethics" (personal communication with Jehana Silverwing, 4 August 1993).

Within the Neo-Pagan community, then, the evolution of community mores, while actively pursued, tends to be seen within a fairly narrow historical context and traced back through Western occultism. When speaking of American Neo-Paganism, however, I think it could fairly be argued that we are continuing a parallel American tradition of self-reliance and philosophical idealism.

One way in which this tradition manifests is the quasi-Transcendentalist language many Neo-Pagans use in discussing their ethical positions. Despite Neo-Paganism's avowed polytheism, the implications of which Pagans are still learning, when it comes to discussing their ethical positions, many use language that echoes Ralph Waldo Emerson's epochal 1838 address at the Harvard Divinity School—an event which caused him to be labeled "heretic" and "pantheist" and which effectively ended his preaching career (Whicher 1957, 98). In his address, an effective repudiation of New England Calvinism, Emerson proclaimed that the "laws of the soul . . . execute themselves. They are out of time, out of space, and not subject to circumstance" (p. 102). Like Emerson, American Neo-Pagans are, in Catherine Albanese's phrase, "the heirs of Puritanism, Platonism, the Enlightenment, and the Revolution [seeking] answers to religious questions in a world in which traditional faith is unraveling" (1990, 80). And to continue Professor Albanese's line of reasoning, they, like the nineteenth-century nature religionists she discusses in *Nature Religion in America*, reflect a tendency to see moral guidance in nature at the same time they attempt to discover what is "behind" nature in a Platonic sense, and attempt to shape a religious tradition that is not hostile to scientific discovery. It is no wonder that Starhawk (Miriam Simos), American Neo-Paganism's nearest thing to a nationally known theologian, describes her ethics as based upon "ordering principles inherent in nature" (1982, 35).

The impersonality of Emerson's "laws that execute themselves," for instance, is echoed in a text used by a Denver-area Pagan group, the Church of Seven Arrows:

> The magician who wishes to practice without "frying" himself must have a *major* interest in what the *Universe* considers to be Right and Wrong, *regardless* of what the cultural morals teach or what he himself has decided prior to becoming a practitioner of magic. (Dew 1979, 3)

From Neo-Pagan writing and conversation, then, the picture we get is that the individual stands alone in a universe of multiple choices and depends on its feedback—usually with an optimistic attitude reminiscent of the American Buddhist saying, "The Universe rewards a right action." As Dew and others have pointed out, the built-in structure of the universe may or may not coincide with a given culture's ethical patterns. This statement should not be interpreted as mere antinomianism. Nor is it necessarily an appeal to a "higher law," as might be used to justify civil disobedience, even though we find the "higher law" argument invoked (Starhawk in essence relies on it to justify her participation in the 1981 blockade of the Diablo Canyon nuclear power plant).

On the other hand, no group has made "celebrate diversity" more of a watchword than Neo-Pagans. Thus it follows that not all endorse the "feedback from the universe" pragmatic view of ethics—that one might, as Dew has it, judge one's degree of good or bad "luck" as an indicator of how well one is following the universe's "rules of the road."

Grey Cat (pen name of a Tennessee Wiccan writer) disagrees:

> I don't think that 'right' or 'evil' behavior is in any sense rewarded or punished by some 'outer universe' . . . being personally satisfied with your own actions as the 'best' you could do under the circumstances as you understand(stood) them is the carrot, and the stick is how loudly you yell at yourself when you fall short. (personal communication, 28 July 1993)

Indeed, the pantheistic streak in modern Paganism helps it to maintain its Emersonian self-reliance, albeit in theological terms foreign to the old Bostonian. "The world-view of immanence values each self as a manifestation of the Goddess, as a channel of power-from-within. . . . Integrity means consistency," writes Starhawk (1985, 34–35).

Today's Neo-Paganism has more to do with Athens—or Alexandria—than with Jerusalem. Perhaps it owes an indirect debt to Geneva, for its "high-choice" standards owe not a little to the broadly diffused Protestant idea that individual responsibility is more important than obedience to authority or tradition. Most importantly, via the Transcendentalist element never absent from American spiritual life, it owes something to Boston as well.

NOTES

1. Hence King Ethelred "the Unready" of England was really "Ethelred the Poorly Advised."

2. Via his teacher Alex Sanders, hence his references to "Alexandrian" Witchcraft.

3. Although it sounds biblical, this maxim probably derives from the seventeenth-century British poet Samuel Butler's *Hudibras*, line 501, perhaps influenced by Matthew 6:25 (King James version).

REFERENCES

Albanese, Catherine L. 1990. *Nature Religion in America*. Chicago: University of Chicago Press.

Clifton, Chas S., ed. 1992. *The Modern Craft Movement*. St. Paul: Llewellyn Publications.

Dew, George. 1979. *Basics of Magic Handbook 1: Psychic Technology*. Wheat Ridge, Colo.: Church of Seven Arrows.

Farrar, Stewart. 1971. *What Witches Do*. New York: Coward, McCann and Geoghegan.

Harrow, Judy. 1993. "Initiation by Ordeal: Military Service as a Passage into Adulthood." In *Modern Rites of Passage*, edited by Chas S. Clifton. St. Paul: Llewellyn.

Kelly, Aidan A. 1991. *Crafting the Art of Magic*. St. Paul: Llewellyn.

Starhawk. 1982. *Dreaming the Dark: Magic, Sex and Politics*. Boston: Beacon Press.

Whicher, Stephen E., ed. 1957. *Selections from Ralph Waldo Emerson*. Boston: Houghton Mifflin.

12

THE BRITISH OCCULT SUBCULTURE: BEYOND GOOD AND EVIL?

Susan Greenwood

INTRODUCTION

THE PRIMARY UNDERLYING PRINCIPLE behind all contemporary Western magical philosophies is the belief that the universe
is an interconnected whole. I would like to examine this philosophy by looking at the notion of evil. David Parkin has claimed that
the concept of "evil" has been useful to social anthropologists by
referring to extreme fear, death, destruction, and also lesser mis-
fortunes. Evil may denote human intention to harm or it may be
seen to have originated in an unintended human or nonhuman
condition (1985, 1). In this chapter I shall attempt to show how
different British magical practices, explicitly or implicitly, use notions of evil as "other" in their self-definition. Christianity, from a
magician's viewpoint, externalizes evil by opposing Satan to God in
the battle between good and evil, so my initial question is how is
evil understood within a holistic cosmology where it must be theoretically integrated?[1] The introduction of sexual politics into the
subculture, primarily through feminist Witchcraft in the late 1970s,
has created a storm of reaction and a fierce debate among practitioners about the basic nature of magical working. Magical practice is perhaps unique among religions in complex societies in the

fact that women and men both participate in magical rituals, and the essence of much ritual work is the notion of sexual polarity. The two topics of evil and sexual polarity may seem quite distinct and far removed from each other, but I hope to show that they are representative of how magical thought attempts to overcome duality in its pursuit of holism. Magical practice is diverse and lends itself to many different groupings ranging from various forms of Witchcraft to chaos magic, but a holistic cosmology is the common uniting thread between the varying practices.

It is my aim here to examine the cosmologies of the magical subculture from the inside through the philosophies of the practitioners themselves, not by any socially sustaining function the practice may have, or as projected by the mass media through a screen of stereotypes of witches and fork-tailed devils that have been erected over the centuries.

Since its inception as an academic discipline, anthropology has been associated with the study and explanation of magic in small-scale societies. One of its nineteenth-century founders, Edward Tylor, claimed that there were three conceptual divisions in viewing the world: magic, religion, and science (1913). Using this same categorization, Sir James Frazer was to write in the early twentieth century that there was an evolutionary move in human thinking from magic to religion and then on to science (1922). Evans Pritchard's 1920s study of the Azande is a brilliant account of Azande magic as a coherent universe of discourse which decides Azande action, but finally magic fails for Pritchard in its comparison with science because it does not meet Western objective standards which are seen to be universal (1985). Because of the dominance of the scientific paradigm in the West, magical practices in themselves have often only been viewed in their relation to the social structure of the particular society in which they occur. This results in the tendency for social scientists to ignore or dismiss the actual beliefs and philosophies of magical practitioners by using functionalist accounts; beliefs thus become subordinated to the sustaining role that magic plays for a society. For example, Mary Douglas claims that a society expresses itself through ritual symbolism. Magic, religion, and pollution beliefs form the same patterns of ordering a society's awareness of its own configuration (1966). Max Marwick, referring to Central Africa, gives social relationships primacy over actual beliefs in his 1964 paper "Witchcraft as a Social Strain-Gauge." More recently,

Richardson, Best, and Bromley, in *The Satanism Scare*, suggest that contemporary Satanism should be understood as a social construction resulting from a structural tension between employment needs and women's traditional domestic role, not as a reality in its own right (1991).

Many historical studies of Witchcraft and Satanism have been examined as a composite of concepts and ideas in relation to Christianity, often as a heresy or as a set of superstitions assembled over the centuries. For example, Geoffrey Scarre suggests that the concept of a witch was a synthesis of elements of Paganism constructed by churchmen (1987). These features, previously attributed to heretics, became incorporated into the stereotype of the witch. Similarly, Norman Cohn has written that during the European witch trials, the Inquisitors interpreted age-old popular beliefs in terms of Satan worship, and that it was this fantasy that was responsible for the deaths of hundreds of thousands of people in the witch trials (1975).

Anthropologists have tended to ignore contemporary Western magical practice, an important exception being Tanya Luhrmann's study of the rationality of contemporary magical practice in England (1989). Anthropology's reluctance to look at European magical practice may stem from the 1970s discrediting of Margaret Murray's work in *The Witchcult in Western Europe* published in 1921. In this book she had sought to prove that the Great Witch Hunt exterminated European Paganism (Hutton 1991). If a pre-Christian Paganism no longer existed, what was the point of examining what must have seemed like a few 'marginal' individual's misconceived beliefs? However, more recently the practice of "invented Witchcraft" has grown enormously, due, in part, to the New Age movement which fosters an internal search for deity and a closer relationship with "nature." It is now well documented that contemporary Witchcraft is a religion conceived in the 1940s stemming from the work of Gerald Gardner, a retired customs official who united folk beliefs with Masonic and high magic ritual to form a new synthesis. While contemporary practitioners generally accept the recent "invention" status of their current practices, they assert that they are reclaiming ancient mystical traditions, elements of which, they say, have survived underground which value the interconnectedness of being—the one with the all, often expressed in the language of myth. Thus the past they honor comes from mythology rather than history as such.

THE MAGICAL UNIVERSE

I will endeavor to show how magical philosophies work for the practitioners concerned. I shall use the term "magician" to mean all practitioners of magic when referring to issues on which there is common agreement, and specific group names to indicate alternative views. For the purposes of my research I have divided the various magical groups in the following way. There is a basic division in the subculture between Witchcraft, a nature-based practice which celebrates the physical creative force symbolized by the Goddess and God, and high magic or Western Mysteries which gains its historical inspiration from alchemy, astrology, and the Kabbalah and which is more controlled in its operation and more inclined to intellectualize its practice. Satanism as practiced by "The Church of Satan" is a separate organization which I will not deal with here.[2] The two practices of Witchcraft and high magic reflect two wider philosophical concepts (Löwith 1967): that of early Greek philosophy whereby the world, and humanity as a part, is an all-embracing and inherently harmonious cosmos (a typical view taken by most contemporary witches), while the other viewpoint is basically Judeo-Christian and concerns the biblical idea that the source of evil is located in humanity's anti-divine will. The practice of much high magic is concerned with the individual magician overcoming the Fall to connect once more with Divinity.

I should at this point make it clear that there are definite differences between the varying forms of Witchcraft and high magic groups, but magical work is open to a great deal of reinterpretation and experimentation and practitioners often move quite freely between different organizations to try out different practices and then gravitate to those which they find most comfortable. The Fellowship of Isis and the Pagan Federation are umbrella organizations which encourage membership from all paths; the former aims very broadly to promote a "closer communion between the Goddess and each member."

Witchcraft divides into two basic groups: the "traditionalists," who derive their way of working from Gardnerian or Alexandrian practices, who ideally work with equal numbers of men and women and aim at harmonizing and balancing the sexual polarities of their members thereby to channel energy. The other group is feminist, which in turn falls into two subdivisions: Dianic, which is restricted to women only, often radical lesbians, having an emphasis on the Goddess (sometimes to the total exclusion of a god); and more liberal variations which work with suitable politically aware men.

In contrast there are many different lodges in high magic which generally base their philosophy and ritual practice on an interpretation of the Kabbalah and the writings of members of the nineteenth-century Hermetic Order of the Golden Dawn, notably Aleister Crowley and others such as Israel Regardie and Dion Fortune. Chaos magick is a notable variation, being an anarchistic practice also influenced by the work of Aleister Crowley and the philosophy of Nietzsche. The central tenet of chaos magick is self-affirmation and the development of the Will (Nietzsche's notion of Superman). Chaos is quite different from other magical practice for a number of reasons, but primarily because it is truly postmodern in that it is completely eclectic, positively not adopting one system, but using whatever elements may be suitable at a particular place at a particular time, even to the extent of using science fiction characters as modern mythological figures, for example. Basically it is a system of *techniques*, as opposed to a belief in deities, the aim of which is to achieve "gnosis" or altered states of consciousness.

The current magical revival has been facilitated by New Age thinking, although many witches are deeply antagonistic to the New Age, believing that it is unbalanced in its emphasis on the light, whereby the dark becomes a repository for all that is chaotic, threatening, or unappealing. Feminist witches also claim that it is patriarchal. The New Age paradigm emerged in Western Europe and North America in the 1970s as a vision of a new world which transcends any particular religion and places emphasis on self-knowledge and inner exploration. It melds particularly well with magical thinking in its emphasis on the interrelatedness of all phenomena, for magicians, like New Agers, are opposed to the dualistic thinking characterized by the Cartesian paradigm in science, believing it to be a limited and inappropriate way of interpreting and understanding the world. Matter, energy, and consciousness are seen as one continuum and all aspects of the whole are seen to be contained within one single part.

AS ONE WITH THE ALL

Aleister Crowley, an initiate of the Hermetic Order of the Golden Dawn, wrote in *Magick in Theory and Practice* (first published in 1929), that theories of Dualism, Monism, and Nihilism are all reconciled and unified in Magical Theory. This is a mystical conception based on spiritual experience obtained through ritual, the aim of which is to unite the Microcosm with the Macrocosm, the individual with the universe. In Crowley's words, "The Supreme and Complete Ritual is therefore the Invocation of the Holy Guardian Angel; or, in the language of Mysticism, Union with God" ([1929] 1991, 11). This union is, however, different from the Christian conception whereby the individual remains separate from God, because the magician actually becomes God. To quote Crowley:

> The magician becomes filled with God, fed upon God, intoxicated with God. Little by little his body will become purified by the internal lustration of God; day by day his mortal frame, shedding its earthly elements, will become in very truth the Temple of the Holy Ghost. Day by day matter is replaced by Spirit, the human by the divine; ultimately the change will be complete; God manifest in flesh will be his name. (p. 182)

According to Crowley, the magician frees himself from transcendent deity and becomes fully conscious of his inner divinity—the magician *is* God. "By the use of this system the magician is able to unify the whole of his knowledge—to transmute, even on the Intellectual Plane, the Many into the One" (p. 5). Likewise, in the traditional Witchcraft ritual of Drawing Down the Moon, the high priest invokes the spirit of the Goddess into the high priestess who then becomes her personification.

The circle is perhaps the most important magical symbol because it represents this idea of the inclusiveness of all phenomena. This is summed up by the phrase in Crowley's Gnostic Mass, "There is no part of me which is not of the Gods."[3] Likewise, the witches' circle is inclusive and represents the four elements: air in the east; earth in the north; water in the west; and fire in the south. These four elements are a psychotherapeutic tool for keeping the witch balanced; for example, the intellect is represented by air and the magical knife, the athame and its cutting action is symbolic of analytic thought. This must be balanced by its opposite, the water of the west which represents emotions. Likewise the north represents the body and the earth which is balanced with the south, the energy of fire and magical will. The feminist witch Starhawk explains it thus:

> The sabbats are the eight points at which we connect the inner and the outer cycles: the interstices where the seasonal, the celestial, the communal, the creative, and the personal all meet. As we enact each drama in its time, we transform ourselves. We are renewed, we are reborn even as we decay and die. We are not separate from each other, from the broader world around us; we are one with the Goddess, with the God. (1979, 169)

The Kabbalistic Tree of Life is like the witches' circle in that it represents the microcosm and the macrocosm. It is a complex symbolic glyph representing human energies, which, if balanced, are said to enable contact with the ultimate source and divine illumination or gnosis. Again, like the witches' circle, it is a tool for becoming "whole." It is taught in some Western mystery traditions that when a person becomes whole they alter the whole of their race and in turn, the Universe; this is said to negate the Fall from an original golden age of magical consciousness.[4]

The idea that it is possible for humans to become God is, of course, the ultimate heresy in Christian terms and primarily the reason why "the occult" is associated with evil. Some Christian groups claim that "the occult" represents a manifestation of Satan's work because magical practice dissolves the boundary between creator and created; during magical practices the practitioner becomes aware of her oneness with divinity. This oneness means that even good and evil are one and an essential defining boundary has broken down.

HOLISM AND EVIL

How do magicians deal with evil in an all-embracing holistic cosmology without rejecting or excluding it? Ideologically magicians tend to follow New Age thinking that there is the potential for good and bad in everyone, and that basically all people are divine but some have histories that make them act in ways "unresponsive to love." Melton writes that the New Age movement was "an attempt to find the social, religious, political, and cultural convergence between the new Eastern and mystical religions and the religious disenchantment of many Westerners" (1986, 107). A key historical factor was the Theosophical, founded in 1878, the originators of which, Madame H. P. Blavatsky and Col. Henry S. Olcott, attempted to integrate Eastern thought into Western life. The doctrine of karma, that a person works out their own good and evil deeds within many lifetimes, is a significant example of Eastern thought that has found its way into Western magical practice.

Magicians tend to stereotype Christian beliefs in the same way that Christians often stereotype Pagan or occult beliefs. To magicians, Christianity is based on a Manichaean split between good and evil. Evil is personified by Satan and externalized, and this is one crucial difference between magical practice and

Christianity. Magical ideologies thus define themselves in opposition to Christianity by their *inclusion* of a notion of evil. What is evil is determined by what is considered to be the "ideal state" of being or existence; evil then becomes the obstruction standing in the way. This, according to Neil Forsyth in *The Old Enemy* (1987), a study of Satan and "The Combat Myth," is the essential role of Satan in Christianity. He, and it is always "he" although he may corrupt "gullible women," is "a stumbling block," whose character, existence, and essence is a function of his opposition to God.

This function clarifies the mythological foundations of both Christian and magical cosmology. An examination of the notion of evil in the magical subculture will show similarities and some important differences between groups.

William Gray, a one-time member of the Fraternity of the Inner Light which was founded by Dion Fortune (one of the most prominent magicians of the 1920s), writes that high magicians believe that in ancient times a very superior race of people made contact with planet Earth and interbred with the then homo-erectus and introduced a new genetic code into the human species that developed into *Homo sapiens* (1989). This is said to be the gene that is responsible for human evolution; its aim is to evolve towards the Ultimate. This is done by a high magician feeling "the call to service." The majority of high magicians that I have spoken to give this explanation when questioned on how they became involved with Western mysteries. One Swedish woman I spoke to explained that she had been led from the street by some unknown force, taken into a bookshop, led up the stairs, and shown a book on ritual magic. Her involvement, which was something of a religious conversion, had started from there.

High magicians utilize the terms Satan and the Devil in a ritual psycho-drama called the Abramelim Ritual, which is a confrontation between what are seen to be the good and evil parts of the personality. To the high magician, life is polarized between Divine and Demonic forces of energy. Evil is seen as a very necessary force whose energy is converted into the power of good by the magician in her attempt to find her "Trueself" in union with the Ultimate pure spirit. If the magician is able to balance the two forces they will combine and transmute to the Divine Being. This is done by direct confrontation with devils on their own ground who are commanded by the magician. Sins or failings are classified into divisions under the heading of some specified fiend, these are then called into consciousness. William Gray writes:

> Listen to me O lord of Life present in every person. I am going to evolve until I link up with you in reality and become one with your Being. To reach you I shall have to expend a lot more energy than I normally have, and so I am embarking on my present plan: to procure the additional energy I need directly from the Devil—to employ those forces in my nature that have been called Evil, which alienate me from you and enslave my soul for their own purposes, so making me into fuel for the Devil's dynamos, providing him with power for working whatever wickedness he wants.
>
> All I need is to learn how to catch, convert, and then place all that power at your disposal, so that instead of causing Evil it will only inspire Good from me and for all my fellow-beings sharing it with me. . . . (1989, 108)

In this account, Satan represents the forces of imbalance and chaos. He has an important role to play in ultimately returning humanity to oneness with Deity, but there is a catch. If the energies of good are directed towards the principle of evil then the "Pseudo Self" can develop into an alternative being the antithesis of good; in short, the Devil or Satan. The Devil or Satan stands for chaos and the antithesis of everything that is ordered, regular, beneficial— that which may conform to control by cosmic consciousness. Thus the power that comes from oneness with Deity is dangerous because the energy that gives power to the good is also the power that destroys and will turn to evil if it is misused or unbound.

Thus the naming of evil outlines a moral and ethical code that explains what is necessary to achieve the desired evolutionary state. William Gray's strategy for combating evil is within the self, to use evil energy for the purpose of good. It was Dion Fortune who stated that the biggest difference between Christianity and magic is that Christianity ignores the rhythm of good and evil, that is, Christianity is antagonistic and static whereas magic is equilibriating and dialectic (1987). The Kabbalistic Tree of Life glyph is arranged on two pillars; these are the symbols of polarity. A candidate for initiation into the Western Mysteries stands between these two pillars which symbolize the candidate's balance between the two. The candidate thus makes a third pillar—the Pillar of Equilibrium. In magical philosophy all things have a dual aspect—positive-negative, male-female, volatile-fixed, mercy-severity, past-future, progress-reaction—all of which are contained within each other and are needed for harmonious functioning of the microcosm and macrocosm. But it would be easy for a magician to get caught in the trap of dualism without managing to transcend it.

A high magician at a recent Western Mysteries conference spoke of the "sinister side" of magical practice. He spoke of how Hitler was initiated into the Thule magical group.[5] "Hitler's spirit visted planes that he shouldn't have visited—he was made to believe that he was the new Messiah and he made a blood sacrifice of his own people to the Teutonic gods of war." This "dark side" is, according to this speaker, "as bad as it gets." He believes that after the defeat of the Nazis by military means the group mind of Nazism still exists on the inner planes, therefore it will always re-emerge. He spoke of how "the distortion of esoteric truths has always been with us" and proceeded to explain how Dion Fortune became a magician to defend herself from psychic attack, and how Aleister Crowley had become addicted to heroin and whose magic had become so distorted and twisted that he "had a history of doing funny things to goats." He intimated that many magicians were not able to cope with their own lives and emotions. Why does the pattern of a magician's power go up and up and then drop? The speaker told of how he had had two full-scale nervous breakdowns due to his esoteric training. This is because it stirs up the unconscious mind—"the dark side is always with you, and the danger of ego inflation." The answer is to "Know Thyself." For this speaker there was no fundamental evil, but only good which was twisted, "a person is incapable of evil when the distortions are stripped away."

Later at this conference, during a Ritual for Planet Earth, the high magus (who had been specially invited from the United States), contacted evil forces; she sank deeper into them and her voice got lower and lower as she proclaimed that no one who was not worthy should be part of this particular mystery school, even if this meant that the school was left with only one person. She eventually toppled over and many were concerned that she was having a heart attack. It was almost as if her spirit could not fight the sheer number of evil entities she was facing. This was not stage managed and there was a general panic as the officiant magicians rushed to her aid; it appeared they had to pull her back from the underworld. We were instructed to chant and sing as she lay moaning. After a very long time she recovered and the ritual continued amid much emotion. This demonstrates the very strong psychological and emotional forces that these beliefs hold. I spoke to a well-known magician afterwards who was most scathing: "if she can't handle the power then she shouldn't be doing this; it gives a bad impression," he said.

According to Dion Fortune (1987), when cosmic forces are invoked, they always come up in pairs—as action and reaction. Every force has its unbalanced or Qliphotic element. Dion Fortune writes that the Qliphoth are inharmonious forces that came into existence before equilibrium was established and have been "reinforced by the mass of evil thoughts ever since" (p. 50). She further states that:

> Those who enter the dark portals which lead to the dread subterranean palaces of Qliphoth, and whose way is no longer that of the normal individual, return from this journey with their bias towards evil intensified. (p. 112)

Not everyone takes this view, however, and I have spoken to a chaos magician who is working on the Qliphoth. He informed me that there are path workings on the Qliphoth just as there are path workings on the other levels of manifestation of the Kabbalah. He described himself as a healer and he was using the Qliphoth to gain control over illnesses as each *sephiroth* has specific diseases which have to be mastered. This involved overcoming its specific demons and monsters, which frequently woke him in the night and which he described as "constructions of mind."

Traditional witches also consider evil to be unbalanced forces. They tend not to use the notion of the Devil or Satan, seeing these as inventions of Christianity, but they do believe, like high magicians, in reincarnation. An individual may take many lifetimes of working out karmic balance until a permanently healthy equilibrium is established. Thus good is harmony of forces and evil is unbalanced equilibrium which is eventually sorted out in the next lifetime; the problem of dealing with evil is postponed theoretically. However, on a practical level the notion of evil is still used in a manner common to many other religious groups: for example, an informant told me how she had joined a particular traditional coven and had problems with the high priest who she felt had inflexible views and was telling her what to think. When she decided to leave he was angry and she could feel his "bad vibes" for some time after. She felt that he was still trying to control her. She eventually confronted him and the vibes stopped for her. But he maintained his intransigent stance and instructed "his" coven not to speak to her or visit her bookshop as she was bad. As so often happens, evil in the shape of dissenters is frequently expelled, rather than being brought into balance as the ideal theory would have it.

HEXING

I have asked my witch informants why they perform rituals. The answers they usually give are for healing both the world and the individual, to aid world peace in specific ways, personal exploration and development, seasonal celebrations to mark the turning of the year, and communication with the gods and goddesses. However, there is a tradition of hexing in most Witchcraft circles. Hexing has to be done carefully, as it is said that hexing the innocent returns tenfold. I spoke to Leah, who is a teacher and a liberal feminist witch in her thirties. She said:

> I am of the tradition which says that you cannot heal unless you can hex. I can do both. I can choose one over the other but my reasons had better be good because everything you do goes out into the cosmos. If you do something that is skewed then that is the energy that goes out to the cosmos for ever, and it goes on and on like Voyager. And I've had that happen. And so you create the larger reality. A huge responsibility. You must have ethics.

The Dianic witch Z. Budapest, in *The Holy Book of Women's Mysteries* ([1980] 1990), says that for women who hex rapists or others who "commit crimes of patriarchy," there is no divine retribution. She gives instructions on how to perform a "Righteous Hex," for "violent criminals only" and for when you "know, not just think" that "someone has harmed you."[6] But I have heard mention of hexing being done between witches for more mundane reasons, over quarrels about money, for example, or to gain retribution from an employer who was unsympathetic.

High magicians do not practice hexing, seeing it as against "cosmic law," which is the law of karma. A person who is out of harmony will precipitate certain effects; these must be dealt with by the individual magician working to balance this within her- or himself, not by apportioning the blame elsewhere. Karma is the consequence of a person's former misdeeds. The wrongdoer *is* the victim; a person must take responsibility for their own suffering and see it as the consequence of natural karmic law. The difference between Witchcraft and high magic may be due to where practitioners view the source of wrongdoing. Southwold (1985) uses Lienhardt's (1961) study of the Dinka to compare external and internal explanations of occult workings. The Dinka tend to project onto supposed external occult agencies much that we attribute to the inward workings of the mind, whereas in Buddhism, for example, the tendency is to reduce all occult agencies to inner psychic phenomenon (1985, 139). For high magicians, confrontations between good and evil do not concern a battle between the self and evil entities, but the conflict between the lower and higher parts of the self; in other words, the struggle is *within the self.* Witches, on the other hand, are more outward looking and are more likely to relate to the outside world and its forces, beneficial or malign. Evil, as well as goodness, is an integral part of the life, death, and rebirth process.

The adept high magician must be able to deal with unbalanced force and handle the "positive" and "negative" aspects of the forces which they invoke; none embrace so-called "black magic" openly, except chaos magicians. Chaos magicians work with black magic very positively. Black magic, to a chaos magician, means deconditioning. This is broadly similar to the Tantric "left hand path," which aims at liberation from disgust or abhorrence of specific images. Gareth Hewitson-May, in the *Dark Doorway of the Beast*, writes that:

> It is the absolute disgust for particular objects, that supports their continuance. Similarly the idea of Satan is advanced, to reassert the necessity for God. If instead of shunning the horrors and thereby causing an exacerbation of their repulsiveness, individuals would accustom themselves to the presence of these substances and situations, ambivalence would soon develop. . . . The considerations of some of the practices shows that there is a definite stream of esoteric knowledge coursing through the system, whose nature is never revealed but often glimpsed by profane eyes. . . .
>
> Tantric practice should be personal and not applicable to the majority view, that is, for an individual well-versed in necrophilia, ritual flaying and murder, Tantric practice would involve charity work, selling jam at Women's Institute stall, or a monastic retreat. (1992, 150, 151)

By combining a power with its opposite it is said the magician gains immense power. For chaos magicians evil is duality which has to be transcended. Evil is manifest everywhere: in the media, "ordinary consciousness" and, in fact, in "ordinary" social life. "Kia," the life force of chaos, is said to be trapped by dualistic mind. Kia is not dualistic; it consists of the will and perception and it is singular. Magic is concerned with giving Kia more freedom and occult power by freeing it from the evil of society. The ultimate aim is the union of kia with chaos, the life force of the universe. An example of how this is done is the Thanateros Ritual. This ritual is a celebration of chaoist principles and is said to invoke the

power of chaos itself. It allows the magician to trick his consciousness into an exalted ecstatic, magical, and creative state beyond
dualism by the "neither-neither effect." The magician meditates
for a time on a particular idea, then on its polar opposite, then on
both qualities. Theoretically the next stage is to meditate on the
simultaneous absence of both aspects, which is supposed to force
conception beyond its normal limits. In the case of the Thanateros
Ritual, it exploits the paradox of the death of self in the act of sex,
and the birth of self in an encounter with death. It is significant
that chaos magicians should choose the two instincts which Freud
claimed it was essential to repress in human civilization.

PATRIARCHY AND ANTI-HOLISM

Magicial practitioners often construct notions of otherness which
then become associated with evil in terms of their self-definition.
One aspect that I would like to focus on is the currently heated
debate about gender roles. This is particularly applicable because
in much magical discourse sexual polarity is of great importance.
The impact of feminism, particularly on traditional Witchcraft,
has been profound, both in the form of negative reaction to its
sexual politics and in the creation of feminist-minded covens which
are either Dianic—women only—or liberal—mixed. The debate
focuses broadly between those who see sexual polarity as central
(and consequently adopt a more or less essentialist position) versus
those who deny sexual polarity, seeing sexuality as a social construction.

The debate has reached its most acrimonious level between
traditional and Dianic Witchcraft, whose practitioners are often
radical lesbians. I quote Una, who is a traditional high priestess in
her early fifties:

> Woman is the power and creation. Woman creates the life force and
> man protects so that knowledge and wisdom can go forward. Man is
> predator, hunter. He has to defend, this is his primeval instinct. The
> God form is Pan who is the personification of all men. The female
> creates power in the circle and the man gives the balance of Yang.
> The role of the High Priestess is totally 100% feminine to call down
> the Mother, to be the Goddess, her personification. In the proper
> Craft all are equal. Man will help woman wash pots, hoover, clean
> the altar, but it is the woman who brings warmth, decorates the altar
> and brings it alive with femininity. . . . You can't have all-female
> groups because you need balance, you need Yin and Yang. Dianic

witches are playacting, there is no ultimate balance, so you get 'bitchcraft.' Everything has to balance and produce, this is what it's all about—reproduction. Lesbians are not happy because they are denying the life force; they are aggressive. It is destroying them.

Traditional Witchcraft is concerned with harmonizing masculine and feminine energies. However, in feminist Witchcraft, the Goddess embodies the empowerment of women, who are reclaiming their spirituality in their own terms against the weight and tradition of centuries of male definition. Dianic Witchcraft represents the most radical form. I quote part of the Manifesto of the Susan B. Anthony Coven No. 1 from Z. Budapest's *The Holy Book of Women's Mysteries:*

> We believe that feminist witches are women who search within themselves for the female principle of the universe and who relate as daughters to the Creatrix.
>
> We believe that, just as it is time to fight for the right to control our bodies, it is also time to fight for our sweet woman souls. . . .
>
> We believe that we are part of a changing universal consciousness that has long been feared and prophesied by the patriarchs.
>
> We believe that Goddess-consciousness gave humanity a workable long-lasting, peaceful period during which Earth was treated as Mother and women were treated as Her priestesses.
>
> We believe that women lost supremacy through the aggressions of males who were exiled from the matriarchies and formed the patriarchal hordes responsible for the invention of rape and the subjugation of women. . . . ([1980] 1990, 2)

It is clear from this that the Goddess represents a spiritual and political weapon against patriarchy and its dualistic religious forms, which are seen as the ultimate evil. Thus the meaning of the Goddess has clearly changed from the way that it is seen in traditional Witchcraft terms: as a symbol of the feminine forces of life who, in partnership with the God, creates polaric balance and harmony in the world. The Goddess, for Dianic witches, represents a political consciousness which may overcome the evil of patriarchy—she has become the symbol of liberation from the male principle. For feminist witches, evil exists in the form of patriarchy, a patriarchy characterized by "estrangement" and oppression which is a long historical process whose roots lie in the Bronze Age shift away from matrifocal, Earth-centered cultures centered on the gods and goddesses embodied in nature, which are for them, the image of goodness.

Liberal feminist Witchcraft groups include men. Many men, like many women, come to feminist Witchcraft as a form of therapy from patriarchy. John Rowan, a humanistic therapist, writes in *The Horned God* (subtitled "Feminism and Men as Wounding and Healing"), that the Goddess represents the image of female power and the Horned God gives an alternative non-dominating masculine image which is necessary in order to change patriarchal society. Rowan explains his first realizations about the Goddess:

> So finding the Goddess was also like coming home. It was like something being restored which had been there before, and had been taken away. . . . I went around noticing so many things I hadn't noticed before—for example, in Athena one day I had the usual reactions to the way women were pictured—sexually objectified, turned into objects for men's use . . . and then I realised it could be looked at quite differently. I could see it as the Goddess insisting on being recognised—as if under all the falsification there was a power which could not be denied, and which would press on through, regardless of anyone's attempt to deny it. (1989, 83)

Leah, the liberal feminist witch, explained the role of the Horned God for men:

> The God can open up things for men like the Goddess does for women, so that they can become unstuck, so they can begin to look at their bodies and feel in a different way as men, not as de-manned men but strong, vital and playful men. I grieve deeply for men because I'd like them to be able to discover their Godself, bound up with the rhythms of life, in a profound way.

Feminist politics have changed the focus of magical practice by their emphasis on the politics of personal discovery—of finding out who you really are, of stripping off layers of patriarchal culture (Starhawk 1979). This is often related to the Sumerian myth of Inanna who journeyed into the underworld to find Ereshkigal, her dark sister. This "descent to the underworld" is when a witch has to face herself or himself. This takes the form of an initiation where a witch has to face her/his own anger, fear, destruction, and death. This is similar to the high magic Abramelim Ritual, but the evil is externalized onto patriarchy. Feminist witches claim that patriarchal religions including high magic and the New Age ignore the dark, destructive, disintegrating aspect of self-discovery by their focus on transcendent light.

At the root of the feminist critique of high magic is the notion that it draws on traditions based on the transcendent principle, the ascent of the light of knowledge from dense matter. This is seen by feminists to be a very patriarchal attitude which fosters hierarchy. In reaction, feminist political consciousness is increasingly located in the body and the "despised matter" of transcendent spiritual ideologies, a development which threatens to produce dualism in reverse in too great an emphasis on the body, the dark, and the chaotic.

CONCLUSION

It is paradoxical that magical practitioners embrace a cosmology that recognizes the interconnectedness of all phenomena—plant, human, and animal—and good and evil, yet, as I hoped I have shown, often exclude the evil like other social groups have done. For example, feminist Witchcraft defines evil as oppression and coercion, which they identify as patriarchy, and thereby deny that power can be misused in a society built on matrifocal principles of immanence.

For high magicians, evil is unbalanced forces located in the nineteenth-century evolutionary idea of spiritual progress and development, which seems strangely dated and elitist in the late twentieth century. Chaos magicians too are trapped, in spite of their beliefs, in projecting evil out onto outsiders. For example Stephen Mace, sounding very Nietzschian, writes in the magazine *Chaos International:*

> [by declining to engage in the clouded vision of the media] we may begin to elevate ourselves above the dual principle and draw in the power that is borne on the wind of this high place. Perhaps this power will even be sufficient to keep those in thrall to duality from breaking down our doors and stealing our children. This much must remain an article of faith. To join them to escape them is to merge with them in slime, and in mutual doom. (CI no 12).

Evil is dualistic society, a society defined by its misguided capability of taking children into care to protect them from "evil Satanists."

While magical ideology in general promotes an all-embracing cosmology, it is clear that particular groups do define themselves against other groups within the subculture, particularly since the introduction of feminist politics. The magical subculture can be seen as a continuum from "conservative" high magical groups and traditional Witchcraft—which both emphasize sexual polarity (the former maintains a holistic view attempting to be non-exclusionary,

while the latter, through the practice of hexing, externalizes malign forces)—to the other extreme: Dianic Witchcraft on the one
hand and chaos on the other. Both of these practices are profoundly non-holistic, Dianic witches by their exclusion of men as
the bearers and perpetrators of patriarchy, and chaos magicians by
their anarchistic view of the evils of "the society machine." Magicians, despite their holistic ideology, are perhaps not so different
from those whom they see as "dualistic."

NOTES

I would like to thank Olivia Harris for her encouragement and for
her detailed and thought-provoking comments on countless earlier drafts.
This chapter was originally prepared for the London School of Economics
Sociology of Religion Graduate Seminar in 1992 and I am indebted to
Eileen Barker for allowing me to present it. The field work upon which
it is based was carried out in England in 1990 to 1992 and I would like
to thank the practitioners of magic whom I interviewed for their gener-
osity of time and information. Gratitude is also due to the University of
London Central Research Fund and the Economic and Social Research
Council (UK) for their financial support.

1. I would like to emphasize that I am not a trained philosopher and
realize that the concepts that I explore are profound, but my main interest
is in how the practitioners themselves perceive their world.

2. Anton LaVey's Church of Satan views Satanism as a secular philosophy of rationalism and self-preservation in opposition to the "compla-
cency of the masses" (Barton 1990).

3. The Gnostic Mass is a ritual celebrating the Mystic Marriage
between priestess and priest, which unites the one with the all:

The Priestess: . . . I who am all pleasure and purple, and drunken-
ness of the innermost sense, desire you. Put on the wings, and arouse
the coiled splendour within you: come unto me!

The Priest: O secret of secrets that art hidden in the being of all that
lives, not Thee do we adore, for that which adoreth is also Thou.
Thou art That, and That am I. (Crowley [1929] 1991, 351)

4. It is taught in Western mysteries schools that the Mysteries originally appeared on the physical plane in the ancient lands of Lemuria and
Atlantis but were eventually destroyed by the evil in the world.

5. According to Nicholas Goodrick-Clarke, in *The Occult Roots of
Nazism*, there is no evidence to support crypto-historical beliefs that Hitler
was initiated into the occult or believed that Germany had a heroic golden

past. However, Hitler was passionately interested in Germany's heroic golden future with himself as the new messiah. He mobilized the nationalistic response of which occult beliefs were a part.

6. Z. Budapest recommends a black altar be constructed and that a doll-shaped form resembling the enemy is cut out:

> . . . sew it around from east to north to west to south (widdershins), and leave only a small part open. Stuff it with boldo leaves . . . Indicate the eyes, mouth, nose, and hair on the doll. On a piece of parchment paper, write the name of your enemy and attach it to the image.

The Goddess Hecate is involved to doom the life of the enemy:

> Goddess Hecate, to You I pray,
> With this enemy no good will ever stay.
> Cut down the lines of his life in three,
> *Doom him, doom him, so mote it be!*

When you pronounce this, take a mallet and break his 'legs' by breaking the herb inside. Dust it with Graveyard Dust; anoint it with Double-Crossing oil, and burn your Black Arts incense. Imagine him totally miserable and with one leg broken . . . Do this three nights in a row. On the third night, burn the doll and bury it. Draw a triple cross over his grave with Dragon Blood power. Walk away without looking back . . .

> Note: Dispose of hexes as far away from your house as possible. Each night you can break something else in him, or stick black-headed pins into his liver or penis. May patriarchy fall! (p. 43).

REFERENCES

Adler, M. [1979] 1986. *Drawing Down the Moon.* 2d ed. Boston: Beacon Press.

Barton, B. 1990. *The Church of Satan.* New York: Hell's Kitchen Productions.

Budapest, Z. [1980] 1990. *The Holy Book of Women's Mysteries.* Reprint, London: Robert Hale.

Carroll, P. [1987] 1991. *Liber Null and Psychonaut.* Me.: Samuel Weiser.

———. 1992. *Liber Kaos, The Psychonomicon.* Wiltshire: Antony Rowe.

Cohn, N. 1975. *Europe's Inner Demons.* New York: New American Library.

Crowley, A. [1929] 1991. *Magick in Theory and Practice.* Castle Books.

Douglas, M. 1966. *Purity and Danger.* Harmondsworth: Penguin.

Evans Pritchard, E. E. [1976] 1985. *Witchcraft, Oracles and Magic among the Azande.* Oxford: Clarendon Press.

Forsyth, N. 1987. *The Old Enemy.* N.J.: Princeton University Press.

Fortune, D. 1987. *Applied Magic.* Northampton: Aquarian.

Frazer, J. 1922. *The Golden Bough.* London: Macmillan.

Goodrick-Clarke, N. 1992. *The Occult Roots of Nazism.* New York: I. B. Tauris.

Gray, W. 1989. *Between Good and Evil.* Minn.: Llewellyn Publications.

Hewitson-May, G. 1992. *Dark Doorway of the Beast.* Yorkshire: New World Images.

Hine, P. 1992. *Condensed Chaos.* Instant Print West One.

Hutton, R. 1991. *The Pagan Religions of the Ancient British Isles.* London: BCA.

Löwith, K. 1967. "The Philosophical Concepts of Good and Evil." In *Studies in Jungian Thought.* Evanstown: Northwestern University Press.

Luhrmann, T. 1989. *Persuasions of the Witch's Craft.* Oxford: Basil Blackwell.

Marwick, M. [1970] 1990. "Witchcraft as a Social Strain Gauge." In *Witchcraft and Sorcery*, edited by M. Marwick. London: Penguin.

Melton, J. 1986. *Encyclopedic Handbook of Cults in America.* New York: Garland.

Morris, B. 1991. *Western Conceptions of the Individual.* Oxford: Berg.

Murray, M. 1921. *The Witch-cult in Western Europe.* Oxford: Oxford University Press.

Parkin, D., ed. 1985. *The Anthropology of Evil.* Oxford: Basil Blackwell.

Parry, J. 1982. "Sacrificial Death and the Necrophagous Ascetic." In *Death and the Regeneration of Life*, edited by M. Bloch and J. Parry. Cambridge: Cambridge University Press.

Richardson, J., J. Best, and D. Bromley. 1991. *The Satanism Scare.* New York: Aldine de Gruyter, Inc.

Rowan, J. 1989. *The Horned God.* New York: Routledge.

Scarre, G. 1987. *Witchcraft and Magic in Sixteenth and Seventeenth Century Europe.* Basingstoke: Macmillan.

Southwold, M. 1985. "Buddhism and Evil." In *The Anthropology of Evil*, edited by D. Parkin. Oxford: Basil Blackwell.

Starhawk, 1979. *The Spiral Dance.* San Francisco: Harper and Row.

Tylor, E. B. [1871] 1913. *Primitive Culture.* London: Murray.

Part V

Christianity and Neo-Paganism

13

EMBRACING JESUS *AND* THE GODDESS: TOWARDS A RECONCEPTUALIZATION OF CONVERSION TO SYNCRETISTIC RELIGION

Christel J. Manning

INTRODUCTION

"I AM A PAGAN—but I also believe in the truth of the gospels," says Cathy, her hand resting on a small stone figurine primitively carved to resemble an ancient fertility goddess.[1] Cathy is a tall, full-bodied woman; she has lively blue eyes and brown hair that is beginning to grey at the temples. In her mid-thirties, she has three children and works full-time as a nurse. Cathy was raised a Roman Catholic but dropped out of the Church in her teens. "I couldn't take their attitude about women," she says. "If Christianity was the truth, how could it be so oppressive?" While in college she experimented with Eastern religions but found Buddhist and Hindu teachers to be no less sexist. Deeply disappointed, she was no longer interested in joining any religious community; instead, she began extensive reading on her own. "Why is it that all religions put women down? Was it always that way? Can I be a religious person without compromising my self-respect?" were the questions she asked herself. She found an answer in Merlin Stone's book *When God Was a Woman* (1976), which asserts that prehistoric peoples all over the world worshiped a female deity associated with Earth and motherhood who was only later replaced by male gods of war and patriarchy.

Other books such as Starhawk's *Spiral Dance* (1979) and Z. Budapest's *Holy Book of Women's Mysteries* (1979) showed Cathy how such a woman-centered religion might be revived today. In conversations with other women, she gradually realized that she was not alone in her interest, and one day decided to begin having a Moon-group, the monthly gathering at which I had first met her. For the past five years, Cathy and about ten other women have been meeting during every full-moon night to celebrate a goddess ritual. At the same time, however, Cathy periodically attends the local Episcopalian church ("they have a woman pastor I like"), sends her kids to Catholic school ("so they can learn good values like I did"), and celebrates Christmas ("Jesus did bring great joy to this world").

What are we to make of Cathy? She claims her conversion to Neo-Paganism is real and sees no inconsistency with her continued commitment to Christianity. Is she a Pagan? Or is she really a disgruntled Catholic experimenting with exotic ideas? In other words, *what effect does blending or syncretism have on religious conversion?* Moreoever, if syncretism is characteristic of Neo-Pagan converts, *are existing models of conversion applicable in this case?* The research intent behind this study was to find an answer to these questions. The chapter has three main parts. Following some remarks on the significance of this research, part one provides a definition and short history of Neo-Paganism and argues that it is itself a highly syncretistic religion and therefore lends legitimacy to further blending. Part two is an analysis of the literature which demonstrates that conversion to Neo-Paganism has not been adequately studied. Part three suggests a new theoretical framework for the study of conversion and outlines a model of how that might be applied to empirical research.

Religious syncretism refers to combination or blending of elements from two or more religions into one coherent worldview. Both individuals and groups engage in this process. At the individual level, each person can create his or her own personal religion from diverse sources (e.g., a woman who calls herself a Christian but also believes in reincarnation, karma, and astrology). At the group level, we see the proliferation of new religions that are themselves combinations of previously separate belief systems (e.g., many New Age groups combine ideas from Eastern religion, such as karma, with concepts taken from spiritualism, such as channeling, or with Native American healing rituals).[2] Both levels reinforce each other by lending legitimacy to the process of combination. Religious syncretism is, of course, nothing new. The blending of

Catholicism with elements from African religion led to the creation of Santeria in Latin America; and simultaneous adherence to several religions is quite common in Asian cultures. What is new about contemporary religious syncretism, at least in the American context, is its individualism and self-consciousness; *anybody* can blend and it's okay to *acknowledge* that you are blending.

How to understand conversion in the context of religious syncretism is an important question because scholars of contemporary spirituality have encountered more and more Cathys in their research.[3] Scholars have debated the nature, causes, and effects of conversion.[4] Yet beneath all this controversy, there has been considerable consensus on the definition of conversion. Conversion means a transformation in worldview in which old beliefs are rejected and new ones take their place. Anything short of that is mere "adhesion" or affiliation, a temporary state that in the long run will either lead to full conversion to the new religion or a return to one's former beliefs.[5] This definition is adequate so long as the convert has a limited selection of distinct traditions from which he/she can choose only one. However, given the contemporary context of religious syncretism in which the individual can mix and match a large number of religions, many of which are themselves already blends of other traditions, a reconceptualization of conversion may be necessary.

This study of Neo-Paganism was undertaken to test the hypothesis that individualistic, self-conscious religious syncretism that exists in the contemporary United States is accompanied by a different kind of conversion process for which new conceptual categories must be developed. Neo-Paganism lends itself to such a study for several reasons. Most American magical groups are not only highly syncretistic, but self-consciously so. Some groups (e.g., feminist covens) permit or even encourage individuals to create further blends, particularly in the area of ritual. Finally, there is evidence that individuals have combined Neo-Paganism with other beliefs and practices.[6] My research suggests that the usual definition of conversion is problematic when applied to many Neo-Pagans.

NEO-PAGANISM: A DEFINITION AND HISTORY

What is Neo-Paganism? Problems in developing a workable conversion model are intensified and at the same time obscured by confusion about what Neo-Paganism actually is. Both academic and popular accounts frequently fail to differentiate diverse strands of what they call "the occult," which includes a broad range of diverse nonmainstream religions such as spiritualism, theosophy, UFO cults, Neo-Paganism, Scientology, and any other group that might be labelled as secret or hidden. Particularly common and most resented by modern Pagans has been the tendency to identify their religion with Satanism.[7]

Several reasons may account for the confusion about what counts as Pagan. The first is fear, reinforced by sensationalistic media reports, which results in the stereotype that all occult movements are satanic and evil. A second is a lack of accurate information due to the secrecy of many of these groups. Ironically, that secrecy is in part a response to public fear and discrimination. Finally, a definitional confusion also derives from the fact that the histories and belief systems of many occult groups do overlap. Unfortunately, although several scholars belief systems of many occult groups do overlap. Unfortunately, although several scholars have provided excellent clarifications (Adler 1986; Marron 1989; Melton 1989; Russell 1980; Truzzi 1974), the confusion persists. Because, as I will show later, this confusion may be an important cause of poor scholarship on the topic of conversion to Neo-Paganism, it is necessary to provide a clear definition and history of the movement at the outset of this chapter.[8]

Neo-Paganism—also referred to as Witchcraft, the Craft, Wicca, or the Old Religion—is a syncretistic re-creation of pre-Christian European nature religions and the medieval Western magical tradition. Neo-Pagans must therefore be distinguished both from other Pagans such as remnants of African nature religions and from other magicians such as Satanists. Resistant to the notion of a unified creed, most Neo-Pagans believe in a polytheistic pantheon in which the high deity is usually female (the Great Goddess) and may or may not have a male consort. Pagans emphasize the cultic dimension of religion. Each group has its own sacred scripture, often called a "Book of Shadows," which contains instructions for ritual and magic. The Pagan code of ethics is simple: "do as thou wilt, but harm none." The community is decentralized. Most groups are organized in covens (which ideally number around thirteen people) or groves (which may be larger), and there is no proselytization. Estimates of the size of the Neo-Pagan movement vary considerably, ranging anywhere from three hundred to thirty thousand covens. The decentralism of the Craft makes concise estimates almost impossible. However, I would concur with Adler's suggestion that there are probably no more than ten thousand people in the United States who identify as Neo-Pagan (Adler 1986, 107–108).

The history of Neo-Paganism has been subject to much debate over whether or not the movement is a new religion.[9] However, the controversy has reached some resolution in the conclusion that Neo-Paganism is a new combination or blending of old themes. One of these themes is the Western magical tradition.[10] This tradition draws on ancient Greek, Egyptian, and Jewish mystical writings as developed by medieval fraternities such as the Knights Templar and the Kabbalists. Maintaining a high degree of secrecy and exclusivity, the tradition has been passed on continuously until the present time. A second theme in the Neo-Pagan combination is the pre-Christian European folk religion or Paganism.[11] We do not know much about this tradition, except that it consisted of a variety a polytheistic nature religions that were practiced openly by most people until Europe was Christianized. There is little reliable evidence that European Paganism continued as a religion after its suppression by the Inquisition. The practice of folk Witchcraft was quietly carried on, and various traditions were brought from England to the American colonies, but it is impossible to determine continuity of lineages to present groups.[12] There is sufficient evidence, however, to distinguish the origins of Witchcraft from those of Satanism, a term first created by the Roman Catholic Church to justify persecution of unbelievers. The linkage of Witchcraft with Satanism in seventeenth-century Salem and the formation of actual Satanist groups in the twentieth century perpetuates the confusion of Neo-Paganism with Satan-worship.

The Neo-Pagan movement was born in late nineteenth-century Great Britain when Gerald Gardner blended elements from Western magic and European folk religion to create what we now know as Wicca or Neo-Paganism.[13] Claiming to have been initiated into a secret coven that represented one of the last remnants of the Old Religion, Gardner initiated into his own tradition hundreds of people, including Raymond Buckland who brought Gardnerian Wicca to America. Americans combined Gardnerian Witchcraft with ideas from science fiction, feminism, and various ethnic sources other than Western Europe, such as Norse, Greek, and Egyptian traditions, so that Neo-Paganism now includes a wide variety of groups ranging from Arian supremacist followers of Norse gods to radical lesbians devoted to the Earth Mother.[14] Syncretism legitimated and therefore increased further combination. As more and more leaders openly combined Neo-Paganism with various other sources, the precedent was clearly set for any individual to combine his or her childhood religion to create yet another syncretistic worldview. What effect did this implied permission to combine have on conversion? It was the hope of finding an answer to this question that motivated my review of the literature presented in the next section.

CONVERSION: AN ANALYSIS OF THE LITERATURE

What do we know about conversion to Neo-Paganism? There are two main bodies of literature relevant to this question: (1) the general (both academic and popular) literature on Neo-Paganism, and (2) social scientific studies (mostly in anthropology, psychology, and sociology) of conversion to new religious movements. My review of both areas indicates that conversion to Neo-Paganism has not been adequately studied.[15] Among social scientific studies of conversion to new religious movements, very few focus on Neo-Paganism.[16] Conversely, among general studies of Neo-Paganism, there is little interest in conversion.[17] When conversion to Neo-Paganism *is* covered in the literature, there are other problems. The study of conversion tends to be unsystematic and speculative,[18] it is often tainted by ideology,[19] and it frequently fails to grasp the phenomenological complexity of Neo-Paganism.[20] This is not to say that the existing literature is worthless; only that, for the most part, it does not provide useful information for the development of a theory of conversion to Neo-Paganism.

The most valuable studies in terms of minimizing these problems are the publications by Margot Adler (1986), Tanya Luhrmann (1989), Frederick Lynch (1977), and Gini Graham Scott (1980). Susannah Miller Lloyd's (1978) dissertation is also worth mentioning, though it is not as frequently cited. These scholars provide accurate definitions of the type of group(s) converted to, they avoid ideology, and each has done empirical research on one or several Neo-Pagan groups (all five employed participant observation and interviews; Adler and Lynch used survey methods as well). Each has also developed some theory of conversion rather than just describing the group.

What do these studies tell us about conversion to Neo-Paganism? In addition to a loose consensus on social correlates,[21] there is significant agreement among these scholars on the process of conversion. They find that most people are not converted out of mainstream religion into Neo-Paganism, but are already religious dropouts.[22] Yet their lack of affiliation with organized religion does not indicate a lack of interest in spirituality. The process leading up to conversion is described similarly by all of these scholars: the individual's interest leads him/her to extensive reading of books about magical practices and/or groups; often there follows a mystical or psychic experience that reinforces what has been read; the individual actively seeks out a group and eventually makes the contact through friends or an ad at an occult bookstore; the experience with the group persuades the individual to either move on or to stay. Conversion, in short, is a gradual, fairly active process.[23]

But what is it that determines whether or not the individual will convert? Given the large number of solitary practitioners of Wicca and magic, not joining a particular group does not necessarily mean not converting to Neo-Paganism. It may be easier to say what is *not* a good explanation of conversion to Neo-Paganism than what is. At least two controversial theories, largely suggested by scholars who studied Neo-Paganism as part of the larger occult movement, are refuted by the five scholars discussed above. First, except for Scott and Lloyd, they firmly reject the deprivation hypothesis; i.e., that conversion is a psychological escape from socioeconomic marginality rather than a deliberate religious choice. Second, with the sole exception of Scott, they reject the counterculture hypothesis; i.e., that conversion to Neo-Paganism is a youthful rebellion against the establishment rather than a larger cultural movement.[24] The rejection of the deprivation and counterculture theories is significant because it implies that conversion to Neo-Paganism may be a permanent end rather than a temporary means of escape or rebellion.

Beyond their agreement on what conversion is not, each of these scholars has a different theory about what it is. Although Lynch (1977, 901) and Scott (1980, 141) both emphasize the appeal of intimacy and emotional support in the group, and Adler (1986, 20) and Luhrmann (1989, 307–310) both stress that conversion to Neo-Paganism is not a matter of changing beliefs but of affirming experiences and actions, their theories differ enough to warrant discussion in some detail.

Scott's (1980) study is based on research conducted from 1974 to 1976 on the Aquarian Age order, a "small, somewhat anarchic Witchcraft group of about 150 members" further organized into several smaller covens, for the purpose of comparing/contrasting it to a "highly organized international spiritual growth group, the Inner Peace Movement, with about 20,000 members."[25] Her conversion theory is essentially a combination of the deprivation and counterculture hypotheses. Converts are young people of marginal socioeconomic status who rebel against establishment values. Feeling different and lacking power, such an individual is drawn to Neo-Paganism because "the Craft offers a supportive family-like environment that celebrates his differences and offers an alternative social vision" (p. 129).

Scott's model has several problems. First, she provides no numerical data to back up her claims. Given the preponderance of evidence presented by Adler, Lynch, and Luhrmann against the deprivation and counterculture hypotheses, we need to know at least approximately what proportion of converts in Scott's study were young and/or socioeconomically marginal. Second, the language of contrast used throughout the study leads one to suspect that her desire to show the differences between the order and IPM may occasionally have cause Scott to oversimplify her conclusions (e.g., when she asserts that Neo-Pagans seek group rather than individual solutions to problems).[26]

Lloyd's work closely resembles that of Scott; thus I will only briefly discuss it here. Lloyd's (1978) study is based on research conducted from 1973 to 1977 in a small Wiccan coven (thirteen members) as well as on sixty-seven other practitioners. Lloyd's theory of conversion is a classic example of the deprivation hypothesis: socioeconomically marginal individuals are drawn to Neo-Paganism because it gives them the illusion of specialness and power (pp. 127–128). Yet even if socioeconomic marginality were generalizable to the entire Neo-Pagan population—which it is not—there are many other marginal individuals who do not become Neo-Pagans. The deprivation hypothesis, therefore, can at best explain why people seek a religious solution rather than, say, a political one, to their problems. The theory does not explain why a person would convert to Neo-Paganism rather than to Pentecostal Christianity or to Islam.

Lynch's (1977) study is based on research conducted from 1975 to 1976 on a single Neo-Pagan organization, the Church of the Sun, of approximately forty members. Having used the John Lofland and Rodney Stark (1965) model of conversion as a general guide in constructing his interview questions, Lynch's theory of conversion to Neo-Paganism clearly reflects the influence of that model. According to Lynch, conversion is the product of a gradual drift into a new worldview that is reinforced through interaction with the group. This drift consists of a sequence of four phases:

(1) intellectual curiosity leads an individual to extensive reading on occult topics; (2) emotional conviction (often caused by a psychic or mystical experience) or tensions and stress lead him/her to search for contact with such a group; (3) contact with a group or guru occurs at the right time and place; (4) the individual's experience of social and intellectual support persuades him/her to stay (pp. 896–908).

While the sequence of conversion phases is a valuable theoretical conceptualization of a process of conversion similarly described by Scott, Lloyd, Adler, and Luhrmann, Lynch's work is itself theoretically inconsistent. He asserts that most converts to Neo-Paganism were former religious dropouts, and he rejects the hypothesis that they were passively manipulated by environmental and social forces. Yet he argues that because converts had a pre-existent interest in the occult, they were not "active seekers" (1977, 897). The implication is that converts more or less passively fell into Neo-Paganism. Lynch never bothers to ask, however, why converts began pursuing their interest in the occult in the first place.

Adler's (1986) revision of her (1979) study is based on a (1985) survey of several Neo-Pagan groups. While her work is primarily descriptive, she does ask questions about what kinds of people become Pagans and why. Her theory is essentially that there is no conversion: Neo-Pagans were already Pagan before they joined the movement, they just did not know it. Calling Neo-Paganism a "religion without converts," Adler asserts that the entry point for "coming home" is provided by a lecture, word of mouth, a book, or an article that "confirms some original, private experience" (p. 14). She assumes that because becoming Pagan is *not* a response to attempts by members to persuade a prospective convert and does not result in a radical change of belief, conversion does not occur. What happens instead is the affirmation of feelings and/or behaviors that were previously repressed or rejected because they were not accepted by mainstream religion.

Adler's coming-home hypothesis presents a valuable challenge to traditional conversion theory in its emphasis on emotion and action rather than on belief and in her suggestion that people may possess a particular worldview long before they join a corresponding organization. Moreover, the parallel of the coming-home experience as Adler describes it and the experience of "coming out" described by many gay people suggests interesting avenues for further research. Her theory is flawed, however, by her excessively narrow definition of conversion, which, ironically, follows the traditional Pauline model that conversion is a drastic change in response to outside influence.

Finally, Luhrmann's (1989) study is based on research conducted from 1983 to 1984 on several magical groups in London, England. Because of America's cultural affinity to England and because Neo-Paganism in the United States originated with a British import, Luhrmann's study is relevant to my topic. Luhrmann develops a model of conversion to Neo-Paganism that is essentially a theory of cognitive dissonance. Conversion to the magical worldview, according to Luhrmann, is a process of "interpretive drift: the slow, often unacknowledged shift in someone's manner of interpreting events as they become involved with a particular activity" (p. 312). This drift consists of three interlocking transformations: (1) a change in interpretation (i.e., the prospective witch, struggling to learn the practice of magic begins to identify evidence for its power by observing patterns that allow her to explain success or failure of a rite); (2) a change in experience (including new feelings and responses, imaginative intensity, self-manipulation, and symbolism) that must be interpreted and rationalized; and (3) a change in rationalization (i.e., the magician "makes sense of powerful experience in ritual by searching for evidence that it has worked"). Rationalization requires employment of the new methods of interpretation that gives the preconvert confidence in further involvement in the practice, which in turn intensifies his or her experiences. Rationalization is reinforced by critical outsiders who accuse magic of irrationality and induce prospective Pagans to argue for their practice, thus increasing their own commitment (pp. 313–314).

Luhrmann's model is consistent with some of the theories discussed above. While she agrees with Scott and Lloyd that converts to Neo-Paganism may share certain personality traits including self-absorption and concern with power, she rejects their deprivation hypothesis (Luhrmann 1989, 99–100).[27] According to Luhrmann, prospective witches or magicians are not marginal individuals drawn into Neo-Paganism to escape a harsh reality, as Scott and Lloyd claim; rather they are middle-class people "searching for a powerful emotional and imaginative religious experience, but not for a religion" in the sense of an "institutional structure that demands commitment to a particular belief" (p. 337). Luhrmann agrees with Adler that Neo-Paganism's emphasis on practice rather than on belief provides the answer to such a search (pp. 335–336). Yet she rejects Adler's assumption that most converts already hold a magical worldview. The preconvert, while intrigued by magic, is also skeptical, and his or her initial involvement is usually the result of curiosity. Thus he/she does not immediately affirm the Neo-Pagan belief system. Rather, it is as "the once-non-magician begins to do what magicians do," that a person "begins to find magical ideas persuasive because he begins to notice and respond to events in different ways" (p. 312). Finally, while Luhrmann agrees with Lynch that conversion to Neo-Paganism is a process of gradual, almost accidental drift, she rejects his conclusion that eventual commitment to this worldview is a result of group reinforcement. According to Luhrmann, it is not "the practice of socializing that produces the primary effects," but the "private phenomenological experience within the practice of magic" (p. 315).

I find Luhrmann's model the most persuasive of the five theories discussed here. The model avoids the pitfalls of the other four studies and is able to answer questions they fail to explain. For example, if we adopt Lynch's group-interaction model, how do we make sense of the large number of solitary Neo-Pagan practitioners? If we generalize from Scott's or Lloyd's deprivation model, how do we explain other more middle-class magical groups? If we accept Adler's "coming-home" hypothesis, then why does the conversion process commonly take so long?

More importantly, Luhrmann's model is useful in understanding the specific issue addressed at the onset of this chapter: the impact of religious syncretism on the process of conversion. Although all five scholars acknowledge the existence of part-time Pagans, these accounts do not sufficiently address the question of multiple allegiances. Luhrmann's study mentions that they exist (several of the individuals in her sample were members of more than one group) and her interpretive drift hypothesis could provide the basis for an explanation. The traditional definition of conversion as a transformation involving rejection of one's previous worldview and its replacement with another is based on the premise that conversion is primarily cognitive, a matter of belief. We assume that beliefs must be consistent and that belief precedes action. If Cathy always acts on her beliefs, then her initiation into a Wiccan coven must mean she has ceased being a Christian. If her beliefs must be consistent, then she cannot believe in both Jesus and the Goddess. Equal multiple allegiances are not possible. Luhrmann's model rejects both of these assumptions. She asserts that most people do not have "coherent clear-cut sets of beliefs" and that they commonly develop beliefs to rationalize previous actions (Luhrmann 1989, 321). Her theory, therefore, is open to the possibility that individuals could hold several different worldviews at the same time.[28]

The five studies discussed above provide useful empirical data as well as interesting theories about conversion to Neo-Paganism. I have argued that the deprivation hypotheses of Scott and Lloyd should be rejected, that Lynch's interactive drift hypothesis is conceptually useful but, unless modified, theoretically inconsistent, and that Adler's coming-home hypothesis provides an important challenge to traditional theory but remains itself based on an excessively narrow definition of conversion. I found Luhrmann's theory of interpretive draft to be the most persuasive general model of conversion to Neo-Paganism, as well as the most useful for testing the specific hypothesis that syncretistic religion will encourage a different kind of conversion. While open to such an application, even Luhrmann's model, however, does not directly address the issue of syncretism's impact on the conversion process.

Why does the existing literature ignore this question? One might argue that conversion to Neo-Paganism is always a complete transformation in worldview in which one's previous religion is rejected. Blending of Judaism or Christianity with Neo-Paganism (e.g., as we find it in feminist spirituality) would be explained as adhesion, i.e., one's primary allegiance to one religion pre-empts true conversion. Yet the existence of organizations such as the Covenant of Unitarian Universalist Pagans and of other individuals who consider themselves both Christian (or Jewish) and Pagan indicates that such an explanation is insufficient. The following section will discuss the directions that future research on this topic might take.

CONVERSION IN THE CONTEXT OF RELIGIOUS SYNCRETISM: SUGGESTIONS FOR FUTURE RESEARCH

The study of conversion in the context of contemporary religious syncretism requires a reconceptualization of the term "conversion." The traditional definition of conversion as a complete transformation in worldview in which old beliefs are rejected and new ones take their place cannot adequately account for the process of blending. Yet, according to David Snow and Richard Machalek's (1984) comprehensive survey of the conversion literature, "the notion of radical change remains at the core of all conceptions of conversion, whether theological or social scientific."[29] The term "radical" here refers to the degree of change, not its speed, cause, or effect. Although scholars have debated whether conversion involves sudden or gradual, active or passive, healthy or unhealthy changes, they have not specified "how much change is enough to constitute conversion" (p. 169).

Snow and Machalek (1984, 169–170) challenge the consensus that defines conversion as radical change and suggest instead a continuum of at least four different kinds of change: (1) *alternation*, similar to A. D. Nock's (1933) adhesion, refers to participation in another religion without giving up one's previous worldview (e.g., a Christian who joins the Theosophical Society); (2) *consolidation* refers to "the adoption of a belief system or identity that combines two prior but contradictory world views or identities" (e.g., "a person raised in a southern Baptist church, who rejected these beliefs for drugs and perhaps Eastern religion, and who then became a Jesus Person"); (3) *regeneration* refers to "the enthusiastic adoption of a belief system" that had been abandoned previously (e.g., St. Augustine); and (4) *dramatic metamorphosis* refers to the transformative experience traditionally labelled conversion.

All four of these terms retain the assumption that an individual must give primary allegiance to one tradition; they do not consider the possibility of equal multiple allegiances. However, in the increasingly syncretistic context of American religion, a convert may be willing to accept more than one belief system as equally valid parts of a combination. I would therefore like to add a fifth type of change to this continuum, *combination*, which refers to the blending of two or more religions into a new syncretistic worldview. Clearly different from regeneration or dramatic metamorphosis, combination is also distinct from alternation in that the individual's former religion does not retain primary allegiance, and from consolidation in that the individual him- or herself self-consciously creates the combination from various sources rather than adopting a single belief system that combines familiar elements.

Reconceptualizing the theory of conversion will have an impact on how it is studied empirically. First, it will affect how we determine whether or not conversion has occurred. Snow and Machalek (1984, 170–173) have suggested that answering the question of where on the change-continuum conversion begins or ends depends not just on the degree of change but on what it is that changes. Even if we adopt the traditional definition and assume that only dramatic or radical transformation constitutes conversion, it is not just beliefs, values, behavior, identity, or interpersonal loyalties that change, but the individual's "universe of discourse" is altered as well. Moreover, in nonmainstream groups, traditional empirical indicators of conversion such as membership status or demonstration events frequently fail to show that conversion has occurred. We should therefore focus instead on what Snow and Machalek call rhetorical indicators. "If it is the universe of discourse that undergoes change during conversion, then that change should be discernible in converts' speech and reasoning" (p. 173). Snow and Machalek's rhetorical indicators of conversion include biographical reconstruction (the convert reconstructs his/her past life in accordance with the new universe of discourse) and the adoption of a master attribution scheme (the convert explains/ interprets feelings, behaviors, or events from his/her new perspective). Such indicators are particularly useful for the study of the combinatory type of conversion that may occur in the context of syncretistic religion.

Combinatory conversion cannot be studied by traditional indicators. A person with a blended worldview may be a member of several organizations or of none at all. He or she may or may not officially demonstrate his/her allegiance to one or more of these religions. Thus membership status and demonstration events cannot indicate conversion for this person. In the case of Neo-Paganism membership status and demonstration events are particularly ineffective. Because of the secrecy and decentralization of most magical groups, membership is almost impossible to measure. Demonstration events such as initiation rituals are equally useless as several researchers have been initiated as witches for academic purposes while many converts have not, either because the group rejects the hierarchy implied in such a ritual, or because the convert has joined a group whose beliefs s/he already shared.

Rhetorical indicators, by contrast, could effectively show if conversion has occurred, because combinatory conversion, if it occurs, is likely to be reflected in an individual's speech and reasoning. Cathy, for example, a woman whose exposure to feminism led her to blend Goddess worship with her pre-existing Christian beliefs, tends to recall her own past as well as to explain the present in ways that reflect her new worldview. Her childhood habit of sitting in silence beneath a particular tree in her family's yard becomes imbued with new significance as she imagines that a goddess was revered there by Native Americans long ago. Yet she also says that "God led me to that place." Her mother and father had been fighting all day, and she had gone to her room and prayed, pleading with God to make them stop. "Suddenly, I got up and went out to this tree and sat down . . . I don't remember for how long . . . but I knew that everything was going to be all right." Cathy feels that many of the worlds problems derive from the "one-sidedness of Christian culture" that leads us to "devalue women and abuse the Earth." If people found a way to "balance their striving for power over or salvation from this world by reverence for the Goddess who resides within it," the world would be a much better place.

Whether or not we adopt the specific indicators suggested by Scott and Machalek, looking at how people talk about themselves and their religious beliefs will tell us more about conversion to Neo-Paganism than we would find by checking the group's list of members (if there is one) or observing who has been initiated. Moreover, because combinatory conversion is usually a rather self-conscious process (telling people you are a Christian witch is bound to lead to a challenge) and Neo-Paganism is a self-consciously syncretistic religion, it is likely that individuals will be able to verbalize if and how conversion took place. Finally, since the magical community is known to be resistant to the standard survey method, one would need to rely primarily on personal interviews with members and prospective converts. Testing for rhetorical indicators is not only consistent with but requires such a method.

Reconceptualizing conversion theory to include the possibility of combination not only affects how we determine whether or not conversion has occurred, but requires a new lexicon to analyze the diverse configurations that result from the blending process. When dealing with religious blends, it is not enough to ask the convert what he or she believes in. We must develop indices to determine the *centrality* of certain elements of belief as well as the *salience* of the elements to one another.[30] We need to ask what is *core* and what is *periphery* in the system of beliefs and whether or not some beliefs legitimate other beliefs. Another important question concerns the relation of belief to practice. In the case of Neo-Paganism it appears that the practice of magic often precedes if not leads to belief in its efficacy. Is this generally true of combinatory conversion? Does a particular belief configuration have anything to do with practice? These and many other questions will have to be further explored before an empirical study of combinatory conversion is attempted.

The reconceptualization of the theory of conversion might be applied as follows. Scholars need to first test the hypothesis that combinatory conversion is likely to occur in the context of syncretistic religion, and then, if so, to understand the psychological meaning of such a process to individual converts. A beginning could be made with participant observation of several Neo-Pagan groups. Testing for combinatory conversion could involve several approaches. (1) One could ask each individual interviewed to label themselves. Do they consider themselves Pagan, Christian (or Jewish), or both? (2) One might make a list of the major elements (important myths, rituals, ethical codes, etc.) of each Neo-Pagan religion and of several mainstream religions. One would then show this list to each individual and ask him or her to select elements embraced, and, if possible, to rank them in order of importance. Patterns could be sought. Are some combinations more frequent? Are there variations among people from different religious backgrounds? (3) Testing for some of Snow and Machalek's rhetorical indicators such as biographical reconstruction or the adoption of a master attribution scheme would also be useful. What kind of language does the convert use to reconstruct his or her past? What kind of causal scheme or vocabulary of motives inform attributions about self, others, and events in the world?

Understanding the psychological meaning of combinatory conversion is more difficult. The psychologist is interested in questions such as what caused the convert to construct a particular religious combination and the effect that combination has on his or her life. The obvious and most commonly employed means of obtaining answers is to ask the convert. However, as Snow and Machalek point out, retrospective "accounts of conversion are social constructions subject to reconstruction with the passage of time and therefore are highly suspect as sources of data about the causes [and effects] of conversion" (1984, 177). We should treat these data as *information* about the convert's current experience rather than as *explanations* of conversion. Unfortunately, in most cases, data derived from converts is all we have. A short-term study can therefore at best understand the subjective meaning of conversion to a convert (what does *Cathy* think are the causes and effects of her conversion?); any objective conclusions (what *are* the causes and effects of her conversion?) would have to await longitudinal research. A long-term study also allows scholars to move beyond individual psychology and take into account historical and/or cultural factors that may affect the meaning of conversion.

Understanding conversion to Neo-Paganism will benefit the study of other syncretistic religious groups as well as the study of individuals constructing their own personal religious combination. Are people adopting an openly syncretistic religion more likely to combine it with yet another worldview than individuals converting to a non-syncretistic religion? Are some types of syncretism more likely to be accompanied by combinatory conversion than others? Are certain combinations more frequent, either at the group or individual level? Hopefully, further research will provide some answers to these and other questions.

NOTES

1. To protect her privacy, I have used a pseudonym.

2. For examples of New Age groups, see Melton (1990).

3. It can be argued that syncretism is the logical outcome of the historical development of American religion. The secularization hypothesis, dominant during the first half of this century, was challenged by the explosion of interest in "new religious movements" in the sixties and the resurgence of evangelical Christianity in the seventies. Some scholars (Bellah 1964; Bellah et al. 1985; Berger 1967) began to talk about a future of increasing pluralization or differentiation and privatization of religion leading in the extreme case to what Robert Bellah and his colleagues (1985) have called Shelaism; i.e., each individual makes up his or her own personal religion. Others (Kelly 1972) predicted that such fragmentation would induce a longing for greater religious homogeneity and spur the continued growth of conservative Christian churches. More recent studies (Roof 1990) support the notion of privatization but suggest that it leads to yet a different trend: religious syncretism.

4. For perspectives on sudden conversion, see works by Christensen (1963), Dewhurst and Beard (1970), James (1902), Salzman (1953), and Starbuck (1915). For the gradualist perspective, see Lofland and Stark (1965) or Pratt (1926). For studies of passive conversion, see Simmonds (1977) or Singer (1979). For active conversion, see Straus (1979). For the view that conversion is healthy, see Allison (1969), Cavenar and Spaulding (1977), or James (1902). For unhealthy conversion, see Dewhurst and Beard (1970) or Salzman (1953).

5. The issue of partial acceptance of new religions, without rejecting and replacing one's previous religion has been addressed, but has traditionally been distinguished from conversion as somehow not real. Thus A. D. Nock first contrasted adhesion, which he defined as the "acceptance of new worships as useful supplements" that does not "involve the taking of a new way of life in place of the old," with conversion, meaning a "reorientation of the soul . . . which implies consciousness . . . that the old is wrong and the new is right" (1933, 7). More contemporary scholars, such as Sheperd (1979) and Travisano (1970) have maintained this distinction.

6. An excellent example of Neo-Paganism's self-conscious syncretism is Budapest's (1989) book, *The Grandmother of Time*. Examples of feminist rituals can be found in Budapest's *Holy Book of Women's Mysteries* (1979) and Starhawk's *Spiral Dance* (1979). Examples of people combining Neo-Paganism with other religions abound, ranging from women's spirituality groups on college campuses to seminars on women's mysteries held at hotel convention centers.

7. Neo-Pagans have sought to defend their public image through organizations such as the Witches Liberation Movement and the Witches Anti-Defamation League, as well as through the publication of numerous popular books about the Craft (see Martello n.d., 23–43).

8. My account relies primarily on Adler (1986), Marron (1989), Melton (1982, 1989), and Russell (1980).

9. Initially, most Pagans (e.g., Gardner 1968; Martello n.d.; Farrar 1971) and some scholars (Eliade 1976) asserted that Witchcraft is the Old Religion of pre-Christian Europe, drawing on evidence provided by anthropologist Margaret Murray. Yet Murray's (1921) work was soon discredited, and most scholars (Russell 1980; Neitz 1990; Truzzi 1974) and some Pagans (Kelly n.d.; Bonewits 1976) argued that Wicca is a twentieth-century invention.

10. My account rests primarily on Marron (1989) and Melton (1989). For additional sources on Western ritual magic, see Melton (1982).

11. My account rests primarily on Adler (1986), Levanthal (1976), and Russell (1980). For additional sources on European Witchcraft, see Melton (1982).

12. Herbert Levanthal distinguishes four types of Witchcraft in America: (1) a variant of Western ritual magic practiced by Pennsylvania Germans: (2) "cunning folk" or "white witches" of traditional English peasant culture who use natural magic to help the community; (3) evil witches who used natural magic for destructive ends; and (4) witches who made a pact with the devil (Levanthal 1976, 118–125). Albanese (1981) provides a good summary of Levanthal's account. For additional sources on colonial Witchcraft, see Butler (1990) and Hall (1989).

13. Both magic and folk religion experienced a revival in the late nineteenth century. The man most often credited with repopularizing Western magic is Aleister Crowley, a member of the Order of the Golden Dawn whose controversial lifestyle and prolific writing stimulated widespread interest in the subject. Interest in European folk religion was encouraged by anthropologist Margaret Murray, who claimed to have found evidence for a unified European Pagan cult of the Horned God and his consort the Triple Goddess, and by writer Charles Leland, who claimed to have been initiated into a tradition of Witchcraft that had been secretly carried on

since the days of the Old Religion. Gerald Gardner was a friend of Crowley's and an avid reader of occult books including Murray's and Leland's. After the repeal of the British Witchcraft laws in 1951, Gardner published two books on the Craft in 1954 and 1957, but claimed that he was keeping the essential ingredients of Wicca secret.

14. Although many American Neo-Pagan groups claim succession to pre-Gardnerian traditions (e.g., Z. Budapest traces Witchcraft in her family back to the thirteenth century, and Martello can trace witches in his family back to 1795), closer investigation shows that virtually all of these groups combine Gardner's structure with beliefs and practices from a variety of other sources. Moreover, Neo-Pagans have become increasingly open about the existence of such blending. As Margot Adler put it, the "primary tradition" of the Craft is "creativity" (Adler 1986, 86). For more information on Neo-Pagan sectarian splits, see Adler (1986) and Melton (1982).

15. Several reasons may account for this lack of research. According to Patricia Hartman (1976, 170), social scientists studying conversion to new religious movements are inhibited from researching Neo-Paganism by methodological problems (e.g., the difficulty in gaining access to secretive groups) and ideology (e.g., the assumption that the occult is a passing fad not worth studying). Yet students of Neo-Paganism are just as unlikely to focus on conversion. Given the definitional confusion discussed earlier, the most pressing task for researchers of this movement has been phenomenological: providing an accurate description of what Neo-Paganism is. Moreover, since they do not proselytize, Neo-Pagan groups have largely remained outside the brainwashing controversy that made conversion such a hot topic in academic and journalistic studies of other new religions. Finally, since Neo-Pagans reject the term "conversion" itself, insider studies of this movement have usually ignored the topic entirely; Adler (1986) is a notable exception.

16. Of 256 behavioral science entries in Lewis Rambo's (1982) bibliography of research on conversion, one study centers on a Neo-Pagan group. James Beckford and James Richardson's (1983) bibliography on new religious movements contains 145 entries pertinent to conversion, but less than 1 percent focus on Neo-Paganism. Both Rambo and Beckford and Richardson cite the same study by Lynch (1977). John Saliba's (1987) bibliography of psychiatric and psychological research on cults contains 75 entries on conversion, none of which discuss the Neo-Pagan movement. His most recent (1990) bibliography of social scientific research on cults does not list any studies of Neo-Paganism among 70 entries on conversion. He does list several studies of Neo-Paganism that are relevant to the theory of conversion, but he apparently does not consider them to be studies of conversion.

17. The bibliography to Margot Adler's *Drawing Down the Moon*, which is widely respected as the best and most comprehensive study of

Neo-Paganism in America, contains only a few items that address conversion. In Gordon Melton's (1982) bibliography of magic, Witchcraft, and Paganism in America less than 6 percent of the entries are pertinent to conversion (and this is a generous estimate since the 695 entries I designated as focusing on Neo-Paganism omit all non-descriptive terms such as songbooks and directories, and the 43 entries I designated as focusing on conversion include sources that only address conversion in passing).

18. The vast majority of accounts of Neo-Paganism are descriptive and concerned more with social trends than with individual experience. Thus they draw only speculative theoretical conclusions about conversion without engaging in systematic study to provide empirical evidence for their claims. The work of historians Ellwood (1988), Nugent (1971) and Russell (1980), and of sociologists Truzzi (1972), Heenan (1973), Tirakian (1971), Greeley (1970) and Penner (1972) exemplifies this issue.

19. A study may be suspected of ideology if it presents conclusions that support the special interests of its author or sponsor but rest on premises that are either untested or insufficiently supported by the evidence provided. Most prominent is a negative ideological stance taken by psychologists, who assume that any religious or magical belief is irrational and must be cured (or at best may itself serve as a therapy to facilitate return to normalcy), and theologians or religious writers who assume that participation in mainstream religion is healthy but involvement in magical groups is deviant and dangerous (e.g., Gay 1989, Oates 1955, Olsson 1985, Pruyser 1977, Scott 1976, and Wilson 1972). Ideology can also be positive as when some feminists (e.g., Christ 1987) assert that a goddess-centered religion is what healthy people, especially women, need.

20. Most researchers have difficulty defining what is being converted to. They talk about conversion to the occult as if all occult groups could be lumped together (e.g., Ellwood 1988, Greeley 1970, Marty 1970, Penner 1972, Tirakian 1971), or they leave the impression that a study of one magical group can be generalized to the entire Neo-Pagan movement (e.g., Moody 1974 a, b; Scheidt 1974).

21. The studies agree that Neo-Paganism is an urban movement, that converts' ages vary ranging from the mid-twenties to fifties; that most converts had completed high school and many had at least some college education, and that Neo-Paganism seems to have a special attraction to women. There is less agreement on class or religious background. Luhrmann and Lynch found that most Neo-Pagans are middle class and hold white-collar jobs, while Lloyd and Scott found most converts to be of lower-income status in unstable, marginal positions such as waitress, dancer, or welfare recipient. Perhaps Adler's assertion that class background of Neo-Pagans varies widely is most accurate. Not surprisingly in the American context, the religious background of converts to Neo-Paganism is most often Protestant or Catholic. There has been some speculation that ex-

Catholics are overrepresented in the Neo-Pagan community because the latter allows them to indulge their love of liturgy without the restrictions of dogma. However, there is no consistent evidence to confirm this hypothesis. Perhaps the most useful data in settling this controversy comes from Luhrmann, who asserts that Neo-Pagans often have a family background that mixes religious intensity with rebellion. This can, but need not, be more likely in a Roman Catholic household.

22. The question of what is being converted from has led some scholars to distinguish between "converts" (change from no religious identification to some) and "switchers" (change from some religious identification to another) (see Bibby and Brinkerhoff 1973; Hertel 1988). According to this definition, Neo-Pagans who were previously unaffiliated are converts. However, depending on the length of time they are unaffiliated they could also be called switchers. I will therefore use the term "conversion" here in its broader sense to refer to both types of change.

23. For more detailed discussion, see Adler 1986, 14–20; Lloyd 1978, 33–59, 81–84; Luhrmann 1989, 19–38; 99–100; Lynch 1977, 893–905; Scott 1980, 127–136.

24. Among other scholars of the occult, the deprivation hypothesis is affirmed by Emmons and Sobal (1981), Nugent (1971), and Stevens (1982); it is challenged by Galbreath (1983) and by Jorgenson (1984). The counterculture hypothesis is affirmed by Greeley (1970), Hartman (1976), and Penner (1972); it is challenged by Marty (1970) and Truzzi (1972).

25. Scott's main point is to show that "while both groups accept monistic spiritual principles," they contrast starkly in values, symbols, structure, and behavior. Thus IPM seeks to "help members adapt and succeed in the world . . . through personal development and achievement." This group appeals mainly to conservative middle-class people from a Protestant background. The order, by contrast, "seeks to reject modern bureaucratic life and create a new tribal society" and appeals to "relatively hip, radical, non-conformist types" often from a Catholic background (Scott 1980, 4, 161). It is in the context of this contrast that Scott develops her theory of conversion to Neo-Paganism.

26. Interestingly, Scott presents some unique data that could form the basis of a different conversion hypothesis. She describes how the newcomer to Neo-Paganism undergoes a prolonged testing/selection process during which a person may participate in rituals and practices that "promote group unity and intimacy" yet at the same time remains an outsider who is regarded with suspicion until sincerity has been proven and the person is permitted to formally join the group. The emotional intensity of the preconvert's experience with the group increases during this period. Scott asserts that many prospective witches drop out during this first year but there are few dropouts after initiation (pp. 131, 156–157). Perhaps

conversion can at least partially be explained by the kind of cognitive dissonance theory applied to explain why hazing increases the desirability of joining a college fraternity. Unfortunately, Scott does not discuss the theoretical implications of the data she presents.

27. Luhrmann (1989, 100) asserts that characteristics such as absorption and power concerns may be descriptive of many Neo-Pagans, but do not indicate a causal sequence. She describes "absorption" in terms such as "imaginative, self-absorbed, intellectual, spiritually inclined, emotionally intense"; she describes "power concerns" in terms such as "rebellious, interested in power, concerned with control of self or world, possibly dreamy or socially ill at ease."

28. Piker's (1972) study of Thai Buddhists argues that people can and do hold mutually inconsistent religious beliefs without experiencing cognitive conflict. Their primary allegiance, however, is to Buddhism—unlike the case I am describing in which allegiance is split.

29. Although most researchers no longer accept the Pauline model (sudden conversion) as normative and reject the brainwashing hypothesis (passive conversion) (see Bromley and Richardson 1983), they continue to assume that conversion means replacement of one belief system by another.

30. According to Roof (1979, 39), centrality refers to the "importance attributed to a given act, belief, or feeling within the total religious system." Salience refers to the relative priority or significance of one element to another.

REFERENCES

Adler, Margot. 1986. *Drawing Down the Moon.* 2d ed. Boston: Beacon Press.

Albanese, Catherine L. 1981. *America: Religions and Religion.* Belmont, Calif.: Wadsworth.

Allison, Joel. 1969. "Religious Conversion: Regression and Progression in an Adolescent Experience." *Journal for the Scientific Study of Religion* 8: 23–38.

Beckford, James A., and James T. Richardson. 1983. "A Bibliography of Social Scientific Studies of New Religious Movements." *Social Compass* 30, no. 1: 111–135.

Bellah, Robert N. 1964. "Religious Evolution." *American Sociological Review* 29, no. 3: 358–374.

Bellah, Robert N., et al. 1985. *Habits of the Heart: Individualism and Commitment in American Life.* Berkeley: University of California Press.

Berger, Peter L. 1967. *The Sacred Canopy: Elements of a Sociological Theory of Religion.* Garden City, N.Y.: Doubleday.

Bibby, Reginald, and Merlin Brinkerhoff. 1973. "The Circulation of the Saints." *Journal for the Scientific Study of Religion* 12: 273–283.

Bonewits, Isaac. 1971. *Real Magic: An Introductory Treatise on the Basic Principles of Yellow Magic.* New York: Coward, McCann and Geoghegan.

———. 1976. "Witchcraft: Classical, Gothic, and Neopagan, Part II." *Green Egg* 9, no. 78: 13–17.

Bromley, David, and James Richardson, eds. 1983. *The Brainwashing/ Deprogramming Controversy: Sociological, Psychological, Legal and Historical Perspectives.* New York: Edward Mellen Press.

Budapest, Zsuzsanna E. 1979. *The Holy Book of Women's Mysteries.* Part 1. Los Angeles: Susan B. Anthony Coven No. 1.

———. 1989. *The Grandmother of Time: A Women's Book of Celebrations, Spells, and Sacred Objects for Every Month of the Year.* San Francisco: Harper and Row.

Butler, Jon. 1990. *Awash in a Sea of Faith: Christianizing the American People.* Cambridge, Mass.: Harvard University Press.

Cavenar, Jesse, and Jean Spaulding. 1977. "Depressive Disorders and Religious Conversions." *The Journal of Nervous and Mental Disease* 165, no. 3, 209–212.

Christ, Carol. 1987. *Laughter of Aphrodite: Reflections on a Journey to the Goddess.* San Francisco: Harper and Row.

Christensen, Carl. 1963. "Religious Conversion." *Archives of General Psychiatry* 9: 207–216.

Cohen, Daniel. 1975. *The New Believers: Young Religion in America.* New York: M. Evans and Company.

Dewhurst, Kenneth, and A. W. Beard. 1970. "Sudden Religious Conversion in Temporal Lobe Epilepsy." *British Journal of Psychiatry* 117: 497–507.

Eliade, Mircea. 1976. "Some Observations on European Witchcraft." In *Occultism, Witchcraft and Cultural Fashions,* pp. 69–92. Chicago: University of Chicago Press.

Ellwood, Robert S. 1988. "Occult Movements in America." In *Encyclopedia of the American Religious Experience: Studies of Traditions and Movements,* vol. 2, edited by Charles Lippy and Peter Williams, 711–722. New York: Charles Scribner's Sons.

Ellwood, Robert S., and Harry B. Partin. 1988. *Religious and Spiritual Groups in Modern America.* 2d ed. Englewood Cliffs, N.J.: Prentice Hall.

Farrar, Stewart. 1971. *What Witches Do.* New York: Coward, McCann and Geoghegan.

Galbreath, Robert. 1983. "Explaining Modern Occultism." In *The Occult in America: New Historical Perspectives,* edited by Howard Kerr and Charles C. Crow, 11–37. Urbana: University of Illinois Press.

———. 1972. *The Occult: Studies and Evaluations.* Bowling Green: Bowling Green University Popular Press.

Gardner, Gerald B. 1968. *Witchcraft Today.* London: Jarrolds Publishers.

Gay, Volney P. 1989. *Understanding the Occult: Fragmentation and Repair of the Self.* Minneapolis: Fortress Press.

Greeley, Andrew M. 1970. "Implications for the Sociology of Religion of Occult Behaviour in the Youth Culture." *Youth and Society,* 2 no. 2: 131–140.

———. 1975. *Sociology of the Paranormal: A Reconnaissance.* Beverly Hills, Calif.: Sage Publications.

Guiley, Rosemary E. 1989. *The Encyclopedia of Witches and Witchcraft.* New York: Facts on File.

Hall, David. 1989. *Days of Wonder, Days of Judgement: Popular Religious Belief in Early New England.* New York: Alfred A. Knopf.

Hartman, Patricia. 1976. "Social Dimensions of Occult Participation: The Gnostica Study." *British Journal of Sociology* 27: 169–183.

Heenan, Edward, ed. 1973. *Mystery, Magic, and Miracle: Religion in a Post-Aquarian Age.* Englewood Cliffs, N.J.: Prentice Hall.

Hertel, Bradley. 1988. "Gender, Religious Identity and Work Force Participation." *Journal for the Scientific Study of Religion* 27: 574–592.

James, William. 1902. *The Varieties of Religious Experience.* New York: The Modern Library.

Jorgensen, Danny L. 1984. "Divinatory Discourse." *Symbolic Interaction* 7: 135–153.

Kelly, Aidan. N.d. *Crafting the Art of Magic: A History of Modern Witchcraft, Vol. 1, 1939–1969.* Santa Barbara, Calif.: Santa Barbara Centre for Humanistic Studies.

Kelly, Dean M. 1972. *Why Conservative Churches are Growing: A Study in Sociology of Religion.* New York: Harper and Row.

Leventhal, Herbert. 1976. *In the Shadow of the Enlightenment: Occultism and Renaissance Science in Eighteenth Century America.* New York: New York University Press.

Lloyd, Susannah Miller. 1978. "The Occult Revival: Witchcraft in the Contemporary United States." Columbia, Mo.: University of Missouri Ph.D. dissertation.

Lofland, John, and Rodney Stark. 1965. "Becoming a World Saver: A Theory of Conversion to A Deviant Perspective." *American Sociological Review* 30: 862–875.

Luhrmann, Tanya M. 1989. *Persuasions of the Witch's Craft: Ritual Magic in Contemporary England.* Cambridge, Mass.: Harvard University Press.

Lynch, Frederick R. 1977. "Toward a Theory of Conversion and Commitment to the Occult." *American Behavioural Scientist* 20, no. 6: 887–908.

———. 1979. " 'Occult Establishment' or 'Deviant Religion?' The Rise and Fall of a Modern Church of Magic." *Journal for the Scientific Study of Religion* 18: 281–89.

Marron, Kevin. 1989. *Witches, Pagans, and Magic in the New Age.* Toronto, Canada: Seal Books.

Martello, Leo L. N.d. *Witchcraft: The Old Religion.* Secaucus, N.J.: University Books.

Marty, Martin. 1970. "The Occult Establishment." *Social Research* 37: 212–230.

Melton, J. Gordon. 1982. *Magic, Witchcraft, and Paganism in America: A Bibliography.* New York: Garland Publishing.

———. 1990. *New Age Encyclopedia.* Detroit, Mich.: Gale Research.

———, ed. 1989. *The Encyclopedia of American Religion.* 3d ed. Detroit, Mich.: Gale Research.

Moody, Edward J. 1974a. "Magical Therapy: An Anthropological Investigation of Contemporary Satanism" in *Religious Movements in Contemporary America,* pp. 355–82. Irving I. Zaretsky and Mark P. Leone, eds. Princeton, N.J.: Princeton University Press.

———. 1974b. "Urban Witches" in *On the Margin of the Visible: Sociology, the Esoteric, and the Occult.* Edward A. Tirakian, ed. New York: John Wiley & Sons.

Murray, Margaret A. 1921. *The Witch-cult in Western Europe: A Study in Anthropology.* Oxford: Oxford University Press.

Neitz, Mary Jo. 1990. "In Goddess We Trust: Witchcraft as a Mystery Religion." In *In Gods We Trust: New Patterns of Religious Pluralism in*

America. 2d ed., edited by Thomas Robbins and Dick Anthony. New Brunswick, N.J.: Transaction Publishers.

Nock, A. D. 1933. *Conversion.* London: Oxford University Press.

Nugent, Donald. 1971. "The Renaissance and/of Witchcraft." *Church History* 40: 69–78.

Oates, Wayne E. 1955. "The Hindering and Helping Power of Religion." *Pastoral Psychology* 6: 43–49.

Olsson, Peter A. 1985. "The Psychology of a Modern Warlock: Rapprochement in a Coven of White Witches." *American Journal of Psychotherapy* 39: 263–276.

Penner, Wes. 1972. "Hippies' Attraction to Mysticism." *Adolescence* 7: 199–210.

Piker, Steven. 1972. "The Problem of Consistency in Thai Religion." *Journal for the Scientific Study of Religion* 11: 211–229.

Pratt, James. 1926. *The Religious Consciousness: A Psychological Study.* New York: Macmillan Co.

Pruyser, Paul W. 1977. "The Seamy Side of Current Religious Beliefs." *Bulletin of the Menninger Clinic* 41: 329–348.

Rambo, Lewis R. 1982. "Current Research on Religious Conversion." *Religious Studies Review* 8, no. 2: 146–159.

Roof, Wade Clark. 1979. "Concepts and Indicators of Religious Commitment: A Critical Review." In *The Religious Dimension: New Directions in Quantitative Research,* edited by Robert Wuthnow, 17–45. New York: Academic Press.

———. 1990. *Narratives and Numbers: Inaugural Lecture.* Santa Barbara, Calif.: University of California, Dept. of Religious Studies.

Russell, Jeffrey B. 1980. *A History of Witchcraft: Sorcerers, Heretics, and Pagans.* New York: Thames and Hudson.

Saliba, John A. 1987. *Psychiatry and the Cults: An Annotated Bibliography.* New York: Garland Publishing.

———. 1990. *Social Science and the Cults: An Annotated Bibliography.* New York: Garland Publishing.

Salzman, Leon. 1953. "The Psychology of Religious and Ideological Conversion." *Psychiatry* 16: 177–187.

Scheidt, Frederick J. 1974. "Deviance, Power, and the Occult: A Field Study." *Journal of Psychology* 87: 21–28.

Scott, Edward M. 1976. "Witches: Wise, Weak, or Wicked Women?" *Journal of Religion and Health* 15: 136–139.

Scott, Gini Graham. 1980. *Cult and Countercult: A Study of a Spiritual Growth Group and a Witchcraft Order.* Westport, Conn.: Greenwood Press.

———. 1983. *The Magicians: A Study of the Use of Power in a Black Magic Group.* New York: Irvington Publishers.

Sheperd, W. C. 1979. "Conversion: Evaluation of a Step-like Process for Problemsolving. *Review of Religious Research* 13: 178–184.

Simmonds, Robert. 1977. "Conversion of Addiction: Consequences of Joining a Jesus Movement Group." *American Behavioural Scientist* 20, no. 6: 909–924.

Singer, Margaret T. 1979. "Coming out of the Cults." *Psychology Today* 12, no. 8: 72–82.

Snow, David A., and Richard Machalek. 1984. "The Sociology of Conversion." *Annual Review of Sociology* 10: 167–190.

Starbuck, Edwin. 1915. *The Psychology of Religion.* New York: Charles Scribner's Sons.

Starhawk [Miriam Simos]. 1979. *The Spiral Dance: A Rebirth of the Religion of the Great Goddess.* San Francisco: Harper and Row.

———. 1987. *Truth or Dare: Encounters with Power, Authority, and Mystery.* San Francisco: Harper and Row.

Stone, Merlin. 1976. *When God Was a Woman.* New York: Harcourt, Brace, Jovanovich.

Straus, Roger. 1979. "Religious Conversion as a Personal and Collective Accomplishment." *Sociological Analysis* 40, no. 2: 158–165.

Tirakian, Edward A. 1971. "Toward the Sociology of Esoteric Culture." *American Journal of Sociology* 78, no. 3: 491–512.

———, ed. 1974. *On the Margin of the Visible: Sociology, the Esoteric, and the Occult.* New York: John Wiley and Sons.

Travisano, Richard V. 1970. "Alternation and Conversion as Qualitatively Different Transformations." In *Social Psychology Through Symbolic Interaction,* edited by G. P. Stone and H. A. Farberman, 594–606. Waltham, Mass.: Ginn-Blaisdell.

Truzzi, Marcello. 1972. "The Occult Revival as Popular Culture: Some Random Observations on the Old and the Nouveau Witch." *Sociological Quarterly* 13 (Winter): 16–36.

————. 1974. "Towards a Sociology of the Occult: Notes on Modern Witchcraft." In *Religious Movements in Contemporary America*, edited by Irving I. Zaretsky and Mark P. Leone, 628–645. Princeton, N.J.: Princeton University Press.

Wilson, Arnold W. 1972. "Magic in Contemporary Life and in Psychoanalysis." *Psychoanalytic Review* 59, no. 1: 5–18.

14

WHERE CHRISTIAN LITURGY AND NEO-PAGAN RITUAL MEET

Rev. Richard E. Kuykendall

THE NOVEMBER 1992 ISSUE of *United Church News* devoted one full page to confessing a wrong that had been committed by the ancestors of the present United Church of Christ.[1] The heading for this page read: "Witch Trials: Reflections from 1692 to 1992."

The articles on this page dealt with the Salem witch trials and the roles played by Congregationalists in this tragic chapter of early American history. To many, such a confession would be considered honorable in view of the fact that, we look back upon the accusations that led to the death of certain individuals as based upon absurd reasoning and a superstitious worldview.

It is one thing for a modern Congregational minister to acknowledge a wrong committed three hundred years ago upon innocent people charged with Witchcraft. To many, however, it would be something altogether different for such a minister to actually embrace rituals practiced by modern self-proclaimed witches, and to even go so far as to incorporate them into Christian worship.

This is the account of how I came to do this very thing. What follows shall therefore of necessity be narrative in nature. This unlikely synthesis, however, has evolved as the result of much research and reflection, and only because I believe that it is "for the good of all concerned."[2]

In 1988 I became the minister of the Community Congregational Church of Tehachapi, California. The Community Church
was a small church with less than one hundred members, and with
99 percent of the congregation over sixty-five years of age.

I, as most any minister, wanted to see my church grow, and
though I love older people, I wanted to see more diversity in the
age make-up of my congregation. We needed young couples, singles,
teenagers, and children, as well as those of retirement age.

The problem, however, was this. In nearly two years I had
found that whenever younger people came to visit our church, they
looked around and saw only older people, and they did not come
back. When I talked with these visitors I heard the same comments
over and over again. They liked my preaching, but they wanted to
go to a church where there were others their own age, and where
their children could be part of a thriving Sunday school. As it was,
my wife and I were the only young couple, and our children and
two or three of their friends were the only children.

As I wrestled with this problem, I decided that one way I
might be able to attract younger people would be to conduct a
second service on Sunday—one geared to a younger audience.
I talked it over with the members of the church council (who were
well aware of the problem) and they gave me the go-ahead.

I began by writing an article for our local newspaper, advertising this service as a "contemporary worship experience." And
I called this service "Spiritwind." I gave it this name for two reasons. First, because both the Hebrew and Greek words in the Bible
for "spirit" could also be translated as "wind," and secondly, because Tehachapi was known for its wind industry. Wind generators
literally cover the hills to the east of the community.

As it turned out, my first service drew only two people. I
concluded that it was because our community already had a number of churches that offered "contemporary worship experiences."
In thinking things over I reasoned that I would have to offer the
community something that it could not get at any of the other
churches, and I had to appeal to an audience that was not interested in what the other churches had to offer, and yet who were
interested in spiritual things. What if I made "Spiritwind" into a
worship experience for these kinds of people?

I told my congregation that our church was originally the
only Protestant church in town, and thus our church had tried to
be, as our bulletin stated, "A House of Prayer for ALL People"—
which actually had meant "ALL Protestants." As time went on,

however, the Lutherans, Episcopalians, Methodists, Baptists, Nazarenes, etc. had established their own churches and thus left the Community Church.

Thus, what was once the largest church in town was now a very small church, left with only a few old Congregationalists. I proposed that what I wanted to do now was truly be what the church had once said that it was—"A House of Prayer for ALL People." I told them that there were many people in town from churches like Unity and the Church of Religious Science—there were also Unitarians, spiritualists, and others—who had no place to worship. What if we made "Spiritwind" a place where those of all faiths could feel free to come? Then we would truly be "A House of Prayer for ALL People."

Though I am sure that there were some who probably felt uncomfortable with my proposal, no one spoke out or voted against my motion to attempt such an unorthodox services. And so it was that our church directory now said that being true to "its commitment to being inclusive," our church offered "Spiritwind, to provide for the community a worship service which is open to those of all religious traditions and spiritual paths."

I immediately took out an ad on the religion page of the local paper which advertised Spiritwind as "A Worship Experience for a New Age." And on the back of the bulletin for Spiritwind's worship service, I printed the following statement:

> We are in a "New Age" because we are now a global community. The days of imperialism—when one nation and its religion saw itself as right and all others as wrong and thus sought to dominate and impose its beliefs upon others is no longer feasible in our global community.
>
> Therefore, religious exclusivism and intolerance must give way to inclusivism and tolerance as well as mutual respect and appreciation. Only through such a course will our world find peace.
>
> What the "New Age" brings is good because it allows us to pool our beliefs and practices in order to deal with personal and global problems through the collective wisdom of all traditions. Beyond this, such an approach enriches us through its inherent pluralism.
>
> It is our intention that "Spiritwind" be such a place where these ideals may find concrete expression.

Then the trouble began. I had definitely gone too far—that is, according to the thinking of the Tehachapi Ministerial Association. They had already had their doubts about me due to my liberal approach to Christianity, but now that I had started Spiritwind they were convinced that I was an enemy of the faith.

This feeling was expressed in a newspaper article entitled, "New Age Service Draws Fire." In this, Tom Brisson, religion editor for newspaper, the *Bakersfield Californian*, said that,

> While other churches in the mountain community southeast of Bakersfield have campaigned against the New Age, Kuykendall has "tried to have a favorable relationship to it" and has created a service he calls "Spiritwind" geared to those with New Age beliefs. (6 April 1990)

And in protest of my "favorable relationship" to the New Age movement, one church had its members go around town and take down all of the flyers I had put up in order to advertise our new service. The following week an officer from the sheriff's department brought one such flyer by my office. It had been turned in to the sheriff's department by a distressed store owner who saw that someone had scrawled the following words across my flyer:

FALSE Prophet CULT
Don't go to that devil church,
ask God to show you a REAL
Holy Ghost filled church.
God loves you and so do I,
that's why I tell you to not go here!

As it turned out most of those who first attended Spiritwind were from the Church of Religious Science and Unity. We also had a Buddhist who had studied under the Tibetan master, Chogyam Trungpa Rimpoche, and who had taught a class in Kundalini yoga which ran for nearly a year. We even had a Pentecostal who attended for a time—believing my work was just a radical form of Christian outreach to these lost souls.

At first I started out by preaching the same sermons I did in my morning service, except with a different emphasis. For example, when preaching on "the Sermon on the Mount" in my morning service, at Spiritwind I preached on the Sermon on the Mount as interpreted by Emmet Fox and Swami Prabhavananda.

But as time went on I eventually dropped the preaching and instead offered "classes" on a variety of subjects, such as: history of philosophy, world religions, paranormal experience, dream interpretation, and holistic health. In addition to this we had guests who led us in guided meditations, showed us how to use tarot cards and the I Ching, and we even witnessed psychics as they "channeled" in trance states.

The *United Church News* printed an article about our service which spoke positively of the fact that "this causal service borrows from many traditions" (July-August 1990). This was certainly no overstatement.

Then my thoughts turned to the Earth. For some time I had been working on my book, *Prophetess of the Earth*, and I was in the process of finishing it up. Thus my thoughts had been fixed for some time upon what I called "the gospel of the way of the earth." And so when I began to prepare for the new liturgical year, the fact struck me that many of the Christian holidays were actually makeovers of ancient "Pagan" holy days connected with the Earth and its changing seasons. Thus I proposed that as I went through the Christian holy year, and celebrated the various Christian holidays with the Community Church over the year to come, we could celebrate our version of the pre-Christian holy days in Spiritwind.

I told those at Spiritwind, as well as the Community Church's church council, that we could do some study into the background of these holy days, and then we would "demythologize" them— ridding them of their references to non-Christian deities. Thus what we would be left with would simply be celebrations of the Earth's changing seasons.

I suggested that when the Christian Church, in its program of evangelization, recast the ancient Earth celebrations in a Christian framework, though they succeeded in the Christianization of the Western world, they also severed our connection to the Earth. No longer did we celebrate the seasons of the Earth, instead we celebrated events in the life of Christ, the Church, and in the lives of the saints. Worse than this, the Earth itself was denounced as the habitation of devils—the very place to which the Devil had been cast down. Furthermore, most Christians believed that the Earth was doomed to be destroyed in the apocalyptic "Day of the Lord." I, however, felt that in view of the environmental crisis and the threat of nuclear holocaust that it looked as if it would be us and not God who would be responsible for the destruction of the Earth.

In order to turn things around, it seemed to me that we must sense once more our connectedness to the Earth. And we must see the Earth as a sacred and living gift, rather than simply an object to be exploited. One way I felt that we could work towards this goal was by celebrating the Earth's "holy days" and changing seasons through the vehicle of liturgy.

What I meant by "the Earth's 'holy days' " was those days
which marked significant changes in the yearly cycle—namely the
solstices and equinoxes, and the seasonal "quarter days"— most of
which had their counterparts in the Christian holy year:

December 21–22	Winter Solstice	Christmas
February 1st		Candlemas
March 21–22	Spring Solstice	Easter
May 1st		
June 21–22	Summer Solstice	The Feast of St. John
August 1st		The Feast of St. Peter's Chains
September 21–22	Autumn Equinox	
November 1st		All Saints' Day

The church council voted to let me go ahead with this "experiment," and so we in Spiritwind excitedly dove into these un-
familiar waters, true to our adventurous spirits.

Another major influence in the recent turn of events at
Spiritwind was my grandfather, Jess McLean. His influence
at Spiritwind was not his involvement—though he did attend, spoke
there on two occasions, and even wrote an article for the paper
defending it against the criticism of the other churches in town.
His influence came more from his love of ritual, as it was practiced
in the Knights of Pythias—supposedly a revival of the ancient
Pythagorean Brotherhood.[3] My grandfather had literally memo-
rized every word and act in all of the rituals practiced within his
order. And since I too was a member of this order, he tried to
instill this same love of ritual in my life.

Thus it was that I began to write Earth rituals based upon my
experience and understanding of ritual in the Knights of Pythias,
and greatly influenced by various Neo-Pagan authors such as: Margot
Adler, Z. Budapest, Laurie Cabot, Gerald Gardner, and Starhawk.[4]
All of this in turn led directly to the "Liturgies of the Earth" which
we began to celebrate at Spiritwind.

The first holy day that we observed was the Winter Solstice.
And though my grandfather really wanted to be there—as did many
others—he, like they, could not come due to the incredible snow-
storm we had.

As it turned out, only seven of us were able to make it. But
we caught it all on videotape thanks to a friend of mine. This
friend was an ordained minister in the United Church of Christ
who was now working as a therapist in Tehachapi. More than this,
it was he and his wife who first suggested that I write a book of our

Earth liturgies. I submitted the idea to a small publishing company that publishes educational and worship resources for churches. They were intrigued by my proposal and agreed to publish my book, *Liturgy of the Earth* (1992a)—after I had performed all of the liturgies recorded therein, so that I could refine them through experience and trial and error. And so it was that we began our journey through the "wheel of the year."

By the time of the Summer Solstice we had already celebrated four of our liturgies, and it had snowed at all but one of these. It had even snowed on May Day, as we danced our Maypole dance in blizzard-like winds. Unlike traditional Christians, who sing, "Just As I Am" in the faith that God would accept them just as they are, we determined to accept the Earth "Just as It Is"—as inconvenient as it sometimes was.

Our journey through the wheel of the year was truly an adventure. In addition to enjoying our snowed-out services, we jumped a broomstick on top of a mountain on the Summer Solstice recalling old wedding rituals,[5] we smoked ourselves out of my house on Loaf Mass (August 1st) as we burned ginger bread figures that symbolized our negative selves, we danced a backwards circle dance next to the Tehachapi Indians' "Creation Cave" on the Autumn Equinox as we focused on what we would banish from our lives, and we decorated our altar with the pictures and keepsakes of our departed loved ones on All Saints' Eve (Halloween) as we recalled what they meant to us—and we even bobbed for apples as if we were snatching our dreams from the womb of life.

There were articles about our "strange goings-on" in the local newspapers as well as in our denominational paper. There were charges of "witchcraft"—a private investigator was even called in on this one.[6] And the rumor mill was working non-stop, day and night, cranking out its bizarre fabrications. We were feared by some, while others saw us as simply eccentric in our practice of religion.

And then, having received a bit of notoriety for the work I was doing with Spiritwind, I was asked to come to Sedona, Arizona—the self-proclaimed center for the New Age movement—to conduct a retreat with our denomination's church there. I showed the members of this church how they could build a bridge across the gulf that separated them from the "New Agers" who were making medicine wheels upon so-called "energy vortexes," by means of the Earth liturgies that we had developed at Spiritwind.

So far they are the only church that had shown any interest in experimenting with Spiritwind's unorthodox worship forms, or in finding ways to worship with New Agers and Neo-Pagans.

Meanwhile, back in Tehachapi, most of those who attended Spiritwind did so selectively, coming only to those classes that interested them. However, almost everyone who attended came to our Earth liturgies. And in June of 1992, just as I was finishing up a class on the tarot,[7] we were invited to perform our Summer Solstice liturgy with the youth who were to attend Southern California's Annual Meeting of the United Church of Christ.

As the annual meeting approached and I realized that the Summer Solstice would occur while we were there, the idea came to me of performing one of our Earth liturgies at the annual meeting. This would be the first time that such a thing had been done at an official gathering of any mainline denomination. I thought that it was unlikely, due to the out-of-the-ordinary nature of such a request, that the conference would feel comfortable with this. But what about the youth? What if we were to do this with the youth?

I called our conference youth program coordinator and told her of my idea. She thought that it was a great idea, but said that the decision was ultimately up to the "youth roundtable" which served as the representative youth leadership for our conference.

She invited me to present my proposal to the youth roundtable at their next meeting. And so I did—amid the melting snows at Pilgrim Pines—our denominational retreat center in Southern California. They agreed to do it, and so a few months later we found ourselves in a public park preparing to celebrate the Summer Solstice, using my *Liturgies of the Earth* as our guidebook.

Once everything was prepared, we formed a large circle around our make-shift altar, beneath spreading trees and flanked by a baseball game to the east, picnickers to the west, and fencers to the north.

We began by invoking the four directions and the four elements with the words:

East: By the fire of the Spirit
South: By the earth—dust we are and unto dust shall we
                 return
West: By the water of life
North: By air, the breath of life
Together: May this place of worship be set apart for our holy
                 purpose. Amen.
Congregation: Give us wisdom O God, that what we do here will
                 be for our good and for the good of all the earth.
                 (Kuykendall 1992a, 40)

And with that we commenced our ritual celebration. I was amazed at how receptive and cooperative the youth were. When I was their age, there would have been no way that I would have participated in something like this—especially in a public place, where others would see. I would have died of embarrassment. But this group of young people all joined in as if this were one of the most natural things one could do in a park. Needless to say, this first was a real success from my perspective—but it was not taken in such a positive light in other quarters of the church.

Prior to the annual meeting, I had been interviewed for an article which was scheduled to come out in the May issue of *United Church News*. In this article the author, Karla Harby, wrote that I would "perform a summer solstice ritual with youth at the annual meeting of the Southern California Conference in June" (May 1992). No sooner had the word gotten out that a debate had begun in the letters-to-the-editor section in the *United Church News*. In the June issue a minister from Massachusetts wrote,

> I read with dismay that the Southern California Conference is allowing a UCC minister to perform a summer solstice ritual with youth at its annual meeting. The observance of summer and winter solstice and the rituals associated with it are deeply rooted in the ancient pagan practice of witchcraft.
>
> One cannot help but think (or lament) that this is yet another indication that in our denomination what is essential (as in 'unity in essential') is that *we have no essentials*. Therefore, anything (like paganism) is perfectly acceptable. Without clearly defined essentials, we cease to be distinctly Christian and instead become *essentially* Christian, or even less.[14]

In the next issue I responded to this minister in his own Christian language, replying in part that,

> Jesus told us that we are not to judge by appearances (John 7:24). He was judged by many to be the servant of the devil (Matt. 9:34) and was consequently put to death. So were thousands of 'witches' who had never even done the things of which they were accused.
>
> Let us not judge according to appearances, but let us judge righteously. (1992)

Also in this issue, a minister in Illinois came to my defense, saying,

> . . . I affirm the minister in California and applaud the openness to explore new avenues of spirituality. The Winter and Summer solstices are rich in beauty and spiritual meaning. Many of Christianity's major holidays, as well as theologies, have pagan origins. What is essential is that spirituality not be confused with creeds and doctrines.

What is essential for many is a spirituality which is a relation-ship to the Eternal, self, others and nature. I hope the UCC can affirm the larger ecumenism (global spirituality) that is on its way. Otherwise we will have more to worry about than pagan(ism). It's time to broaden our horizons and listen to others in our midst. (Kucera 1992)

In the above letter to the editor, Kucera says that he hopes "the UCC can affirm the larger ecumenism (global spirituality) that is on its way. Otherwise we will have more to worry about than pagan(ism)." I believe that the New Age movement and Neo-Paganism must be included in this larger ecumenism. To restrict "deep ecumenism" only to "world religions" such as Judaism and Buddhism is to continue in a kind of spiritual arrogance. As I wrote in Spiritwind's bulletin statement,

> . . . religious exclusivism and intolerance must give way to inclusivism and tolerance as well as mutual respect and appreciation. Only through such a course will our world find peace.

More than this, I have found that "such an approach enriches us through its inherent pluralism" (Spiritwind bulletin).

Thus it is that I, a modern Congregational minister in the United Church of Christ, have come to not only acknowledge the wrong committed three hundred years ago upon those who were charged with Witchcraft, but to embrace modern self-proclaimed witches, and to even incorporate their rituals into Christian worship.

NOTES

1. The United Church of Christ was formed in the year 1957 as result of a voluntary union of Congregational Christian Churches and the Evangelical and Reformed Church.

2. Some of what follows is an adaptation of part 3 of my book, *The Wind Blows Where It Wills.* (1991).

3. Modern Witchcraft is no more a continuation of what was called Witchcraft back at Salem, than the Knights of Pythias is a revival of the ancient Pythagorean Brotherhood. Nor do either of these find the origin of their rituals in their supposed ancient predecessors.

4. I actually began my study of modern Witchcraft in 1983.

5. This particular observance was announced publicly in an article by religion editor Tom Brisson in *The Bakersfield Californian,* 21 June 1991, entitled, "New Age Rises Above the Trendiness of the Late '80s."

6. See "Pastor Unearths Reasons to Celebrate." *The Bakersfield Californian,* 20 January 1992.

7. This class was the basis for my book, *Tarot Meditations: A Christian Reflection.*

8. Richard E. Kuykendall, "Recommends Book of Liturgies." *United Church News,* July/August 1992b.

9. Dean Kucera, "Spirituality is Not Creeds." Ibid.

10. See: p. 5.

11. See: p. 5.

REFERENCES

Harby, Karla. 1992. "Both Advocates and Critics Agree: 'New Age' Meets Spiritual Needs." *United Church News* (May 1992).

Hoffnagle, Grant. 1992. "No More Essentials." *United Church News.* (June 1992).

Kucera, Dean. 1992. "Spirituality Is Not Creeds." *United Church News* (June 1992).

Kuykendall, Richard E. 1992a. *Liturgies of the Earth.* Phoenix, Ariz.: Educational Ministries, Inc.

———. 1992b. *Prophetess of the Earth.* New York, N.Y.: New Paradigm Books.

———. 1992c. "Recommends Book of Liturgies." *United Church News* (July-August 1992).

———. 1991. *The Wind Blows Where It Wills.*

———. 1991. *Tarot Meditations: A Christian Reflection.*

15

WORKS OF DARKNESS:
OCCULT FASCINATION IN THE NOVELS
OF FRANK E. PERETTI

James R. Lewis

The night is far gone, the day is at hand. Let us then cast off the
works of darkness. . . .

—Romans 13: 12

ON HALLOWEEN NIGHT OF 1990, Evangelist Larry Lea led
an assault on San Francisco's local demons. A popular televangelist
and a leading proponent of "spiritual warfare," Lea ordered his
prayer warriors to descend on the city to do battle with the ruling
spirits of Witchcraft, drugs, and sexual perversion. The San Francisco assault had been preceded by earlier campaigns: In Anaheim,
California, six thousand freelance exorcists had attended a three-
day crusade intended to "inflict serious damage" on the forces of
darkness in Southern California. In Chicago, seven thousand Christian
warriors had turned up "to clobber the devil." At these meetings,
Lea's followers shouted, stomped, brandished imaginary swords,
and spoke in tongues. While even Christian critics such as Ron
Enroth, the Evangelical scholar, have described Lea's dramatic
campaigns as "supernatural sideshows," and while his crusades have
yet to inflict noticeable damage on the powers of darkness, his

tactics *have* been highly successful at packing auditoriums. The sense of high drama in the war against Satan is heightened when Lea shows up in military fatigues. The pastor-warrior also distributes "prayer army dog tags" to help his soldiers feel that they have been *officially* inducted into heaven's regiments.

Bay area witches, and an ad hoc group calling itself GHOST— Grand Homosexual Outrage at Sickening Televangelists—organized themselves to oppose Lea's Halloween crusade. Eric Pryor, high priest of the New Earth Temple, was quoted as saying, "The witch-hunts are over, and I, for one, don't intend to be burned at the stake." GHOST organizer Mark Pritchard asserted that "Lea's message is, 'Perverts are bad and we're going to destroy perversity.' People in San Francisco want a chance to stand up against fundamentalists. Larry Lea has made himself a convenient target."

Despite the preacher's claim that the angry militancy generated by his campaigns was "not directed at flesh and blood," it was widely rumored that Lea's prayer warriors were planning to roam the streets and physically assault witches and gays following the prayer meeting in the civic auditorium. Anti-Lea protests began on the day preceding the crusade, when a crowd of approximately one hundred people assembled for a "public cursing." Pagan leader Eric Pryor led the "cursing," burning and eventually decapitating a black candle representing pastor Lea. In a scene that mixed medieval pomp with countercultural flamboyance, the crowd danced in a circle and chanted, "Never again the burnings." At one point in the ritual the entire civic center was sealed off with an ancient spell of "binding," designed to constrain the negative energy of Lea's assault. On the actual night of crusade, a large crowd of protesters gathered outside the civic center. To reach the auditorium, charismatic Christians were forced to run a gauntlet of more than one thousand angry gays and pagans. Protestors chanted, blew whistles, and occasionally tossed eggs at the prayer warriors. Invoking a highly charged image from Christian history, some members of the crowd shouted, "Throw them to the lions!" In Civic Center Plaza on the other side of the street, a large banner reading "Born Again Bigots, Go Home" was raised over mock gravestones bearing the names of Lea and other Christian evangelists. San Francisco police were barely able to prevent the opposing sides from coming to blows.

☆   ☆   ☆

Although the basic notion of "spiritual warfare" has biblical roots, Lea's campaign was directly inspired by the novels of bestselling Christian author Frank E. Peretti.[1] Peretti's works, especially *This*

Present Darkness (1986) and *Piercing the Darkness* (1989), have fu-
eled the imaginations of certain conservative Christians with bloody
visions of angelic crusades against demonic evil. The action in
these novels moves back and forth between two interacting levels:
While angels and devils cross swords in the spiritual realm, Peretti's
human heroes and heroines do battle with New Agers, witches,
psychologists, secular education, and the American Civil Liberties
Union.

One of the keys necessary for understanding Lea's crusades is
the belief—directly inspired by Peretti—that the concentrated prayers
of God's earthly saints provide power and protection for warrior
angels. This "prayer energy" empowers God's angels to win their
battles against supernatural demons. A decisive defeat of Satan's
legions in the spiritual realm disempowers Satan's earthly minions
(i.e., everyone opposed to Christian fundamentalists), which in turn
leads to their defeat.

The climax to the final confrontation in *This Present Darkness*
provides a good example of how this "prayer power" is viewed as
working. In the concluding scene of the battle, Tal, leader of the
angelic host, crosses swords with Rafar, leader of the demonic forces.
At the same time, the Remnant of God's human "warriors" engaged in the earthly struggle are distracted by the dramatic damage inflicted by their crusade. This distraction interrupts the flow
of "power" to Tal, so that Rafar almost gets the better of him. At
the last possible moment, these Christians feel impressed by the
Lord to direct their prayer power against the demon they can
sense but cannot see:

> *[Event in spiritual realm:]*
> Tal could only back away from the fearsome onslaught of the
> demon prince, his one good hand still holding his sword up for
> defense. Rafar kept swinging and slashing, the sparks flying from
> the blades as they met. Tal's arm sank lower with each blow. "The
> Lord . . . rebuke you!" Tal found the breath to say again.
> *[Appropriate Christian "prayer" response, intuited by an elderly lady:]*
> Edith Duster was on her feet and ready to shout it to the heav-
> ens. "Rafar, you wicked prince of evil, in the name of Jesus we
> rebuke you!"
> *[Effect of "prayer energy" in spiritual realm:]*
> Rafar's blade zinged over Tal's head. It missed.
> *[Further "prayer" action in physical realm:]*
> "We bind you!" shouted the Remnant.
> *[Effect in spiritual realm:]*
> The big yellow eyes winced.

[Action in physical realm:]
"We cast you out!" Andy said.
[Effect in spiritual realm:]
There was a puff of sulfur, and Rafar bent over. Tal leaped to
his feet.
[Action in physical realm:]
"We rebuke you, Rafar!" Edith shouted again.
[Effect in spiritual realm:]
Rafar screamed. Tal's blade had torn him open. (Peretti
1986, 370)

While Christians have always believed in the power of prayer, the
Darkness novels picture prayer as having a fantastic, magical efficacy against fallen angels. Such melodramatic invocations of God's
power—resembling exorcisms more than prayers—provide the paradigms for Lea's frenzied crusades. Whatever may be the effects of
these tactics on the "powers of darkness," Peretti's vision of spiritual combat has powerfully influenced certain segments of the
conservative Christian community. In effect, Peretti's writings have
encouraged charismatics and fundamentalists to adopt an attitude
of greater hostility to the non-Christian world by providing quasi-
theological justifications and dramatized prayer-exorcism tactics for
attacking Satan's forces. How is the widespread appeal of these
novels, which are reshaping the face of convervative Christianity,
to be understood?

In the first place, Peretti, in sharp contrast with many other
Christian authors, is a gifted writer. Even the harshest critics will
find themselves drawn into the narrative action of the *Darkness*
novels. In the second place, Peretti is able to weave together be-
lievable, this-worldly stories with fantastic, "Dungeons and Dragons" struggles between other-worldly angels and demons. The results
of this skillful juxtaposition are novels with an eerie narrative landscape that Evangelical scholar Irving Hexham has described as
"sanctified Stephen King" (1992, p. 156). In the third place, Peretti
chooses to portray the anti-Christian forces in his stories in terms
of the single most popular target of conservative Christian ire,
namely the New Age movement. The capsule summary of *This
Present Darkness* on the book's back cover, for example, describes
Peretti's story in the following manner:

> Ashton is just a typical small town. But when a skeptical reporter
> and a prayerful pastor begin to compare notes, they suddenly find
> themselves fighting a hideous New Age plot to subjugate the towns-
> people, and eventually the entire human race.

Unknown to most people outside of the conservative Christian subculture, "New Age" has become the catch-all category for everything despised by fundamentalists. (Contemporary Neo-Pagan witches are viewed by writers like Peretti as the controlling forces behind the New Age.) The major steps by which this came to pass are not difficult to trace.

If one peruses the shelves of any Christian bookstore, one will almost always find a section devoted to volumes that critically analyze secular humanism, "cults," and other heresies. As might be expected, these works run the gamut from even-handed treatments that discuss various groups and movements in terms of their deviations from correct doctrine, to hysterial books that portray everything outside of a rather sharply delimited circle of light as a demonic conspiracy aimed at destroying true Christianity. While the ostensible purpose of such volumes is to alert Christians and to equip them to convert the heathen, they are probably best viewed in terms of "boundary maintenance"—compositions that allow a community to strengthen its own sense of identity by contrasting itself with "others" who are portrayed as being the exact opposite of themselves.

The 1980s saw the emergence of a new topic for such works—the New Age movement. Beginning rather modestly in 1983 with the publication of Constance Cumbey's *The Hidden Dangers of the Rainbow*, the number of conservative Christian books on the New Age increased rapidly until a complete collection would now fill several library shelves. The event that appears to have crystalized the topic of the New Age as a target of attack was Benjamin Creme's highly public advertising campaign for Maitreya, the New Christ who Creme presented in terms of Alice Bailey's Theosophy. Creme's widespread advertising began in 1982. The first book-length responses directed explicitly at the New Age emerged in 1983. The one other clearly identifiable event to stimulate the growth of this genre was the televised version of Shirley MacLaine's *Out on a Limb* in 1987. While Creme's campaign was important for giving birth to Christian anti–New Age literature, MacLaine's televised miniseries was responsible for establishing the New Age as *the* most popular topic for Christian polemics.[2]

As the first of its kind, Constance Cumbey's book suggests itself as a useful focal point for analysis. *The Hidden Dangers of the Rainbow* (1983) is a mixed work in which one finds a few insightful criticisms juxtaposed with many accusations of the least responsible sort. As the earliest work in this genre, Cumbey set the agenda, both positively and negatively, for later writers. For instance, her conspiracy theory and her focus on certain "buzz words" as identifying New Age conspirators (including certain Christian ministers) are points which most succeeding authors have felt compelled either to affirm or to deny.[3]

The very vagueness of the New Age movement has allowed it to become a catchall category for everything conservative Christians perceive as threatening. In Constance Cumbey's case, after asserting that "this Movement has infiltrated all of Christianity, as well as Judaism" (p. 39), she goes on to imply or to assert that the New Age conspiracy is the motivating force behind ecumenism, holistic health centers, New Thought, humanistic psychology, Montessori schools, modernism, secular humanism, and zero population growth. In her conspiratorial vision, Unitarian churches and health food stores become "New Age recruiting centers" (p. 127), and the Guardian Angels become one of the New Age movement's "para-military" organizations. Her least cautious assertion is that "the New Age Movement has complete identity with the programs of Hitler" (p. 56), and the link to Nazism is a theme to which she returns over and over again throughout *Hidden Dangers*.[4] The basis for this collapsing of boundaries between widely disparate phenomena is, with few exceptions, not empirical; rather, it is transparent that Cumbey is simply lumping together anything that departs from a rather strict interpretation of Christianity.[5]

Peretti's writings draw much of their nourishment from this polemical literature.[6] As one might anticipate, his novels reflect many of the characteristics of this literature, such as the tendency to lump together everything outside of conservative Christianity as part of a satanic conspiracy. In the words of one of Peretti's protagonists:

> "It's all a con game: Eastern meditation, witchcraft, divination, Science of Mind, psychic healing, holistic education—oh, the list goes on and on—it's all the same thing, nothing but a ruse to take over people's minds and spirits, even their bodies" (1986, 314)

Over the course of the two *Darkness* novels, Peretti mentions many other facets of the satanic threat, such as environmentalism, feminism, channeling, sex education, humanism, the ACLU, liberal Christianity, yoga, psychology, belief in ET's, belief in karma and reincarnation, and belief in mother earth and mother goddesses. These various threats are woven together in such figures as the evil genius behind the plot to take over the town of Ashton in *This Present Darkness*, Juleen Langstrat.

As a woman with advanced degrees in psychology, Prof. Langstrat directly embodies two "fundamentalist bogey-men" (to again borrow an expression from Hexham): feminism and secular education. While Peretti does not put strong feminist statements in her mouth, Langstrat's feminism comes across in the titles of some of the non-credit courses she teaches at the university, such as "In the Beginning Was the Goddess" (p. 94). Peretti's disdain for higher education comes through in the reflections of one of his chief protagonists, Marshall Hogan, who, while waiting for his daughter to get out of class, happens to overhear fragments of Langstat's lecture. He reflects,

> Yeah, here was more of that college stuff, that funny conglomeration of sixty-four-dollar words which impress people with your academic prowess but can't get you a paying job. Marshall smirked. . . . (p. 37)[7]

Not one for subtle distinctions, Peretti locates the central lair for the demons plotting to take over Ashton in a psychology department conference room—a room described in language suggesting that the department is an outpost of hell itself:

> In this dismal nether world the ceiling was low and oppressive, and crawling with water pipes and heat ducts that seemed like so many huge snakes waiting to drop. Everything—walls, ceiling, pipes, woodwork—was painted the same dirty beige, and light was scarce. . . . (p. 48)[8]

Beyond her already un-Christian status as a psychologist with feminist inclinations, Prof. Langstrat teaches other non-credit courses on topics that serve to identify her more deeply with the dark forces. Such topics include how to meet your own spirit guides, how to experience past lives, spells and rituals, and Eastern meditation techniques. Langstrat is clearly a damned figure who eventually meets an ignoble death at the hands of a semi-possessed henchman.

Peretti's narrative campaign against the forces of darkness does not, however, stop with attacks on obvious deviations from a rather narrowly circumscribed fundamentalism. While the psychology department's conference room may be the principal gathering place for evil entities in Ashton, lesser demons stalk such dens of iniquity as video arcades:

> Here were kids of all ages, with few other places to go, congregating after school and all through the weekends to hang out, hang on, play games, pair up, wander off, do drugs, do sex, do whatever. Hank

knew this place was a hell hole; it wasn't the machines, or the decor, or the dimness—it was just the pungent spiritual stench of demons having their heyday. He felt sick to his stomach. (1986, 149)

Subjected to Peretti's discerning gaze, such superficially innocent entertainments as spring carnivals reveal their true nature as festivals of evil:

> Most would . . . take in the festivities, the street disco, the carnival rides, the nickel movies, and whatever else could be had, over or under the table, for kicks. It was a wild time, a chance to get drunk, pregnant, beat up, ripped off, and sick, all in the same night . . . On this warm summer night the roaming, cotton-candied masses were out to enjoy, enjoy, enjoy. . . . The streets, taverns, stores, alleys, and parking spots were jammed, anything was allowed, and the illegal was ignored. . . . The festival, reaching a crescendo now on its last night, was like a terrible storm that couldn't be stopped. . . . (pp. 9–10)

If even arcades and carnivals are hell holes, one might well ask what pleasures are left for good, God-fearing folk. Peretti obviously disapproves of the urge to "enjoy, enjoy, enjoy," and leaves very little to entertain weary spiritual pilgrims. Beyond the righteous pleasures of prayer and family life, the only excitement left is the joy of trouncing Satan's forces. The angel Guilo, for example, takes obvious pleasure in bloodying his sword with the gore of God's enemies:

> The demon warriors fell upon them like an avalanche, but for Guilo this was good sport. Tal and the General could hear his uproarious laughter through the thudding sounds of his blade going through demon after demon. (1986, 358)

Spiritual Combat is good, wholesome fun—one of the few forms of enjoyment Peretti can unequivocally endorse. This explains much of the attraction of his writings within fundamentalist circles: Because of their edifying themes, the *Darkness* novels allow conservative Christians to indulge in reading good horror/adventure stories without the pangs of guilt they might feel reading secular stories. Much the same can be said about Larry Lea's campaigns: One can release one's emotions by cheering on the home team without the twinges of guilt one might feel getting worked up over a secular sporting event.

Peretti's art has created an exciting imaginative world that enables Christians to understand and respond to the demonic threat, but the cost of this literary tour de force has been to bring conservative Christianity closer in spirit to the very phenomenon in which the forces of darkness are most clearly evident: the New Age movement. Peretti's narratives have imaginatively transformed the realm of the ordinary and the everyday into a kind of real-life Dungeons and Dragons game, replete with supernatural phenomena, psychic intuitions, quasi-magical powers, and sword-swinging warriors. A fascination with the occult is evident in Peretti's descriptions of demons, for example:

> He was like a high-strung little gargoyle, his hide a slimy, bottomless black, his body thin and spiderlike: half humanoid, half animal, totally demon. Two huge yellow cat-eyes bulged out of his face, darting to and fro, peering, searching. His breath came in short, sulfurous gasps, visible as glowing yellow vapor (1986, 36).[9]

While Christians have always believed in the power of prayer, the *Darkness* novels picture prayer as having a fantastic, magical efficacy against demonic warriors:

> "Lord God," she said, and the warmth of the Holy Spirit flowed through them, "I build now a hedge around this young couple, and I bind the spirits in Jesus' name. Satan, whatever your plans for the town, I rebuke you in Jesus' name, and I bind you, and I cast you out!"
>
> CLUNK! Rafar's eyes darted toward the sound that had interrupted his talking and saw two swords fallen from their owner's hands. (1986, 113)

While Christians have traditionally believed in the guidance of the Holy Spirit, the vivid picture Peretti draws of highly personal angels conveying guidance to the minds of God's saints makes "Christian" inspiration appear a close relative of New Age psychism.[10] Peretti also pictures angels as capable of materializing to help God's chosen, as when the angel Betsy materializes to give one of the heroines, Bernice Krueger, a short motorcycle ride. Once Bernice has reached her destination, Betsy evaporates like some eerie figure out of an occult novel:

> She turned back to Betsy and stiffened. For a moment she felt she would stumble forward as if a wall had suddenly disappeared in front of her. Betsy was gone. The motorcycle was gone. It was like awakening from a dream and needing time to adjust one's mind to what was real and what was not. But Bernice knew it had not been a dream. The tracks of the motorcycle were still plainly visible in the gravel, leading from where it had left the highway to the spot directly in front of Bernice. There they ended. (1986, 303)[11]

As with many of the events that take place in the *Darkness* novels, such eerie encounters reflect a fascination with the supernatural and with supernatural powers. And the net effect, for readers who buy into Peretti's version of Christianity, is to bring Christians closer in spirit to the very form of occult spirituality they claim to despise: The New Age movement.

NOTES

1. "Many of the more popular Evangelical books on the New Age are more akin to fiction than serious scholarship. It is not surprising therefore to learn that by far the most popular Evangelical book on the New Age is a novel by Evangelical author Frank E. Peretti. His surrealist work *This Present Darkness* has sold over a million copies and is rumored to be under consideration as a major motion picture." (Hexham 1992, p. 156)

2. The rise of "New Age" as the most popular category for Christian polemics can be seen in such areas as the name change of Paul C. Reiser, Teri K. Reisser, and John Weldon's *The Holistic Healers: A Christian Perspective on New-Age Health Care* (1983) to *New Age Medicine: A Christian Perspective on Holistic Health* (1987) when it went into its second edition.

3. In *The Seduction of Christianity: Spiritual Discernment in the Last Days* (1985), Dave Hunt and T. A. MacMahon pick up on one of Cumbey's most controversial points—that Christianity is being subtly infiltrated by the New Age, causing the church to fall into apostasy. *The Seduction of Christianity* went so far as to attack by name certain conservative Christian leaders, and as a consequence evoked more than a few critical responses.

4. As hysterical as *Hidden Dangers* might appear, however, Cumbey's work is conservative when contrasted with such works as Randall N. Baer, *Inside the New Age Nightmare* (1989); Texe Marrs, *Dark Secrets of the New Age: Satan's Plan for a One World Religion* (1987); and Paul de Parrie and Mary Prind, *Unholy Sacrifices of the New Age* (1988).

5. Cumbey's tendency to group together everything and everybody she dislikes is *cautious* compared with the assertions of certain other authors, such as the following: "Globalism, humanism, socialism, feminism, illuminism, New Age, etc. are all the same animal: the differences are semantic and inconsequential" (Bowen 1984, 15).

6. At the same time, the popularity of the anti-New Age genre has prepared his audience to understand certain suggestive allusions without requiring the author to lay out further explanation. Thus, for example, when a villain asserts that "Omni Corporation is about to establish still another foothold for the coming New World Order and the rule of the New Age Christ," no elaboration is necessary for Peretti's

audience to understand that the "New Age Christ" is the anti-Christ (Peretti 1986, 257).

7. While Hogan's comments here are the most disparaging expression of Peretti's dislike of higher education, one can find more subtle disparagements elsewhere in the novel, as well as in *Piercing the Darkness* e.g., 1989, pp. 248–249.

8. A psychologist is also brought in as an expert witness in *Piercing the Darkness*, which is about a satanic plot to destroy a Christian school. Dr. Mandanhi's remarks are interesting in the way they convincingly express how an ultra-secularist psychologist might evaluate fundamentalist education, e.g.:

"The pervasive religious overtones of the school's curriculum would be, in my opinion, sufficient to exacerbate Amber's preexistent emotional turmoils. The Christian doctrines of sin and of a God of wrath and judgment, as well as Christianity's imposition of guilt and accountability, would immediately assimilate into the child's preestablished identity structure, producing a whole new set of reasons for her to be insecure and fearful of her world." (1989, p. 232)

9. A lengthier and more dramatic description of a demon can be found on p. 11.

10. For example, when the pastor Hank Busche considers praying for a possessed young man, he eventually responds to the prompting of the angel Krioni:

"I *would* like to pray for you, okay?" Hank asked, just to check. "No, don't," Ron said, and then pleaded, "Please pray, c'mon. . . . " "Do it," Krioni prompted. "Pray!" "No!" the demons cried. "You can't make us leave him!" Hank knew he had better take charge of the situation and pray for this boy. (1986, 152)

11. There are a number of places in the *Darkness* novels where angels reach through from the spiritual realm to help God's chosen (e.g., 1989, 265–267).

REFERENCES

Baer, Randall N. 1989. *Inside the New Age Nightmare.* Lafayette, La.: Huntington House.

Bowen, William, Jr. 1984. *Globalism: America's Demise.* Shreveport, La.: Huntington House.

Cumbey, Constance. 1983. *The Hidden Dangers of the Rainbow: The New Age Movement and Our Coming Age of Barbarism.* Shreveport, La.: Huntington House.

de Parrie, Paul, and Mary Prind. 1988. *Unholy Sacrifices of the New Age.* Westchester, Ill.: Crossway Books.

Hexham, Irving. 1992. "The Evangelical Response to the New Age." In *Perspectives on the New Age*, edited by James R. Lewis and J. Gordon Melton. Albany: State University of New York Press.

Hunt, Dave, and T. A. MacMahon. 1985. *The Seduction of Christianity: Spiritual Discernment in the Last Days.* Eugene, Oreg.: Harvest House.

Marrs, Texe. 1987. *Dark Secrets of the New Age: Satan's Plan for a One World Religion.* Westchester, Ill.: Crossway Books.

Peretti, Frank E. 1986. *This Present Darkness.* Westchester, Ill.: Crossway Books.

———. 1989. *Piercing the Darkness.* Westchester, Ill.: Crossway Books.

Reiser, Paul C., Teri K. Reiser, and John Weldon. 1983. *The Holistic Healers: A Christian Perspective on New-Age Health Care.* Downers Gove, Ill.: InterVarsity Press.

———. 1987. *New Age Medicine: A Christian Perspective on Holistic Health.* Downers Grove, Ill.: InterVarsity Press.

Part VI

Literature Reviews

16

RATIONALIZING THE MARGINS: A REVIEW OF LEGITIMATION AND ETHNOGRAPHIC PRACTICE IN SCHOLARLY RESEARCH ON NEO-PAGANISM

Sarah M. Pike

IN RESPONSE TO ACCUSATIONS of satanic sacrifice and child abuse, Neo-Pagans portray themselves as the most recent victims in a long history of persecuted people, including massacred Native Americans and martyred seventeenth-century witches.[1] Misunderstanding and ignorance about what witches and Neo-Pagans do often have tragic consequences—people lose their children, their businesses, and their property.[2] No wonder, then, that most scholarly work is concerned first of all with demonstrating that witches and Neo-Pagans are not devil-worshipers who sacrifice babies.

Interpretations of contemporary Americans' involvement with "magical" and "occult" activities hinge on the assumption that it is the role of scholars and social scientists to legitimize these groups.[3] Scholarly studies are framed by attempts to show why individuals involved with the occult are "rational" and thus "legitimate" rather than evil or insane. However, journalists, social scientists, and other "authorities" on Neo-Paganism proceed as though they have already decided on the nature and definition of rationality, ignoring the cultural specificity of such concepts.[4]

"Neo-Paganism" is as much a self-descriptive label as it is a scholarly definition for the many groups and individuals who are engaged in reviving and inventing pre- or non-Christian religions. Journalist Margot Adler explains that

> most Neo-Pagans sense an 'aliveness' or presence in nature. They are usually polytheists or animists or pantheists, or two or three of these things at once. They share the goal of living in harmony with nature and they tend to view humanity's 'advancement' and separation from nature as the prime source of alienation. They see *ritual* as a tool to end that alienation. Most Neo-Pagans look to the old pre-Christian nature religions of Europe, the ecstatic religions, and the mystery traditions as a source of inspiration and nourishment.

Because much of the knowledge of these traditions is seen as "hidden" or the groups themselves are somewhat secretive, they have also been labelled "occult" and "esoteric." I will use whatever label appears in the book or article I am discussing.

Public suspicion of Neo-Pagans and occultists results from their apparent strangeness, hiddenness, and "irrationality." Even contemporary anthropological approaches based on extended participant observation focus on questions of legitimacy and rationality such as, "Why do otherwise rational people believe in magic?" Or as T. M. Luhrmann puts it in *Persuasions of the Witch's Craft: Ritual Magic in Contemporary England*, "the purpose of this book is to examine a case in which apparently irrational beliefs are held by apparently rational people, and to identify the elements which seem important to explaining how they do so" (1989, 13).[6]

Questions of rationality/irrationality framed by sympathetic researchers as well as suspicious outsiders have determined the agenda of the academic study of Neo-Paganism. In the 1970s, sociological descriptions of occult groups responded to public anxiety about the flourishing of new religious movements. Most of these studies define and categorize different practices and beliefs so as to distinguish "destructive" from "harmless" rituals, "white" from "black" magic, and "witch" from "satanist."[7] Yet a survey of scholarly literature on occultism, Witchcraft, and Neo-Paganism testifies to the fact that three decades of categorizing different groups and defining their differences has done little to clear up public confusion.[8]

Supposedly "objective" studies of occult or Neo-Pagan groups are similar to polemical writings on Neo-Paganism and Witchcraft in that they determine which issues and events get looked at. Much of the scholarly research reviewed in the following pages is sym-

pathetic rather than oppositional to Neo-Pagans.⁹ Yet the predetermined questions that these researchers bring to their studies
shape their interpretations and thus make difficult a direct encounter with Neo-Pagans and their communities.

Overemphasis on rationality and belief in the past thirty years
of academic scholarship on Neo-Paganism results from the defensive agenda I have already alluded to. In the process of exposing
this agenda I highlight gaps in coverage and suggest avenues for
further research.¹⁰ Interpretations emerging from the encounter
between researcher and subject as well as the researcher's intimate
knowledge of and extended experience with Neo-Pagan culture
look at what people "do" instead of the rationality or danger of
what they "believe." I argue that a more "experience-centered"
approach is increasingly evident in recent scholarship on Neo-
Paganism, although it often co-exists with legitimizing projects.
Scholarly approaches to Neo-Paganism are "experience-centered"
in two ways. First, the researcher is aware of and makes use of his
or her experiences in order to illuminate method, foci, and possible biases in the research process. Second, I contend that the
experiences of the research subjects, such as dancing and other
techniques of the body, personal stories, visions, and ritual practices, should not be seen as supporting data for the understanding
of belief, but rather as central and important activities in their
own right.

Sociological research of the 1970s is characterized by the
imposition of preconceived agendas on Neo-Paganism, or as many
sociologists labelled it, "occult" culture. Nevertheless, several of
these early essays make necessary and important distinctions between different kinds of occult groups and activities. They include
very little, if any, ethnography. Because they attempt to map and
describe general trends, sociological studies of "the occult revival"
are characteristically distant from rather than immersed in the cultures
they analyze.¹¹

The title of sociologist Edward Tiryakian's collected volume
of essays, *On the Margin of the Visible* (1974), attests to the distanc-
ing of occult groups from more visible and less "marginal" society.
The collection of essays edited by Tiryakian and his own essay on
"esoteric culture" illuminate aspects of twentieth-century occult
culture obscured by public ignorance. In order to do so, Tiryakian
attempts to clarify the relationship between what he calls "esoteric
culture" and mainstream society. This relationship, however, has
already been established by Tiryakian and his sociological prede-

cessors as a binary opposition of margin to center. While Tiryakian reassures his readers that these "marginal" groups are not necessarily "evil" or destructive, he does not question the dualistic perspective that equates them with everything considered "other." What is the cultural context in which occult practices are thought of as "deviant" or "irrational?" Why do educated and often, but not always, privileged Americans choose labels like "witch" or "Pagan?" How do they go about giving these labels meaning?

On the Margins of the Visible contains three sections: the first, "classics of esotericism," includes writings by Carl Jung, P. D. Ouspensky, W. B. Yeats, and Rudolph Steiner; the second focuses on the social setting of Witchcraft in different eras; the third section deals mostly with theoretical approaches to the occult and includes several articles about the contemporary "occult revival." The connections between these three areas are suggestive but undeveloped. In what ways do participants in the occult culture portrayed by Tiryakian use classic texts by Jung and other earlier occultists? In what ways have the European witch persecutions or other historical events affected more recent groups and individuals? What kinds of interpretations and judgments do contemporary Neo-Pagans make of this history? These are questions which Tiryakian's book does not address but which seem essential to understanding Neo-Pagans' views of history, authority, and tradition, as well as the ways in which individual Neo-Pagan practitioners incorporate these elements into their identities.

In "Towards a Sociology of Esoteric Culture" Tiryakian (1974) contextualizes his own approach to the study of contemporary occultism with brief and helpful descriptions of previous work on this topic: Marcello Truzzi (1974b), Martin Marty (1970) and Andrew Greeley (1970). Tiryakian refines the concerns of these earlier efforts and alludes to the broader sociological significance of "esoteric culture." He argues that issues emerging from the study of the occult revival go beyond frameworks established by the sociology of religion. He claims that scholarship on Neo-Paganism is relevant to the study of secularization and the nature of societal change. For instance, outbursts of enthusiasm for esotericism coincide with major shifts in cultural paradigms, such as the fall of the Roman Empire and the Reformation/Renaissance. But what exactly is the relationship between revivals of occult activity and paradigm shifts or processes of modernization? What particular factors in recent American cultural history account for the upsurge of interest in the occult? Knots of occult activity appear in particular historical and cultural contexts as a result of a confluence of forces which Tiryakian alludes to but does not account for.

Tiryakian's essay introduces important questions about the relationship between symbols or concepts and social action: "the problem of indicating linkages between esoteric symbolisms, imageries and conceptions of reality to purposive symbolic behavior, that is, the question of how conceptions of the structure of reality translate into paradigms of social action and social imagery is also laden with serious methodological difficulties" (1974, 268). Perhaps these difficulties account for why Tiryakian privileges belief over action and assumes that belief precedes action. He writes more about what people think and say about their symbols and images, than what they *do* with them. More personal contact with practitioners of the occult might have demonstrated to Tiryakian and the many other sociologists who follow this model that ritual practice and other experiential aspects of occult involvement exist in an interdependent relationship with belief. Systems of belief cannot be fully understood apart from the ways in which they are expressed and experienced.

Tiryakian suggests that sociologists might turn to linguistics and structural anthropology for tools to use in understanding the relationship between belief and Neo-Pagan practices. Structural anthropology, however, while it is based in ethnographic practice, denies the significance of intentional subjects on social and cultural processes.[12] It attempts to universalize its findings in ways that negate cultural particulars. It is attention to cultural practitioners and their experience that could further understanding of the issues highlighted by Tiryakian.

Zaretsky and Leone's *Religious Movements in Contemporary America* appeared in 1974, the same year as *On the Margin of the Visible*. It includes information on a wide variety of "marginal" religious movements and on theoretical issues such as altered consciousness and the relationship between ritual and belief.[13] Several of the essays included in this volume touch on Neo-Paganism, but remain within the limits established by earlier studies.[14] They categorize and differentiate between different kinds of Witchcraft, other types of Neo-Paganism, and Satanism. None of these essays includes ethnographic research into occult or Neo-Pagan groups, although in "Towards a Sociology of the Occult: Notes on Modern Witchcraft" Marcello Truzzi writes, both analytically and empirically, witchcraft is a highly multidimensional form of occultism and generalization is most difficult. In any case, it would certainly be premature, for much more research is needed into the basic ethnography of these groups before fruitful generalizations can be stated. It is hoped that this introduction to these social forms might help stimulate interest in this vital area and that more social scientists will turn their attention to these increasingly significant forms of marginal religious patterns in American life. (1974b, p. 642)[15]

Unfortunately, few social scientists took this advice and ethnographic research remains scarce. They continue to offer "introductions" to and "generalizations" about these "social forms" without conducting ethnography. Moreover, the handful of researchers who did field work in the 1970s and 1980s remain within a Durkheimian framework which emphasizes an oppositional relationship between ritual and social structure and between occult groups and mainstream society without exploring the nature of this opposition.

Scholars view their task as validating the existence of occult groups, thus focusing on issues of rationality or the legitimacy of conversion and the "deviant" or "mainstream" character of occult groups. Consequently they have made little progress in describing how individual participants experience involvement with occult activities. How do groups and individuals describe their own "marginality?" Why do some Neo-Pagans seek respectability and widespread acceptance while others revel in their otherness? How do they understand the political reasons for reclaiming "deviant" labels like "witch?"

Cult and Countercult: A Study of a Spiritual Growth Group and a Witchcraft Order (1980), Gini Scott's comparative study of two new religious movements, responds to Marcello Truzzi's call for ethnographic research. However, the titles of her book and the dissertation upon which it is based betray a method which does not allow interpretations to emerge from her own ethnographic inquiry or from the experiences of the people she worked with. Her analysis focuses too much on the opposition between the two groups and between "cults" and "traditional religions." At the beginning of her first chapter Scott asks, "Why have so many deserted the old faiths? Are the followers of these new groups being exploited? Are the new gurus offering false religion? Will the Guyana tragedy recur in other groups if nothing is done to control cults?" (p. 3). Like other scholars of new religions, she feels compelled to respond to public paranoia precipitated by Jonestown by enumerating ways in which the coven does not pose the same kind of threat to its members. Scott concludes her study with a discussion *not* of the title subject but of the dangers accompanying certain kinds of socialization and social control in cults:

> In the Craft, the traditional safeguards derived from mainstream links are not there, and the group's isolationist, retreatist stance could fan the flames of excess should conditions be ripe. There are also certain characteristics of the group that might make violent excesses more likely. For example, the group's paranoia and victims' posture toward the establishment might, under appropriate circumstances, lead members to strike out against that establishment in direct or in symbolic ways. For instance, a Manson-like response to a perceived establishment threat might be a theoretical possibility. (p. 179)

The title of Scott's 1976 doctoral dissertation, "Social Structure and the Occult: A Sociological Analysis of the Social Organization, Behavior Patterns and Beliefs of Two Occult Groups: A Spiritual Growth Group and a Witchcraft Coven," upon which her book is based, reveals a distant analyst observing patterns of behavior and discovering beliefs. Her defensive methods obscure the real-life experiences of her subjects—what they do in ritual, what they feel and think about their involvement with the group, and what kinds of conflicts they have.

Furthermore, Scott's study, while a sympathetic and often insightful account of this particular Neo-Pagan group, is limited by the comparative framework she employs. The first half of *Cult and Countercult* describes a socially and politically conservative, highly commercial, and hierarchically organized "spiritual growth group." Her analysis of the first group determines her interpretations in the second half of the book; her questions are fixed prior to her investigation of the Witchcraft coven. Where previous scholars legitimize these groups in response to popular misconceptions, Scott's understanding of the Witchcraft group is shaped by her responses to the spiritual growth group. Questions about the nature of participants' involvement in the Witchcraft group are not dealt with at all because of this bias.

F. R. Lynch's thoughtful ethnographic study of an urban California Neo-Pagan group, conducted several years after Scott's original research on "the Aquarian Age Order," is documented in two essays: "Toward a Theory of Conversion and Commitment to the Occult" (1977) and " 'Occult Establishment' or 'Deviant Religion?' The Rise and Fall of a Modern Church of Magic" (1979).

Lynch's is one of the few early sociological studies of Neo-Paganism to move beyond simply describing and categorizing different groups. He examines the processes by which individuals become involved with "the Church of the Sun," an occult group incorporating Jewish Kabbalah and Egyptian mythology, as well as the meanings they make out of their involvement.

The first of Lynch's essays, published in 1977, describes the process of "conversion" to this group as a complex combination of reading, "mystical" experience, and ritual work. Lynch's account of members' conversions is neither of radical departure from their former beliefs to new ones nor of slow and gradual progress towards commitment to the group. Lynch outlines the vicarious and often subtle movement by which people become members of this group. Collective ritual work, he explains, encourages reading and "mystical experience," such as "precognition, astral projection, déjà vu, and telepathy" (p. 898). Psychic and mystical experiences in turn lead to increasing interest in ritual work. Lynch argues that the interactive dynamic of belief and practice results in deeper commitment to the group. Lynch acknowledges the importance of this dynamic but then asserts his Durkheimian bias: "collective rituals were highly effective in promoting cohesion and in the formation of individual self-concepts. Symbolic social ritual was at the heart of the dynamics of the church" (p. 903). Following Durkheim, Lynch assumes that personal religious identity is formed by this kind of collective experience.

"Did the membership of the Church of the Sun reflect the 'respectable' middle-class nature of Marty's 'Occult Establishment,' or did it comprise 'deviant' individuals similar to those whom Lofland and Stark found attracted to the 'deviant' perspective of the Doomsday Cult?" (1977, 281), is one of the three questions that begin Lynch's study. And while he challenges the depiction of these groups as deviant, he fails to call into question the limitations of categories such as "deviant" and "normal" (Campbell and MacIver, 1987). In order to legitimate occult involvement Lynch argues that it shows a search for spiritual meaning and collective experience in an increasingly secularized and individualistic culture. According to Lynch, the emergence of occult groups and other new religions can be seen

> as the reflections of the problems of American society rather than of the deviance which is so quickly attributed to members of these groups. In the specific case of the Church of the Sun, the strong

sense of communal solidarity and the lack of active participation in other organizations of any type by members or ex-members alike, evinces the continuing atomization, rationalization, secularization, and demystification of American society. (1979, 297)

Like his predecessors, Lynch continues to emphasize the reasons why individuals join and leave these groups, rather than the meanings they make out of their participation. Finally, he is interested in the legitimacy of their involvement. He writes in the concluding sentence of "Toward a Theory of Conversion and Commitment to the Occult," that "it is high time we devoted more study to how and why people are drawn into the occult subculture, and to how they may be harmed or benefited by such experiences" (1977, 905). Both Scott's and Lynch's research is driven by issues involving legitimation, such as the extent of the "dangers" posed by Neo-Paganism. The sociologist's project of judging relative social harm prescribes an analysis of belief systems and involvement patterns, rather than personal experience and individual action.

Both Lynch and Scott begin to move beyond the questions of belief which arise whenever "rationality" is the focus of one's investigation. But they are constrained by a Durkheimian approach which emphasizes the relationship between group ritual and social cohesion. Thus they do not confront the varieties of individual experience within ritual or the tensions, conflicts, and disruptive effects of ritual. In "Toward a Theory of Conversion and Commitment to the Occult," Lynch argues from a Durkheimian perspective that ritual is essentially a *collective* experience. He focuses on the collective experience of ritual rather than the conflictive and cooperative relationships between individual participants. Thus the varieties of individual experience within ritual, the tensions, conflicts, and disruptive effects of ritual, are not dealt with by these authors. And moreover, their interpretations of ritual practice fail to employ any of the work by their contemporaries in the field of anthropology—Victor Turner for example.[16] While both Lynch and Scott acknowledge the central importance of ritual, neither explores its significance.

Lack of attention to ethnography and overemphasis on "deviance" is likewise characteristic of Nachman Ben-Yehuda's *Deviance and Moral Boundaries: Witchcraft, the Occult, Science Fiction, Deviant Sciences and Scientists*. Though Ben-Yehuda's work updates sociological studies of the 1970s, it lacks the theoretical insights of Tiryakian and the ethnographic descriptions of Scott and Lynch.

Like most earlier analyses of the occult, Ben-Yehuda's ethnographic research is general and cursory.

However, his book is useful for its evaluation of the relationship between involvement with the occult and the everyday anxieties and uncertainties which characterize contemporary American culture. According to Ben-Yehuda, occult activities such as astrology and palm reading allow individuals to "recenter the world." Occult participation is thus a response to existential problems that cannot be answered by other forms of religion and science. He attempts to explain why and how participants in occult groups and activities seek new ways to redefine moral boundaries and to recenter their worlds: "both science fiction and the occult . . . flourish in a pluralistic, complex society, offering a variety of ways to define and change not only one's suggestive output but societal moral boundaries" (1980, 74). Ben-Yehuda's study reveals the values and meanings that participants give to occult practices. The personalization of occult activities allows participants to draw their own moral boundaries and thus contextualizes the concept of "deviance." The redrawing of moral boundaries by individual participants, however, also affects social boundaries and thus social definitions of deviance.

Ben-Yehuda describes the notion of deviance non-judgmentally, and defines it in relation to "mainstream" religious and scientific views. Even when deviance is not understood as a negative judgment, however, its use indicates that the researcher's job is to legitimize and defend occult groups. Furthermore, in his conclusions, Ben-Yehuda judges the objective "validity" and "viability" of claims made from an occult paradigm. He clearly misses the point; that is, what makes these activities valid and viable to those who engage in them?

Margot Adler's *Drawing Down the Moon* (1986) goes a long way toward answering this question. First published in 1979, *Drawing Down the Moon* is a richly detailed ethnography authored by someone who is both a trained journalist and a self-proclaimed witch. Yet it is less defensive and apologetic than sociological studies conducted by many supposedly objective "outsiders." Adler's research agenda emerges out of her extensive involvement with Neo-Paganism, rather than being driven by questions framed within academic disciplines.

As is the case with most other book-length studies of Neo-Paganism, she sacrifices depth of analysis for breadth of coverage. Adler's book is an example of the ongoing attempt to classify different elements of Neo-Paganism, rather than focusing on detailed examination of specific issues and events. But what this book sets out to do it does very well. In the second edition (1986), Adler identifies several major trends that have occurred in the Neo-Pagan movement since her first edition. She observes, for instance, that Neo-Paganism has become increasingly self-aware of itself *as* a movement. She suggests this is largely because of the increase in size and number of Neo-Pagan festivals where festival-goers gather together in a temporary community to share information and stories, to exchange goods, to dance and play music, and to create rituals. But, exactly how do these festivals decrease the isolation of small groups and solitary occult practitioners? In a festival setting, what kinds of tensions exist between the desires and needs of individuals or between individual groups and the larger Neo-Pagan community? Also, I would add that electronic discussion lists and bulletin boards have had an enormous impact on the accessibility of Neo-Paganism. How have these forms of community shaped the broader Neo-Pagan movement? In what ways have they been channels by which individuals connect with Neo-Paganism?

Drawing Down the Moon is unmatched in its sweeping survey of Neo-Pagan culture and for the historical perspective it provides on the emergence of various small groups within the larger movement. More a report from the trenches than rigorous analysis, Adler's straightforward account of these groups is not an attempt to justify their existence or to explain them away. Her examination of the meanings that individuals make out of their lives through the encounter with and construction of Pagan culture is a welcome shift away from the focus of sociologists on questions of "deviance" and "conversion"—all concepts defined from outside. And let me be clear here that I am *not* critical of outside labels per se. What I like about both Adler's book and T. M. Luhrmann's *Persuasions of the Witch's Craft* (1989) is the presence of self-reflexivity and in particular, attention to the problems of approaching these groups with predetermined assumptions. Adler's thoroughly researched study and combined insider/outsider perspective should continue to prove useful and inspiring to Pagans seeking information as well as for teachers and students of new religions.

Like *Drawing Down the Moon*, Canadian writer Kevin Marron's survey of Canadian Neo-Paganism, *Witches, Pagans and Magic in the New Age* (1989), attempts to be as all-encompassing of Neo-Paganism as possible. Marron too describes a landscape of invented practices and beliefs. Perhaps because his journalistic perspective

aims to entertain as well as educate, Marron's tone is overly con-
ciliatory and simplistic at times. By trying to please Neo-Pagan
sympathizers as well as skeptics and critics, he often contradicts
himself. This is clearly the case when he is trying to legitimate
Wicca and more "positive" Neo-Pagan groups. In his conclusion
he writes: "I think it is time that we got away from the notion of
a black and white world," and then three sentences later, "I believe
that the only other reason to fear magic is if one is susceptible to
the influence of a proponent of black magic" (p. 224).[17]

Marron challenges oppositions between black/white and good/
evil, and yet his study, like those of Tiryakian, Scott, and Lynch,
takes a defensive stance. Much of his book is concerned with distinguishing witches and "harmless" Pagans from occult practitioners he considers to be dangerous Satanists. Marron's work thus
moves into another important and related topic that I have not
dealt with in this chapter: the rumored connection between Satanism
and ritual abuse.

Sociologists, religious studies scholars, psychologists, and police
officers as well as journalists, deprogrammers, and Christian fundamentalist polemicists have written extensively on the topic of
alleged satanic crimes.[18] Although the investigation of contemporary Satanism is well beyond the scope of this chapter, its relevance
to the issue of scholarly legitimation cannot be strongly enough
stated. Clearly scholars of Neo-Paganism confront the task of explaining issues revolving around the "Satanism scare" to their students and the broader public. But explanation too often gives way
to judgment and legitimation. Marron and many other scholars
tend to position themselves with the "good" Neo-Pagans and witches,
who like the Christians before them mark the bounds of their own
communities by attacking those they are not, i.e. "Satanists" or
"black" witches. Scholarly critiques of scapegoating such as Jeffrey
Victor's *Satanic Panic* (1993) and some of the essays contained in
the edited volume *The Satanism Scare* (Richardson, Best, and Bromley
1991) look closely at social contexts in which the construction of
myths and rumors about satanic ritual abuse take place. More field
work is needed on the processes by which witches, Neo-Pagans,
and Satanists distinguish among themselves. Why do groups who
already feel persecuted scapegoat others within their own ranks?
Moreover, why and in what ways do conservative Christians cast
most "New Age" and occult practices as satanic?

Academic research on Neo-Paganism drops off between 1980
and 1989, with the exception of Adler's updated second edition of

Drawing Down the Moon, published in 1986. To my knowledge, no anthropologically informed ethnographies of Neo-Paganism were published until T. M. Luhrmann's *Persuasions of the Witch's Craft* in 1989, though several dissertations on Witchcraft appeared (Ludeke 1989; Orion 1990). During this period feminist, goddess-centered spirituality flourished. Theologians and other spiritually motivated scholars published feminist critiques of Western religions and often uncritically adopted "goddess religion," which was modeled on Witchcraft and other forms of Neo-Paganism.[19] Until the explosion of feminist spirituality in the late 1970s and 1980s, Neo-Paganism was a marginal topic in religious studies, with the important exception of its appearance in the classificatory work of J. Gordon Melton (1982). No scholar in religious studies or any other fields in the humanities has published a book-length analysis of Neo-Paganism.[20]

By the end of the 1980s, Neo-Paganism was no longer the province of sociologists alone. A reorientation towards the West and the increasing self-reflexivity of anthropological studies has encouraged more attention to the nature of the researchers' own experience: "Ever more anthropologists are turning inward to study their own society. But they have tended to focus on the immediate problems of urban life: ethnicity, acculturation, religious revitalization. Few have continued to ask traditional anthropological questions, to look for the exotic and learn from it about the familiar" (Luhrmann 1989, 4). Through careful, context-sensitive investigation of ritual activities, T. M. Luhrmann's ethnography of London magicians and witches explores the relationship between belief and practice and the various paths by which people come to give meaning to their Neo-Pagan identities.

Her description of the interdependent relationship between belief and experience redirects the thrust of earlier sociological studies which prioritize belief. She convincingly argues for a model of commitment to magical practice which she calls "interpretive drift": "ideas and beliefs drift, in a complex interdependency of concept and experience. This interdependency is often given passing acceptance as a cliche, but it is rarely genuinely appreciated when people settle down to analyse the nature of apparently irrational ideas and action" (1989, 353). Influenced by the psychological anthropology of Vincent Crapanzano and Gananath Obeyesekere, she focuses on the psychological effects of entering into and living within the world of magic and ritual.[21] Although her book offers detailed descriptions of this world and is rich in material for further investigation, many of her insights get lost in her digressive writing style. *Persuasions of the Witch's Craft* attempts to cover post-structuralist theory, linguistics, psychoanalysis and parapsychology, to name a few of the disciplines she delves into. Nevertheless, the experiential basis for relief and the mutual interaction between belief and practice remain a constant theme throughout Luhrmann's often confusing narrative.

Luhrmann should have dealt more completely with the ambiguities and tensions that accompanied her role as participant-observer. She discusses what she shares with the London magicians and yet disavows an identity as magician or witch. Such disclaimers are problematic when studying within one's own culture where, as she puts it, "I was honest about my enterprise, but my intention was to fit in, to dispel outsider status, and I was rather relieved when people forgot what I had so carefully told them" (1989, 17). More clarity on her part about the nature of her ambiguous role as insider/outsider would have been helpful.

Like the other authors reviewed here, Luhrmann feels compelled to comment on the legitimacy of occult involvement. After initiations and extensive and intimate involvement with several different London magical groups, Luhrmann writes that she is not an insider though she shares many experiences with the people she studies. "I am no witch, no wizard, though I have been initiated as though I were." She describes her childhood enchantment with fantasy series such as Lloyd Alexander's *Mabinogian* and concludes that "I was enchanted by the imaginings, and yet I always knew, when I was a child, that the make-believe was never real. I never have and do not now 'believe' in magic" (1989, 18).[22] What she means here by belief remains unclear; what is the point of this comment? Does not the process of "interpretive drift" apply to her own experiences as well as those of others? But just as the witches she worked with forgot she was an outsider, readers will forget her initial disclaimers as they become immersed in London's magical communities.

Because Neo-Paganism is underrepresented in scholarly literature, researchers are tempted to cover as much of its vast territory as they can, but what is needed is more specificity. Attention to particular groups, events, and issues often illuminates larger theoretical problems. For instance, aside from Luhrmann, no scholars have closely looked at the processes involved with ritual invention. What sources do Neo-Pagans use to create rituals? Where do they find these sources and how do they use them? What kinds of conflicts come up during the process of putting together and performing rituals? How do they deal with charges of "stealing" the rituals of other cultures?

The study of Neo-Paganism is no longer solely the province of sociologists. Hopefully the researchers from other disciplines such as folklore, cultural studies, gender studies, history, and religious studies who are beginning to look at Neo-Paganism will study it with the thoroughness it deserves. Scholarly work that categorizes and labels Neo-Pagan beliefs and practices tends to ignore overlapping identity boundaries. A multiplicity of approaches will reveal the complexities of occult involvement as it is lived by its participants. Certainly definitions are important, but how helpful are they when framed as responses to attacks and misunderstandings? Analyses that attempt to defend and legitimate Neo-Paganism are more likely to legitimate their own enterprise than the groups they study.

NOTES

1. Due to the increasing visibility of witches and Pagans, the growth of feminist spirituality and the New Age movement, and a large body of literature by Christian fundamentalists and others about the dangers of the occult, Neo-Paganism is fast becoming a popular topic of research for undergraduate papers and graduate theses.

2. See for example the story of Terry and Amanda Riley of Jonesboro, Arkansas who lost the lease on their occult bookshop ("Do You Believe in Magick?" *Newsweek* [23 August 1994]: 32).

3. Much debate revolves around these labels as they carry different meanings depending on who is using them. "Magic" has often been used as a grabbag, i.e., anything not religious must be magical. "Occult" is often used by conservative Christians to mean "evil" or "satanic."

4. Most scholarly research appears to be sympathetic to Neo-Paganism. Some are skeptical of its validity, while others romanticize its egalitarian self-presentation. One recent example of uncritical praise for Wicca is Joan Ludeke, "Wicca as a Revitalization Movement Among Post-Industrial, Urban, American Women," (1989). Ludeke argues that Wicca offers an alternative to hierarchical religions like Christianity which she classifies as a religion of "power over." She fails to examine the power dynamics and points of contention within Wicca. See also Loretta Orion, "Revival of Western Paganism and Witchcraft in the Contemporary United States." As her title suggests, this is an ambitious study which attempts to cover too much ground. She focuses on three main themes, each deserving

book-length treatment: the efficacy of alternative healing; Gardnerian Witch-craft on American soil; and the creative art of invention. While her in-sights on healing are carefully thought out and convincingly argued, much of her study lacks critical depth. It focuses mainly on positive examples of the efficacy and meaningfulness of healing and it neglects tensions and conflicts within Neo-Paganism.

5. In chapter 1, "Paganism and Prejudice," Adler (1986) provides an excellent discussion about definitions of Neo-Paganism and Witchcraft.

6. Luhrmann's book is a theoretically sophisticated ethnography of London Neo-Pagans. Luhrmann's book on "ritual magic" is somewhat mistitled, because many of the people she discusses would *not* call them-selves "witches," but rather "magicians."

7. Scholarly work on the occult contains many such distinctions. See for instance Marcello Truzzi, "Nouveau Witches" (1974a).

8. See the recent collection of essays on stories about satanic abuse and conspiracies edited by sociologists James T. Richardson, Joel Best, and David G. Bromley, *The Satanism Scare* (1991).

9. A male witch told me that if he ever revealed his religious iden-tity to his parents, he would give them a copy of Luhrmann's *Persuasions of the Witch's Craft*, both the most theoretical and ethnographic of any study of Neo-Paganism published to date. He also pointed out that Luhrmann's study was most compelling because it did not, like Adler's *Drawing Down the Moon* (1986), gloss over tensions and conflicts within Witchcraft and Neo-Paganism (conversation with Michael, February 1994).

10. I will generally confine my comments to academic research on the "occult revival" which began in the 1960s and is now a loosely orga-nized network or movement called Neo-Paganism. Computer mediated discussions of Neo-Paganism include participants from all over Great Britain, Western Europe, Australia, New Zealand, and even Eastern Europe.

11. Scholars dubbed the apparent growth of interest in astrology, tarot, and nature-based religious practice as well as other occult traditions such as Theosophy the "occult revival." Material dealing with early twen-tieth-century occultists like Aleister Crowley and occult groups such as the Golden Dawn is beyond the scope of this chapter. What does merit research is how Neo-Pagans *use* the writings of Crowley upon which many of their rituals are based. See Aidan Kelly's *Crafting the Art of Magic* (1991) for an analysis of the roots of contemporary Witchcraft.

12. Sherry Ortner identifies these two critiques of structuralism in her excellent review "Theory in Anthropology in the Sixties" (1984).

13. Other collections of essays on new religious movements which include essays on Neo-Paganism or occult groups are: Joseph Fichter, ed.,

Alternatives to American Mainline Churches (1983) and Robert Ellwood, *Religious and Spiritual Groups in Modern America* (1973). The Fichter volume includes "Thelemic Magick in America" (pp. 67–88), by J. Gordon Melton, a short history of the O. T. O. (the Ordo Templi Orientis founded by Aleister Crowley) in the United States. Melton, director of the Institute for the Study of American Religion, observes that the followers of Crowley, or "Thelemites," are at the margins of the occult movement, the fringes of the fringe.

14. *Religious Movements in Contemporary America* covers groups as diverse as the Church of Latter Day Saints, Christian Science, Scientology, and Spiritualism. Articles on occult groups include Edward J. Moody, "Magical Therapy: An Anthropological Investigation of Contemporary Satanism"; Marcello Truzzi, "Towards a Sociology of the Occult: Notes on Modern Witchcraft"; and Harriet Whitehead, "Reasonably Fantastic: Some Perspectives on Scientology, Science Fiction, and Occultism."

15. Patricia Hartman's "Social Dimensions of Occult Participation: The Gnostica Study" (1976) presents her research on Neo-Paganism in the Minneapolis–St. Paul area. Hartman likewise calls for more ethnographic research on Neo-Paganism. And yet, instead of drawing on her several years of participant observation, Hartman's interpretations are shaped by the survey she conducted.

16. Turner's *The Ritual Process* was published in 1969. Since anthropologists have specialized in studying "strange" and foreign cultures, scholars who research the "strange" within their own societies should find useful the application of some anthropological methods.

17. Marron's book might be called a "demystification" of Neo-Paganism and contemporary Witchcraft.

18. Gray and Cavender's "Cauldrons Bubble, Satan's Trouble, But Witches Are Okay: Media Constructions of Satanism and Witchcraft" is one of the many essays included in Best, Richardson, and Bromley's edited volume, *The Satanism Scare* (1991), which is a good place to start reading about the state of current research in sociology, psychology, and criminal justice. Also see Jeffrey Victor, *Satanic Panic: The Creation of a Contemporary Legend* (1993) for a thorough documentation of rumor-spreading and police officer Keith Lanning.

19. Some of the earliest and most influential work in this area was published by feminist academics. Carol Christ, a religious studies professor, authored several books in this area. Among those dealing specifically with goddess religion are *Womanspirit Rising: A Feminist Reader in Religion* (1979) and *Laughter of Aphrodite: Reflections on a Journey to the Goddess* (1987). Other important work was published by Naomi Goldenberg, *Changing of the Gods: Feminism and the End of Traditional Religions* (c1979), and Mary Daly *Gyn/Ecology, The Metaethics of Radical Feminism* (1978), among many

others. A recent essay by Nancy Finley (1991) takes more of a social scientific view of feminist spirituality. In "Political Activism and Feminist Spirituality," Finley uses information gathered from field work with Dianic Wiccans to challenge the pervasive Marxist view among sociologists that religion is apolitical. She argues that religion, here in the form of Wicca, can become a tool for political activism and social change. And her essay does reflect briefly on individual experience as it effects political involvement.

20. Scholars of North American religion such as Catherine Albanese (1990) have begun to include discussions of Neo-Paganism in their historical and cultural studies.

21. Crapanzano's *Tuhami* (1978) is a highly self-reflexive study of the relationship between anthropologist and subject, problematizing the legitimizing practice of the anthropologist and portraying the relationship of observer and informer as a dialogue rather than an interrogation. Obeyesekere's *Medusa's Hair* (1981) likewise criticizes the anthropologist's outsider status and foregrounds the meaning-making practices of personalized ritual.

22. The relationship between involvement with magic and the "culture of childhood" is worthy of further investigation. Do Neo-Pagans use the playfulness and creativity of ritual practice to reclaim or re-invent their pasts? And if so, what kinds of stories do they tell about this kind of invention? How does the use of favorite childhood books and other remnants of childhood discussed by Luhrmann, fit into the personal histories of occult practitioners? M. D. Faber's *Modern Witchcraft and Psychoanalysis* (1993) explores the parallels between childhood experience and contemporary Witchcraft. Faber argues that tension between union and separation is a theme in both worlds.

REFERENCES

Adler, Margot. 1986. 2d ed. *Drawing Down the Moon*. Boston: Beacon Press.

Albanese, Catherine. 1990. *Nature Religion in America: From the Algonkian Indians to the New Age*. Chicago: University of Chicago Press.

Ben-Yehuda, Nachman. 1980. *Deviance and Moral Boundaries: Witchcraft, the Occult, Science Fiction, Deviant Sciences and Scientists*.

Campbell, Colin, and Shirley McIver. 1987. "Cultural Sources of Support for Contemporary Occultism." *Social Compass* 34: 41–60.

Christ, Carol. c. 1979. *Womanspirit Rising: A Feminist Reader in Religion*. San Francisco: Harper and Row.

———. 1987. *Laughter of Aphrodite: Reflections on a Journey to the Goddess*. San Francisco: Harper and Row.

Crapanzano, Vincent. 1978. *Tuhami.* Chicago: University of Chicago Press.

Daly, Mary. 1978. *Gyn/Ecology, The Metaethics of Radical Feminism.* Boston: Beacon Press.

Ellwood, Robert. 1973. *Religious and Spiritual Groups in Modern America.* Englewood Cliffs, N.J.: Prentice Hall.

Faber, M. D. 1993. *Modern Witchcraft and Psychoanalysis.* Rutherford, N.J.: Fairleigh-Dickinson.

Fichter, Joseph, ed. 1983. *Alternatives to American Mainline Churches.* New York: Rose of Sharon Press.

Finley, Nancy. 1991. "Political Activism and Feminist Spirituality." *Sociological Analysis* 52, no. 4: 349–363.

Goldenberg, Naomi. c. 1979. *Changing of the Gods: Feminism and the End of Traditional Religions.* Boston: Beacon Press.

Greeley, Andrew. 1970. "Implications for the Sociology of Religion of Occult Behavior in the Youth Culture." *Youth and Society* (December 1970): 132.

Hartman, Patricia. 1976. "Social Dimensions of Occult Participation: The Gnostica Study." *British Journal of Sociology* 27, no. 2: 169–183.

Kelly, Aidan. 1991. *Crafting the Art of Magic.* St. Paul, Minn.: Llewellyn.

Ludeke, Joan. 1989. "Wicca as a Revitalization Movement Among Post-Industrial, Urban, American Women." Ph.D. dissertation, Iliff School of Theology.

Luhrmann, T. M. 1989. *Persuasions of the Witch's Craft: Ritual Magic in Contemporary England.* Cambridge, Mass.: Harvard University Press.

Lynch, F. R. 1977. "Towards a Theory of Conversion and Commitment to the Occult." *American Behavioral Scientist* 20, no. 6: 887–908.

———. 1979. " 'Occult Establishment' or 'Deviant Religion'? The Rise and Fall of a Modern Church of Magic." *Journal for the Scientific Study of Religion* 18, no. 3: 281–298.

Marron, Kevin. 1989. *Witches, Pagans and Magic in the New Age.* Toronto: Seal Books.

Marty, Martin. 1970. "The Occult Establishment." *Social Research* 37: 212–230.

Melton, J. Gordon. 1982. *Magic, Witchcraft, and Paganism in America: A Bibliography: Compiled from the files of the Institute for the Study of American Religion.* New York: Garland Publishing.

Obeyesekere, Gananath. 1981. *Medusa's Hair.* Chicago: University of Chicago Press.

Orion, Loretta. 1990. "Revival of Western Paganism and Witchcraft in the Contemporary United States." Ph.D. dissertation, State University of New York at Stony Brook.

Ortner, Sherry. 1984. "Theory in Anthropology in the Sixties." *Comparative Studies in Society and History* 26, no. 1: 126–166.

Richardson, James T., Joel Best, and David G. Bromley, eds. 1991. *The Satanism Scare.* New York: Aldine de Gruyter.

Scott, Gini. 1976. "Social Structure and the Occult: A Sociological Analysis of the Social Organization, Behavior Patterns and Beliefs of Two Occult Groups: A Spiritual Growth Group and a Witchcraft Coven."

———. 1980. *Cult and Countercult: A Study of a Spiritual Growth Group and a Witchcraft Order.* Westport, Conn.: Greenwood Press.

Tiryakian, Edward, ed. 1974. *On the Margin of the Visible.* New York: John Wiley and Sons.

Truzzi, Marcello. 1974a. "Nouveau Witches." *Humanist* 34, no. 5: 13–15.

———. 1974b. "Toward a Sociology of the Occult: Notes on Modern Witchcraft." In *Religious Movements in Contemporary America*, edited by Irving Zaretsky and Mark Leone. Princeton: Princeton University Press.

Turner, Victor. 1969. *The Ritual Process.* Ithaca: Cornell University Press.

Victor, Jeffrey. 1993. *Satanic Panic: The Creation of a Contemporary Legend.* Chicago: Open Court.

Zaretsky and Leone. 1974. *Religious Movements in Contemporary America.*

17

PRACTITIONERS OF PAGANISM AND WICCAN SPIRITUALITY IN CONTEMPORARY SOCIETY: A REVIEW OF THE LITERATURE

Dennis D. Carpenter

THIS CHAPTER IDENTIFIES, summarizes, and critiques the research that has focused on the practitioners of contemporary Paganism and Wiccan Spirituality. While numerous books and articles have been written in recent years by practitioners describing their own Pagan and Wiccan beliefs and practices, this body of information will not be dealt with at length. Rather, the focus of this chapter centers on research that utilizes formal methods (e.g., participant observation, interviews, surveys, questionnaires, etc.) to facilitate understanding of those involved in contemporary Paganism and Wiccan Spirituality.

The first section of this chapter describes the means by which material was obtained for this literature review. Since a variety of terms are used in this chapter that have many meanings depending upon the context in which they are used, definitions of these terms are provided. Following these basic definitions, the historical context of contemporary Paganism and Wiccan Spirituality is briefly touched upon. Following this, the subjects and methods used in each of the studies are described. Then, the results of the research are summarized in answer to the questions, "who is involved, how did they become involved, and why are they involved?" After this, a methodological critique including a discussion of ethical issues is presented. This chapter closes with a discussion of the research findings from this writer's perspective of having been involved in Paganism and Wiccan Spirituality for nine years. Throughout this chapter, various terms (i.e., Pagan, Paganism, Witch, Witchcraft, Craft, Wicca, Wiccan, and Neo-Pagan) are capitalized in recognition of their religious reference.

STRATEGY FOR CARRYING OUT LITERATURE REVIEW

In order to obtain references to dissertations, journal articles, and books that reported research on contemporary Paganism and Wiccan Spirituality, several computerized bibliographic databases were searched. The Memorial Library reference facilities on the University of Wisconsin–Madison campus were utilized in carrying out these searches. The databases selected for searching included Dissertation Abstracts (1861 to present), PsychInfo (1967 to present), Religion Index (1949 to present), Social Sciences Citation Index (1972 to present), and Sociological Abstracts (1963 to present). In addition, the University of Wisconsin–Madison computer catalogue was used to search the holdings of the various university libraries for relevant books. Such words as Wicca, Wicce, Pagan, Neo-Pagan, Neopagan, Witch, and magic were utilized. In addition, the computer was told to find all instances where such words were also parts of larger words. Bibliographies from all the primary references obtained were also closely scrutinized for relevant entries.

DEFINITION AND DISCUSSION OF TERMINOLOGY

The terms (i.e., Pagan, Neo-Pagan, Wicca, Witch, and magic) used in this chapter often have different meanings depending upon who is using them. In fact, the way in which these terms are defined and used by practitioners sometimes stands in marked contrast to common public usage. Definitions from the second edition of the *Oxford English Dictionary* (OED) are used as starting points to identify the commonly accepted meanings. Discussions of the various ways each of the terms are actually used by practitioners follow the OED definitions.

Pagan
According to the OED, Pagan is defined as follows: (*a*) derived from the Latin "paganus" meaning villager, rustic, civilian, non-

militant; (*b*) one of a nation or community which does not hold the true religion, or does not worship the true God; (*c*) worshiping idols, heathen; (*d*) nature-worshiping, pantheistic.

In its popular usage in this country, the term Pagan is frequently associated with the OED definition of not worshiping the true God. In fact, the term Pagan is sometimes considered to be synonymous with God-less. The OED definition of nature-worshiping and pantheistic reflects how the term Pagan is actually utilized by those who use it to describe their beliefs and practices. Adler (1986) reflected this nature-worshiping theme in defining Pagan as a member of a polytheistic nature religion, such as the ancient Greek, Roman, or Egyptian religions, or, in anthropological terms, a member of one of the indigenous folk and tribal religions. Adler further identified the following three main beliefs which serve to define Pagan and seem to underlie the Pagan resurgence in contemporary society: (*a*) animism—a reality in which all things are imbued with vitality; (*b*) pantheism—divinity is inseparable from nature and deity is immanent in nature; (*c*) and polytheism—reality (divine and otherwise) is multiple and diverse. A significant aspect of the appeal of polytheism for many contemporary Pagans is the recognition of female forms of the divine as well as male forms.

Neo

The OED defines "neo" as denoting a new or modern form of some doctrine, belief, practice, language, etc., or designating those who advocate, adopt, or use it. Consistent with this definition, Neo-Pagan is frequently used by practitioners as well as scholars to refer to the modern-day forms of expression of the mythologies, beliefs and practice of various ancient Pagan (i.e., pre-Christian) cultures (e.g., Greek, Roman, Egyptian, Celtic, Norse, Native American, etc.). In this chapter, Pagan, rather than Neo-Pagan, is used to refer to the collection of contemporary spiritual expressions broadly characterized as nature-worshiping, animistic, pantheistic, and polytheistic.

Witch

The OED provides the following definitions of Witch: (1) a man who practices witchcraft or magic; a magician, sorcerer, wizard; (2) a female magician, sorceress; in later use, a woman supposed to have dealings with the devil or evil spirits and to be able by their cooperation to perform supernatural acts. Consistent with the later use in the second definition, the word Witch carries strong

negative connotations in its popular usage. One of the most pervasive images of a Witch in American culture is that of the "Wicked
Witch of the West" in the *Wizard of Oz*, despite the character of
the good Witch in the same film. Consistent with the OED definition, a Witch is thought by many to be a malevolent practitioner
in league with Satan.

According to the OED, the term Witch is derived from the
Old English terms "Wicce," the feminine form, and "Wicca," the
masculine form. Adler (1986) pointed out that considerable debate
exists among modern-day Witches regarding the derivation of Wicca
and Wicce. Some Witches claim that these two words derive from
the root "wit" meaning wisdom. Other Witches claim that the
word derives from the Indo-European roots "wic" and "weik,"
meaning to bend or turn. According to this derivation, a Witch
would be a person skilled in the craft of shaping, bending, and
changing reality. Despite these differences of interpretation, Adler
indicates that many practitioners define Witchcraft as the "Craft of
the Wise" and view the Witches of previous times as the wise
people of the village, often women, who were skilled in healing
and practical arts. In line with this viewpoint, many feminists, both
female and male, have reclaimed the word Witch to describe themselves as a political statement in recognition of the history, since
the Middle Ages, of the oppression of women and folk healing by
male-dominated society and medicine.

In actual usage, the term Wicca is commonly used by practitioners as a generic term to describe both female and male
practitioners. Wicca or Wiccan Spirituality are preferred by many
over Witch or Witchcraft because they don't carry with them the
same immediate "knee-jerk" associations with evil and Satanism.
Incidentally, the OED defines a white Witch as being of a good
disposition; one who uses Witchcraft for beneficent purposes; one
who practices "white magic." While this OED definition more
accurately reflects the benevolent nature of those using the term
Witch to describe themselves, Wiccans seldom use the words "white
magic" or "white Witch" because of the frequent popular use of
black and white as racial connotations.

Magic

The OED defines magic as "the pretended art of influencing the
course of events, and of producing marvellous physical phenomena, by processes supposed to owe their efficacy to the power of
compelling the intervention of spiritual beings, or of bringing into

operation some occult controlling principle of nature." The use of the term "pretended" in this definition reflects the common associations of magic with stage magic and sleight of hand. In contrast to this, Pagans, Wiccans, and magicians use the term magic to refer to what they claim to be a very real ability to influence events and bring about change in the world. Adler defined such magic in the following manner:

> Magic is a convenient word for a whole collection of techniques, all of which involve the mind. In this case, we might conceive of these techniques as including the mobilization of confidence, will, and emotion brought about by the recognition of necessity; the use of imaginative facilities, particularly the ability to visualize, in order to begin to understand how other beings function in nature so we can use this knowledge to achieve necessary ends. (1986, 8)

Relationship of Terms

Those who use the words Wiccan and Pagan to describe themselves can be generally described as drawing from pre-Christian roots that are pantheistic, animistic, and polytheistic. However, differences do exist regarding which pre-Christián spiritual traditions and mythologies are used for inspiration and what forms current spiritual expression takes. Some Pagans and Wiccans use these terms interchangeably, while others view Wiccan Spirituality as one of the many forms of contemporary Paganism. Yet others, such as Luhrmann (1989) and Kelly (1991), distinguish between the two by asserting that Wiccans are trained and initiated into a closed fraternity or coven, while Pagans are not. In recognition of such variability of usage and attempting to be all inclusive, both of these terms will be utilized in this chapter to refer to the broad collection of individuals who represent the focus of this chapter.

HISTORICAL PERSPECTIVES

Much has been written about Witchcraft from a historical perspective. In fact, this literature is so vast that it is beyond the scope of this chapter to deal with it in any significant way. In short, a great deal of historical material has been published regarding Witchcraft in the Middle Ages in American and Europe, particularly with regard to the persecution of alleged Witches. In the twentieth century, a variety of works are considered standards with regard to the history of Witchcraft and to the re-emergence of Witchcraft in modern culture (e.g., Gardner [1954] 1970 [1959] 1971; Graves 1948;

Leek 1971; Leland [1897] 1974; Murray [1921] 1971, [1931] 1970; Valiente 1962, 1973). The works of Murray and Gardner are particularly important and deserve further attention here.

Margaret Murray was a British anthropologist who published her first book in 1921 based on her research into the origins and history of Witchcraft. Murray claimed to have discovered the existence of a pre-Christian fertility religion which she called the ancient religion of Western Europe. A major aspect of this religion described by Murray was the recognition of the divine as female as well as male. Considerable debate centers around the legitimacy of Murray's claims. In the foreword of the 1971 reprint of Murray's 1921 book, Sir Steven Runciman described how Murray's work was generally discounted by those who could not accept her claims for various theological reasons and by anthropologists who claimed that she jumped to conclusions which her data did not support.

The 1951 repeal of the Witchcraft Acts of 1735 forbidding Witchcraft in England set the stage for Gerald Gardner, in 1954, to publish *Witchcraft Today* in which he supported Margaret Murray's claims that Witchcraft was an ancient religion by maintaining that he was a Witch. Gardner claimed that he was initiated into a Witchcraft coven whose traditions had been passed along from generation to generation surviving the inquisition of the Middle Ages. Debate exists in the literature regarding whether Gardner was actually initiated into a coven of continuous lineage as he described it or whether he created the tradition he wrote about by synthesizing that which he read from a number of previously published sources. The reader is referred to Kelly (1991) for an in-depth discussion of this controversy. Despite the debate regarding the authenticity of the claims made by Murray and Gardner, their work is generally considered to be highly significant in contributing to the contemporary interest in Paganism and Wiccan Spirituality.

The counterculture revolution of the 1960s and early 1970s created an atmosphere of rebellion against social injustice and exploration of social and spiritual alternatives for many. By the early 1970s, a wide variety of new religions flourished in the United States. While historians of religion (e.g., Kerr and Crow 1983; Melton 1978, 1982, 1985, 1988) identify an earlier and continuous evolution of alternative spiritual forms in the Western world, the sociocultural backdrop of the 1960s contributed to a widespread explosion of interest in new religions. As part of the broader climate of religious experimentation and innovation which gained momentum in the late 1960s and early 1970s, interest in Paganism and Wicca began to increase and has continued to grow ever since. The year 1979 is regarded by some to be a highly significant turning point in the growth of Paganism because of the publishing of such important works as *The Spiral Dance* by Starhawk, *Drawing Down the Moon* by Margot Adler, and the first edition of the *Circle Guide to Wicca and Pagan Resources* by Selena Fox. The 1980s witnessed dramatic growth in Paganism and Wicca in terms of the number of individuals and groups involved, the number of periodicals and books published, the number of gatherings, the proliferation of computer networking activities, and the attention of the media. A rapidly expanding body of printed material (i.e., books and periodicals), written by a variety of contemporary practitioners of Paganism and Wiccan Spirituality, exists which documents the most recent evolution of Pagan and Wiccan mythologies, lore, beliefs, and practices. While this information written by Pagan and Wiccan practitioners will not be dealt with further in this chapter, its role in the growth of the movement is significant.

REVIEW OF THE RESEARCH ON PAGANS AND WICCANS

A relatively small amount of research has examined those involved in Paganism and Wiccan Spirituality. The bulk of this research is ethnographic research carried out by sociologists and anthropologists and is highly descriptive of the beliefs, practices, and characteristics of those involved. This chapter focuses on the characteristics of Pagan and Wiccan practitioners and reviews this body of research in three stages. First, the populations studied and the methods utilized are summarized. Then, the results of the research are summarized in answer to the questions "what are some of the characteristics of those involved, how did they become involved, and why did they become involved?" Finally, a methodological critique is provided as well as a discussion of ethical considerations.

DESCRIPTION OF THE SUBJECTS AND METHODS

This section presents fairly detailed descriptions of the subjects and methods utilized in the research. These descriptions include such information as who were selected as subjects, how the subjects were located, how the research objectives were communicated to the subjects, and what research methods were employed.

Adler (1986)

For the first edition of her book, published in 1979, Adler carried out "observer-participant" research during five years of involvement with Pagans and Wiccans and three months of intense travelling to groves and covens in the United States and Britain during which she attended ritual gatherings, conducted interviews, and met hundreds of people. Data collection techniques included observations, a questionnaire with more than seventy items, and interviews. Approximately 100 questionnaires were returned; however, the number circulated was not reported. For the second edition of her book, Adler utilized a revised and briefer questionnaire which was published in a journal and passed out at three Pagan festivals in 1985. Four hundred and fifty questionnaires were circulated in addition to being published and 195 responses were obtained.

Hartman (1976)

Involvement with astrologers, palmists, and spiritualists for a number of years and participant observation work with Witches and Cabalists (magicians) for two years provided the background for Hartman to develop a survey instrument. Grappling with the problem of how to obtain a representative sample of such a diverse group, the researcher learned of Llewellyn Publications, a St. Paul based "occult" publishing house that published books and a monthly newspaper, *Gnostica*, sent to book purchasers and subscribers. Due to the nationwide nature of the *Gnostica* mailing list, the researcher decided that such an information source represented the easiest and most economical way for her to obtain data from a large group of individuals who might otherwise be difficult to find. The editor of *Gnostica* granted permission for the study in exchange for receiving the results of the study. From the 40,000-name list, the researcher obtained approximately 800 responses to her survey. The researcher did not report how many surveys she mailed out to get this number of responses. Hartman acknowledged the diverse nature of this population selected for study due to the wide variety of interests represented in the books published by Llewellyn.

Jorgensen and Jorgensen (1982)

These researchers conducted an intensive participant-observation study of tarot readers in a large western city between 1976 and 1978. This study was judged by this writer to be applicable to this chapter due the prevalence of interest in the tarot among Pagan and Wiccan practitioners. Jorgensen and Jorgensen compiled a card index of individuals and groups obtained from casual conversations, information from bulletin boards in occult/metaphysical book and supply stores, advertisements, and several local publications (two of which contained lists of members). A list of 100 groups and 125 practitioners was compiled. Through telephone interviews, observation, and conversation with members and informants, information was collected regarding the size, range, and type of activity, leadership, nature of beliefs and practices, location, and relation to other individuals and groups. Observation and analysis of actual networks (friendship, mutual awareness or recognition, overlapping memberships, business connections) revealed about 300 people and 35 groups networked in some way.

The researchers carried out their roles as participant-observers by assuming the roles of seeker and client, i.e., they participated by having tarot readings done by a variety of tarot readers at psychic fairs. In order to gain more entry into the community, they learned the tarot through a process of self-study and attendance in various classes. Eventually they were invited to participate in psychic fairs as tarot readers and became accepted as fully participating members of the community.

Kirkpatrick, Rainey, and Rubi (1986)
The subjects in this research included 144 Pagans from North America, whose names were obtained by mailing questionnaires to the editors of 76 English-language Pagan journals and periodicals, and to leaders of 260 Pagan temples, churches, covens, and associations listed in two directories. Snowball sampling expanded the population to include both public and private Witches who were independent or members of a coven. Snowball sampling is a procedure by which questionnaires are passed along to acquaintances of the original respondents. These researchers described their methodology as participative sociology "in which members of the community of focus participate in counseling and guiding the research project from the questionnaire design through data analysis and coding" (Kirkpatrick, Rainey, and Rubi 1984, p. 32).

Lloyd (1978)
From July 1973 through May 1974, Lloyd was a member and observer of a LaCrosse, Wisconsin, coven. She utilized case histories of each of the coven members as a source of data and included these histories in her dissertation. During the next year and a half, Lloyd contacted and interviewed, either in person or

by letter/cassette tape mailings, 67 additional Witches. She made contact and collected additional information from some of the original informants through December, 1977. The coven members combined with the additional Witches interviewed resulted in a total sample of 80.

Lloyd initially presented herself to the Witches she was able to find as a person who wanted to be a Witch. The members of the coven she joined were not told of her research objectives. In fact, Lloyd described her covert role as researcher as one of camouflage, like a double-agent in spy films. After group meetings, she wrote down the details coven members revealed about their personal lives and included this information in her case histories.

Ludeke (1989)

Ludeke utilized interviews, life histories, and participant observation at training sessions, religious ceremonies and rituals, lectures, and periodic gatherings throughout the United States. Over a period of ten years beginning in 1978, Ludeke interviewed 623 women, many of them several times. Snowball sampling was utilized in which the recommendations of the initial informants led to contacts with others. Ludeke selected the life histories of three women for inclusion in her dissertation.

Ludeke first approached the task of finding Wiccans by advertising in several college newspapers. Minimally successful with this approach, Ludeke then frequented occult shops, leaving her name, address, and a short description of her research project on bulletin boards in the shops. Ludeke considers her breakthrough in making contacts to have occurred when a colleague referred her to a Wiccan woman. Ludeke became a student of this woman and this contact served to open the door to the Wiccan scene in the United States.

Luhrmann (1989)

Through a friend of a friend of a friend, Luhrmann was given the name of a woman who was instrumental in providing the initial contacts by informing her of a conference in London. As a result of attending this conference, Luhrmann came to know a large number of individuals and groups throughout England. Luhrmann utilized a combination of extensive participation, socializing, formal and informal interviews. She immersed herself in the world of those she studied by reading books, taking courses, becoming initiated into magical groups, writing and leading rituals, reading Tarot cards, and interpreting astrological charts. Luhrmann focused her investigation on a very diverse population of individuals whose beliefs and practices she categorized into four broad groups—Witchcraft, Western Mysteries, ad hoc ritual magic, and non-initiated Paganism. Luhrmann regards magical practice to be the thread that unites what she referred to as this "floating, ill-defined collection of people, practices, and organizations" (p. 32).

The primary purpose of Luhrmann's study was to examine the process by which people come to believe in the efficacy of magic and ritual, i.e. "that mind affects matter, and that in special circumstances, like ritual, the trained imagination can alter the physical world" (p. 7). Luhrmann asserted that the purpose of her study was not to explore the truth behind claims that magical rituals can alter physical reality. Instead, Luhrmann appeared to study magical practitioners as a means to examine the broader topic concerning the process by which people become persuaded of ideas and speak of them as true. Luhrmann developed a very detailed and comprehensive model of what she calls "interpretive drift," the slow shift in someone's manner of interpreting events, making sense of experiences, and responding to the world. Luhrmann's work on "interpretive drift" will not be investigated further; however, her ethnographic information relating to the purpose of this chapter will be cited where applicable.

Lynch (1977, 1979)

This researcher made initial contact with an occult organization, referred to by the pseudonym of the Church of the Sun, by enrolling in a six-week course on "basic Wicca" which was taught during the summer of 1975 at an occult supply store in a metropolitan area of California. Following this course, the researcher was invited to attend weekly services that offered a variety of lectures, meditation exercises, hypnosis demonstrations, and magical rituals. Detailed observations were written immediately following each service. During this time, the researcher was known to the others as a professor, but his research activities were not communicated. After a while, the researcher questioned the leader about studying the organization. The leader agreed to a combination of interviews and continued participant observation. The researcher conducted interviews with 32 individuals (22 members and 10 ex-members) during the early summer and fall of 1976. Interviews and a set of open-ended questions related to the topic of religious conversion were utilized.

Orion (1990)

Orion conducted intermittent participant observation at yearly gatherings of Witches and Pagans over the course of seven years during the 1980s. The researcher was also a member of two covens for a few years. A questionnaire was passed out at gatherings and to one of the covens resulting in 189 responses. Orion reported that she set up a tent and served cookies and iced tea to attract respondents. As a facilitator of one of the gatherings where Orion carried out her research, this writer recalls her research activities and remembers how forthright she was with the gathering partici-pants regarding the nature of her research. Orion designed her questionnaire to provide a demographic profile, to discover the beliefs of the subjects regarding magic, healing, and the efficacy of their own healing and professional medicine.

Scheidt (1974)

Scheidt carried out a comparative study examining the social psy-chological variables of deviancy and power. He conceptualized deviancy in terms of primary and secondary aspects, a primary deviant being an actor whose initial behaviors have come to be labeled as deviant by others and a secondary deviant being an in-dividual whose self-concept and activities have come to conform to the deviant image that others have of him or her. In his study, Scheidt viewed Witches, Magicians, and Spiritualists as possible secondary deviants and hypothesized that such individuals would display a greater degree of negative behavioral labeling by others prior to their entrance into their present belief systems than would more traditional religionists. Scheidt conceptualized power in terms of being latent or manifest and related power to internal-external locus of control. He defined latent power as a disposition, attitude, set, or expectancy toward creating changes within the environ-ment. He further characterized high latent power as being synony-mous with internal control or the perception that reinforcement is contingent upon one's own actions. Viewing Witchcraft and magic as involving assumptions of influence and influence attempts in that materials, rites and spells are believed to be effective for ful-filling desires, Scheidt predicted that Witches, Magicians, and Spiritualists would exhibit a greater degree of latent power and internal control than would more traditional religionists.

Scheidt utilized 32 subjects (9 Methodists, 10 Pentecostals, 7 Spiritualists, and 11 Witches-Magicians) from large Midwestern cities in his comparative analysis. None of the subjects were obtained through random sampling, although an attempt was made to achieve rough comparability of age and socioeconomic status across groups. A thirty-two-item interview schedule and participant observation strategies were utilized. Scheidt did not describe the origin of the interview schedule or describe any information regarding the validity and reliability of this schedule in measuring the variables of deviance and power.

Scott (1980)
Scott studied two new religious groups of very different character from 1974 to 1976: the Inner Peace Movement (IPM), a highly organized international spiritual growth group; and a Witchcraft group of about 150 members called by Scott the Aquarian Age Order to preserve anonymity. The Aquarian Age Order organized into several covens located in the San Francisco Bay Area and linked informally with other Witchcraft groups in California and nationally. Scott participated in a variety of coven study-group meetings and rituals. She also conducted interviews with about 20 informants.

CHARACTERISTICS OF PAGANS AND WICCANS

These studies focusing on contemporary Paganism and Wiccan Spirituality and related topics have sought to identify some of the demographic characteristics of those involved. The following variables have been selected for discussion: age, sex, ethnic background, educational background, socioeconomic/occupational status, previous religious affiliation, and the psychological characteristics of overall adjustment, power, conformity, and creativity.

Age
Hartman (1976) found the mean age of her subjects to be thirty-five years. Lynch (1977) reported that his subjects tended to be middle-aged, with a median age of thirty-seven years (some subjects were in their twenties and others were in their fifties and sixties). Lloyd (1978) reported that 60 percent of her subjects were between the ages of twenty-five and thirty, 19 percent were under twenty-five, and 21 percent were over forty. Jorgensen and Jorgensen (1982) found their subjects to be middle-aged with the majority between thirty and forty years of age. Luhrmann (1989) reported that the individuals she studied tended to be middle-aged. Ludeke (1989) reported that 49 percent of her subjects were twenty to

thirty-five years old, 38 percent were thirty-six to fifty years old, and 13 percent were fifty-one years and over.

The age data presented by these studies is difficult to interpret because the studies occur over a thirteen-year period and age is reported in a number of ways (i.e., mean age, median age, varying age ranges with associated percentages). However, the majority of the subjects seemed to be in their twenties, thirties, and forties at the time the information was collected. Individuals born between the years 1946 and 1964 have frequently been referred to as the "baby boom" generation. If one looks at the age data within the context of the time periods of data collection for each of the studies, it seems that the largest group of individuals could be considered "baby boomers" in that they were born during that time period. In these studies, the next largest group was born since 1964 and the smallest group was born before 1946.

Sex

Hartman (1976) reported her sample to be comprised of nearly two-thirds females. Lynch (1977) identified 72 percent of his subjects as female and 28 percent male. Lloyd (1978) reported her sample to be made up of 66 percent females and 34 percent males. Jorgensen and Jorgensen (1982) found their subjects to be about equally divided between the sexes, with only a few more females than males. Kirkpatrick et al. (1986) found Wiccans to be equally divided by sex. Orion (1990) found her sample to be comprised of 38 percent males, 57.8 percent females, and 4.3 percent who reported themselves to be androgynous. The subjects in Ludeke's 1989 study were all women since they were the focus of her study.

While two of the studies (Jorgensen and Jorgensen 1982; Kirkpatrick et al. 1986) reported equal sex distribution, others reported higher percentages of females (Hartman 1976; Lynch 1977; Lloyd 1978; Orion 1990). These studies suggest that more women are involved than men with women making up somewhere between 50 and 66 percent of the total population involved with Paganism and Wiccan Spirituality.

Ethnic Background

Hartman (1976) reported that the ethnic background of her subjects included 80 percent northern and central European (including English, Scottish, Irish, and Welsh) and 20 percent other continental Europeans, Orientals, African-Americans, and others. Jorgensen and Jorgensen (1982) found their subjects to be predominantly Caucasian, but did not specify the ethnic backgrounds of the non-Caucasians. Kirkpatrick et al. (1986) found 65 percent of their respondents to be of European ancestry with the rest from Canada, Mexico, and India. Ludeke (1989) reported that 74 percent of her subjects were Caucasian with the rest fairly evenly divided among Asian, Black, Hispanic, and Native American. With the exception of one Chicano, all of the subjects in Lynch's 1977 study were Caucasian. Adler (1986) reported that most Pagans and Wiccans are Caucasian, with the rest representing a variety of ethnic backgrounds. These studies suggest that the majority of those involved in Paganism and Wiccan Spirituality are of European ancestry with a much smaller percentage of individuals from a variety of other ethnic backgrounds.

Educational Background
Hartman (1976) found that 13 percent of her respondents had obtained less than a high school education and 63 percent had at least some college work. Hartman also discovered that nearly half of the fathers of the respondents had less than a college education and one-third of the fathers had at least some college. Hartman concluded that the population sampled was more educated than the general population and that it was upwardly mobile (defined as obtaining more education than their fathers).

Jorgensen and Jorgensen (1982) found their subjects to be at least high school graduates with half claiming some college education and a few claiming graduate degrees. Kirkpatrick et al. (1986) found their subjects to be more highly educated than the general population as indicated by the United States census, with college degrees reported by 66 percent and advanced degrees reported by 38 percent. The subjects in Lynch's 1977 study were all high school graduates, 23 percent had obtained or were close to obtaining master's degrees, and 6 percent had doctorates. Orion (1990) found that 69.8 percent of her subjects had four or more years of education beyond high school (compared to national statistics of 19.4 percent in 1986 of those twenty-five years or older reporting four or more years of college education). High school as the highest phase of education completed was indicated by 23.8 percent of Orion's subjects. Lloyd (1978) reported that five out of eighty of her subjects had attended colleges or universities and only two had graduated. Lloyd further reported that fifteen out of eighty had attended vocational or technical schools and seven of these graduated. Ludeke (1989) reported that 22 percent completed high school only, 23 percent had some college background, and 55 percent had college degrees.

The educational data from these studies strongly suggest that those involved in Paganism and Wiccan Spirituality are considerably more educated than the general population in the United States.

Socioeconomic/Occupational Status

Adler (1986) found the job profiles of her 1985 informants to be very diverse with 16 percent being either computer programmers, technical writers, or scientists, and the rest ranging from doctors and lawyers to cooks, waitresses, and nannies. Hartman reported that 40 percent of her subjects held professional or managerial jobs, compared to 10 to 15 percent of the general population. Jorgensen and Jorgensen (1982) reported considerable variation among occupations with overrepresentation in the human-service fields of counseling, social work, teaching, and health care. Kirkpatrick et al. (1986) found that Witches and Pagans tend to have relatively high-status occupations; however, they were underrewarded in that 80 percent earned below the national median income for 1983. Ludeke (1989) reported that 32 percent of her subjects were white-collar workers, 29 percent were housewives, 23 percent were blue-collar workers, and 16 percent were professionals.

Lynch (1977) reported the following occupational characteristics of his subjects (twenty-three females and nine males); 35 percent of the females were housepersons (some with part-time sales jobs); 30 percent of the females were employed in low-level white-collar work; 22 percent of the females were teachers; three of the nine males were self-employed, one male was a college professor, three males were in low-level white-collar jobs; one male was a maintenance man; and one male was a graduate student. The median yearly family income for Lynch's subjects was $15,000, the median individual income was $12,500, and slightly more than 80 percent had annual incomes in excess of $10,000. Lynch further characterized his subjects as middle-class and middle-of-the-road in terms of political views and lifestyles.

Orion (1990) reported the following occupational characteristics of her subjects: 21.6 percent were engaged in "helping and healing" jobs; 13.7 percent were employed in arts and entertainment; 5.9 percent were writers; 9.8 percent held computer-related jobs; 6.5 percent were students; 6.5 percent held business-related jobs; 5.9 percent were office workers; and 31.1 percent held some other miscellaneous job. With regard to income, Orion found that, of the 56.3 percent of her total respondents during this information, 49.6 percent earned less than the median income for households (1986 median income = $24,900), and 29.1 percent of individuals earned less than $7,000 annually.

Lloyd (1978) reported that 75 percent of her female respondents had worked outside the home, and 80 percent of these held non-professional jobs. Ninety-three percent of the males in Lloyd's study held non-professional jobs. Of the working individuals in Lloyd's study, two reported incomes of more than $10,000/year, thirty reported incomes between $7,000 and $10,000/year, and twenty-five reported incomes between $4,000 and $7,000. Luhrmann (1989) described her informants as ordinary middle-class English people and maintained that if any profession predominated it was the computer industry.

The occupational data from these studies clearly indicate that Pagans and Wiccans as a group are involved in a wide range of occupations. Consistent with their tendency to be more highly educated than the general population, many hold jobs requiring considerable educational background. The income data is more difficult to interpret because of the varied ways the data is reported, the lack of standards of comparison, and the changing value of the dollar due to inflation.

Religious Background
Lynch (1977) found that 47 percent of his subjects were once Protestant and 16 percent were once Catholic. Virtually all of these former Protestants and Catholics had stopped attending church in their teens. Lynch further reported that 25 percent moved into the Church of the Sun from either recent or lifelong participation in either Christian Science or the Church of Religious Science. Lynch did not report the backgrounds of the rest of his subjects.

Orion (1990) reported the following regarding childhood religious upbringing: 24.5 percent Roman Catholic, 58.8 percent various Protestant, 9.1 percent Jewish, 4.2 percent Unitarian, 1.4 percent Greek Orthodox, 2.1 percent self-designed religious path. In Lloyd's 1978 study, 45 percent had Roman Catholic background, 27.5 percent had Protestant background, 25 percent reported a hereditary Craft background, and 2.5 percent reported no religious background. Ludeke (1989) reported that 49 percent of her subjects were previously Catholic, 40 percent Protestant, 10 percent Jewish, and 1 percent non-affiliated.

Based upon her 1985 questionnaire, Adler (1986) reported the following religious backgrounds of her informants: 23.5 percent Catholic, 9.0 percent Anglican or Episcopalian, 30.2 percent other Protestant, 7.8 percent mixed (Catholic and Protestant or Catholic and Episcopalian), 5.4 percent Jewish, 3.0 percent Unitarian, 8.4 percent non-religious, 1.8 percent other (Greek Orthodox, Craft, etc.), and 1.8 percent Religious Science, Science of Mind, etc.

The religious data of these studies clearly suggest that the majority of those involved in Paganism and Wicca have previously been involved with Protestantism or Catholicism, with a smaller but substantial number from Jewish backgrounds. Relatively small percentages have been involved with other religions or had no religious background. With the exception of the subjects in Lloyd's 1978 study with hereditary Craft background, those involved in Paganism and Wiccan Spirituality in these studies did not grow up in Pagan or Wiccan families.

Psychological Characteristics
Overall adjustment, power, conformity, and creativity have been chosen for discussion as most representative of the psychological characteristics addressed in the research on Pagans and Wiccans.

Scheidt (1974) found that occultists (Witches, Magicians, and Spiritualists) evidenced a greater degree of negative behavioral labeling prior to their entrance into their belief systems than the traditional religionists. In other words, they tended to be rated more deviant by others prior to becoming involved in the occult. Scheidt's conclusions should be interpreted cautiously due to sampling limitations and the lack of information regarding the scales of measurement utilized and their reliability and validity. Jorgensen and Jorgensen (1982) reported their subjects to be sincere and devoted with no indication of serious social, psychic, or economic deprivation or psychopathology. Luhrmann (1989) also reported that the individuals she studied did not display significant socioeconomic or psychological maladjustment. While little confidence should be placed on Scheidt's work due to its limitations, the results of the other studies point in the direction of adequate overall adjustment. However, this information is too sketchy and limited to warrant any definitive conclusions.

Regarding power, Lloyd (1978) concluded that the Witches she studied were relatively powerless within the environments they occupied and resorted to Witchcraft and magic in order to have a sense of power and specialness. Luhrmann (1989) also concluded that magicians seem concerned with control in the sense of self-mastery and mastery over the environment. Using a powerlessness scale from the work of Neal and Seaman (1964), Kirkpatrick et al. (1986) hypothesized that Wiccans would score high on powerlessness since Witchcraft is a practice oriented toward mastery and control over the events in one's environment and personal life and one would expect powerless people to be attracted to such practice. Kirkpatrick et al. concluded that their data did not support such a notion, with scores falling in the moderate range. Defining latent power as a disposition, attitude, set, or expectancy toward creating changes in the environment, Scheidt (1974) found that occultists (Witches, Magicians, and Spiritualists) exhibited a greater degree of powerfulness or internal control (latent power) than persons participating in more traditional religious systems as demonstrated through thematic content analysis of interview data.

The information presented here regarding the issue of power seems to be inconsistent and inconclusive. First of all, the validity of the models and scales used to measure power can be questioned. Kirkpatrick et al. (1986) and Scheidt (1974) do not provide sufficient justification for their theoretical models of power and the scales used to assess this variable. Secondly, these studies reflect differences in how a powerful Witch or Pagan is conceptualized. Kirkpatrick et al. and Lloyd (1978) hypothesized the Witch to be a powerless individual who compensates by resorting to magical practice in order to affect change in his or her environment, yet these studies arrived at conflicting conclusions. In contrast, Scheidt hypothesized that such individuals are powerful to begin with and magical practice represents a manifestation of that personal power. Differing from both these points of view, Starhawk defined power as energy and maintained that a Witch's power does not manifest itself as control over others and the environment. Rather, it manifests as power-within, which she defined as the "ability to control ourselves, to face our own fears and limitations, to keep commitments, and to be honest" (1989, 51).

Scott (1980) generally described the Witches she studied as seeking to reject modern bureaucratic life and create a new tribal society, and valuing close personal relationships and old social values, such as love for nature and the land. She concluded that the primary appeal of Witchcraft was to relatively hip, radical, and nonconformist types. Ludeke (1989) provided three case studies from which she concluded that the women had made strenuous efforts to conform to the status quo and could not. Inner conflict and tension resulted in their breaking away from their nuclear families which, in turn, created hostility and sadness toward the former environment. Ludeke maintained that feminist Wicca offers a sense of community for such individuals who have rebelled against the status quo. In contrast to Scott and Ludeke, Adler (1986) maintained that most adherents of Paganism and Wicca are adults whose lives, with the exception of their religious practices, are fully integrated into the mainstream of society. Thus, the information presented here regarding conformity is limited and inconsistent.

Orion concluded that the core issue that clarifies all of the characteristics of Paganism and Wiccan Spirituality is the creative process. She found Pagans and Wiccans to be creative individuals and the movement to be one that fosters the acquisition and use of creativity. In fact, she found very few Pagans and Wiccans who did not engage in some form of art, craft, or performance media as an avocation, if not primary occupation. Orion maintained that Pagans and Wiccans take "the creative process beyond the mere fabrication of a work of art into the creation of the conditions of their personal and social lives" (1990, 5). In addition, Orion noted that these individuals use the creative process for healing and in so doing evolve alternatives to the existing health care system. Orion also attributed the creativity and individualism of Pagans and Wiccans to being responsible for an apparent "awe-inspiring" diversity in beliefs and practices. Orion was apparently so struck by the creative potential of the Pagans and Wiccans she met that she said, "I can with confidence say that the Neopagans are poets, artists, and visionaries and cannot be understood in terms of religious phenomena unless this is taken into consideration" (p. 59).

Luhrmann concluded that "magic gives magicians the opportunity to play—a serious play, but nevertheless a rule-defined, separate context in which they identify with their imaginative conceptions, and act out the fantasies and visions of another world" (1989, 13). Luhrmann further noted that real psychotherapeutic benefits result from such play. In addition, Luhrmann indicated that her findings suggested that people who become involved in modern magic are searching for powerful emotional and imaginative religious experiences, without having to adopt an explicit creed or some authority's belief. Similarly, Adler (1986) concluded that Pagans and Wiccans maintain a childlike wonder at the world and that the primary bond between these individuals is one of imagination.

These studies that have considered aspects of creativity seem to consistently describe Pagans and Wiccans as creative and imaginative individuals. The creative potential of these individuals manifests itself in a variety of aspects of their lives including occupation, avocation, personal growth, healing, religious beliefs and practices, and personal characteristics.

THE PROCESS OF BECOMING INVOLVED IN PAGANISM AND WICCA

Some studies have addressed the ways in which individuals become involved in Paganism and Wiccan Spirituality. Unlike members of some religions, Pagans and Wiccans do not proselytize, i.e., attempt to convert others to their religion. Since one is not likely to find Pagans and Wiccans on street corners, in airports, or going from door to door spreading their beliefs, the initial aspect of becoming involved centers upon actually finding out about the existence of Pagan and Wiccan practitioners. Ludeke (1989) asked her subjects how they found out about Wicca and received the following responses: 13 percent heard about it from a friend, 32 percent heard about it in a school setting, 28 percent read books about Witchcraft, 17 percent saw a notice for seminars at local bookstore, coffeehouse, or other places, 9 percent attended women's spirituality gatherings, and 1 percent found out in some other way. Adler provided the following account of how one finds out about and becomes involved with Paganism and Wicca:

> There are few converts. In most cases, word of mouth, a discussion between friends, a lecture, a book, or an article provides the entry point. But these events merely confirm some original, private experience, so that the most common feeling of those who have named themselves Pagans is something like "I finally found a group that has the same religious perceptions I always had." A common phrase you hear is "I've come home," or, as one woman told me excitedly after a lecture, "I always knew I had a religion, I just never knew it had a name." (1986, 14)

Lynch (1977) focused most directly on the process by which individuals become involved in the occult. Lynch developed a four-phase descriptive model of this process. While the four phases are presented sequentially, Lynch does not regard the process of conversion and commitment he describes to necessarily follow such a linear and sequential pattern. Lynch considered each phase, described in the following paragraphs, to act upon all other phases in some regards.

During the first phase, Lynch maintained that an individual reads occult books because of questions about the nature of the self and the universe which are left unanswered by conventional religious perspectives. The second phase begins with the development of a firsthand, personal psychic or mystical experience and/ or encountering a group of people with similar interests. Lynch concluded that such psychic or mystical experiences were important even though only 40 percent of the members and 30 percent of the ex-members of the Church of the Sun described such experiences as a major turning point in their lives. Lynch maintained that book-bred curiosity becomes fused with emotional conviction and a desire to know more emerges. Lynch described the third phase as beginning when the individual makes contact with others who share similar interests. Unlike the first two phases which emphasize the role of reading and inner experience, this phase involves social interaction with others.

The fourth phase of Lynch's model focuses upon the reasons individuals stay involved. Lynch concluded that emotional bonds are important in keeping people involved. Forty-seven percent of his subjects stated that the group was like a family or like home to them. Twenty-two percent stated that one of the major reasons for continued involvement was that they like the people. In fact, according to Lynch, the social lives of those involved may revolve solely around the group's activities. Sixty percent of Lynch's subjects reported that they belonged to no other social, political, or cultural groups. Membership in such groups for the rest tended to be nominal. Very few had social lives unrelated to church activities. Even the activities of ex-members centered around contacts with other ex-members. Lynch also reported reasons for staying involved other than emotional bonds. Sixty percent of Lynch's subjects reported that involvement gave them a sense of inward or spiritual development. Forty-four percent mentioned that they had obtained a new or more positive self-image. Twenty-eight percent emphasized that they remained in the Church of the Sun because of the continuous sense of mystery, curiosity, and excitement they felt during church activities.

With regard to the interaction of these four phases, Lynch noted that the processes of the fourth phase feed back into other aspects of the model, producing increased reading of occult literature and more frequent sensations of the supernatural order, which in turn, fostered further community solidarity and self-knowledge, which led to more reading and psychic experiences, and so on.

Both Adler (1986) and Lynch (1977) described the process by which some information such as that obtained by reading a book confirms some sort of inner experience. Adler described this experience as original and private while Lynch describes this experience as psychic or mystical. Such confirmation of inner experience, whatever form it might take, serves to stimulate further involvement. Adler describes the power of this confirmation in the phrase "I've come home." Adler's description of the process of becoming involved stops at this point, while Lynch's model goes on to describe the role of encountering others with similar interests.

REASONS FOR BEING INVOLVED IN PAGANISM AND WICCAN SPIRITUALITY

Kelly maintained that "the creating of new religions is a normal, healthy, and universal activity by which creative people (that is, the educated middle class, not the outcasts), in all societies attempt to meet their religious needs" (1991, 3). Kelly went on to identify the following unmet needs in our society to which contemporary Paganism and Wiccan Spirituality is a creative response: (*a*) the need for a sacramental experiencing of sex; (*b*) the need for ordinary people to have practical paths for personal and spiritual development; (*c*) the need for flexible, viable, and autonomous religious organizational structures; (*d*) the need for anti-dogmatic approaches which do not require acceptance of a set of beliefs for membership; (*e*) the need for polytheistic theologies to accompany the growing pluralism of societies throughout the world; and (*f*) the need for individuals to have a religion which they are creating for themselves continually.

Adler (1986) asked Pagans and Witches why they were involved and obtained six primary reasons: (*a*) quest for and involvement with beauty, vision, and imagination; (*b*) intellectual interest and satisfaction with the wide dissemination of strange and fascinating books; (*c*) personal growth through pursuit of the mystery traditions, initiations into the workings of life, death, and rebirth; (*d*) interest in exploring the spiritual aspects of feminism through emphasis on Goddess worship; (*e*) reverence for nature and concern about the environmental crisis; and (*f*) freedom of religious belief and expression.

Central to their involvement, Orion (1990) found that Pagans and Witches: (*a*) value inner freedom and an individual approach to religion; (*b*) desire a sense of responsibility for one's part in the unfolding of historical events; (*c*) believe that individuals can and should be powerful in the sense of reclaiming the powers of the mind (i.e., intellect, imagination, will, intuition, and other mental faculties); (*d*) value free time to create and celebrate, to the point of often being willing to sacrifice material rewards for this freedom; and (*e*) believe that life should be playful as well as purposefully creative, and that one's work should be a true expression of one's sensual nature.

Ludeke (1989) asked her subjects questions related to why they were involved in Wicca and received the following responses: 9 percent needed to get in touch with the inner woman, 19 percent wanted a "women-only" religion, 30 percent were angry and frustrated with patriarchal religion, 10 percent felt a love for Mother Earth, 28 percent because lesbians were welcome, 3 percent loved to create rituals, and 1 percent for some other reason. Ludeke also asked her subjects why they thought other women became Wiccan and obtained the following responses: 47 percent because of a need for a women's religion, 22 percent because of spiritual growth, 18 percent because the world needs changing, 11 percent because of personal growth, and 4 percent because of other unspecified reasons. Ludeke also reported that many women considered what they were getting out of Wicca was the same as why they had become involved in the first place, which included: (*a*) Wicca provided an opportunity to play an active role in ritual work which led to the self-empowerment they felt was denied them in patriarchal religions; (*b*) Wicca helped them make the mind, body, spirit connections that were absent in mainstream religions; and (*c*) Wicca presented other women in the light of strength, friendship, cooperation, and trust which facilitated a bonding between women that they did not perceive existed outside of Wicca.

Lloyd (1978) asked the twenty hereditary Witches in her study questions regarding what is most important about the Craft and their reasons for staying with it. Their responses fell into four main categories in the following order of importance: (1) the issue of family associations; (2) identification with the Goddess; (3) the Craft's emphasis on harmony and balance with nature; and (4) the importance of controlling one's life through magic. Lloyd asked the sixty non-hereditary Witches in her study questions regarding what first interested them in the Craft and what currently seems most important about it. Their responses fell into the following four categories in order of importance: (1) the excitement of being a powerful person; (2) their supposed ability to control their environments through magic; (3) enjoyment of Wicca's ceremonial life; and (4) pleasure in working with a female deity.

These studies reveal a variety of reasons why individuals become involved in Paganism and Wicca. While all the reasons cited apply to some individuals, certain themes do emerge as more prevalent. Above all, a need for religion that recognizes the feminine as divine in the form of the Goddess seems to be the most commonly cited reason for involvement. The need for creative approaches to spirituality that value individual freedom of belief and expression also appears to be a predominant reason for becoming involved. Reverence for nature and living in harmony with nature also represent important reasons for involvement. Finally, quests for personal enrichment and spiritual growth also lead many individuals to Paganism and Wicca.

METHODOLOGICAL CRITIQUE OF THIS BODY OF RESEARCH

The Problem of Representative Samples

In order to provide an ethnographic description of contemporary Pagan and Wiccan culture, the studies focused on in this chapter have utilized a variety of methodological approaches, including participant observation, questionnaires, surveys, and interviews. The confidence that one might place in the results of these studies may be questioned because of the methodological problem of obtaining representative samples.

In discussing survey research, Fowler noted that "data from a properly chosen sample are a great improvement over data from a sample of those who attend meetings, speak loudest, volunteer to respond, or happen to be convenient to poll" (1988, 11). Unfortunately, the data about Wiccan and Pagan practitioners has come from those who attend gatherings, who volunteer to respond, or who are convenient to poll (e.g., names listed in a directory, subscribers to a periodical, and those encountered by circumstance). Thus, all of the data that has been collected from Pagans and Wiccans may be regarded as biased. While this biased nature of the data calls into question the confidence one may place in this information and its interpretation, it does not mean that the data is useless. The data does describe certain aspects of some of the individuals and groups involved in Paganism and Wiccan Spirituality. However, any attempt to make generalizations about contemporary Pagan and Wiccan practitioners as a whole may be regarded as intellectually risky due to the limits of the research.

In defense of these studies, they appear to be designed out of necessity. The question of how one conducts valid survey research on such a diverse collection of religious practitioners is central. No organizational structure exists through which one has access to all those involved. Some Pagan/Wiccan periodicals have large subscriber lists, yet these lists can probably not be regarded as totally representative samples of the movement as a whole. Many Pagan and Wiccan practitioners regard their spirituality as private, something to be kept secret from others. Such individuals are going to be difficult to find and their cooperation hard to solicit. Problems of harassment and discrimination still face many of those involved in Pagan and Wiccan practices. Such individuals are not likely to reveal their identity to researchers and some even choose not to subscribe to Pagan/Wiccan periodicals. Many Wiccans and Pagans seem to be highly individualistic and mistrustful of conventional power structures and authority. Such people are not likely to react favorably to research efforts. All of these characteristics of Wiccans and Pagans interfere with the ability to obtain representative samples for research purposes.

Ethical Issues

Most of the researchers mentioned in this chapter grappled with the problem of making contact with and gaining the confidence of those they wished to study. Great variability exists in how the researchers approaches this task of obtaining data, ranging from being straightforward and honest to being totally deceptive. Important ethical issues emerge when examining this range of strategies.

In 1971, the Council of the American Anthropological Association adopted a set of ethical principles to guide ethnographers (Spradley 1980). In discussing these principles, Spradley pointed out they generally require that the ethnographer do the following: consider informants first; safeguard informants' rights, interests, and sensitivities; communicate research objectives to the informants; protect the privacy of informants; not exploit informants; and make reports available to informants.

Concealment and deception seem to be directly proscribed by this set of ethical principles. As Spradley indicated, participant observation represents a powerful tool for invading other people's way of life. If a researcher conducts interviews or uses questionnaires, the subjects are likely to be aware that something is going on. With participant observation, the subjects may not be aware that their comments and actions are being noted for research purposes. This kind of research can result in the researcher playing the role of an undercover secret agent. Kennedy noted that the possibility of betraying confidence increases as the researcher builds a relationship with the people being studied. Kennedy went on to state that "the problem is constantly one of striking a balance between being a good friend and a psychological snoop, of using information one has gathered in order to gather more information without betraying the trust of the informants" (1982, 17).

Some of the researchers did not appear to conform to the ethical principles described by the Council of the American Anthropological Association. The research of Lloyd (1978) represents the most obvious example of disrespect for the sensitivities and privacy of the individuals studied. Lloyd did not explain her research objectives to participants at the outset. Furthermore, it does not seem that she informed her subjects after the fact or provided them with any kind of research report. Scott (1980) made the point that she was not able to use survey data because the subjects were suspicious of outsiders, which causes one to wonder how aware the subjects were of her observations and note taking. Jorgensen and Jorgensen (1982) presented themselves as seekers and later actually became tarot readers in order to collect information for their research. Infiltration under the guise of being a seeker also does not seem consistent with clear communication of research objectives to the informants. Playing the role of tarot reader also brings up some interesting ethical concerns since tarot readers approach their work much like more traditional counselors and are concerned about the well-being of their clients as well as respectful of the confidentiality of the client-counselor relationship. The idea of someone providing such divination services for the sole purposes of collecting research information does not seem to hold the well-being of the client as the primary concern.

The issue of confidentiality is particularly pertinent to these studies of Pagan and Wiccan practitioners since such individuals are often very secretive about their beliefs and practices because of fear of persecution. The bulk of the researchers ensured that the confidentiality of their informants was maintained through a variety of means including using pseudonyms of the groups and individuals, disguising the actual names of the cities in which the

research was conducted, and using questionnaires in which personal identity was not revealed.

The research conducted by Lloyd does not appear to have
adequately protected the privacy of the subjects. She carried out
her research in LaCrosse, Wisconsin, where, at the time, she was
a faculty member in the department of sociology and anthropology
at the University of Wisconsin. Lloyd addressed the manner in
which she dealt with the issue of confidentiality in the following:

> Among the problems of doing research in one's own home commu-
> nity is that of protecting the identities of informants, people who
> might be socially injured—even years in the future—by the revela-
> tion of their names in connection with Witchcraft. Therefore, al-
> though the names of the communities where my information was
> gathered are not disguised, the Witches are referred to by their
> personally chosen "Witch" names. (1978, viii)

While Lloyd seems to believe that she has adequately protected
the confidentiality of her informants, she has overlooked the significance of Witch names and the possibility that identity could be
revealed by reference to these names. Lloyd provided fairly extensive personal case histories for each of the individuals who were
members of the coven she participated in and studied. Since many
individuals are at least known to other Witches by their Witch
names and often become known to outsiders by these names, too
much personal identifying information was provided by Lloyd to
ensure the long-term privacy of the informants.

DISCUSSION

The studies mentioned in this chapter have examined a variety of
aspects regarding the beliefs, practices, and characteristics of those
individuals involved in Paganism, Wicca, and related paths. I have
selected, from this broad and descriptive body of information, studies
that deal with who is involved, how they became involved, and why
they are involved. From this, I have focused on the variables that
were addressed more frequently throughout the studies or that
seemed most significant. I have approached this task from the
perspective of nine years of personal involvement in Wicca and
Paganism. While I have attempted to stick to the data throughout
this chapter, this section discusses the research from the perspective of my direct involvement.

A composite picture of a typical Pagan and Wiccan emerges from the demographic information. The contemporary Pagan or Wiccan tends to be an adult individual most commonly born during the "baby-boom" years 1946 to 1964 or more recently. The majority of these individuals are of Caucasian ancestry with the rest made up of individuals from a variety of other ancestries. Somewhat more of these individuals are female. The contemporary Pagan or Wiccan grew up in a family that was most frequently either Catholic, Protestant, or Jewish. This individual tends to be more highly educated than the general population and frequently holds a job commensurate with such educational background. Based upon my experience, this composite picture seems to accurately portray contemporary Pagans and Wiccans in a very general sense.

The research regarding psychological characteristics seems to offer an inconsistent and inconclusive portrait of the typical Pagan and Wiccan, particularly with regard to overall adjustment, power, and conformity. While some maladapted individuals end up being involved with Paganism and Wicca after not fitting in anywhere else, the bulk of those who are involved do seem to display typical patterns of psychological adjustment. While some ineffectual individuals seem attracted to the magical lure of power in order to control others as well as their environment, the majority of individuals seem to be appropriately interested in improving themselves as individuals and making life's circumstances better for themselves and others. While individuals may display nonconformity in certain aspects of their life such as religious beliefs and practices, they may seem to conform quite well in other aspects of their lives such as occupation. Thus, it is particularly difficult to categorize the general tendencies of Pagans and Wiccans along such dimensions as overall adjustment, power, and conformity. The studies that focused on the issue of creativity, on the other hand, clearly point in the direction of consistently describing Pagans and Wiccans as creative and imaginative individuals, a finding I would have to concur with based upon my experiences.

Process of Becoming Involved

One of the most important factors in becoming involved seems to rest in actually finding out about Paganism and Wiccan Spirituality. This task has become much easier over the past ten years due to a dramatic increase in the number of books and periodicals published, the number and scope of networking organizations, the number of stores selling books and other religious items, the number of people involved whom one might encounter, and exposure in the mass media. What is encountered strikes some kind of chord with the inner experience of those who become further involved. In meeting numerous individuals new to Paganism and Wiccan Spirituality, I have often heard comments similar to those mentioned by Adler in which the individual is ecstatic to discover that there are others who believe the same things that he or she does. My experiences do not support Lynch's claims that interpersonal interaction with others is necessary for continued and more extensive involvement. A fair number of Pagans and Wiccans regard themselves to be solitary practitioners and rarely, if ever, have direct face-to-face contact with other Pagans and Wiccans. While many of these individuals may deeply desire such interaction, it is not a necessary prerequisite for personally committing oneself to Pagan and Wiccan beliefs and practices. My experiences also do not support Lynch's findings regarding exclusive social interaction for those Pagans and Wiccans who are involved with a spiritual group. While such groups can be very close, most individuals tend to maintain other social contacts.

REASONS FOR INVOLVEMENT

Perhaps the most interesting topic that has been touched upon is why people become involved with Paganism and Wiccan Spirituality. Such involvement is not often an easy process. Some individuals in American society still consider any religious beliefs and practices different from their own to be inspired by Satan. In addition, many open-minded individuals still react in stereotyped ways to the terms Pagan and Witch. Thus, those who become involved often keep their beliefs and practices secret for fear of discrimination and persecution. This fear is not irrational, for a growing number of cases involving Pagans and Wiccans have been documented recently pertaining to job and housing discrimination. Those who do reveal their interests have also often suffered rejection by their families and experienced various forms of harassment from others. Furthermore, many individuals express a sense of loneliness and alienation because of the lack of like-minded individuals in their area to associate with. It is interesting then, to consider, why individuals become involved and stay involved if these are the kinds of experiences that may be encountered.

A variety of reasons for involvement were mentioned in the studies. Just as there are a diverity of individuals involved so too are there a variety of reasons for being involved. My experiences generally support the following general themes as reasons for involvement for many: (*a*) recognition of the divine as female as well as male; (*b*) the need for creative approaches to spirituality which value individual freedom of belief and expression; (*c*) reverence for nature and living in harmony with nature; and (*d*) quests for personal enrichment and spiritual growth.

None of the studies that have examined the practitioners of Paganism and Wiccan Spirituality have really explored in an in-depth fashion the reasons why individuals become involved and stay involved. The reasons cited in the studies are very descriptive, cover a wide range of possibilities, and fall into a number of inter-related categories including spiritual beliefs and theology, religious practices, religious political structures, ethical guidelines, relationship to social and political causes, social identification, interpersonal relationships, and personal psychological adjustment. None of the studies seem to have captured the complexity and interrelatedness of factors and reasons underlying the current growth of interest in Paganism and Wiccan Spirituality.

CONCLUDING REMARKS

Despite the methodological limitations of the studies dealt with in this chapter, taken as a whole they offer some apparently accurate and descriptive insights into the characteristics of the practitioners of contemporary Paganism and Wiccan Spirituality. However, it is important to again emphasize the pitfalls in drawing sweeping generalizations about Pagans and Wiccans based upon this body of information. Based upon my experiences, I can't stress enough the diversity represented by these individuals and groups.

Since the late 1960s and early 1970s, interest in and involvement with Paganism and Wiccan Spirituality has steadily increased. During the past few years, this growth seems to have accelerated. This spiritual movement and those involved represent fertile ground for further research and exploration. Metzner (1991) noted that existing cultural paradigms cannot adequately deal with the issues humans are facing, particularly with regard to the ecological crisis. Metzner further described an emerging ecological worldview with very different perceptions of the role and place of the human in the scheme of things. Further investigation into the growing appeal of Paganism and Wiccan Spirituality may yield important insights into various aspects of such changing worldviews and cultural paradigms.

REFERENCES

Adler, M. 1986. *Drawing Down the Moon: Witches, Druids, Goddess-Worshippers, and Other Pagans in America Today.* Rev. ed. Boston: Beacon Press.

Fowler, Jr., F. J. 1988. *Survey Research Methods* (rev. ed.). Newbury Park, Calif.: Sage Publications.

Fox, S. 1979. *Circle Guide to Wicca and Pagan Resources.* Madison, Wisc.: Circle Publications.

Gardner, G. B. [1954] 1970. *Witchcraft Today.* Reprint, New York: The Citadel Press.

———. [1959] 1971. *The Meaning of Witchcraft.* Reprint, London: The Aquarian Press.

Graves, R. 1948. *The White Goddess: A Historical Grammar of Poetic Myth.* New York: Farrar, Straus and Giroux.

Hartman, P. A. 1976. "Social dimensions of occult participation: The Gnostica study. *British Journal of Sociology* 27, no. 2: 169–183.

Jorgensen, D. L., and L. Jorgensen. 1982. "Social Meaning of the Occult." *The Sociological Quarterly* 23: 373–389.

Kelly, A. A. 1991. *Crafting the Art of Magic: A History of Modern Witchcraft, 1939–1964.* St. Paul, Minn.: Llewellyn.

Kennedy, R. 1982. "Participant Observation as a Method for Humanistic Psychology. *Saybrook Review* 4, no. 1: 9–22.

Kerr, H., and C. L. Crow. 1983. Introduction. In *The Occult in America: New Historical Perspectives,* edited by H. Kerr and C. L. Crow, 1–10. Chicago: University of Illinois Press.

Kirkpatrick, R. G., R. Rainey, and K. Rubi. 1984. "Pagan Renaissance and Wiccan Witchcraft in Industrial Society: A Study of Parasociology and the Sociology of Enchantment." *Iron Mountain: A Journal of Magical Religion* (Summer 1984): 31–38.

———. 1986. "An Empirical Study of Wiccan Religion in Postindustrial Society." *Free Inquiry in Creative Sociology* 14, no. 1: 33–38.

Leek, S. 1971. *The Complete Art of Witchcraft.* New York: The World Publishing Company.

Leland, C. G. [1897] 1974. *Aradia: Gospel of the Witches.* Reprint, New York: Samuel Weiser.

Lloyd, S. M. 1978. The Occult Revival: Witchcraft in the Contemporary United States. *Dissertation Abstracts International*, 39: 6205A. (University Microfilms No. AAC7906899)

Ludeke, J. C. 1989. Wicca as a Revitalization Movement Among Post-Industrial, Urban, American Women. *Dissertation Abstracts International* 50: 2951A. (University Microfilms No. AAC9004182)

Luhrmann, T. M. 1989. *Persuasions of the Witch's Craft.* Cambridge, Mass.: Harvard University Press.

Lynch, F. R. 1977. Toward a Theory of Conversion and Commitment to the Occult. *American Behavioral Scientist* 20: 887–908.

———. 1979. " 'Occult Establishment' or 'Deviant Religion'? The Rise and Fall of a Modern Church of Magic." *Journal for the Scientific Study of Religion* 18: 281–298.

Melton, J. G. 1978. *The Encyclopedia of American Religions.* Wilmington, N.C.: McGrath Publishing Company.

———. 1982. *Magic, Witchcraft, and Paganism in America.* New York: Garland Publishing.

———. 1985. "Modern Alternative Religions in the West." In *A Handbook of Living Religions,* edited by J. R. Hinnells. New York: Viking Penguin.

———. 1988. "A History of the New Age Movement." In *Not Necessarily the New Age,* edited by R. Basil, 35–53. Buffalo, N.Y.: Prometheus Books.

Metzner, R. 1991. "Reclaim Our Environment." *Meditation* 6, no. 3 (Summer 1991): 24–26, 28.

Murray, M. A. [1931] 1970. *The God of the Witches.* Reprint, London: Oxford University Press.

———. [1921] 1971. *The Witch-cult in Western Europe.* Reprint, Oxford: Oxford University Press.

Neal, A. G., and M. Seaman. 1964. "Organization and Powerlessness: A Test of the Mediation Hypothesis." *American Sociological Review* 29: 216–226.

Orion, L. L. 1990. Revival of Western Paganism and Witchcraft in the Contemporary United States. *Dissertation Abstracts International* 52: 1799A. (University Microfilms No. DA9128573)

Scheidt, F. J. 1974. "Deviance, Power, and the Occult: A Field Study." *The Journal of Psychology* 87: 21–28.

Scott, G. M. 1980. *Cult and Countercult: A Study of a Spiritual Growth Group and a Witchcraft Order.* Westport, Conn.: Greenwood Press.

Spradley, J. P. 1980. *Participant Observation*. Fort Worth: Holt, Rinehart and Winston.

Starhawk [Miriam Simos]. 1989. *The Spiral Dance: A Rebirth of the Ancient Religion of the Great Goddess* Rev. ed. San Francisco: Harper and Row.

Valiente, D. 1962. *Where Witchcraft Lives*. London: Aquarian Press.

———. 1973. *An ABC of Witchcraft Past and Present*. London: Robert Hale Limited.

INDEX